MING CHO LEE

To David
from Ming Cho Lee 李名覺

April 2015

ARNOLD ARONSON

MING CHO LEE

A LIFE IN DESIGN

Theatre Communications Group
New York 2014

Ming Cho Lee: A Life in Design is published by Theatre Communications Group, Inc.,
520 Eighth Avenue, 24th Floor, New York, NY 10018-4156

Image credits appear on page 319.

Printed and bound in China

This publication is funded in part by the Educational Foundation of America, with additional funds from the Tobin Theatre Arts Fund and the New York State Council on the Arts with the support of Governor Andrew Cuomo and the New York State Legislature.

TCG Books are exclusively distributed to the book trade by
Consortium Book Sales and Distribution.

Library of Congress Cataloging-in-Publication Data

Aronson, Arnold.
Ming Cho Lee: A Life in Design / Arnold Aronson.
pages cm
ISBN 978-1-55936-461-4 (hardback)
1. Lee, Ming Cho. 2. Set designers–United States–Biography. 3. Theater–Stage-setting and scenery–United States. I. Title.
PN2096.L44A86 2014
792.02'5092–dc23
[B]
2014004073

Book design by Bob Stern

First edition, October 2014

for Lorie Novak

CONTENTS

Preface

I FIRST MET MING CHO LEE in November 1983 when I interviewed him for my book *American Set Design*, which profiled eleven designers. In deciding which to include, Ming was the most obvious choice. Already known as the dean of American designers, his career spanned Broadway, regional theatre, and opera and dance at home and abroad. And of course he was head of design at Yale School of Drama. I chose the book's other ten designers for a variety of reasons, trying to capture a cross section of American set design, but what I did not realize at the time was that eight of those ten had been Ming's former students or assistants, and one other had worked with him professionally. It was clear to me then that Ming deserved a book of his own. It has obviously taken me a while to achieve that goal, but if there is a silver lining to the delay, it is that I am now able to encompass an entire career.

Starting in 2010 I began regular visits to Ming and Betsy's legendary apartment where we sat at the dining room table and went through his life year by year and show by show. As anyone who knows him will attest, Ming is never at a loss for words. I would turn on the recorder, ask a question or name a production, and Ming was off and running, recalling productions in extraordinary detail. He has a phenomenal memory. Because Ming sees his designs in the larger context of the production, he usually started his discussion of each show by identifying the other creative artists, the major actors or singers and often the technical personnel. This was frequently followed by a précis of the piece at hand. I would like to say that I didn't need these synopses, but there were times when I was quietly appreciative. Once I confused the operas *Manon* and *Manon Lescaut*, and Ming launched into a half-hour disquisition on the differences between the two and the respective styles of Massenet and Puccini. It was largely irrelevant to the discussion of design, but I felt privileged to have enjoyed a mini-seminar on opera. Almost every show came with a treasury of anecdotes—far more than I was able to include in this book—but as Ming admits, he has told many of these stories over and over and several can be found in other publications and are well known to his students and colleagues.

But there were moments that proved the memory wasn't merely the result of years of narrative repetition. We usually discussed each production with some sort of visual material in front of us—photos or sketches—but there was nothing available for the 1965 Juilliard production of *The Magic Flute*. As Ming began to describe the set he asked for a piece of paper. I tore a sheet out of my notebook, he picked up a Pilot Razor Point pen and, with a somewhat shaky hand, sketched out seven scenes (one of which is included in this book). When I asked in astonishment how he could remember an entire production in such detail after more than forty-five years he said, simply, "I thought it was a pretty good design." Of course, Ming has a unique aide-mémoire—his wife and partner of fifty-five years, Betsy. She was usually in the room or nearby as we spoke, ready to fill in the blanks, confirm or correct Ming's remembrances and miraculously dig out sketches from hidden recesses. This is, of course, a book about the designs of Ming Cho Lee, but insofar as it is also about Ming's life and artistic practice, this is a book about Betsy as well.

I wound up with some 150 hours of recorded interviews, so I want to begin by thanking my transcribers, Jess Applebaum, Jason Fitzgerald and Naïma Phillips, as well as my research assistants at Columbia University, Neil D'Astolfo and Emily Madison. I spent some time in archives and libraries and would like to thank Jeni Dahmus at the Juilliard School, Dale Stieber at the Occidental College Library, John Pennino of the Metropolitan Opera Archives and Barbara J. Wohlsen of New York City Opera.

There are two people who preceded me in writing about Ming. The first is David Nils Flaten whose 1979 unpublished dissertation, "Ming Cho Lee: American Stage Designer," was the most comprehensive study of Ming's work to that time. It proved to be a vital resource. In particular, as part of his research, Dr. Flaten photographed just about every sketch and model in the studio, and that visual documentation most often provided the basis for the discussions Ming and I had about his early work. Because some of the original artworks have disappeared for one reason or another, these photos provide the only available record we have of those productions and some are reproduced here. I thank David Flaten for his generosity in allowing us to use them. Second is Delbert Unruh's *The Designs of Ming Cho Lee*, published in 2006 as part of the U.S. Institute for Theatre Technology's monograph series. The thorough chronology guided us through our interviews, and the illustrations provided important reference points. I am grateful to Del and to David Rodger, publisher of Broadway Press, for making the illustrations from that book available as well.

Many people spoke to me about Ming, and I hope they will forgive me for not mentioning them all by name, but there are a few I want to single out: Marjorie Bradley Kellogg, who also read and commented on drafts of a couple of chapters; Jerry Freedman, who spent two days with me at the University of North Carolina School of the Arts; and Omar and Helen Paxson, who were charming and generous and provided invaluable insights into Ming's first years in the United States. (Omar Paxson died in December 2013, eight days after his ninetieth birthday.) They wisely preserved Ming's earliest design efforts. I am also indebted to Richard and Christopher Lee, who graciously discussed family life in the Lee household.

Unlike much of the rest of the world, where publishing books on living designers is not an unusual endeavor, American publishers shy away from such undertakings. I am therefore enormously grateful to Terry Nemeth, publisher at TCG, who was enthusiastic about the idea from the time I first proposed it and who has tirelessly supported this large and expensive undertaking. To that end TCG obtained assistance from the Tobin Theatre Arts Fund and the Educational Foundation of America, without whose generosity this book would not exist. I don't think any of us realized the magnitude of the operation when we began. There is a whole team of people at TCG to thank: Russell Dembin, who meticulously researched the chronology; Zach Chotzen-Freund, who has organized, collected and kept track of the 500 illustrations in the book and the even greater number that didn't make it in, and who now knows every nook and cranny of Ming's studio; Bob Stern, whose elegant design of the book accommodated more images and words than initially planned; and my editor, Sarah Hart, who patiently saw this text through numerous versions and iterations, always offering superb advice. Additionally Monet Cogbill, who scanned much of the original artwork; Kitty Suen, who oversaw the retouching and color correction of all the images within; and Ted Thompson for photo research.

For past support in writing I thank the Bogliasco Foundation and the Rockefeller Foundation Bellagio Center. I am forever grateful to my wife, Lorie Novak, who read through drafts of every chapter and provided encouragement, advice and loving support.

And finally, as anyone who has ever worked on any project with Ming would say—including Ming himself—this would not have been possible without Betsy, whose support, assistance and input in every conceivable aspect of this book (not to mention endless cups of tea) was crucial in bringing it to publication.

Arnold Aronson

Introduction

1 Ming Cho Lee's signature (Lee Ming Cho) in pre-1949 traditional Chinese characters.

MING CHO LEE is one of the most important figures in modern American theatre. This is, admittedly, a large, even grandiose, claim, but, as I hope this book will demonstrate, a fair one. Few would question his significance in the field of set design. In the 1960s and '70s he radically and almost single-handedly transformed the American approach to scenography,[1] particularly through his work at the New York Shakespeare Festival, New York City Opera and Arena Stage in Washington, D.C. Even on Broadway, where he was associated with a run of musical theatre failures of epic proportions, reviews often began with praise for his sets. He may be the only set designer nominated for a Tony for a play that closed in one night. Lee drew upon the work of his mentors—Jo Mielziner, Boris Aronson and, to a degree, Rouben Ter-Arutunian—his training in Chinese watercolor painting, Brechtian aesthetics and contemporary German opera and theatre to forge a new American scenic vocabulary. He was a pioneer in introducing new or unusual materials to the stage, from erosion cloth and raw wood, to spray foam, Styrofoam and Sculp-metal, to space-age Mylar.

Even if that were the sum of his contributions, it would still earn Lee a place in the top tier of American designers, but his influence reaches well beyond that. As a teacher of stage design at New York University's School of the Arts in the late 1960s, to more than forty years at the Yale School of Drama, Lee has trained more set designers than anyone in American theatre history. And because costume and lighting design students at Yale also take his classes, as do playwrights, stage managers and directors, his ideas, approaches and aesthetics have seeped into virtually every aspect of theatre production and creation. Lee's students hold leading roles in the worlds of theatre, opera and dance design, as well as in education, occupying positions at many, if not most, significant training programs at colleges and universities across the country. Over the course of his career Lee has given hundreds of lectures and workshops in the U.S. and abroad. He was an organizer of the design portfolio review and its eponymous successor—"Ming's Clambake"—for graduating MFA students. Given all this, there is a very good chance that anyone who studies theatre, participates in theatre or attends theatre or opera performances across the country, is directly or indirectly affected by Ming Cho Lee.

But there is yet another aspect of Lee's approach that is rare in any American theatre artist: a passionate commitment to artistic freedom and social justice and a concomitant dedication to instilling in his students the idea that art and politics are inseparable. As one story goes, while conducting a master class, Lee devoted much of his presentation to the state of contemporary American society and politics. Afterward a student said, "I thought we were coming to hear a talk on design," to which Lee replied, "I *have* been talking about design." At election times Lee exhorts his students to vote and has not only been known to excuse students from class in order to return to their home districts to do so, but on at least one occasion he offered to pay the airfare for a student who couldn't afford to go. One of the qualities Lee admired most in his mentors was the breadth of their knowledge and interests. While their professional lives may have been thoroughly immersed in theatre, their conversation was not. They could talk about art, culture, food, politics—about the world. Lee bemoans the fact that so many theatre artists today are narrowly focused in their range of interests and talk only of theatre. Lee's assistants from over the years recall the lunch break, or the glass of scotch at the end of the day, when the conversation usually revolved around politics or current events, not theatre. Jon Jory, former artistic director of Actors Theatre of Louisville, summed it best, calling Lee the "guardian of the ethics and morals of the profession."

AMERICAN DESIGN AT MIDCENTURY

To understand Lee's impact on American design it is necessary to look at the theatrical world that he stepped into in the early 1950s. At the beginning of the twentieth century, American theatre was dominated by melodramas, well-made plays, musical revues and a limited selection of plays from the Shakespeare canon (although virtually no other classical drama), all presented on a proscenium stage. Interior scenes often employed box sets (a three-walled room viewed by the audience through the missing fourth wall). The room might be filled with real furniture, but the walls were generally made of canvas or muslin flats with practical doors, but with much detail—wallpaper, moldings, wood paneling, bookcases, even windows—depicted through illusionistic painting. Most other settings were created through the use of painted backdrops and borders, perhaps with freestanding two-dimensional elements, such as trees. Thus, until the early twentieth century the scene painter was the de facto designer.

All of this began to change, if slowly, in the second decade of the twentieth century with the emergence of the Little Theatre or Art

Theatre Movement in New York and in several cities around the country. This precursor to Off Broadway consisted of small theatres with a more experimental profile that served as an entry point for new forms of European drama, especially symbolist and expressionist works, as well as new developments in American dramaturgy, with the early work of Eugene O'Neill among the most notable examples. In many cases the art theatres provided a home for new scenographic approaches as well, influenced largely by European design, particularly the work of Adolphe Appia and Edward Gordon Craig, that rejected detailed naturalism and painted pictorialism in favor of abstraction, stylization, atmospheric scenography and simplified or suggestive realism. In the U.S. this approach became known as the New Stagecraft and quickly found its way from the small theatres onto mainstream stages. The most influential figures of the American New Stagecraft were Robert Edmond Jones, Lee Simonson, Joseph Urban and Norman Bel Geddes—modern American scenography is often dated from Jones's design for the 1915 Broadway production of *The Man Who Married a Dumb Wife*. Nonetheless, despite the anti-naturalist plays of O'Neill, Susan Glaspell and a few other playwrights, American drama at the time remained largely within the domain of realism. This resulted, during the interwar years, in a peculiar mix of realistic, often psychologically based drama contained within a physical and visual environment that was semiabstracted, suggestive, symbolic or emblematic.[2]

After the Second World War a new generation of dramatists emerged, and many plays moved away from the hard-edged realism of prior decades. Most notably with Tennessee Williams's *The Glass Menagerie* and *A Streetcar Named Desire* and Arthur Miller's *Death of a Salesman* a style best described as poetic realism emerged, typified by heightened poetic language, a cinematic structure and fluid movement between dream and reality, past and present. Even the ostensibly naturalistic dramas of William Inge in the 1950s had ethereal aspects as they explored the emotional lives of their characters. With Edward Albee in the late fifties an American brand of absurdist drama entered the mainstream. These plays demanded a scenography capable not merely of establishing place but of conveying mood, suggesting inner states of mind and accommodating dreamlike transformations—a scenography that could create a unified framework for nonlinear narrative. This was also a golden age of the musical theatre. Like the dramas, musicals

2 Jo Mielziner, sketch for *Look Homeward, Angel*, Broadway, 1957.

2

such as *Oklahoma!* and *South Pacific* in the late 1940s, and continuing in the 1950s with *Guys and Dolls*, *West Side Story* and *Gypsy*, among many others, required nuanced creation of mood and tone, as well as complex and sophisticated visual and physical transformations between scenes. Because movies could create an unsurpassed literal reality, theatre design moved more toward the suggestive, the fragmentary, the poetic and the frankly theatrical. Further contributing to a movement away from literal and illusionistic design was the emergence of New York as the focal point for modern dance. Dance demanded a sophisticated approach to lighting—as did the new scenography of drama and musicals—and the art of lighting design came into its own during this period, developing in the U.S. long before it did elsewhere in the world.

The designer who, more than anyone, established this new scenic vocabulary was Jo Mielziner (1901–75), probably the most influential designer of the American theatre in the mid-twentieth century. He was also the first designer Lee assisted when he moved to New York in 1954. In a fifty-year career that began in the 1920s Mielziner designed the sets and usually the lighting for the majority of the landmark plays and musicals of the period, including *Street Scene*; *Winterset*; Tennessee Williams's *The Glass Menagerie*, *A Streetcar Named Desire* and *Cat on a Hot Tin Roof*; Arthur Miller's *Death of a Salesman*; and the musicals *Pal Joey*, *Carousel*, *Annie Get Your Gun*, *The King and I*, *The Most Happy Fella*, *Guys and Dolls* and *Gypsy*—a small sampling of his some three hundred productions. Mielziner apprenticed with Joseph Urban and Lee Simonson and, even more important, was an assistant to Robert Edmond Jones for five months in 1925—not a long time, perhaps, but it had a powerful impact on his subsequent work. Having trained as an artist, most of Mielziner's designs embodied a strong painterly style that softened and romanticized the naturalism of early twentieth-century American theatre. His use of scrim in plays like *The Glass Menagerie* and *Salesman* allowed for shifts between reality and memory through changes in lighting alone while also enhancing the dreamlike aura of the settings. Although Mielziner was not the first person to use scrim in the theatre—the practice probably dates back to the eighteenth century—he transformed its use into an art, and it became a signature element of many of his designs. His use of skeletal scenic elements—suggesting place without solidity while allowing it to be seen within a larger visual and spatial context—became a significant motif in midcentury American scenography. Mielziner's designs made an indelible impact on American theatre; in some cases, particularly with *The Glass Menagerie* and *Death of a Salesman*, his designs were so integrally bound up in the texts and so closely identified with the productions that it took decades for later generations of designers to overcome those visual motifs. To a large extent, when one looks at the visual record of American theatre in the 1940s and '50s, one is looking at Jo Mielziner.

Another theatre artist with an important influence on the theatre of this period (and on Lee)—although without the commercial success of Mielziner until late in his career—was the Ukrainian-born Boris Aronson[3] (1898–1980), who had a distinctly different approach to design. Instead of the pictorial, Aronson's designs emphasized architectural structure, plasticity, the emblematic and, a bit later in his career, the use of collage. In Russia he had apprenticed with artist and designer Alexandra Exter and witnessed the work of Vsevolod Meyerhold, and thus absorbed the revolutionary ideology of constructivism firsthand. He moved to Berlin in 1922 where he studied art and participated in the first foreign exhibition of Soviet art. (While there, he wrote a treatise on the work of his friend, the painter Marc Chagall, whose iconography Aronson would later incorporate into his designs for *Fiddler on the Roof*.) Aronson immigrated to the U.S. in 1923 and embarked on an eclectic, innovative and distinguished career that included early work with Yiddish theatre companies in the 1920s and the Group Theatre in the 1930s. As Frank Rich has pointed out in *The Theatre Art of Boris Aronson*, his superb and thorough study of the designer's work, Aronson's eclecticism was in part a result of having to adapt his avant-garde scenography to the decidedly conservative realm of the American theatre.[4] He, too, designed works by Tennessee Williams (*The Rose Tattoo*), Arthur Miller (*The Crucible, A View from the Bridge, The Price*) and William Inge (*Bus Stop* and subsequent work), though in each case he was following in the wake of Mielziner, who had designed the landmark or breakout plays for each of those writers. Within the theatre world Aronson was considered a brilliant and versatile designer, but in 1958, when Lee began working in his studio, he hadn't yet achieved the renown that would come from his collaborations with producer and director Harold Prince on a string of major musicals, starting with *Fiddler* in 1964. Nonetheless, Aronson was largely responsible for introducing constructivism, cubism, the fantastical elements of Chagall and other nonobjective art movements into the American theatre, and this work provided an important counterpoint to the poetic realism of Mielziner. As profound as Aronson's scenographic impact would be on Lee, his attitude towards his art was equally important. "For Boris," Lee has said, "designing for the theatre was not just a question of design but of the play's relationship to history, society, politics, religion—to life itself. His approach was often complex, ambiguous and very personal."[5]

3 Boris Aronson, *The Firstborn*, Broadway, 1958. The figures on the posts would appear in several of Lee's designs in the 1960s and '70s.

3

Two more designers deserve particular mention, not because of any direct influence on Lee, but because of their role in shaping American scenography during this period. One is Donald Oenslager, whose career began in the mid-1920s and who, in addition to his scenographic work in theatre, opera and ballet, was Lee's predecessor as head of design at Yale, where he taught for forty-five years. Oenslager's work was eclectic; there was no single dominant style, but it blended elements of neo-romanticism typified by elegant curving lines, heightened realism and symbolism.

The other designer is Oliver Smith, whose musical theatre oeuvre, beginning in the 1940s, was second only to Mielziner. Among the shows he designed were *Brigadoon, My Fair Lady, West Side Story, The Sound of Music, Camelot* and *Hello, Dolly!*. He began his career with designs for modern ballets such as *Rodeo* and *Fancy Free* and served as co-director of American Ballet Theatre for more than thirty-five years. There was a strong graphic element to his predominantly painterly style, but it was his ability to create a flowing, seemingly choreographed movement of decor from one scene to the next that made him an ideal designer of midcentury musicals. (This was one aspect of design at which Lee never really excelled.)

It is impossible, of course, to neatly categorize American design of the postwar era. Looking at a cross section of work from the era one would find examples of the fragmentary, suggestive, expressionist and, perhaps above all, neo-romantic. But the 1950s witnessed the onset of changes to the American theatre that would come to fruition in the 1960s and be at least as radical as those of the 1920s. Lee, like many artists of the period, noted that the American theatre was ready for something different: "From the fifties to the sixties everything was changing. Our way of looking at the world was changing."[6] Some of these changes were driven in part by financial factors and led to the emergence of Off Broadway as a site for new dramas that could no longer find a home on Broadway. Some had to do with shifting demographics as the middle class began to move out of the city and into suburbs, where television became the dominant form of entertainment. And some had to do with the beginnings of an American avant-garde theatre whose influences came from the world of art and music as much as from theatre. One thrust of this avant-garde, strongly influenced by the writings of Antonin Artaud, placed an emphasis on neo-expressionist acting and use of language whose power derived as much from its sound as its literal meaning. The energetic and kinetic sensibility of abstract expressionism, which had become the dominant style of postwar American art, crossed over into performance and contributed directly to the emergence of Happenings. The formalism of certain art movements also found a counterpart in emerging avant-garde performances.

While Lee readily admits that he did not always understand new trends in art, these upheavals in art and performance were contributing to an investigation of the very notion of what constituted a stage, as well as the relationship of the stage to the auditorium. As a result, traditional approaches to scenography were disrupted. These changes were, not surprisingly, slow to reach the mainstream theatre, but Off and Off-Off Broadway sought out new spaces, new structures and at times even abandoned the physical theatre and traditional design altogether. If one looked to Europe, however, the scenographic change was more visible and more radical. A major factor in new European design, particularly in both East and West Germany and Great Britain, was the work of Bertolt Brecht and the Berliner Ensemble. (The Berliner Ensemble did not perform in the U.S. until 1999, so Brecht's influence in the U.S. in the 1950s and '60s came initially through his dramatic and theoretical texts, which were frequently misunderstood or selectively interpreted by American practitioners.)

4 Teo Otto, model for Giorgio Strehler's production of Luigi Pirandello's *I Giganti della Montagna*, 1947.

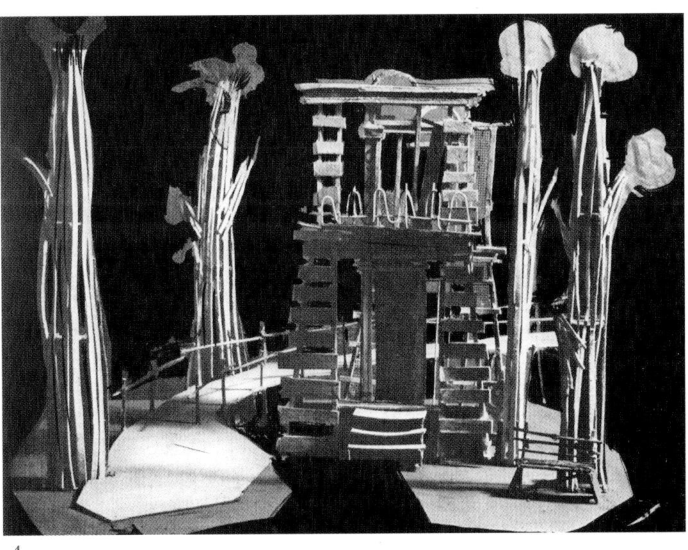

4

Lee cites Boris Aronson's observation that American theatre was "all about relatives" (by which he meant the family), and the new generation of theatre artists were eager to move beyond this and "were impatient to put personal life into a larger context." Brecht's theatre seemed to provide the perfect structure to accomplish this goal. A central element of Brecht's epic theatre was the *verfremdungseffekt* or alienation effect—an approach to text, acting and scenography intended to create aesthetic distance, thus making the familiar strange so that ideas could be seen afresh. Brecht believed that the model of Western theatre was dominated by the emotional engagement of the audience within an illusionistic framework that eliminated the possibility of rational judgment and response, thereby making the spectator feel instead of think. The scenographic techniques he employed to defamiliarize the stage included eliminating the front curtain, exposing the lighting equipment and revealing the offstage spaces and mechanisms—emphasizing the stage as stage, not a place of illusion.

LEE'S INFLUENCES

Although Lee is not sure how or when he became aware of Brecht or even how he came to understand what Brechtian design might mean, Brecht nonetheless became the most important force in Lee's thinking through the first few decades of his career. He regularly resisted the decorative in his designs, even when it might have been

5 Isamu Noguchi, model for Martha Graham's *Errand into the Maze*, 1947.

5

appropriate, opting for a modern presentational approach. He is sure that no one at Occidental College, where he was an undergraduate, knew about Brecht. Jo Mielziner was certainly not Brechtian. Boris Aronson had designed *Love Life* in 1948, by composer Kurt Weill who had been Brecht's collaborator in Germany, so he had a connection to Brecht's ideas. Frank Rich, who cites *Love Life* as a precursor of the "concept musicals" of the 1960s, refers to the genre as "Americanized Brechtian musicals," noting that Aronson "was born to design" them.[7] But Aronson never thought of himself as a Brechtian per se and Lee recalls no discussion of Brecht in the studio. Yet by the time Lee designed the Jerome Robbins–directed *Mother Courage and Her Children* in 1963, he would express his unhappiness with Robbins's un-Brechtian approach.

Lee thinks his first exposure to Brecht might have been during his one year of graduate school at the University of California, Los Angeles, where he read a bit of Eric Bentley. He remembers in particular a student director who talked about Brecht and who did plays with a strong political point of view. (Lee even acted in one of these productions, an original play that opened his eyes to some of the issues in the Middle East.) For one class Lee read Mordecai Gorelik's influential book, *New Theatres for Old*, which focused on Soviet and German theatre innovations, if not Brecht in particular. While Lee complained about the "turgid" writing, he was nonetheless intrigued by the notion of the politically and socially engaged theatre that Gorelik championed.

And somewhere along the line—again he's not sure where or when—Lee began to look at *Opernwelt*, the German opera magazine. He could not read the articles, but the images were an eye-opening exposure to a scenography radically different from almost anything in the American theatre: more spatial, architectonic, emblematic and, of particular relevance in terms of Lee's work, more vertical. As he has said, the ideas were there for the taking—he didn't discover some hidden secret—but he seemed to be the only one paying much attention. Of particular note were the productions of Wieland Wagner at Bayreuth Festspielhaus, but there were others as well, particularly work by Hannes Meyer and Rudolf Heinrich, that grabbed his attention.

By the early 1960s Lee was definitely aware of two of Brecht's major designers, Caspar Neher and Teo Otto. Lee claims that Otto had the greater influence on him: "I thought Teo Otto's designs were fantastic. I never quite figured out what Caspar Neher's designs were about because it was all so much line drawing that it didn't come together for me. I understood what Neher was doing, but unlike Teo Otto I couldn't copy it." Lee was consciously influenced by Otto's richly textured yet stripped-down settings with their isolated scenic units, and he took one very specific idea from Otto that he would use repeatedly over the years: abstract, stick-like trees that he saw in a photo of Otto's model for Giorgio Strehler's production of Luigi Pirandello's *I Giganti della Montagna*.[8] But even if he was not consciously copying Neher, there were striking similarities. Using natural materials, Neher created seemingly rough-hewn, drab settings that were the perfect complement to Brecht's plays, placing an emphasis on the props or scenic elements crucial to the characters and their actions, and indicating the rest through suggestion. Brecht could have been referring to Lee when he described Neher's sketches as "small and delicate work[s] of art."[9] Interestingly, Lee was also attracted to the work of American painter Ben Shahn whose social-realist murals and paintings of workers and urban scenes were politically in line with Brechtian ideas.

Ultimately, what allowed Lee to develop a unique style was his ability to absorb a wide variety of disparate influences, many from outside the American scenic vocabulary, and synthesize them into a coherent approach. The most obvious influence, that no one else in the American theatre could possibly have had, was Chinese landscape painting, which he studied as a teenager in Shanghai. That training instilled in him a minimalist aesthetic and a penchant for distilling an image to its essence. It is not abstraction because Chinese watercolors depict a kind of reality—mountains, trees, waterfalls, clouds, people

6 Eugene Berman, backdrop for *Don Giovanni*, 1957.

6

and so forth—but they are often achieved with a single brush stroke and only those elements necessary to achieve the desired image, tone and theme are presented. Space is not treated in naturalistic manner. Furthermore, poetry and calligraphy are incorporated into Chinese painting and, as a result, says Lee, "I have problems with totally non-objective abstraction; there is too much separation between visual symbols and words."[10]

A third designer with a significant influence on Lee was Rouben Ter-Arutunian (1920–92). The set and costume designer was born in Tbilisi, Georgia (to Armenian parents) and studied and worked in Berlin and Paris before moving to the U.S. in 1951. He never had the impact on American theatre that either Mielziner or Aronson had, and he did more opera and ballet than theatre, but he played a role in Lee's development. Part of his impact on Lee was simply through his work—in the 1950s he designed numerous productions for the American Shakespeare Theatre in Stratford, Connecticut, as well as New York City Opera, many of which Lee saw. But Lee also assisted him on a Broadway show, *New Girl in Town*, in 1957 and on *Blood Moon* for San Francisco Opera in 1961. Ter-Arutunian was one of the only designers working in the U.S. at the time to make fully painted models, and Lee adopted this practice. Designers dating back to the Renaissance created models of their sets, so model-building in itself was hardly new, but until the 1950s the general practice in American theatre was to construct "white models"—structures made from paperboard in ⅛", ¼" or ½" scale. A painted model gave more information to the director and the shop, but perhaps more important, allowed the designers themselves to get a better understanding of the role of color within their design and allowed a more meaningful experimentation with light. Lee's models are legendary in their detail and perfection, and when Lee began teaching he placed a greater emphasis on model-making than most design teachers of the time, and certainly was among the first to require fully painted models from his students. In fact, the way in which the construction and painting of models became central to design training in the U.S. was largely a result of Lee's practice.

Yet another influence on Lee was Japanese sculptor Isamu Noguchi (1904–88), who designed nearly two dozen works for modern dance choreographer Martha Graham over a thirty-year period beginning in 1935. The demands of modern dance are very different than for opera and theatre. There is generally no narrative or at best a minimal story reduced to essentials. Much of the stage must be left clear for the movement of the dancers, and it seldom requires illusionistic or pictorial scenery. The design, particularly for Graham, emphasized the sculptural aspect of the space and the volume of the stage, sometimes accompanied by emblematic images that foregrounded tonal or thematic elements. Noguchi's designs for Graham generally consisted of carefully crafted sculptural objects that created a suggestive though nonobjective environment. Many of the Noguchi-Graham designs included a single vertical structure amidst the more earth-hugging geometric forms. These had a profound impact on Lee's work, and he has acknowledged that "the sculptural sets of the 1960s and early 1970s, especially at the New York Shakespeare Festival Delacorte Theater, were perhaps my attempt at bringing the theatre of Martha Graham to the legitimate stage."[11]

Finally there was the Russian-born painter Eugene Berman (1899–1972), whose neo-baroque stage designs for ballet and opera, with their ethereal line and hauntingly mysterious tone, were seemingly antithetical to Brechtian aesthetics or the sculptural work of Aronson or Noguchi—yet Lee gravitated to this work and found it inspirational.

One can trace a line from Adolphe Appia and Edward Gordon Craig through Robert Edmond Jones to Jo Mielziner to Ming Cho Lee; from Russian directors Vsevolod Meyerhold and Alexander Tairov via Alexandra Exter to Boris Aronson to Ming Cho Lee. From less identifiable sources there is the influence of Bertolt Brecht and postwar German opera design. Add to that Chinese landscape painting, the sculpture of Isamu Noguchi and the painting of Ben Shahn and Eugene Berman. Mix it all together with Shakespeare; Italian, French and Russian opera; and modern dance—and one has the makings of modern American scene design.

CHAPTER 1

From East to West 1930–54

1

2

3

4

5

1 From left, Lee's maternal grandmother; maternal uncle, Tang Yulu, who was killed in an assassination attempt on T.V. Soong; mother, Ing Tang; and maternal grandfather, early 1920s.

2 Lee's father, Tsu Fa F. Lee, c. 1980.

3 From left, Lee's grandmother, great-grandmother and mother, early 1930s.

4 Ing Tang in posed portrait, pre-1930.

5 Ing Tang in theatrical costume as Lady Precious Stream, c. 1935.

CHINA

Ming Cho Lee points out that the Mandarin name for America is Měi Guó—"beautiful country"—and he believed that one day that's where he would be, a place where "the grass is greener, the sky is bluer and the moon is bigger." He grew up in a Westernized household—his father had attended college in the U.S. and, he says, "I felt I knew the U.S." He achieved his goal when he was nineteen, coming to Los Angeles to study at Occidental College, but at the time he had no particular objective, no idea of what to major in, no specific career plans. His mother had been a well-known amateur actress, he had spent two teenage years learning watercolor painting, and relatives had introduced him to Western opera, yet it never occurred to him that any of this might be the basis for a career—and his father would have objected in any case. Yet once at Oxy, language difficulties propelled him to the art department and from there to theatre, even though he had never before set foot on a stage. His trajectory from that point was astonishing: A dozen years after his move to New York City in 1954, Lee was designing for the New York Shakespeare Festival, the Juilliard Opera Theater, the Joffrey Ballet, Martha Graham, the Metropolitan Opera National Company, New York City Opera and Broadway.

Lee was born in Shanghai on October 3, 1930. The city at the time had a population of about three million, making it the fifth-largest city in the world. A center of trade and commerce, Shanghai prospered while much of the world suffered through the Great Depression. After the First Opium War in 1842, so-called treaty ports forcibly opened China to Western trade, and Shanghai was partitioned into American and British Concessions north and south of Suzhou Creek (administratively combined into the International Settlement in 1863) and the French Concession south of the British sector, leaving only Greater Shanghai, more or less north of the Huangpu River, under Chinese control. The foreign sectors, particularly the French quarter where Lee's family lived, were wealthier and contained restaurants, nightclubs and Western-style architecture, much of which is still evident today. Because of its strong Western characteristics, Shanghai became a popular refuge from the European upheavals of the early twentieth century, adding further to the cultural mix. White Russians fleeing the revolution settled there, and in the late 1930s and early 1940s it became a destination for some twenty thousand Jews fleeing the Nazis. However, while Shanghai thrived, China as a whole was in a state of turmoil following the establishment of the Chinese Republic, the ongoing battles of the warlord era and a power struggle between Sun Yat-sen's Guomindang (the Nationalist Party) and the Chinese Communist Party. Meanwhile, after World War I, the Japanese seized territory in Manchuria and elsewhere, even attacking Shanghai in 1932. The Second Sino-Japanese War erupted in 1937 and one result was the Japanese occupation of the Chinese sector of the city, although the international concessions remained untouched, and Lee's family was largely unaffected until the Japanese entered World War II in 1941. (Meanwhile, less than two hundred miles away in Nanjing, in December 1937, some three hundred thousand Chinese were massacred by Japanese troops.)

The Lee family was large. His paternal grandfather had two wives; the first had eight sons and two daughters, while the second had seven sons and one daughter. His father was son number four. In contrast to this family of eighteen siblings, Ming Cho[1] was an only child, though from the age of twelve he would have two younger stepsiblings. Several members of the family studied abroad. Tsu Fa Lee, Lee's father, enrolled at Miami University of Ohio in 1917 and transferred to Yale University, graduating in 1919 with a degree in economics. (One uncle also attended Yale and another went to Virginia Polytechnic Institute.) In Shanghai he ran a construction company with brother number three and a cousin, was involved in an import-export business and was a general agent for the Occidental Life Insurance Company. He was, in Lee's words, "disciplined and practical," with no interest in the arts and little patience for young Ming Cho's artistic inclinations. The arts, after all, were not a way to make money. Lee's mother, Ing Tang, on the other hand, was artistic and outgoing and is still remembered as part of a golden age of Shanghai theatre and fashion. Lee adored her and credits her with shaping the direction of his life: "My mother was fun! My father was not. She was very beautiful, amazingly beautiful. She came into a room and before you know it you had a party."

At home the family often ate Western-style food, and English was frequently spoken, though unfortunately not so much that Lee could become fluent. Ing Tang briefly gave up the theatre to devote herself to motherhood, but when Lee was four she returned to acting, and when he was six she divorced his father. At the time this was highly unusual, even scandalous, and Lee thinks she may have been one of the first women in China to initiate a divorce. "My mother was a 'new woman' of China, an educated woman. She was having problems with my father and, like Nora in Ibsen's *A Doll's House*, she just

6

7

8

9

10

6 Lee at about three years old with his mother and baby ducks.

7 Lee at age four or five with his mother.

8 Lee at age five or six with his mother in a park in Shanghai.

9 Lee with his mother in 1947.

10 Lee, right, with his cousin Diane Tong Woo, daughter of Tang Yulu, c. 1935.

walked out, and I'm the child that's left behind." Because his mother was the one who sued for divorce—she was leaving Tsu Fa Lee for another man—custody was given to the father. "One night I woke up and my mother was gone," Lee recalls. "I cried and kept asking where is my mother, but my aunts and everyone told me to be quiet. A door opened and I saw her in the other room but it closed again and that was the last time I saw her [for four years]." She left Shanghai with her lover, H.L. Yung; they were married in Singapore and moved to the U.S. Over the next few years Lee was sickly, frequently missing school—which he now suspects was psychological. After retiring from designing in 2005 Lee spent a great deal of time doing watercolors, and something about painting brought him back to that time in his life. "I found myself suddenly having memories...evenings or nights when I was seven or eight or nine years old, desperately missing my mother. And suddenly those feelings, those emotions, just flooded back in vivid Technicolor."

Lee's father didn't really know how to relate to children and he and Lee fought a great deal. "On the other hand," says Lee, "I think he had great love for me, something that he was unable to express or perhaps a little ashamed to express. But the older I got, the better he and I got along—as long as we didn't talk about politics. He had a wicked sense of humor and loved to provoke me. When he was ninety-five he said to me, 'All artists are morally degenerate.' I must say, though, I couldn't have a better friend." From a material perspective, Lee wanted for nothing. The family had a cook, a chauffeur and a maid, and he was sent to a private school. He started studying English in third grade, but with the Japanese occupation his father transferred him to a French Catholic school, reasoning that the Japanese were less likely to interfere there than at an elitist Chinese school. But Lee flunked out of the French school—"I didn't let anyone know, I just said, 'I'm sick of French school'"—and began ninth grade at a Baptist school located near the Bund.

When Lee was twelve his father remarried—to a beautiful woman (in Lee's words) named Esther (she called herself Eta), eighteen years younger and only twelve years older than Ming. She had been married previously and had two children whom Lee's father adopted: Ming Sing (Ernest), age five, and Sylvia, age three. So Lee suddenly had two younger siblings. H.L. Yung, Lee's stepfather, also had children, three girls and a boy, but they were older and not really part of Lee's life (although much later, in New York, he would become very close to one stepsister, Fay Loo, whose involvement with Chinatown politics and education in New York City led, in part, to Lee's own political engagement).

From the time his mother left, Lee would visit his maternal grandmother every Saturday. They would go to the movies—she particularly enjoyed the ones with Nelson Eddy and Jeanette MacDonald. "They would all sing 'Sweetheart,' and she always had a good cry—that was the purpose of going to see movies," Lee recalls. "I would go home and tell my uncle, 'Wow, really terrific singing.' And my uncle would say, 'Oh, they're terrible singers, you should listen to some really good singing.'" This uncle had studied in Japan and brought back records of Enrico Caruso, Amelita Galli-Curci and Antonio Scotti. "To my surprise they were indeed very much better. So I began to learn all the opera arias, and I loved them. They sang the same arias so many different ways. I loved the tenors' voices, but I did not like baritones because they sounded too much like my father." Lee's knowledge of Western music also came from a cousin who would later become a well-respected pianist and from another uncle, a tenor who sang German lieder.

In 1940, when he was ten, Lee's mother and stepfather returned to Shanghai, and he spent Saturdays with her, an almost magical time that was among the happiest of his youth. "We sometimes went to the dog races or jai alai. She gambled and never lost when I was with her." She also took him to theatre, opera and art galleries, "all of the things that my father would have nothing to do with." The first opera Lee saw with his mother was *Rigoletto*.

> ***Rigoletto*** **changed my life because my impression from listening to all the arias [on recordings] was that the tenor had to be the protagonist. Then seeing the opera I realized that actually the tenor was a philanderer and was a really, really bad person. And here was this baritone [the jester Rigoletto] who was a hunchback whom I always avoided, but when I listened to it all the way through he made me cry at the end.**

Lee says, bluntly, "Without my mother I would not have been anything. I would never have gone to the theatre or studied painting. She was tenacious in getting me involved with the arts." It was as if she and Lee's father battled for his soul. Tsu Fa Lee was not merely opposed to a career in the arts—he was very concerned about the general influence of Ing Tang, whom he saw as "a wild and uncontrolled woman." He was afraid that under her influence Ming would turn out like her brother Tang Yulu. Tsu Fa Lee had roomed with Tang at Yale and came to dislike him. Moreover, in 1931, Tang, who was the private secretary to T.V. Soong, a major figure in the Guomindang government, was killed in a botched assassination attempt on Soong. "So that's another reason why he felt that my mother was going to purposely mislead me into a life of evil or whatever."

Soon after his mother returned to Shanghai, Lee had an attack of appendicitis and spent several weeks in the hospital—which turned out to be a transformative experience. "Several good things happened in the hospital," recalls Lee. "I had a lot of visitors and my mother came and stayed with me. My future stepmother came to visit me. Suddenly I thought I was a pretty popular person. And then after that I became quite healthy, and I became a very different person." When he returned to school he was a much better student and far more sociable.

During the Japanese occupation of Shanghai, Hollywood movies were banned and, says Lee, "None of us would be caught dead seeing Japanese movies, and the Chinese movies were a little embarrassing. So there was a great renaissance of theatre, Western theatre spoken in Chinese. And because of the German and Italian Jews escaping from Europe, there was a fairly sizable number of singers, and we had frequent performances of operas and sometimes ballet." The Japanese did not censor classical drama, and it became a means of surreptitious political protest. Lee cites in particular productions of *The Inspector General* and even Sardou's *La Tosca*—with the setting changed from Rome to Beijing.

The most important event in Lee's artistic development came in 1944. He had been dabbling in art, so his mother arranged for him to apprentice with the landscape painter and calligrapher Chang Kwo Nyen. He began by cleaning brushes and observing, then carrying out assignments from the master, including shaping the proper point of the brush, a task done with the teeth which, of course, turned them black. This only served to aggravate his father. Practicing painting at home, "I drove my father and stepmother crazy because I had to take over the whole dining room table and spread out paper and then the ink would seep into the table." He apprenticed with Chang for two years and the technique he learned would have a profound impact on his later development as a designer. Chinese watercolor is all about the brushstroke—knowing how much paint to put on the brush and how much pressure to apply so that each stroke is complete and of appropriate weight. "The thing that allowed me to become a decent watercolorist was my technique of using the brush. I was not afraid of having a brush filled with water and I was taught very early that, say you were doing a snow scene in a landscape, you had to have enough water on the brush to do a wash across the paper without letting the paper soak it up so that you can't continue. This became second nature to me." Lee's apprenticeship, in a sense, also laid the foundation for an approach to design that was neither realistic nor abstract.

> **There is no such thing as total abstraction in Chinese art, just as you can never find total abstraction in Greek vase painting. It may look abstract but it is not. It's about design, proportion. You're not pretending to represent a three-dimensional illustration on two-dimensional terms. Chinese landscape painting is completely two-dimensional, but it has subject matter. In fact, the subject matter and the words are so important that many paintings have written poetry as part of the painting. The brushstroke or the calligraphy is in the service of putting down something quite real. Somehow you put it together and it creates an image. A man is on the mountain meditating. The man is a real man but is expressed by only three brushstrokes. The excitement really is the calligraphy.**

Lee also notes that the Chinese painters were totally removed from the reality of their subject matter. Chang, for instance, lived on the second floor of an old-style Chinese house in an alley. Yet the subject matter was "all these mountains and waterfalls, a scholar walking around, and so forth—so far from his own reality. It's all about copying past masters, all about reproducing a way of thinking, way of life, way of interpreting the relation between people and nature—and nature in relation to philosophical thinking about what life should be. He doesn't even have a photo of the mountain. Just past painting."

Lee was not unaware of Western art. When his mother took him to art supply stores he would buy picture postcards of paintings, mostly the English romantic artists J.M.W. Turner and John Constable. However, he knew nothing of impressionism or the Western modernist movements. Western realism, on the other hand, saturated popular culture and magazine advertisements. (Lee's painting would later be influenced by the Chinese American watercolorist Dong Kingman. Many of Lee's early works are, in his words, "nearly dead-on copies"—note in particular Lee's painting of Seventy-Second Street and Broadway [see page 287]. Lee feels that Dong "was almost reckless with his sky wash, and his freedom in leaving a white area of the paper in depicting landscape or architecture.")

In ninth grade the high school Lee attended was in the French Concession, so he could ride his bicycle there. But in tenth grade it became a boarding school and moved to a residential campus in Greater Shanghai, north of Suzhou Creek, and that put an end to his Saturdays at Chang's studio. (Lee jokes that he gave up art to play soccer. "I was a decent right wing. The only reason I was no good is I never gathered enough courage to use my head to hit the ball. Probably I was wise, otherwise I might be a zombie now.") The wife of one of the school's missionaries began offering drawing classes in her living room. "After a week or so she decided I was way outclassing her and said, 'I'm going to leave you alone.' So I just got paper and I copied Constable postcards or I would draw things." But the classes had the advantage of getting him out of the dormitory area and making him a familiar presence among the missionary households, which were in a separate part of the campus. In eleventh grade Lee was in charge of soliciting advertisements for the class yearbook, which meant going into the city to talk to merchants. "Since I knew the guard at the residence gate I could ride my bicycle through that entrance and go downtown and spend the afternoon visiting my uncles or my stepmother, sometimes staying for dinner and coming back late. I was pretty much a free agent in eleventh grade." Once, upon seeing Lee's stepmother drive up in a Packard to pick him up, a schoolmate exclaimed, "You're not living a normal life!" Unfortunately, this also led to a drop in his grades.

World War II had some effect on the Lee household. Although the Japanese largely left the French Concession alone—the Vichy government collaborated with the Axis states—the Lees' apartment building was appropriated by the Japanese army. The family—Lee's father and stepmother, his two stepsiblings, a cousin and two servants—moved to a small ground-floor apartment in the British sector consisting of one large room, a small bedroom and a kitchen. All the children and the servants slept in the large room.

In 1947, while he was still in high school, Lee's mother and stepfather moved back to the U.S. to work for AIG, the international insurance company founded in Shanghai in 1919 by C.V. Starr. Meanwhile, Lee's father realized that the Nationalist government was not likely to survive and that the Communists would soon take over Shanghai, so he moved his business operations to Hong Kong, leaving Ming with his young stepmother. But soon, realizing that Shanghai was no longer safe, he started sending urgent messages that they should leave the city. "I was in twelfth grade, and I said, 'It's just six months until graduation, why don't I finish?' My father replied, 'It's up to you, but I can't guarantee I'll get you out.' Very smart guy!" Lee and his stepmother moved to Hong Kong where Lee's father hired a tutor to help improve his English. The tutor started him off reading *Julius Caesar*—"my introduction to Shakespeare." Despite the tutoring, however, Lee's English was not adequate to gain entry into the English-language University of Hong Kong, so his father drew on his business connections to the president of Occidental College in Los Angeles. Lee applied and was accepted for the fall semester of 1949.

Getting a passport was not a simple task. The Nationalist government had already evacuated Nanjing and moved to Canton, so that is where he had to go to apply. He and his father flew from Hong Kong to Canton, made the application at the Ministry of Foreign Affairs, and were told to return in a week. Lee returned the following week on his own. "I went to the ministry and they said, 'It's not ready, come back tomorrow.' The next day, still no passport." This continued for three or four days, and his father began sending telegrams saying to forget the passport and just come home because the Communists were right outside the city getting ready to invade. The day Lee got his passport was the day the government offices evacuated the city. Passport in hand Lee rushed to the airline office.

I had a return ticket—but they said, "Good luck. The plane may be gone, it may not be coming in, it may be full." I said, "Holy shit, what do I do now?" They said, "You should take a train." So I rushed to the train station. It was like those French movies after World War II where all the refugees were having car trouble on the road with German planes coming overhead. The train station was crowded and there were people hanging off the train. I thought, I'll never make it. I tried to buy a ticket and they laughed and said, "Get on if you can." One of the train people said, "I think you are better off going to the airport because on the train we take anyone, but on a plane if you have a seat you have a seat." I went back to the airport and they said, "You are in luck, there are two seats left." Meanwhile, my father and stepmother were fit to be tied. So I got on the plane and got to Hong Kong and they were at the airport waiting for me. They said that may have been the last plane, "You might have been lost in Canton forever."[2]

So at the end of September 1949, Lee left Hong Kong for California. There was no such thing as nonstop in those days; his Pan Am flight went through Manila, Midway, Guam and Honolulu, and

Lee was airsick at every landing. In Honolulu he had to go through immigration where in return for helping an immigration officer with translation for another Chinese passenger he was given a tour of Honolulu. The final leg of the journey was on a TWA double-decker Stratocruiser. In Los Angeles he was met by Carl Neprut, a friend of his father's who had formerly run the customs office in Shanghai and would serve as Lee's guardian. Neprut greeted him, "Howdy, Ming." Ming Cho Lee had arrived in the United States.

OCCIDENTAL COLLEGE

Arriving on October 3, his nineteenth birthday, Lee had already missed the first few classes of the semester. He was terribly lonely and scared and called his mother in New York City almost every other day. Occidental was a small college of fourteen hundred students, of which three were Chinese, as Lee recalls. Lee was the only one of the three who kept his Chinese name—"for some reason I felt extremely nationalistic." He made a slight concession, however. His true middle name is difficult for English speakers to pronounce—in the Pinyin system of romanization it would be spelled Jue, and in the older Wade-Giles system as Chü—so he opted for Cho. The name means "to detect; to became aware of; to awake, to be awakened; to come to understand, to be enlightened"—an apt name, indeed.

Having grown up in a family where Western culture predominated, Lee expected to fit right in, but he quickly discovered that whatever his level of English in China, it was vastly inadequate in the U.S. "My first class at Oxy was History of Western Civilization. I didn't understand one word. I didn't expect the U.S. to feel like a foreign country. I was very much by myself. But for some reason I said, 'I belong here.'" Socializing did not come easily. At his high school boys and girls were completely separate, but "at Oxy there were all these co-eds and I had great difficulty talking to them." Lee took studio art classes nine hours a week to counterbalance bad grades in academic classes, and this helped pave the way to greater social interaction—a transformation that he attributes in large part to his art teacher, Dick Swift. He accompanied a studio art group on a trip up the coast, painting scenery along the way; he participated in a California Watercolor Society exhibition; he joined the staff of a campus magazine for which he designed a cover. But he soon came to realize that he would not make it as an artist, especially because his aesthetic was very different from American art, which was dominated at the time by abstract expressionism. Also, as he later explained, "I was frightened by the fact that painters are supposed to have this great big piece of canvas and just create. In set designing, at least you rely on a script. There is something to grab onto first."[3] He thought about a career in the movies and enrolled in a summer film program at the University of Southern California after his second year at Occidental, but he hated USC; more to the point, he discovered that film was artistically about superrealism and specialization among the crafts, neither of which appealed. He remained at Occidental but switched from art to the speech department, which housed the theatre major. It was a transformative experience. He felt at home and relaxed. He made friends, occasionally played bridge, which he had learned from his stepfather, and became more comfortable having conversations.

The head of theatre at Occidental was Omar Paxson who, as in so many small departments then, did everything: direct, design, build and teach academic classes. It was Paxson who turned Lee into a designer. Every artist has many influences, but simply stated, without Paxson, there would be no Ming Cho Lee. Because it was such a small department, everyone was engaged in all aspects of production. Lee started by doing publicity for a show in 1951, then began working on all the crews, and even acted and directed. Paxson didn't care that Lee's English was difficult to understand. "He cast me in every goddamned show," recalls Lee.

> **Couldn't care less if nobody understood my English. The first show I was in was *Peer Gynt* and I was one of those guests in Morocco and also painted all the sets. In the scene we were all sitting there having this dinner and he said, "Do something funny. Why don't you eat a grape and spit the seeds out?" Which I did and he was, "Ha ha ha ha, funny"—he laughed at everything. But he was so encouraging, and it seemed that you could never do anything wrong.**

As the only theatre major with training in art, Lee became the scene painter and then the designer for all the shows, although he knew nothing about set design. "All the basics came from Omar Paxson: how to construct a flat; how to stretch canvas; how to lay in the flat base coat on the flat; how to use a stage brace; how to hang a light and don't hang it upside down or whatever because it will blow up."

The first show he designed was Robert E. McEnroe's *The Silver Whistle* in the spring of 1952. He was also cast as the undertaker. The play concerns a charlatan in an old-age home and Lee's design was based on Los Angeles Victorian houses, which he loved.

11

11 ***The Silver Whistle***, Occidental College, 1952, sketch. Lee's first theatrical design.

The Adding Machine
Occidental College, 1952

12 Cemetery, scene 6. Lee's sketch indicates a watercolor wash for a sky, but the actual set just employed the plaster cyclorama of the theatre: "I fell in love with a plainly lit cyc. I was fascinated by it. Just a white wall with colored light. Sometimes if you kind of squint your eyes, and people in front happen to be silhouettes, it looks like the space is miles away. I was completely in love with having just a bare sky. That carried through even all the way through my time at UCLA. I just used the bare cyc. It was Mielziner who kicked me out of the habit."

13 Sketch of scene 4.

12

13

LEE ON SKETCH VS. RENDERING

Most people would refer to the seemingly finished painted images on these pages as "renderings," but Lee refers to all his theatre drawings, from 1/8″ pencil sketches to fully painted scenes, as sketches. "I hate the word rendering," he declares.

A rendering represents the finished design. It is a recording of what you have set out to do, what you have discovered in the sketches. By the time you get to the stage of rendering your creativity has been spent and all the life is drained out of it. It is a lie. Sketching is the process of discovering what the design is, the crystallization of the idea, the transformation of the idea into a visual statement.

I learned from Rouben Ter-Arutunian that the final step of the process tends to be in the 1/4″ or 1/2″ scale model. Taking the visual expression of a two-dimensional illustration into the engaged space of a three-dimensional model is part of the discovery of what the stage set has to be. When you get into the model your process of discovery has not stopped; you're still working. Once you have finished the model to go back and do a two-dimensional illustration is absolutely a waste of time.

I never start a sketch just drawing people because in drawing people you need to define what the hell those people are doing. Are they floating in air or are they standing? And if they're standing there will be some kind of a floor. You need to commit to a starting point to allow you to develop the design. I tend to have certain amount of preconceived space and architectural character or definition, but I would stop immediately if in the process I begin to draw things that are actually replacing the actor.

I instinctively say, "Oh, oh I took the wrong turn." I'll have an onionskin overlay with people to push the architecture and spatial illustration into the background so that the people take prominence.

14

The difference between Southern Californian Victorian versus the Victorian in San Francisco is that the San Francisco Victorian buildings are all white. In Los Angeles they are all yellow ocher with red roofs. And there were tons of them; the hill where the Music Center is now was covered with the best examples in Los Angeles. When we had watercolor classes we'd quite often take field trips and I would paint a lot of Victorian buildings.

The production scripts were usually the ones published by Samuel French, which included a photo of the original production and a ground plan and common practice was simply to copy the original. "But sometimes you'd say, 'Gee, this ground plan doesn't make sense.' I remember looking at the photo of *Silver Whistle* and saying, 'Oh, I can do better than that.'"

The sketch for *The Silver Whistle* is still striking, as are all of Lee's scenic sketches from Occidental. There is a subtle blending of color, a clarity of line, while retaining the impressionistic feel of watercolor—a strong sense of mood and also an implicit dynamism. One might attribute this to Lee's well-developed skill as a watercolorist, but there is something else—this is a stage set, not a semiabstract landscape. There is a careful balance of elements while creating a space for acting. Of course Lee had seen opera and theatre in Shanghai, but he had never studied theatre, let alone stage design before. Yet the sketch is of a quality that many designers today would be proud to achieve.

The next show was Elmer Rice's *The Adding Machine*. By this time Lee was looking at *Theatre Arts Monthly*, which was filled with photos of current Broadway productions, often showcasing the latest by Jo Mielziner. Also, the students had been assigned to read *The Stage Is Set* by Lee Simonson, the show's original designer. The nearly six-hundred-page tome, which Lee found "unreadable" and "wordy," combined a history of design with a philosophy of designing. But Lee also stumbled across Simonson's *Part of a Lifetime* in the campus bookstore—a pictorial autobiography, as it were, documenting Simonson's work from 1919–1940. This, says Lee, "became my bible." Simonson's *Hamlet* included a graveyard scene with a fence made of sticks that clearly influenced Lee's *Adding Machine* design.

As was true throughout his career, Lee's commitment to the play was thoroughly based in the text. Paxson remembered speaking to the cast about the play at the first rehearsal. "When I had finished and they left, Ming Cho stayed. He told me 'Mr. Paxson, I think you have totally misinterpreted *The Adding Machine*.' That's what he told me! And we started talking, and he was right. I'll never forget that." It is remarkable that despite Lee's struggles with English he read the text thoroughly and could engage in a detailed analytical debate. As a theatre major Lee had to do a senior recital, a solo performance. Helen Paxson, Omar's wife, but also a fellow actor with Lee at the time, remembers that he was "so suave, so sophisticated." The art department faculty who came to the recital, she recalls, were "stunned. They said, 'You did something for him we could never have done if he'd stayed an art major.'"

With his mother and stepfather in New York, Lee spent at least part of every summer and most Christmas holidays visiting there, as well as exploring other parts of the country. (Lee would not return to China until 1978.) At his first Christmas break he took a train to New York, which entailed a change in Chicago. Lee took advantage of the long layover to discover burlesque. It was only on the second trip that he thought to visit the Art Institute: "Over the years I saw more of the Art Institute and fewer burlesque shows." (He now jokes that seeing striptease was research for *Gypsy*, which he later worked on as an assistant to Mielziner.) Just as his mother had taken him to see theatre in Shanghai, she now took him to Broadway.

Following his first year at Oxy, Lee got a summer job working as a pantry boy in charge of desserts at a resort in Lake Geneva, Wisconsin. His second summer, following the class at USC, he went to New York, where he spent a lot of time painting watercolors at his mother's apartment. And after his third year at Oxy, he got a job at the Camden Hills

14 ***The Madwoman of Chaillot***, Occidental College, 1952, sketch. This was only a couple of years after the Broadway production, designed by Christian Bérard, which had a set with a large bed and many birdcages. "But I was too young to understand why there should be birdcages. I think I had begun to see Jo Mielziner's designs, so for the basement all the skeletal things began to get in there, like the skeletal door. I was in love with having people coming down long staircases, then entering through a doorframe and then keep going and exit down into the underground. I didn't know much about the history of interior design but things stuck in my mind. It's all very naïve; I must confess that it's a college production."

Playhouse, a summer stock theatre in Maine, where he played a pageboy in *Henry VIII* and, more important, designed *Lady in the Dark* (with some help from the resident designer, Arch Lauterer).

UCLA

In the fall of 1953 Lee enrolled in the graduate design program at UCLA which, as a large state university, was a very different environment. "At Occidental College I was very much protected," recalls Lee, "and then at UCLA the world just fell apart on me." But he also feels that it forced him to grow up, and it exposed him to students of a wide age range and from diverse social strata. But in terms of the academic curriculum:

I don't think I really learned anything from the design department at UCLA. Aside from flunking out of all the classes because I found it difficult to read [Mordecai Gorelik's] *New Theatres for Old*—Gorelik is a very turgid writer—I spent a good deal of the time following a very old scenic artist who taught scene painting. He was one of those film scenic artists who is a master at wood graining. Sometimes he'd do a wood graining and you'd be standing right there and think it's real. He kind of took me under his wing, and I would assist him, doing a lot of the wood graining and learning all the technique. So I didn't do too much designing.

Lee believes that the department simply wasn't ready for a graduate design program. Looking at a few of his surviving projects it is clear that Lee's work at UCLA lacks the fluency, imagination and even technique of his work at Occidental. The watercolor is gone, replaced by crayon on tracing paper. The lightness and subtlety of mood and color is similarly missing. It is as if everything that gave his undergraduate designs energy and aesthetic beauty was somehow drained out of him.

Lee did create one truly successful design, however, for *The Pearl*, a dance piece based on John Steinbeck's novella. There was a competition open to both students and faculty to design the show and Lee's proposal was selected. Although he may not have learned much about design at UCLA, he was absorbing the work of painters, sculptors and designers, either through seeing performances or through books and magazines. His strongest scenic influences at the time came from the Russian-born neo-romantic painter and designer Eugene Berman ("I loved his kind of stylized but superreal painted architectural approach to the Italian Renaissance") and painter Ben Shahn ("the really pure graphics"), as well as from Mielziner and sculptor Isamu Noguchi (Lee had seen his design for Martha Graham's *Seraphic Dialogue*). Elements from several of these artists appear in the designs for *The Pearl*—in fact each scene is almost in a different style. The extant renderings, however, are not the originals. Because of the success of this production Lee thought it could be his "calling card," the basis for a portfolio. But to make them more professional looking, he later redid them using the techniques he learned from Mielziner, especially how to draw people. Lee bemoans the fact that the rough drawings no longer exist. "All the elaboration after working for Jo took away from what was a very simple idea," he declares.

At UCLA Lee continued to act and direct—and the highlight of his time there may have been winning an acting award. All students were required to audition for every show and he was cast in a new one-act play.

It was about a political prisoner—a terribly boring two-person play with a lot of long speeches, and this crazy director cast me to play one of the prisoners. I took it very seriously—a real method actor. I needed to know every goddamn question and motivation and got myself really involved. UCLA always had an end-of-school party at one of the smorgasbord restaurants in Beverly Hills or Sunset Boulevard. I didn't go because it turned out to be one of those Los Angeles nights where it was raining cats and dogs. In the middle of the night people knocked on the door and a whole group of kids came in saying, "How come you weren't there? You won the acting prize!" So that's the only time that all the acting at Occidental paid off. After that I thought I understood acting.

I also directed, but I discovered that I spent too much time on blocking. I realized that I could never really be a decent director because I was still way too shy and I couldn't deal with scenes that remotely had any kind of obvious overt sexual implications or whatever. I couldn't do it. All I could think of are those British movies where people are holding hands yards apart.

If UCLA did not contribute much to Lee's development as a designer, it did open him up to contemporary politics and social issues and the possibilities for theatre as a sociopolitical tool. He began to read Eric Bentley, whose writings at the time had a strong political focus and may have introduced Lee to the ideas of Bertolt Brecht. Nonetheless, with the success of *The Pearl*, which Lee felt was entirely his work, uninfluenced by his UCLA classes or teachers, and also because "I was sick of studying and I was really not a good student," he made the bold decision to leave after his first year. In the summer of 1954 he moved to New York.

15

16

17

15 ***Much Ado about Nothing***, Occidental College, 1953, production photograph with Lee as Leonato, third from right. "By then I'd become rather stubborn in terms of functioning as a set designer, having my own ideas. I wanted to design a set that had an Italian fresco look, everything is white and all rubbed away. But how did I know how to do that? What books did I look at? I didn't even know how to use the library. I must have found a book on Renaissance art. I remember the director saying, 'Oh, you're not going to have a typical set up of above and below and so forth?' And I said, 'No, I just want to have a town with a white stucco wall." And she said okay. It didn't work very well; I should've listened to the director. I also played Leonato. It's the first time that I actually really fell in love with a Shakespeare play. I never thought that Shakespeare could be that funny."

16, 17 ***Lady Audley's Secret***, Occidental College, 1953, sketches. This is a nineteenth-century melodrama and Lee created a set in the appropriate style of the period. He built an apron over the orchestra pit with fake footlights and drops painted in the flat style of stock scenery—although he spent a day mixing fourteen shades of lavender for one of the drops. The program, done in the style of a nineteenth-century playbill, stated, "Mr. M.C. Lee respectfully announces to the ladies and gentlemen of the audience that he has prepared for representation in a style of splendor never before witnessed here the following pieces of New Scenery: A view of the Lime Tree Walk all in lavish shades of green. A conservatory in the Audley House accomplished in a beautiful rose color with a correct representation of a garden water fountain, and an unbelievable scene divide into two rooms with a ladder which is supposed to lead to a hayloft and the correct representation of a great fire."

18 The Oxy Players from the 1952 Occidental College yearbook.

19 Lee as Sir Michael Audley in *Lady Audley's Secret*.

20 Lee receiving an honorary doctorate from Occidental College in 1975, with his former teacher, Omar Paxson.

oxy players

row 1: Diane Woodford, Rosemary Mixon, John Utzinger, Dorothy Davis, Guy Steiner, Marilyn Burn, Errol Allan, Omar Paxson.

row 2: Carl Ginet, President; Joan Lunoe, Ming Cho Lee, Dee Sharpe, Willis McKenzie, Arlene Franck, Helen Imrie.

Although the '51-'52 season had the best attendance since the war, profits did not exceed $100 a production. Because of the increasing costs of production materials, this average must be improved.

Occidental Players is a group built on limited membership with intense interest in dramatics. The emphasis has been on work and service to drama.

This problem, along with keeping members busy on sets and publicity, is one which faces future Players groups.

18

19

20

PASSING THROUGH THE CHURCH TO THE DOCTOR'S HOUSE

21

KINO'S HOUSE THE SCORPION BITES

22

UNDERWATER SC THE PEARL BED 4

23

LEE ON POLITICS

Growing up I was aware of what was going on around me because my father and uncle always talked about politics. My father did not have any trust in the Nationalist government. He felt that the Communist government was going to take over, and he had the foresight to be prepared for it. And while he eventually became a Goldwater-type conservative, my mother had many Communist friends, especially the intellectuals. So when I came to the U.S., I was a very confused person, politically. At that time you had a lot of really conservative anti-Communist Republicans, like senator [William F.] Knowland, who was known as "the senator from Formosa" [because of his uncompromising support of the Nationalists], and the House Un-American Activities Committee. And of course I developed a big hatred for Nixon while I was in Los Angeles. But even at that time I knew that the situation was much more complex than anyone realized. I knew that the truly corrupt Nationalist government was not the hero. At the beginning, when they occupied Taiwan, they massacred a lot of Taiwanese natives. I would have been for the Communists, except that when they went into Shanghai their behavior was brutal and it affected many of my relatives, especially my favorite uncle number seven who sang Schubert. When the Communists came in he became a translator for German tourists, and I guess he got a little bit free complaining about the government, and he was forced to commit suicide by jumping out a window. Do I have anything good to say about Chinese Communists? Not really. But in the U.S. you have someone like my guardian, Carl Neprut, who was a Republican from Wisconsin and the most conservative person I have ever met, and he called everyone at the State Department "pinkos." I never really argued with him, but I kept saying: I will never be caught dead being one of the Nepruts of politics. I was extremely happy about the Warren Court, which said that even if you preach about violence, as long as it's preaching, the First Amendment protects you. So politically I was leaning towards the left after I came here, but I would have nothing to do with the Chinese Communists. And because I was on the West Coast, I was not very much affected by all the Chinese [in New York] who are actually all right-wingers because they all escaped from China to avoid the Communists. By being on the West Coast, I was politically more radical than my stepfather would like. I was a very mixed bag when I was in California. In my own mind, all these things managed to fit together.

ONE-ACTS

In building 3K-7, a temporary building in Site Three, the Theater Arts Department produces two rounds of one-acts each semester, giving a total of thirty-six one-act plays throughout the school year. These many faculty-supervised shows are ably written, directed and acted by the students.

MING CHO LEE and AL COHEN were the two central characters in ROBRET BARROW's prison-cell one-act, A CUP OF HEMLOCK, directed by MANUEL LEONARDO.

24

25

21–23 ***The Pearl***, UCLA, 1954, sketches for, from top, the town, Kino's house (closely based on Noguchi's design for *Appalachian Spring*) and the underwater scene, all as redrawn by Lee after he began to work for Jo Mielziner. For the underwater scene "all the fishnets and all that were added later. It looks like I'm copying Jo Mielziner's underwater scene from *Fanny*. But the vertical elements were part of the original." The redone sketches have Lee's signature watercolor sky washes, but for the actual production he continued to use a white cyc.

24 Lee acting in *A Cup of Hemlock*, a student-written play at UCLA, for which he won an acting award, in a photo from the UCLA yearbook.

25 ***Fumed Oak***, UCLA, sketch.

CHAPTER 2

First Years in New York
1954–58

1

1 ***Guys and Dolls***, Grist Mill Playhouse, 1955, paint elevation for the drop. Lee's first professional design. Lee did not know he needed to protect the elevation with acetate, which is why it is covered in paint splotches.

SINCE THE TIME THAT NEW YORK CITY emerged as the theatre capital of the United States in the nineteenth century, young people have moved to the city with hopes of making a life in the theatre. Few, however, have been as successful as Lee. We now live in an era in which theatre training is dominated by master of fine arts programs and, particularly in design, an MFA is just about the only route to a professional career. In the 1950s there were a handful of programs around the country, including UCLA, but from a professional standpoint there were really only two: Yale School of Drama and Carnegie Institute of Technology (now Carnegie Mellon University). But a talented individual could still carve out a career by becoming an assistant to a professional designer, not unlike the apprentice system of medieval trade guilds, and this was the route Lee chose. In fact, he believes that if he had gone to Yale at the time he might not have had the success he did. Luck certainly played some role in his development, as did incredible talent—but Lee also made astute choices. Despite some shyness and insecurity in certain social situations, he was extremely self-confident and outspoken when it came to things theatrical and artistic.

As Lee was planning to move to New York in late summer 1954, three of his closest female friends from Occidental were planning to move as well, so he joined them in a third-floor walk-up apartment in Greenwich Village. "It made my stepfather enormously nervous for two reasons. One was to be living with three young American women; and the other is, since nothing is happening, I must be gay. That made him even more nervous!" His Oxy friends in New York were his theatregoing companions, but he also had friends from his year at UCLA. One of the UCLA acquaintances was the soon-to-be-famous theatre and television star Carol Burnett, and Lee played a small role in launching her career. In March 1955, together with Burnett's fiancé, Don Saroyan, they raised money to rent Carl Fischer Concert Hall, across the street from Carnegie Hall, to put on a showcase entitled *The Rehearsal Club Revue*. The show led directly to Burnett's television debut. "We all knew she was the best comedian we'd ever seen," says Lee. "And I spent thirty dollars renting lighting instruments, so I was part of putting Carol Burnett on the map!"

JO MIELZINER

Eddie Kook, founder of Century Lighting, one of the major Broadway lighting firms, had given a seminar at UCLA and suggested that Lee contact him once he got to New York. Lee brought Kook his portfolio with work from Occidental, *The Pearl* from UCLA and some Ben Shahn–inspired watercolors and gouaches. "He looked at it," recalls Lee, "and called Jo Mielziner saying, 'I have a Chinese chap here'—I remember that very well—'and I think you should see him.'" But Mielziner was preparing for the out-of-town tryouts for *Fanny* in Philadelphia, and it was a nerve-rackingly long time before Lee heard from him. Meanwhile, Lee's stepfather, assuming this call would never come, somehow got him an interview with the theatre and film producer Mike Todd who, in turn, sent him to see the designer George Jenkins (who had been an assistant to Mielziner in the late 1930s). Lee would later work briefly for Jenkins, but nothing came of the meeting at the time. Mielziner, of course, did eventually call in late October 1954 (*Fanny* opened in New York on November 4). Looking through Lee's portfolio Mielziner said, according to Lee, "You are a very good watercolorist and a painter. You're really very good. But you don't know a thing about what's going on in the theatre."

Mielziner took Lee on as an unpaid apprentice at his studio in the Dakota apartment building on West Seventy-Second Street. From its start the Dakota attracted elite figures of the cultural world, and Mielziner had an apartment on the fourth floor and his studio on the ground floor. Lee's apprenticeship began by helping out longtime associates John Harvey and Warren Clymer, filing and other office tasks. Since Lee was not a member of United Scenic Artists, the designers' union, he was not permitted to work as a formal assistant, and Mielziner made it very clear that when anyone visited the studio Lee was only to be seen filing—office assistant work. Over the next months Lee followed Clymer getting props for *Silk Stockings*, and Harvey gave him all the ¼" ground plans to draft. "I made tons of mistakes and John said, 'That's no good. Draw it again.' So I kept drawing ground plans over and over again. Occasionally I'd do a little section elevation. Then I would go and mix Jo's paints—all the studio apprentice jobs. Rather similar to what I did for the Chinese landscape artist." Mielziner began to teach him about light and the way in which colored gel would transform painted colors. And, of course, he saw rehearsals: *Fanny*, *Silk Stockings* and the first rehearsal of *Cat on a Hot Tin Roof*. For the latter show, in the spring of 1955, Mielziner took Lee on as a paid assistant at seventy-five dollars a week, a good salary at the time, and gave him his own drafting table, though he still had to pretend to be doing office work if other designers visited.

The first thing I did on *Cat on a Hot Tin Roof* was the layout of the fresco on the ceiling. Jo had done a rough ¼" thing and a very

2

2 ***Romeo and Juliet***, an exercise done for Mielziner in preparation for the United Scenic Artists exam. The similarity of style to the redrawn *Pearl* sketches is apparent, particularly the delicate pillars and arches, attenuated human figures and watercolor sky.

3 Jo Mielziner, Betsy Lee and Ming Cho Lee at Mielziner's apartment in the Dakota, 1963.

4 Program from *Guys and Dolls* at Grist Mill.

3

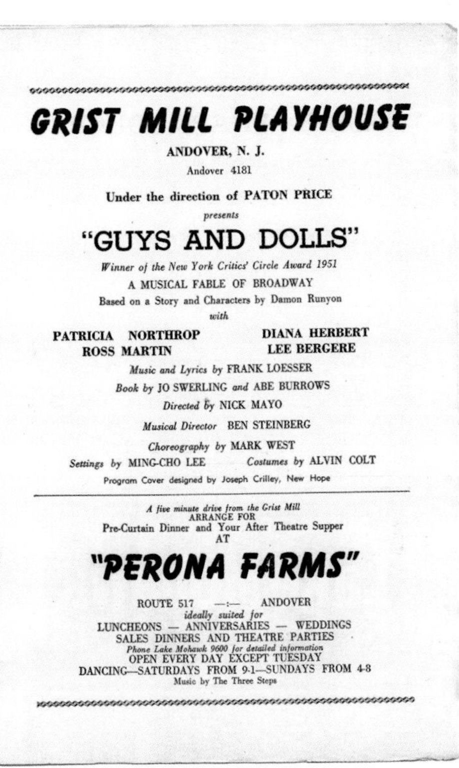

GRIST MILL PLAYHOUSE

ANDOVER, N. J.

Andover 4181

Under the direction of PATON PRICE

presents

"GUYS AND DOLLS"

Winner of the New York Critics' Circle Award 1951

A MUSICAL FABLE OF BROADWAY

Based on a Story and Characters by Damon Runyon

with

PATRICIA NORTHROP DIANA HERBERT
ROSS MARTIN LEE BERGERE

Music and Lyrics by FRANK LOESSER

Book by JO SWERLING *and* ABE BURROWS

Directed by NICK MAYO

Musical Director BEN STEINBERG

Choreography by MARK WEST

Settings by MING-CHO LEE *Costumes by* ALVIN COLT

Program Cover designed by Joseph Crilley, New Hope

A five minute drive from the Grist Mill
ARRANGE FOR
Pre-Curtain Dinner and Your After Theatre Supper
AT

"PERONA FARMS"

ROUTE 517 —:— ANDOVER
ideally suited for
LUNCHEONS — ANNIVERSARIES — WEDDINGS
SALES DINNERS AND THEATRE PARTIES
Phone Lake Mohawk 9600 for detailed information
OPEN EVERY DAY EXCEPT TUESDAY
DANCING—SATURDAYS FROM 9-1—SUNDAYS FROM 4-8
Music by The Three Steps

4

5

rough drawing. My job was to do a very carefully drawn-out layout for the color elevation. Then I did the drawings for the floor, for the carpet. The tricky part was the bar—it needed to lift and turn, and it was on a raked floor. Jo said to John, "Well, do you think Ming can draft the bar?" And John said, "Let's give him a try." Joe Lynn, the famous prop master, came and got the prints and said, "Hey, this is very good drafting. I can build from it." I think at Joe Lynn's recommendation my pay increased to $100 or $125.

The next project was the bus-and-truck tour of *Can-Can*, for which he did most of the drafting—"that was real training." This was a remarkably rapid transformation. Within five years Lee had gone from a nineteen-year-old college freshman just arrived from China, who spoke little English and who had never worked in the theatre, let alone designed a set, to assisting the most important designer in the American theatre on some of the landmark shows of the era. It was, Lee declares, "absolute magic."

Lee studied for the rigorous exam to become a member of United Scenic Artists, which he would pass in June 1955. The process at the time demanded competence in set, costume and lighting design, as well as scene painting, as part of a two-day written and practical exam. Mielziner let him borrow any book he wanted from the studio and also gave him exercises to do in preparation for the exam, including a *Romeo and Juliet.*

In May and June both Mielziner and Harvey went on vacation, leaving the studio to Lee and the secretary. One day Paton Price, the producer of the Grist Mill Playhouse, a summer stock theatre in Andover, New Jersey, came by to ask Mielziner for a recommendation for a designer. With no one else around, Lee showed Price his own portfolio. Price hired him and Lee had his first professional job. The initial show of the season was *Guys and Dolls* which, of course, Mielziner had designed on Broadway five years earlier. The advance director was Bernard Gersten, who, within a few years, would become associate producer of the New York Shakespeare Festival. Gersten remembers primarily the backdrop: "It was very good-looking because Ming was always an excellent painter. It was a collage so that you could play any one of the scenes in front of that one drop. And because the resources of the summer theatres were slight, and it was a big and demanding production, one backdrop for the entire production was about as much as the traffic would bear." There were also scenic pieces that could be put together in front of the drop to form the necessary locales. The then-unknown Jerry Orbach was credited in the program as "technician" and helped paint the drop.

The design of the second show, Edward Chodorov's *Oh, Men! Oh, Women!*, "bankrupted the goddamn theatre," proclaims Lee. "I had no problem getting the set designed and built, but I did not know how to handle props, how to pace it. I ran out of money and it almost ended up a propless show. We barely opened, and I was fired from the theatre. I was just not a summer stock designer."

Following the Grist Mill debacle, Lee worked for George Jenkins on *Too Late the Phalarope*, based on the novel by Alan Paton—Lee's first introduction to South African politics and apartheid. The show was postponed and Jenkins was getting more film work, so Lee returned to Mielziner's studio to work on Rodgers and Hammerstein's *Pipe Dream*, followed by Paddy Chayefsky's *Middle of the Night* and Frank Loesser's *The Most Happy Fella*. Dissatisfaction with the latter show—"he was distressed by musicals that became increasingly operatic," recalls Lee—led Mielziner to conceive and

6

5, 6 ***The Infernal Machine***, Phoenix Theatre, 1958, sketches for the opening scene (opposite) and final scene. The Phoenix used the E.B. Dunkel Studios for scene construction. "George Dunkel was completely unscrupulous and a terrible scenic artist," Lee recalls. "For the bedroom of Jocasta and Oedipus, I had the bed and a lot of metallic little things and an oval mirror over the bed—it was supposed to be, at the time, very sexual and all that. The set was symmetrical—a mistake that I'll never do again. The model was complete but the drawing showed half the set with the instruction, 'repeat, reverse.' On the day of the load in we discovered that they built only half the set. There was only half a mirror; everything was complete on stage right and nothing on stage left. We had to let everyone go home and the shop quickly made the other half."

produce *Happy Hunting*, which opened in December 1956. The show, with a book by Howard Lindsay and Russel Crouse, was loosely inspired by the hoopla surrounding the recent marriage of Grace Kelly and Prince Rainier of Monaco. Ethel Merman's star power kept the show running for a year, but many agreed with Lee's assessment that "it was a terrible musical." Mielziner designed the sets and lighting, but the demands of producing the troubled show occupied much of his time so Lee, who could duplicate Mielziner's watercolor style, did all the paint elevations along with the drafting. The process, however, caused him to begin to question Mielziner's approach to color and lighting. In Mielziner's studio was a small room that, with Eddie Kook's help, was turned into a light lab where he could test the effect of different colored gels on paint elevations, fabrics and the like. One scene required a drop of a forest with yellow leaves. The paint elevation was brought into the light lab and lit with a blue gel, which meant the leaves turned red.

Jo said, "I have a feeling you may have to make the yellow less red and go to kind of greenish yellow." Suddenly I was painting a green drop in order to get a yellow result, and I thought: Well, this is really a stupid way of designing a show because you have no idea what you're looking at. That was an important lesson. The thing is, when you're painting a drop you really shouldn't be thinking about lighting. You should just paint the drop and then let the lighting make it look the best it can.

The experience of working on this show altered Lee's perception of New York theatre. "My work with Jo began to change," he recalls, "and I began to have my own aesthetics." Lee's colleagues on *Happy Hunting* included Pat Zipprodt, the future Tony-winning costume designer, who was assisting Irene Sharaff; Word Baker, Mielziner's secretary, who would go on to fame as the director of *The Fantasticks*; and Paul Libin, a production assistant, who would become the producing director of Circle in the Square and then executive vice president of Jujamcyn Theaters.[1] With the arrogance of youth Lee and his *Happy Hunting* compatriots concluded that they could do just as well and decided that they would produce a play. Rather than find an original script, they looked at plays that had not worked for one reason or another in their original productions and that might benefit from a revival, and settled upon Arthur Miller's *The Crucible*. Although the play won the Tony Award for best play in 1953, it had received very mixed reviews.

7

FIRST PROFESSIONAL CREDITS

As this somewhat naïve group of young theatre artists began to plan their production, another job fell into Lee's lap. At Mielziner's recommendation Norris Houghton, co-artistic director of the Off-Broadway Phoenix Theatre, hired Lee to design *The Infernal Machine*, Jean Cocteau's 1934 version of *Oedipus*. The director was Herbert Berghof, a Viennese-born actor who was ultimately best known for the acting studio he ran with his wife, Uta Hagen. "I had a terrible time," says Lee.

I had no idea how to be a designer. I made Herbert Berghof so angry he almost strangled me. I would have a fresh idea and call him up at three in the morning and he would say, "Who are you? Why are you calling me up this hour?" We had fights not to be believed. I insisted on designing in the style of Eugene Berman, very heavy and architectural, but somewhat simplified and minimalist looking, and a unit that turned around. He went along with it.

The costumes were by Alvin Colt, who had designed with Lee at the Grist Mill Playhouse, and Tharon Musser designed the lights. "It turned out nobody had a good time with Herbert Berghof—except that I really asked for it." Lee's semiabstract setting contained no walls and the main raised platform sat island-like in the midst of the stage. The horizontality of the basic ground plan was strongly offset by vertical scenic units and posts—one of the earliest examples of the verticality that became so closely associated with Lee's work. Brooks Atkinson, in his *New York Times* review, waxed eloquent over the set. Lee was singled out in the opening paragraph while Berghof received a perfunctory mention in the third. Atkinson went on to say, "Although the production is relatively simple, it has extraordinary splendor. Mr. Lee's plastic stage designs have warmth and repose—a sort of inevitability of mass, an unself-conscious indifference to details.... Mr. Lee and Mr. Colt have given the Phoenix its most stunning physical production" (February 4, 1958). This established a pattern that would be repeated often in Lee's Broadway and Off-Broadway reviews: His designs were praised even as the show itself was criticized. Lee was concerned that outshining the director might be detrimental to his career. Even Musser told him, "This is the worst thing you could have done. For the next four years you will not get one design job." Mielziner was a bit more reassuring: "Well, actually it's pretty good, but don't let it go to your head."

At the same time Lee got a call from the Metropolitan Opera. Among the interviews that Lee had had when he first came to New York was one with Herman Krawitz, the assistant general manager of the Met. At the time, Krawitz told Lee, "You're pretty good, you've got talent. When you have something come and show me." Now the Met was planning a new production of *Madama Butterfly* for February 1958 (two weeks after *The Infernal Machine*), supported by none other than C.V. Starr, the insurance magnate for whom Lee's stepfather worked. Starr wanted a new production because, according to Lee, he "couldn't stand all the fake Japanese scenery with tons of flat cutout flowers." The creative team was Japanese, directed by Yoshio Aoyama with sets and costumes by Motohiro Nagasaka. Starr apparently told Met general manager Rudolph Bing that he wanted Lee involved, and since the United Scenic Artists regulations required that a union designer be hired in a supervisory capacity if the designer of record were not a union member, this seemed like a perfect solution. Krawitz took Lee to lunch and explained that essentially this was featherbedding and Lee didn't even have to come to rehearsals. But Krawitz also offered some professional advice: "No one is going to hire you if they can get Jo. And definitely you will never get into the Met. From now on you better start finding out where opera productions are being done across the country, because people like Bobby O'Hearn did tons of opera [outside New York], and now he is going to design for the Met."

But Charles Elson, a well-established Broadway designer who had already designed four shows for the Met, wanted to be the supervisory set designer and told Lee that he should be the costume supervisor. Aside from his disappointment at losing the scenic credit, Lee panicked because, "I'd never touched a costume in my life." Elson assured him that he didn't need to worry—"You don't need to

7 ***Madama Butterfly***, Metropolitan Opera, 1958, costume sketch for Kate Pinkerton.

8 ***The Crucible***, 1958, sketch showing Elizabeth and John Proctor at dinner. Because of budget issues the set was never built and Lee took his name off the program.

8

9

9 ***Missa Brevis***, José Limón, 1958. Although the image is identical to the one used in the original projection, this is actually a sketch for a backdrop created for a memorial performance for Limón at the New York State Theater in 1972. The backdrop was painted but then never used.

do anything." Of course things did not turn out so simple. Nagasaka refused to design the costumes of the American characters—Pinkerton, Sharpless and Kate Pinkerton—and the job fell to Lee, who researched naval uniforms of the period. Having no experience he assumed that he was also required to create the patterns, a cause for further panic, until he was assured that that was not his responsibility. So Lee had his first opera credit, at the Metropolitan Opera no less. But he realized that he would have to get opera design work outside the city if he truly wanted to work at the Met in the future, and he needed to design on his own, not merely assist.

The Crucible was finally set to open March 11. So through the first months of 1958 Lee was working on three productions simultaneously: *The Infernal Machine*, *Madama Butterfly* and *The Crucible*. Lee's mother had agreed to invest in *The Crucible*, and she even held a backers' audition at her apartment to help raise money, although Lee and his soon-to-be-wife, Betsy, with whom he was now sharing an apartment, had tickets for *West Side Story* that evening and missed the party. The production was initially planned for the Off-Broadway Carnegie Hall Playhouse. Lee designed a beautiful set for the proscenium stage: a raised platform of whitewashed wood and planking, accessed by steps on either side, with a gallows stage left. Lee conceived of it as an "architectural, formalized playing space." The sketching style was admittedly influenced by Mielziner—"there couldn't be any better way of storyboarding lighting." The almost ghostlike appearance of the characters was achieved by applying white highlighting to the back side of the tracing paper on which the sketches were drawn, giving the whole image a strongly expressionistic tone. But while the technique was Mielziner, the overall style of the set more strongly reflected Eugene Berman.

However, budget issues forced a change of venue to the Martinique Theatre, which was the ballroom of the Martinique Hotel on West Thirty-Second Street. The bulk of the budget was spent converting the space into a theatre-in-the-round, and most of the original design was sacrificed. By the time it opened Lee was so upset that he took his name off the program as set designer (though he retained credit as lighting designer). The production turned out to be a hit, running

10 Ming and Betsy at their wedding dinner at Ming's mother and stepfather's apartment, March 21, 1958. Ing Tang can be seen at center reflected in the mirror behind them.

for 571 performances, and Lee vowed never to take his name off a production again.

Meanwhile, his *Infernal Machine* colleague Tharon Musser was designing lights for choreographer José Limón's *Missa Brevis* at Juilliard and needed a projection of a ruined church. Musser could not paint well, so she recommended Lee. The dance, to music written by Hungarian composer Zoltán Kodály at the end of World War II, deals with the indomitable human spirit in the face of destruction. Lee's skeletal image suggests a bombed ruin of a church, yet one that retains its soaring verticality. The silhouette was outlined with a thin white line to increase the contrast, and Lee adjusted for the throwing angle of the projection. When he first brought a sketch to Limón the choreographer liked it so much he asked Lee to design costumes as well, which Lee did, assisted by June Dunbar, the young assistant director of Juilliard's dance division. He came up with rehearsal clothes for the women—leotards and skirts with kerchiefs on their heads—and khaki pants and shirts for the men. Lee says, only partly joking, that he was "*way* ahead of Twyla Tharp." (In 1975 Santo Loquasto designed stylish rehearsal clothes for Tharp's production of *Sue's Leg*, which set off a whole new trend in modern dance costuming.) Lee now had his second costume credit.

Thus, by the spring of 1958 Lee had two major Off-Broadway credits as scenic and lighting designer, costume design experience at the Metropolitan Opera, projection and costume design credits for José Limón, two summer stock productions, an assistant credit with George Jenkins, another with Rouben Ter-Arutunian (for 1957's *New Girl in Town* on Broadway), and some dozen shows with Jo Mielziner. To top it off, he and Betsy got married.

MARRIAGE

In the fall of 1955 Lee was living on West Ninety-Seventh Street between Broadway and West End Avenue. One Saturday afternoon he was carrying a roll of drawings for *Pipe Dream* as he was heading home to listen to the Metropolitan Opera radio broadcast. He stopped in a supermarket where he ran into Judy Tucker, Jenkins's administrative assistant.

> **Judy is a very outgoing lady and I was a little bit shy. I was a little bit flustered after seeing her, and I left my drawings at the supermarket. When I got home, I said, "Oh, shit, I left my drawings someplace and I'll be fired by Jo." But right off the bat Judy called me saying, "Don't worry, I've got your drawings. But in order to get them you have to come to dinner." And it turned out that Betsy was Judy's roommate. I had actually met Betsy once before—she came to Jo for an interview and Jo introduced Betsy to all the assistants in the room. So that's how we met again.**

Betsy Rapport was a graduate of Smith College and, in her words, a "budding designer." She had done some technical and lighting work Off Broadway and, at the time she was introduced to Lee, she was working in the costume shop for Joseph Papp's Shakespeare Workshop (the precursor to the New York Shakespeare Festival). They were married three years later, March 21, 1958, at City Hall in the midst of a blinding snowstorm. (For the next ten years it always snowed on that date. "We panicked the first year it didn't snow," says Betsy.) On the morning of their wedding day Lee had a costume design meeting with Limón about *Missa Brevis*. When he returned to their apartment, Betsy asked him how it went,

> **and he said, "Oh it went fine, I'm going back at five o'clock." I said, "I think you're forgetting something." And he said, "Oh, what?" And I said, "We're getting married at four." He said, "Oh, well, that's okay, we can get married and then I'll go to my meeting." So that's what we did. We got married and then he went to his meeting with José Limón and I went to the party at his mother's apartment.**

Lee continues the story:

> **I was showing the costumes and I was getting increasingly impatient. José said, "Ming, why are you so impatient?" And I said, "Well I just got married and there's a party." They looked and me and said, "So what are you doing here? Go away." So I came to the party. That was an auspicious beginning.**

"The moral of the story," concludes Betsy, "is don't take any of it too seriously."

The marriage, as everyone in the theatre world knows, went on to be one of the great collaborative partnerships.

CHAPTER 3

The Career Begins 1958–61

1

1 ***The Pearl Fishers***, Peabody Conservatory and Empire State Music Festival, 1961, ½" model. This is one of the earliest examples of Lee's use of verticals and grid structures.

BORIS ARONSON

The burst of design activity over the first months of 1958 suggested a career about to take off (and, surprisingly, possibly launch Lee as a costume designer), but it would be more than a year before Lee would fully leave behind his days as an assistant. He continued to work for Jo Mielziner, as assistant designer on *The World of Suzie Wong* and *Whoop-Up*, and, through Mielziner's recommendation, designed *Triad*, a triple bill of one-act operas by composer Mark Bucci produced Off Broadway. But most significant, toward the end of the year he began to assist Boris Aronson. This would provide Lee with a whole new vocabulary and new methods of working.

Aronson had seen some of Lee's paint elevations for Mielziner at Imperial Scenic Studios, one of the two leading scenery construction studios in New York. According to Lee, Aronson could not do a watercolor wash: "It always looked very awkward, which meant that he was always kind of envious of Jo. He saw that I could do Jo Mielziner's wash without an airbrush [which Mielziner used], which is one step more pure." Aronson called, and because there was a lull in Mielziner's studio at that moment, Lee eagerly went.

When Lee joined the studio in December 1958, Aronson was working on Peter Hall's production of *Coriolanus* with Laurence Olivier and Edith Evans for the upcoming season at Stratford-upon-Avon, England. Earlier that year Aronson had designed Christopher Fry's *The Firstborn* and Archibald MacLeish's *J.B.* With its "sculptural, abstract design of complete plasticity,"[1] *The Firstborn*, in particular, had made a very strong impression on Lee and he later declared it to be "way ahead of its time." Aronson's work on *Judith*, produced at Her Majesty's Theatre in London in 1962, was another highly textured, sculptural design that would have a major impact on Lee. To Lee's great disappointment, however, his first assignment was not a theatre project but the ark for the new Temple Sinai in Washington, D.C. Aronson felt that in order to work on this Lee needed to learn about Jewish tradition and its iconic elements, and this would best be done by a visit to the Jewish Museum. It was pouring rain the day Lee arrived at Aronson's studio, and he quickly learned something about the difference between Mielziner and Aronson:

> **When you travel on a field trip with Jo Mielziner you always come out of One West Seventy-Second and hail a taxi and you go wherever you go. But Boris took buses. Both of us were standing in front of a bus stop and finally the stupid bus came and we were drenching wet; I was not prepared for this. So we get on the bus, get off at Ninety-Sixth Street and Central Park West, wait for the crosstown bus, get off at Fifth Avenue and Ninety-Sixth and then wait for Fifth Avenue bus, then get off at Ninety-Second. I was absolutely wet. And after, we repeat the whole process of bus-bus-bus. I thought: Uh-oh, this is really a stupid thing I have gotten myself into.**

Aronson had made a small wooden sculpture of the ark and then created a separate model of sorts out of melted wax crayons on shirt cardboard for the decorative elements. Lee later explained that Aronson "thought the menorahs [at the Jewish Museum] were like Giacometti sculptures, and soon he was creating a similar look by melting down crayons and letting them run—I had never thought of that."[2] But none of the elements were in scale and neither Aronson nor his wife, Lisa, who also worked in the studio, could figure out how to draft it. So Lee drew it and made a model out of balsa wood.

Aronson was impressed and put Lee to work on *Coriolanus*, doing some elevations, sketches and a model. Aronson had a reputation for discussing ideas but then letting the assistants figure it out. This was, of course, an exaggeration—but with a grain of truth. "When you worked for Boris," explains Lee, "you felt he was never doing any work. But sometimes, when you left in the evening things were all over the place, and when you got there the next day he showed you something and said, 'What do you think?' And you would say, 'Very beautiful.' 'Well, I carved it last night, but it's not in scale, so now you take this and make it into scale.' This is the way Boris worked."

Lee also continued working for Mielziner, most notably on *Gypsy*, one of the landmark productions of the American musical theatre, which opened in May 1959. Mielziner was brought into the project relatively late and the studio became a scene of frantic activity, especially as director Jerome Robbins was constantly changing his mind about scenic elements. Lee redrafted the dressing room scene innumerable times.[3] And in June, Lee and Betsy's first son, Richard, was born.

Lee worked on *Flowering Cherry* and *A Loss of Roses* in Aronson's studio, but his major assignment came a year later for the musical *Do Re Mi*, which opened in December 1960. Aronson appreciated Lee for his drawing and painting skills, but he would not believe that Lee was technically competent to do the drafting. "You are a real artist," he told Lee, "which means that technically you are not very good." Despite Lee's protests Aronson insisted that a technically competent artist simply did not exist. He brought Robert Randolph in to do the technical drawings and told Lee, "You will just do the artistic thing." According to Lee, "Boris is a very secretive person," and he often kept the assistants apart in separate rooms, "so we were always kind of in a limbo." Randolph and Lee worked without seeing each other. Eventually even Lisa Aronson agreed that the different efforts were a waste of time, so Aronson relented and allowed Lee to do the drafting, and ultimately made him the assistant designer on *Do Re Mi*. Although the set was well received critically, Lee believes "it was a failure; nobody understood it." The problem, for Lee, was that this was one of the first shows in which Aronson used collage in a substantial way, and the shop did not know how to execute it. "Instead of cutting pieces out of plywood, doing collage, or pasting it together, they tried to paint it—and of course it all looked fake."

Aronson would have a profound effect on Lee's work, particularly in developing the sculptural and emblematic aspects, which allowed him to break away from the pictorial influence of Mielziner. He taught Lee to experiment with nontraditional materials and he also demonstrated that accident and disorder could be very important in generating ideas. "Jo was a quintessential professional," declares Lee, "while Boris was anti-professional"—an opinion further supported by an anecdote Lee relates from designer and scenic artist Lester Polakov:

> **Boris told a scenic artist, "This is a luxurious ballroom and it should be shiny and have gold leaf and ornaments and so forth," although the scenic artist protested that it was supposed to be an old, fading ballroom. But Boris insisted and the scenic artist painted all the beautiful things. Boris came to look at it and said, "Very good painting, but it's all wrong." "Mr. Aronson," replied the scene painter, "why is it wrong? I followed your instructions." "It is all wrong because this room should be all destroyed. You have to take opaque gray and black and purple paint and you need to cover all this." Two days later the scenic artist said, "I did what you asked, but I think it looks terrible." And Boris said, "Well, you're right, it looks terrible. What's wrong is you covered all the stuff. Now you need to wash it away and let the original painting come through." Finally, of course, Boris got what he wanted. He wanted the real thing.**

By contrast, Lee notes, Mielziner would start with a perfect paint elevation for the scene shop to work from. Aronson improvised. "He would do a little sculpture, and you would discover that the soul of the play was in that little sculpture. But from then on he was, in a way, incompetent, because he didn't know anything else. It was always about the visual soul of the work. With Boris, it's about philosophy, about the condition of the society, about aesthetics. Essentially it's about the world. I learned that to be absolutely, carefully professional isn't all that important. When things get too predetermined that may not be such a great idea."

JOSÉ LIMÓN AND THE MET ONCE MORE

During the summer of 1959, as part of the twelfth American Dance Festival at Connecticut College, Lee designed his second production for José Limón, *Tenebrae, 1914: Episodes in the Life of Edith Cavell*. For the dance, based on the story of the British World War I nurse who was executed by the Germans, Lee created a Ben Shahn–inspired backdrop of ghostlike figures rising up from the ground behind somewhat abstracted barbed wire.

The lighting was by Tom Skelton, who was also designing the revival of *Missa Brevis*. Skelton had a reputation for using a lot of oversaturated colors and Lee, who described himself as "a noncolor designer," was worried about what this would mean for *Missa Brevis*. Skelton reassured him saying, as Lee remembers, "There are different ways of achieving a sense of no color. One is you use *no color*, and that is the lazy man's way. You turn the dimmer down and it all turns yellow. Another is you use hundreds of colors and you make white light out of color. And for *Missa Brevis* I can promise you that, except for some scenes that need to be red, it will be almost white." "I realized," says Lee, "that Tom was a great lighting designer."

Meanwhile, following Lee's work on *Madama Butterfly* at the Met, Herman Krawitz hired him as an assistant—this time on sets—on two more productions: British designer Oliver Messel's Met debut, *Le Nozze di Figaro*, and *Il Trovatore*, designed by Elizabeth Montgomery, one of the three sisters who founded the design firm Motley. Messel's way of working was very different from Lee's experience with Mielziner or Aronson. Messel had done a *Figaro* at the relatively intimate Glyndebourne Opera in England and decided to use the same design. Lee's assignment was to enlarge it to fit the Metropolitan Opera stage. Working from the drawing—which was done on graph paper—and a very rough model "things got all screwed up because a chair rail which was three feet at Glyndebourne turned out to be four foot six and so on. Oliver said, 'Oh, it doesn't matter, you just go for it and adjust it.' That took me the longest time.

2

3

2, 3 ***Tenebrae, 1914***, American Dance Festival, 1959, sketches.

All these curlicues needed to be enlarged, and I was not very good at these rococo details. Eventually I drafted the whole thing, but Oliver was not that happy because it got a bit stiff and he just wanted it very loose. I was steeped in Brecht, and Oliver Messel was not the person for me to work with." (British designer John Bury once told Lee, "Oliver Messel is just a watercolorist; he is not a theatre designer.")

Montgomery, on the other hand, was primarily a costume designer and therefore was very much in need of an assistant for the set. "Liz Montgomery doesn't draft at all. Her model feels like a costume for a homeless person—a lot of crappy paper pasted together. Even looser than Boris Aronson." Lee drafted the show and took it to the Met shop where the shop foreman, a man called Big Tex, told him the details would all get lost in the Met house. Lee felt that a scene outside the dungeon keep could be set in-one. On Broadway an in-one scene is usually six feet deep—enough room, as Lee puts it, "for Ethel Merman to sing and a follow spot." For the Met he doubled it to twelve feet. But at the tech rehearsal everyone still felt that was too small. "I said, 'You only have two people on the stage, why do you need so much room? It's much more intimate.'" To which the baritone Leonard Warren replied, "Kiddo, you've been working on Broadway too long. When I take even one step, ten feet is not enough." The scene got pushed farther upstage, and Lee added more scenery. "The set design was horrible. But everyone felt that I actually had done a lot more work than the usual assistant and Liz Montgomery thought I should take a curtain call along with all the others, but I decided that I was way too young and this would go to my head." Lee would work with Montgomery again a few years later on *Mother Courage and Her Children*.

PEABODY CONSERVATORY

Tharon Musser, who had brought Lee in to work on *Missa Brevis*, became his entrée into the world of regional opera as well. She had been asked by Laszlo Halasz to design productions for the Peabody Conservatory in Baltimore (now the Peabody Institute of the Johns Hopkins University), but was not available. Since Lee could do lights as well as sets she recommended him. Halasz was a Hungarian-born conductor, most famous for being the first music director of the New York City Opera from its founding in 1943. Halasz had ongoing disputes with the City Opera board of directors, often over his choice of modern operas in the repertory, and he was finally fired in 1951. "He had a temper like not to be believed," notes Lee. "He also mistreated singers." Halasz offered Lee a rather paltry $250 per production, but he accepted. As for transportation to Baltimore, Halasz would drive Lee—which actually became a time for pleasurable conversation, given Lee's deep knowledge of opera, including ones outside the standard repertoire.

Halasz's practice at his previous posts had been to rent old scenery from other opera companies; similarly, the Baltimore Civic Opera, then under the direction of Rosa Ponselle, also rented old-fashioned scenery from Anthony Stivanello's warehouse. But Peter Mennin, the newly appointed director of the conservatory—and later president of Juilliard—wanted professional-looking productions with new sets. In a sense, Lee did for Peabody what he did at Occidental: replace stock scenery with original designs for each production. So when Lee's first Peabody production, Rossini's *The Turk in Italy*, opened, the sets were the focus of glowing reviews. "The first aspect of this production which made its impact was the setting," proclaimed the *Baltimore Sun* reviewer Weldon Wallace. "In twenty years of going to the Peabody, this writer has not seen anything so ingenious and imaginative as the transformation of the Peabody stage wrought by the scene designer, Ming Cho Lee" (December 16, 1959).

The design was a fascinating combination of the pictorial and architectural. Lee built the set onto the apron beyond the ponderous proscenium and obliterated the proscenium columns with slats that were frankly copied from Rouben Ter-Arutunian's designs for the American Shakespeare Theatre at Stratford, Connecticut. Two pairs of Moorish-style pavilions flanked the stage, and plain white gonfalons against a black background framed the central stage, which depicted the Bay of Naples. However, it all had a flat, cartoonish style influenced by the work of illustrator Saul Steinberg. The slats recurred in *The Fall of the City*, a twelve-tone opera by James Cohn, along with a variety of platforms, ramps and step units, and again in Gian Carlo Menotti's *The Old Maid and the Thief*.

Each of the Peabody productions exhibits a slightly different approach and style. Lee, just at the start of his career, was experimenting, investigating and discovering himself as a designer, and opera provided a broad canvas for exploration. His sketches for *La Bohème*, for instance, show a strong influence of Mielziner. "I became nervous about sketching," Lee claims. "Every time I did sketches it made the work become a mess because I did the opera trying to reproduce the sketches in the Mielziner style."

Amahl and the Night Visitors, directed by Menotti later the same year, with its semi-expressionist shapes and blocks of color, looked remarkably like Ignati Nivinsky's design for Evgeny Vakhtangov's 1922 Moscow production of *Turandot.* Interestingly, this time the *Baltimore Sun* reviewer (Wallace, again) felt that the designs for the double bill of *Amahl* and *The Old Maid and the Thief* were "too dominant. They impose themselves too insistently on the eye. The operas seemed to be created for the sets rather than the other way around" (December 9, 1969).

La Bohème was the largest production Lee did at Peabody. The local shop could not handle it, and it was sent to a shop in Mount Vernon, New York. "I stayed all night in Mount Vernon painting the set," Lee recalls. "It was raining outside and the paint wouldn't dry. It was just a mess." The real disaster came in the third act on opening night. The women's chorus entered over a bridge. "All the women got on the bridge and it collapsed. Boom! And I ran out of the theatre and took a train back to New York." (No one was hurt, and the set was fixed for the subsequent performances.)

Because of his work at Peabody and the connection with Halasz, Lee was hired to design two opera productions in the summer of 1960 at the Empire State Music Festival in the Hudson River Valley: Deems Taylor's *Peter Ibbetson* and the American premiere of Leoš Janáček's *Kátya Kabanová,* conducted by Halasz and directed by Christopher West (who would soon head the opera program at Juilliard). Lee says that his design for *Kátya Kabanová,* based on Alexander Ostrovsky's *The Storm,* was inspired by Mielziner's design for *All Summer Long* in 1954. Lee was struck by Mielziner's translucent drop of a winding river behind a skeletal house. He also created a backdrop of Chinese landscape painting–inspired leaf shadows. Despite Mielziner's influence, though, Lee took his rough sketches to Aronson for critique, perhaps because, in Lee's words, the design was "pretty abstract—a constructivist kind of thing." A curving ramp spiraled in from upstage right to downstage left behind an oblong, octagonal raised platform. It did, in fact, have echoes of the work of Soviet directors Vsevolod Meyerhold and Nikolay Okhlopkov from the 1920s. Aronson enthusiastically approved.

For the 1960–61 season Lee continued to work at Peabody and at Aronson's studio. The spring production at Peabody was Georges Bizet's early work, *The Pearl Fishers.* Influenced by his UCLA production of *The Pearl,* Lee made the daring choice to set it in Mexico instead of Ceylon. The set was remarkably simple: a group of irregularly shaped platforms framed by symmetrical, shutter-like slats once again masking the proscenium, a seemingly jerry-built structure of vertical and horizontal rough wooden poles, and some screens of irregularly shaped and broken slats. Lee also designed the costumes and lights. "Everyone said, 'Is that it? *Pearl Fishers* is supposed to be oriental, with Buddha and all that stuff.' But I said, 'No, no, it's happening in Mexico.' And they checked and said, 'You're right, because Bizet originally wanted to set it in Mexico.'" When the production was restaged at the Empire State Music Festival that summer the reviewer for *Time* magazine applauded the altered locale. "Most productions follow the original Paris staging, in which the fishing village became as elaborate as a movie set, and the fishermen went about like oriental chieftains in turbans and silk robes. In last week's production, Chinese-born set designer Ming Cho Lee wisely changed all that—and made the opera far more credible. His sets, strewn with fishermen's huts, were starkly simple, and his costumes were equally plain" (July 21, 1961).

Lee's scenography extended even to the staging. For this production he created a storyboard—beginning a lifetime practice. A storyboard allowed him to plot out not only scene changes, but the movement of actors through the set, giving him a greater understanding of the spatial demands of a show. Even now, he cannot conceive of creating a design without this tool, and is baffled by designers who do not follow this practice. It also means that to at least some degree Lee is thinking like a director, and his design inevitably influences the staging. Hugh Thompson, the director and baritone lead, came to Lee with the problem of staging the ending of *The Pearl Fishers.* Lee suggested a *West Side Story*–like fight: "three students running towards you and you flip one that way—whoosh—and one another way, and while you flip the other one, someone from the back stabs you. And that's how it went on." Lee recalls Thompson commenting, "I've never worked with a designer like that. He tells you everything you have to do."

The final show of the season at Peabody, in May 1961, consisted of three one-act operettas by Jacques Offenbach—*The Magic Fife, Le Mariage aux Lanternes* and *The Island of Tulipatan*—under the umbrella title *Three Times Offenbach.* The *Baltimore Sun* critic described the setting simply as "imaginative but quite waggly and very insistent on attention from the spectator" (May 5, 1961).

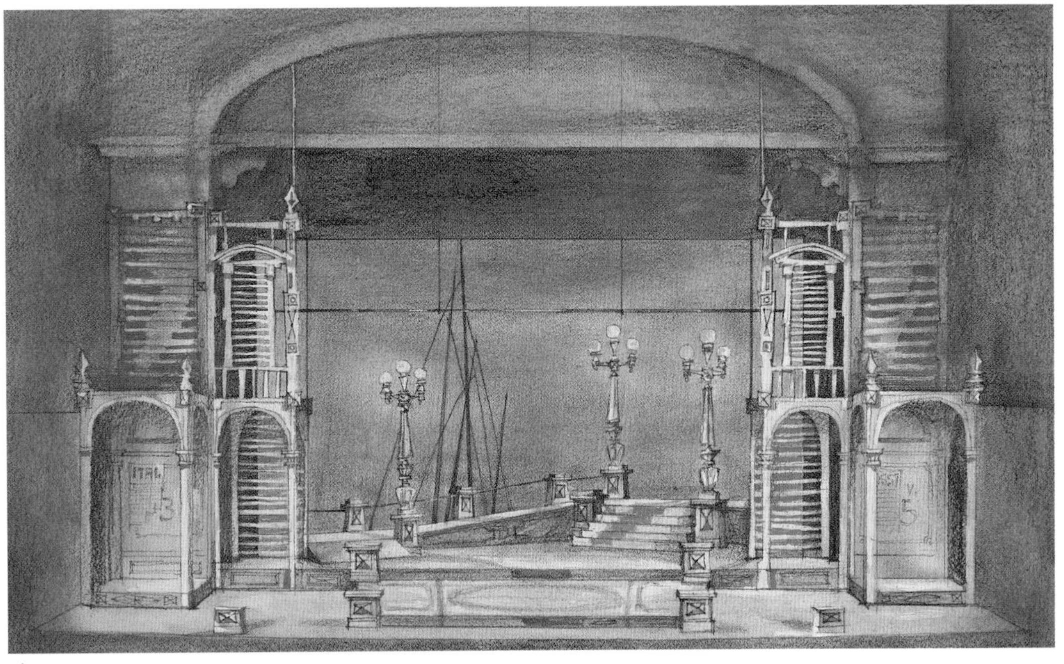

4

5

6

4 ***The Turk in Italy***, Peabody Conservatory, 1959, sketch. Note slats covering the proscenium.

5 ***The Fall of the City***, Peabody Conservatory, 1960, sketch.

6 ***The Old Maid and the Thief***, Peabody Conservatory, 1960, photograph. Structurally the set resembles *The Turk in Italy*, with slats masking the proscenium and framing a central, cartoonish setting. Lee jokes that those were his "slats years." Since Ter-Arutunian had abandoned slats in favor of "what we call his potato chips, I said, 'Well, if Rouben doesn't want the slats, I'll use them.'"

7

8

7, 8 ***La Bohème***, Peabody Conservatory, 1960, sketches for the garret, act 1 (top) and Café Momus, act 2, showing the strong influence of Jo Mielziner.

9 ***Amahl and the Night Visitors***, Peabody Conservatory, 1960, photograph.

9

10

11

12

13

14

15

10–12 ***Kátya Kabanová***, Empire State Music Festival, 1960, sketches. The design was inspired by Mielziner's *All Summer Long*, but was ultimately more influenced by Aronson's constructivism.

13–15 ***Peter Ibbetson***, Empire State Music Festival, 1960, sketches.

16

16, 17 ***Un Ballo in Maschera***, San Francisco Opera, 1961, sketches for act 1, scene 2, Ulrica's cave (left) and act 3, scene 3, the royal ballroom. The production was Lee's one original design as the company's resident designer.

But aside from these operas Lee had no projects of his own, so he returned to work for Aronson on a play called *The Queen and the Rebels* by Ugo Betti. For all his admiration, Lee found Aronson increasingly difficult and frustrating to work for. Lee resented being excluded from the meetings with directors, and it seemed that nothing he did would please Aronson. "He wanted me to do a sketch for him that looked like Jo Mielziner's, so I did and he said it looks too much like Jo. And then he messed it up." On several shows Aronson had Lisa make models out of shirt cardboard and then asked Lee to "clean it up—but then he wouldn't like it, and I began to complain. So he sat me down and said, 'Ming, you are so wonderful to work with, but lately you have become so angry. Why are you so angry?' I said, 'Perhaps I shouldn't work for you anymore because I'm getting absolutely filled with rage.' He said, 'Take it easy. You are so good.' So we became again a happy family." Unfortunately, the funding for the Betti play did not materialize and the show was canceled, and suddenly Lee found himself unemployed, with a family to support—his second son, Christopher, had been born in November 1960. "Boris just gave me $150 and called it a day." Desperate, he contacted Pete Feller at Imperial Scenic Studios as well as Nolan Scenery Studios to see if he could work as a scene painter, but it was the end of the Broadway season; the shops would not start up again until June for the fall shows.

SAN FRANCISCO OPERA

Remarkably, just at that time Kurt Herbert Adler, the general director of San Francisco Opera, asked Mielziner to design a new opera, *Blood Moon* by Norman Dello Joio. Mielziner could not do it so it was offered to Rouben Ter-Arutunian, who accepted on condition of having an assistant hired for him. Adler hired Lee for the season as "art director," or resident designer (or, as Lee puts it, "glorified assistant"). Lee had assisted Ter-Arutunian back in 1957 on his first Broadway show, *New Girl in Town*—"and I swore I would never work for him again. He is a weird guy. He is obsessed with neatness. Every time you quit you have to quit half hour early to clean your table; everything put in the right place. Absolutely opposite to my personality." Nonetheless, as Lee has acknowledged, Ter-Arutunian's designs had a major impact on his development. The designs for San Francisco had to be completed in a mere four weeks. The arrangement was that Lee would work with Ter-Arutunian for two weeks in New York and then bring the completed designs out to San Francisco and remain there for the season, which ran through December. Betsy packed up the apartment and, with the two children, joined Lee in San Francisco. Lee had been apartment hunting while staying with a cousin in Berkeley. "It turns out that in San Francisco if you have kids it's like having a dog—it's very difficult to get an apartment."

Lee worked on almost every show in the season—some new ones but mostly those brought out of the warehouse—"really 1920s and

17

'30s old-fashioned design." The practice at San Francisco was for the resident designer to oversee the scene changes and generally run the backstage. Lee arranged to split this task with the technical director, alternating nights, meaning that he was backstage at every other performance. Lee did make a few original contributions, however. When it was discovered at the last minute that there was no set available in the company's stock for *Lucia di Lammermoor*, they hired German designer Leni Bauer-Ecsy. Perhaps because of the very small budget, Bauer-Ecsy sent in a very rough model depicting "the weirdest *Lucia* I've ever seen." It was essentially a curved wall with some small openings, which became known as the "Swiss cheese *Lucia*." But this production was going to be Joan Sutherland's American debut, and when director Dino Yannopoulos saw the design, he insisted that there be a staircase for Sutherland's mad scene. Bauer-Ecsy refused, and Yannopoulos said, "Oh, have the kid design the staircase." So Lee designed a staircase in Bauer-Ecsy style coming out of hole in middle of the set.

The company also did a two-week season in Los Angeles every year—Lee had seen them several times during his student days—and this season included Verdi's *Un Ballo in Maschera*, for which no viable scenery existed in the warehouse. The standard practice, when there was no existing set, was to cannibalize scenery from other productions, but virtually every piece was in use for other operas. Lee managed to salvage one scene from *Rigoletto* and another from *Boris Godunov*, then designed the rest from scratch on a budget of $700, most of which went to paying scene painters.

While in San Francisco Lee received a call from Mielziner, offering him a Broadway show that Mielziner had to turn down. The show was *The Moon Besieged*, and it promised to be Lee's first Broadway credit. Scheduled for the spring (it was subsequently postponed), work needed to begin immediately, and the director, Lloyd Richards, wanted to meet Lee before agreeing to hire him. Richards had been the director of the groundbreaking *A Raisin in the Sun* in 1959 and was the first African American to direct on Broadway. (Lee and Richards would meet again when Richards was appointed dean of the Yale School of Drama from 1979–91.) Lee took the redeye to New York on a night when he was not running the backstage and returned on a flight back to San Francisco the next day, arriving in time to run the show that evening. This would be the first of many, many such rapid turnaround flights that Lee would take during his career, flying across the country or literally from the other side of the world to meet a class or fulfill a design obligation. There were a few more redeyes over the following weeks for design meetings before Lee returned to New York at the end of the San Francisco Opera season, stopping in Dallas along the way to oversee a production of *Lucia di Lammermoor* that was using the "Swiss cheese" set. The coming year would change his life.

CHAPTER 4

1962—The Annus Mirabilis

1, 2 ***Tristan und Isolde***, Baltimore Opera Club, 1962, sketches of the ship in act 1 (top) and the garden scene in act 2 with hanging abstract metallic foliage pieces. The entire design was inspired in part by designs for the Bayreuth Festspielhaus that Lee had seen in German opera magazines.

1

2

IT WOULD BE HARD TO IMAGINE a more eventful year in the development of Lee's career—or anyone's, for that matter—than 1962. The family returned to New York from San Francisco and found an apartment at 121st Street and Amsterdam Avenue which, despite its proximity to Columbia University, was not at the time a particularly safe or appealing neighborhood. The year began not only with work on *The Moon Besieged* (which was ultimately postponed to the fall because of fundraising difficulties), but with Lee's final season at Peabody Conservatory: *Tristan und Isolde* (done in conjunction with the Baltimore Opera Club) and *Werther*. But this would not be another year of commuting to Baltimore. Almost as soon as he settled back in New York, there was a call from Sarah Caldwell, founder of the Opera Company of Boston and a notoriously adventurous and idiosyncratic conductor and director. On Jo Mielziner's recommendation she asked Lee to design a *Madama Butterfly*. Then Martha Graham's office called to say she wanted to meet with him. "Why would she call me?" Lee wondered, "I'm totally unknown." Graham's regular designer, Isamu Noguchi, was unavailable and, as Lee heard it, Graham wanted to work with an Asian designer—of which there were very few. She contacted the Union and, says Lee a bit facetiously, he was the first, perhaps only, on the list. She asked him to design *A Look at Lightning*. And not long after that, he received a call from Joseph Papp that would change his life and lead not only to his long association with the New York Shakespeare Festival, but to the emergence of a new design vocabulary for the American theatre.

Less than a year earlier "I couldn't get anyone to say hello. As Boris said to me, 'Ming, you are at the stage when not even a wrong number is going to call you.' But then I am back, and Boris called saying, 'Ming, can you work for me?' And I said, 'Boris, you are too late; I'm busier than I can handle.' I could hear Lisa in the background saying, 'Boris, leave the boy alone.'" Less than six months after working as a "glorified assistant," Lee was on the verge of becoming the most influential designer in the American theatre.

MARTHA GRAHAM

From the mid-1940s, Graham's productions were usually presented on Broadway, and because the opening of *The Moon Besieged* had been postponed, *A Look at Lightning* would become Lee's Broadway debut on March 5 at the Broadway Theatre. The dance, with music by Egyptian-born composer Halim El-Dabh, was a collection of short pieces on the theme of inspiration. Lee has said that designing for dance is "designing in its purest sense. You are designing a visual statement in a space that is compatible to a human form moving, expressing a theme, and that is pure set designing.... It is totally nonliteral because dance itself is nonliteral. It is theatre expressed through movement; therefore, if your form is compatible to the movement, you have achieved the impact of the work."[1]

At this point Lee's dance experience was still limited—two pieces for José Limón and *The Pearl* at UCLA. But despite the pressure of working for Martha Graham on Broadway, it was "the easiest goddamn thing I have ever experienced." There was very little discussion; Lee was simply asked to watch rehearsals and come up with the design. One end of the rehearsal room was stacked with a lot of Noguchi tables, with their iconic organic shape, a ladder—her dances often had a vertical element—and a drum. The dance took on a triangular shape within which she placed the ladder, one of the tables and the drum. "And that's the dance. What you do is you religiously measure this drum. For the Noguchi flat table you design an abstract flat piece, and a vertical thing, and a drum is a drum is a drum. Jeannie Rosenthal [Graham's lighting designer] said Martha hates painted drops. So a blue scrim, and call it a day." Lee acknowledges the influence of Boris Aronson on the design, particularly *J.B.*, with its abstracted circus tent, circular platform and vertical pole. Rosenthal, who in the 1930s practically invented the profession of lighting designer, was enormously supportive. When Lee brought his design to Graham it was Rosenthal who said, "Wonderful, exactly what we wanted." "I had never had that kind of experience before," recalls Lee. "Everyone was treated so gracious—like a treasure, like an artist. Very low key, very little talk."

Ironically, Lee could not attend his Broadway debut because it fell on the same night as *Tristan und Isolde* in Baltimore—and given that Birgit Nilsson was singing Isolde he was not about to miss it. The *Tristan* set consisted of a long platform with a ship's rigging and a sail. The backdrop for the second act used what would become a Lee signature in his early work—floating branches and leaves and circular treetops with spiky metallic foliage that he referred to as "hostile trees." By this point Lee was regularly looking at *Opernwelt* and *Theater Heute*, and what he saw in the German designs was a total rejection of decorative and illustrative design in favor of a presentational style, an emphasis on the three-dimensional form and texture, the use of emblematic and iconic elements, bold use of lighting as a scenic element as well as projections, and experimentation with new materials, particularly metal. Some of that influence could be seen in this production, particularly in the metallic trees.

The final production of the Peabody season and, for all intents and purposes, the conclusion of Lee's career there, was Jules Massenet's *Werther*, a seldom-produced opera that Lee himself had proposed to Laszlo Halasz. "It was not that good a set," Lee recalls. "Typical minimal thing with abstract leaves that I was already overusing." It is unlikely Lee would have done another season, but an incident with Halasz finalized that decision. "In act three the mezzo has a famous letter aria, and suddenly during the performance Halasz goes tap tap tap tap on the podium and says out loud, 'Don't sit on the music, you duck!' And I walked out of the theatre and never returned." (There would actually be one more production in the fall, but Lee's participation was minimal.) Despite his feelings about Halasz, Lee acknowledges that it was because of him that he learned how to design opera.

THE NEW YORK SHAKESPEARE FESTIVAL

The experimentation, transformations and new spirit in the theatre of the 1960s is usually associated with names such as the Living Theatre, Open Theatre, Caffe Cino, La MaMa, the Performance Group, etc.—the theatrical avant-garde of the time. But innovation was not limited to the world of Off-Off Broadway. What was happening at Joseph Papp's New York Shakespeare Festival would have a profound impact on American theatre, and it was at the Delacorte Theater in Central Park that American scenography was radically transformed by the work of Ming Cho Lee.

There are slightly varying accounts of what led Papp to call Lee. Lee thinks that the company manager, Hilmar Sallee, may have recommended him. Lee had actually interviewed with Papp once before, but at that point he had no Shakespeare experience and very little in his portfolio that was relevant. Meanwhile, director Gerald Freedman believes that *he* urged Papp to see Lee. Based on the recommendation of his Northwestern University schoolmate Omar Paxson, Freedman had met with Lee several years earlier when he was looking for a designer for an Off-Broadway revival of *On the Town*. "It soon was apparent," Freedman recalls, "that Ming wasn't of that

3 Lee with Joe Papp at the Delacorte Theater, 1966.

3

sensibility. But his portfolio was so outstanding, so gorgeous, I still talk about it, and I said, 'We're going to work together.' I introduced him to Joe Papp, which then led to our long collaboration there." Whatever the impetus for the call, Papp was obviously impressed by this second encounter. Lee remembers Papp ending the interview with, "All right, you sound pretty good. Go for it!"

The New York Shakespeare Festival had begun as the Shakespeare Workshop in 1954 in a Sunday school room of Emmanuel Presbyterian Church on the Lower East Side of Manhattan and in 1957 found a home at the Heckscher Children's Center in East Harlem in a theatre last used by the Federal Theatre Project in the 1930s. During the summers the company toured the city, and wound up by Belvedere Lake (now Turtle Pond) in Central Park when their touring truck "broke down" there in 1958. Through the famous drawn-out battle with parks commissioner Robert Moses, Papp succeeded in getting the city to construct an outdoor theatre on that site for the presentation of free Shakespeare: the Delacorte Theater, named in honor of benefactor George T. Delacorte Jr. Lee had seen only two Festival productions, *As You Like It* at the Heckscher Theatre and *Twelfth Night*, designed by Eldon Elder, in the pre-Delacorte theatre in the park. He had, however, seen several Rouben Ter-Arutunian designs at the American Shakespeare Theatre at Stratford, Connecticut. Despite his limited experience with Shakespeare and total lack of experience with outdoor theatres, Lee nonetheless felt that he was ready.

The 2,300-seat Delacorte was designed by Elder, who had been the Festival's resident designer since 1958. The stage resembled that of the Tyrone Guthrie–designed Stratford Shakespeare Festival in Ontario, Canada, with a polygonal thrust and broad steps leading down to the auditorium on five sides. But Elder was fired by Papp before the opening because he was also helping to design the new stage for the American Shakespeare Theatre and had done so without informing Papp.[2] Now Papp wanted Lee to make some changes:

> **The man would come out like a cannon ball. The minute I was hired he said, "Come with me!" They were still constructing the Delacorte Theater, and I had never seen the plan. He said, "That goddamn Eldon Elder, he went to Connecticut and then left me with this thing here. And I don't think it works!" I said, "Joe, give me some time, I don't know if it works or not." He said, "Here, in the middle of the auditorium, is the foundation that's supposed to have two lighting towers. So what happens to the sightline?" I was so shook up and I said, "I guess people sitting behind it would have a tough time." He said, "Well, Ming, you'd better fix it!" And that was literally my first job—moving those foundations. With Joe you just kind of jump in.**

The towers were actually an Erector Set–like lighting bridge fifty-five feet tall and forty feet wide. Aside from potentially blocking sightlines it generated complaints that it was marring "the beauty of the Belvedere Lake" (*New York Times*, April 6, 1962).

The Delacorte stage was forty-eight feet wide, had six permanent lighting towers, and twenty poles across the rear of the stage, each twenty-one feet tall, at five-foot intervals, intended for hanging scenery.[3] "It was really a wretched stage," says Lee, "but I had to work with it." Lee had the light towers moved behind the seating and eliminated several of the upstage poles. Given the relation of the seating to the stage, most of the audience could see the stage floor, which made it a significant scenic element. Elder had covered the floor with ribbed rubber, intended to keep the actors from slipping. The height of the scenic poles—too low in relation to the width of the stage—created a sense of vast openness that was hard to overcome, so it was difficult to create intimate, interior scenes. It is virtually impossible to obscure the natural surroundings of the Delacorte—and to do so would be antithetical to the notion of Shakespeare in the Park—but every designer and director must determine just how visible and integrated the park will be. Belvedere Castle, perched on a high rock across the lake, looks down on the theatre, and the skyline of Manhattan can be seen beyond that. From the beginning, Lee chose to let the surroundings bleed through much of the set, while always trying to maintain a focus on the stage. Also, in the early summer, performances began before sunset, meaning the ambient light would change over the course of the evening which, of course, affected the lighting design (which Lee was responsible for through the first season).

What tends to be forgotten now is that thrust stages were not all that common in the American theatre at that time. Off Broadway's Circle in the Square Theatre had a very deep thrust, as did a few of the emerging Off-Off Broadway and nascent regional theatres. So staging for the thrust was an evolving art. Freedman recalls, "When we started, there was an encrustation of Theatre Guild productions of Shakespeare. They were all proscenium dominated. What I know I brought to the collaboration was not the idea of the thrust, but how you use a thrust. Some of that came from my work on Broadway musicals. I brought a musical theatre sensibility, which meshed with my understanding of classical theatre. It was presentational." Lee grasped the need to frame the action so that the thrust would be understood as an extension of the upstage scenery.

Lee's solution for *The Merchant of Venice*, which opened the Delacorte on June 21, 1962, directed by Papp and Gladys Vaughan, was to frame the stage with two latticework towers upstage right and left, with Venetian lancet arches, shutters and "airy flights of steps," as Arthur Gelb described them in his *New York Times* review the following day. The towers were connected by a moveable bridge (with slats below the platform echoing the shutter motif) that altered the spatial configuration for each scene. The sense of locale was further suggested by two large panels painted like tapestries that unfurled upward from the stage floor between slender upstage poles, providing appropriate scenic backdrops for Portia's house and the courtroom scene. The set was thus transformable to create multiple locations and two acting levels, yet it was utterly simple, with a delicate scaffolding structure that evoked a Venetian locale while allowing the lake, the castle and the nighttime park to be continuously present.

The delicacy of the latticework made the towers appear like tracery against the cityscape. There was real architectural detail, yet the overall effect was almost abstract. Lee also created an elaborate design to be painted on the floor. But he soon discovered that the ribbing defeated the paint: "It all depends on which direction the rib goes. If you look at it from one direction you see the painting; but from the other, you might as well not do any painting because you can't see a damned thing. And then we discovered that no matter how much the stage is raked you really don't see that much detail anyway."

No single element of this was new for Lee. Vertical poles, skeletal sets, horizontal shutters and slats had all been used before. Looking back, it was as if Peabody, *The Crucible* and *The Moon Besieged* were a research and development laboratory. Certainly the skeletal framework and poetic sensibility of Mielziner, the structural and emblematic vocabulary of Aronson and the stylistic motifs of Ter-Arutunian can all be seen within this work. But now it came together in an identifiable style and became a template of sorts for subsequent Delacorte productions. In retrospect, it seems an obvious, almost inevitable solution to the demands of Shakespeare in the Park, but it was Lee's discovery.

Although the English Renaissance stages of Shakespeare's time may have been "open-air," they were enclosed and intimate. Creating the intimacy in the park required by many of Shakespeare's plays posed an enormous challenge. Judith Crist, in her review of *Merchant* in the *New York Herald Tribune*, noted the spatial problem created by the vast open stage. "The stage…is somehow bare; the Rialto is deserted, with only a couple of players pausing to converse from time to time. Only in a masque scene…is any use made of the afar reaches of the stage" (June 27, 1962). Lee was aware of the problem: "When I was trying to create an interior, or a sense of interior, let's say the scene between Shylock and Jessica, no matter how we moved the damn bridge in, it still looked like they were outside the house." It was for precisely this reason that Lee sought to redesign the stage for future seasons.

Lee also learned about lighting in the park. The light focus and cueing took place from midnight—at the end of rehearsals—to four A.M. "It all looked great at four in the morning. The next day we'd start the technical rehearsal and you couldn't see the lighting because it's daylight. We realized that you can't light the show at night. At the beginning of the show, you just turn everything on and then begin to set some light cues while the show was going on. When we set the light cues carefully for the whole damn show, like in the opera, it was a total waste of time."

The second show of the season was *The Tempest*, a play which Lee did not know. Directed by Freedman, it brought together three-quarters of the creative team that would be responsible for sixteen productions at the Shakespeare Festival (both in the park and at the Public Theater) over the next ten years: Freedman, Lee and costume designer Theoni Aldredge. Lee's lighting assistant, Martin Aronstein, would become the fourth member the team the following year. "We talked the same language, we seemed to understand each other, and we enjoyed working with each other," Lee would later say of the team. "I had a feeling at that time that we were breaking new ground, not only for ourselves, for the New York Shakespeare Festival, but in terms of the American theatre. We were doing things that were not normally done. It was very strong, very gutsy. We felt that we were on a mission. There was a company spirit. It was a real high."[4] All told, the design team of Lee-Aldredge-Aronstein worked on thirty-five productions together, at the Festival and elsewhere. Freedman asserts, quite rightly, that the notion of a creative ensemble in the mainstream theatre of that time was unusual, and that its contribution has been overlooked. Soon after there would emerge the team of Harold Prince and Boris Aronson, and a decade later the collaborative ensemble of choreographer-director Michael Bennett, set designer Robin Wagner, Aldredge and lighting designer Tharon Musser, who created *A Chorus Line* and several other musicals. But Lee, Aldredge and Aronstein (with and without Freedman) were the first to work on such a scale over such an extended period of time.

The floor was repainted for *The Tempest*, but the basic framing units of the two towers remained. Partly this was determined by budget and time constraints. In those days there were three productions in the park each summer, rather than the current schedule of two, so changeover time was limited. More important, the stage demanded some sort of framing device as well as great scenic height in order to focus the spectators' gaze. The environment must "control the action," as Lee puts it. "When people sitting in the front row look up at an actor, if they see the park, Fifth Avenue and the sky, they lose all interest. But if they look at the actors' faces and there is some surface or line or whatever that belongs to the environment of the show—through which you see the sky—then you feel that the performers are acting within something.[5] The scenery creates an inner volume and nature is the other volume." The early sets were twenty-one feet tall—very high for the time—and ultimately reached thirty-two feet. In

4

6

5

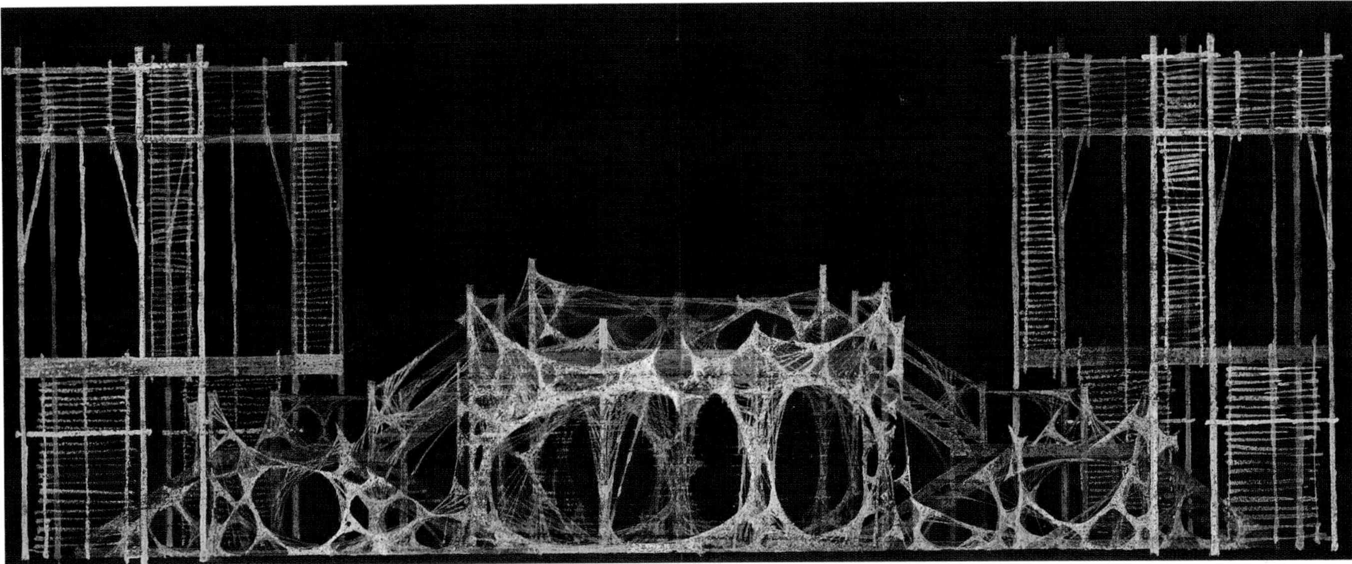

7

8

9

10

The Merchant of Venice

New York Shakespeare Festival, 1962

4 Production photograph. The boxes around the front of the stage hid the floor microphones, which were essential because of the theatre's poor acoustics (and long before the age of body mikes). There were also microphones hidden within the scenic units. "In designing for Shakespeare in the Park," notes Lee, "the first thing you do is figure out where to put the microphones. It was all very primitive. All the staging was controlled by where you are in relation to the mikes." Gerald Freedman declares this "one of Ming's most brilliant inventions—hiding the floor mikes in terms of the aesthetic of the particular show. I could use them as sitting places. You could have a three-dimensional staging space without putting furniture out there." Note the tapestry hanging up center.

5 Sketch. Although it would go through many variations over the next ten years, this shows the basic "Elizabethan stage" used by Lee: a raised platform upstage providing an "above" and a "below," and stairs and vertical structures on the sides.

6 Color elevation for the tapestry for the Belmont scene.

The Tempest

New York Shakespeare Festival, 1962

7 Sketch of the ship in scene 1.

8 Production photograph of scene 1. To achieve the change into scene 2, the flat piece representing the ship was carried offstage and the mast sunk into a trough at the rear of the stage.

King Lear

New York Shakespeare Festival, 1962.

9 ½" model.

10 Production photograph.

the post-Lee era designers went even taller. The towers also provided multiple acting levels, in keeping with contemporary understandings and practices of producing Shakespeare.

The structural and utilitarian towers also reflected Lee's Brechtian aesthetic, which steadfastly resisted the illustrative and pictorial, but Freedman wanted, says Lee, "a pretty set." He wanted a realistic ship and island, "not a bunch of scaffolding." Lee's solution was a cobweb-like construction from which trees seemed to emerge supporting the upper stage on the bridge. The bridge allowed for realistic ship elements at the beginning but at other times both the upper and lower stage had an almost surreal quality. For the masque scene more neoclassical elements were added. The floor was painted with what appeared to be bubbles or perhaps a stylized impression of sea foam. Freedman remembers the set evolving from discussions about texture, with particular inspiration coming from a meeting at Lee's apartment: "Richard was in his high chair, spilling food, and Betsy was cleaning it up. I know that's where the inspiration for the piece came from because suddenly there was a sponge and I said, 'That's what I want!'"

While the set received positive mentions in the reviews, the combination of styles did not really work. The skeletal towers with their fragmented slats or shutters and the weblike and globular elements seemed to come from different productions. Lee's unhappiness with Freedman's approach seemed to be echoed in the *New York Times* review which noted that Freedman rejected any deep investigation of themes in favor of "lightness and grace" (July 17, 1962). Lee and Freedman went on to a productive artistic partnership as well as a lifelong personal friendship, but at the time, Lee believes, Freedman did not want him rehired for the Festival.

The third and final production of the ambitious 1962 season was *King Lear*, again co-directed by Papp and Vaughan. Lee had seen pictures of Norman Bel Geddes's Stonehenge-like designs for an unproduced *King Lear*, and even though he thought it was the wrong atmosphere for the play, "I didn't have a better idea and thought: Why not?" Most important, with *King Lear* Lee began to tackle the problems of the Delacorte stage. First, he eliminated the side towers and actually widened the stage a bit. He added two stepped levels that replicated the shape of the stage, so that the basic stage became a kind of wraparound apron. By eliminating the side towers, the asymmetrical, semiabstract "Stonehenge" monoliths actually created a more emphatic center, allowing for more intimate interior scenes.

Lighting the monoliths was problematic. Lee wanted shafts of light coming through them, but was having difficulty achieving this without the overhead lighting positions one has in a regular theatre. "It looked like a mess. We refocused this way and that, but the more we focused on the posts the worse it got. Then Marty [Aronstein] said, 'You know, I'm beginning to learn something here. The sidelight should avoid the vertical posts close by, and instead shine through and hit the vertical posts on the other side of the stage.' What an insight! Then the lighting came together."

For designing sets and lights for three shows that summer, Lee was paid $900.

Lee's final obligation at Peabody was an opera by Sergius Kagen based on *Hamlet*. In terms of his career, Lee calls this a "footnote." Between the Shakespeare Festival, the Sarah Caldwell *Butterfly* and the on-again *The Moon Besieged*, he had no time, and designed a "kind of scaffolding set." The true footnote, however, was the director: Joseph Papp. "I said to Joe, 'Do you want to do opera?' and he said, 'Why not?' I said, 'Here's your chance. You go and direct it, but I'm busy doing your work so I can't be there. I'll send Bob Guerra [Lee's assistant from the Shakespeare Festival], and you just have some fun doing the opera. Just don't take the Hungarian too seriously.' It's the first time and the last time that I gave Joe Papp a job."

Lee's first summer in the park was also the start of his long association with legendary scene builder Pete Feller.

When Joe Papp hired me, Pete came to visit me—I mean, the great Pete Feller actually came to visit me—and said, "You're going to do Shakespeare in the Park, and I'm opening up a new shop. There's no work in the summer, so I'd like to have work just to break even." I thought: Wow! Pete Feller doing my shows. I introduced Pete to Joe and they got on immediately. So Pete Feller became the shop for the Shakespeare Festival. Later, when we began to look for a location for the Public Theater, Pete would come along with us and say, "Yes, this is possible, or this is not possible." He became very much a part of the New York Shakespeare Festival, and he and I became very, very good friends.

SARAH CALDWELL

Music critic Anthony Tommasini has referred to Sarah Caldwell as "an indomitable but chaotic force," and that would certainly apply in the case of her *Madama Butterfly* (*New York Times*, March 25, 2006). But Lee loved the opera and jumped at the chance to do it. Caldwell described the set in her memoir:

> **Ming and I talked a great deal and I showed him books, and he had a lot more books and we talked more. He designed the most versatile and appropriate set for *Madama Butterfly* I have ever seen. A small Japanese house is set in the midst of a bamboo grove. In the back there's a bridge that leads up a hill and goes over a small stream. Downstage toward the conductor there is a little garden. The house has shoji screens that open and close. The colors are beige, brown, and the very pale waxy color of bamboo.**[6]

The main inspiration for Lee was a Japanese house he saw at an exhibition in the sculpture garden of the Museum of Modern Art in New York with "wonderfully finished wood, tatami platform and shoji screen. Extremely abstract, which is the essence of Japanese architecture. And I fell in love with it. I said, 'That is the way to do *Butterfly*.'" Lee saw that minimalist approach as a way to remove the sentimentality of the opera. In a radical move for the time, he eliminated the usual cherry blossoms that were a standard aspect of every *Butterfly* set and just used bamboo poles. "I thought I was actually designing an abstract *Butterfly*, of course nowadays that is so old-fashioned."

The production was initially done for only three performances at three venues in and around Boston—two high school auditoriums and the Harvard Square Theater in Cambridge. However, it continued to be revived for decades, more than any other opera in the company's thirty-two seasons.[7] The set was constructed on the sixth floor of an old factory, and Lee's assistant, Richard Hay, who painted the set, remembers it as a cold, miserable experience. Caldwell had not paid the rent—Lee says this was not atypical for her—so the building was padlocked and Lee and his assistants had to break in and lower the set out a window down to a truck. She never paid the final portion of his fee, either. Lee left Boston before the opening, leaving Hay to oversee the production—including redesigning the lighting at Caldwell's insistence.

THE MOON BESIEGED

Finally, at the end of 1962, Lee made his theatrical Broadway debut with sets and lighting for *The Moon Besieged* by Seyril Schocken at the Lyceum Theatre. The play, about the radical abolitionist John Brown and his conflict with his sons, closed after two previews and one performance. As with *The Infernal Machine*, Lee's design was praised while the play was critically demolished. The failure was all the more frustrating because when it looked as if it might not be able to open for lack of funds, Lee had even helped rescue the show financially: "I was not about to let my first Broadway show disappear." He appealed to his father in Hong Kong to put in three or four thousand dollars, emphasizing the connection to the civil rights movement and its social relevance. "That was when I discovered that I can actually do a publicly rousing speech."

While the play itself turned out to be insignificant, the design was a kind of watershed for Lee, in which he explored the full gamut of his influences and in which could be seen harbingers of what was to come. At root was a steadfast insistence on avoiding illustration and realism. The large number of preliminary sketches reveal hanging abstract backdrops, sculptural units, a more or less realistic interior, a raked wooden platform, a forest of abstract trees and a hanging spikey tree sculpture. The final design included a platform with skeletal posts and a backdrop of floating leaves and branches. One of the things Lee discovered from studying German productions was that "if you put in a raked platform, the job is half done," a discovery he had already put to use at the Delacorte. The skeletal quality of the set was influenced by Mielziner's *Salesman*, but it was equally influenced by Aronson "in terms of the design being very iconic. The term icon or emblem was not in my vocabulary, but that was what I was doing. And I was literally forcing it on Lloyd. If you don't do any realistic sketches, the director has no way to get into it. And I just didn't do any."

By this time Lee had also developed an interest in scaffolding and the way in which it framed the unfinished buildings behind. Hints of this are visible in some sketches. Most important, Lee felt that the scaffolding and iconic elements were a step towards modernizing design. "I felt that I had a kind of theatrical vocabulary that said contemporary world." As he increasingly applied this vocabulary to opera and Shakespeare, he brought a contemporary sensibility to classical forms.

11

12

13

The Moon Besieged

Broadway, 1962

11 ½" model, act 1. A scrim consisting of panels of loose-weave burlap was placed in front of the set. To create a more complex texture, holes were cut in the burlap which were then covered with bobbinet.

12 ½" model, act 2, with hanging "hostile" branches.

13 ¼" sketch; not used.

The part that absolutely tears me apart in *Butterfly* is the letter reading scene in act two. Sharpless says, "Let me read the letter." Cio-Cio-San says, "Let me kiss the letter." When I was growing up in Shanghai, for many years I was essentially brought up by servants because my mother was elsewhere. My servant, when she received a letter from her village, would always take the letter to the street where there were tables set up and scholarly looking men with beards and inkwells and sheets of paper and so forth. The maid would bow to him, and she would sit on one chair, and he would be sitting opposite, and I would have a little stool sitting beside the maid. And this person would read the letter. When he finished reading the letter, the servant would dictate a letter. It is *exactly* like the opera. The letter reader would say, "Now, this is from your sister." "Oh! It's from my sister, oh, let me smell it." And the sister might have written, "Your niece is now in high school," and the maid would say, "Oh my god, my niece is in high school." It would be a conversation. Then the maid would cry. And I was sitting there! And then the maid would dictate her letter. Essentially, it was like she was talking to her sister. When I heard that part of it in the opera, I broke down. I don't know how Puccini got it. But it is so real—when people who are uneducated communicate by having someone read or write your letters. Also, you think of *Madama Butterfly* as kind of icky sentimentality, which it's not. Cio-Cio-San is a woman who has no self-pity at all. I have never encountered in any show a leading lady that has so much spunk. I have always thought that while Pinkerton had some very beautiful music to sing, he is really a schmuck. The idea that a Westerner could actually write a story about a Westerner and a Japanese Geisha girl, in which the Westerner, the Caucasian, is so unsympathetic, such a lout—I always loved that opera.

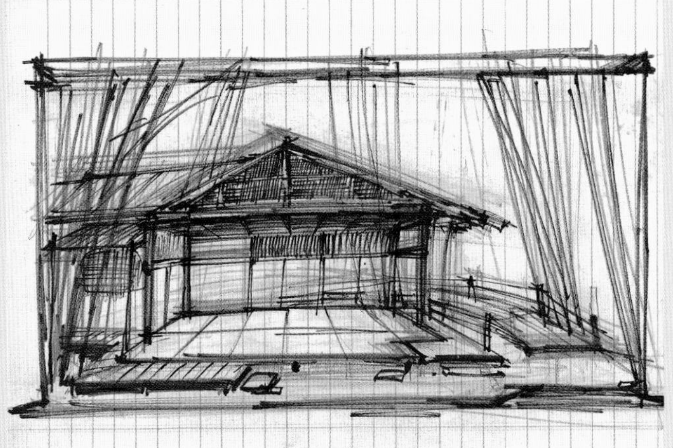

14

15

14, 15 ***Madama Butterfly,*** Opera Company of Boston, 1962, sketch and ½" model. In a radical step for the time Lee designed it without cherry blossoms. Between the time of the preliminary sketch and the model Lee flipped the ground plan.

CHAPTER 5

The Emblematic Stage 1963–64

1

1 ***Antony and Cleopatra***, New York Shakespeare Festival, 1963, ½" sketch, gouache, modeling paste and wax pencil on paperboard.

SOMETIMES WHAT WE THINK of as revolutionary is really, in retrospect, a question of making the immanent obvious; the revolutionary leader is often the person who sees connections among disparate ideas or practices that no one else has recognized. This is, in fact, what Ming Cho Lee did following that first summer in the park. All the influences he had absorbed to that point—the skeletal and pictorial settings of Jo Mielziner, the textured designs of Rouben Ter-Arutunian, the emblematic and sculptural work of Boris Aronson, the spatial organization of Isamu Noguchi, the presentational aspect of Brecht and contemporary German design—coalesced over the next two years into a singularly recognizable Ming Cho Lee style that moved American scenography once and for all out of the world of illusion and illustration.

MOTHER COURAGE

The year 1963 began with Lee's second Broadway play, Brecht's *Mother Courage and Her Children*, directed by Jerome Robbins. Robbins was notoriously difficult to work with, as Lee had discovered while assisting Mielziner on *Gypsy*. No matter how Mielziner changed the model for that show, Robbins rejected it. It was Lee who realized that Robbins, as a dancer, did not know how to read a model but would be able to interpret a ground plan taped out on the floor. Lee's solution may have worked then, but it did not prepare him for the experience of *Mother Courage*.

Ironically for Lee, given his devotion to Brecht, Robbins wanted a set that had absolutely no reference to the Berliner Ensemble production. He wanted none of Brecht's scenic devices or techniques, and he definitely did not want a wagon that looked like the famous one pulled by Helene Weigel—though as Lee noted, "a wagon is a wagon." In actuality, Robbins was trying to avoid the cliché perception of Brecht as, in Lee's words, "all gray and no sense of humor." But while Robbins emphatically stated what he did *not* want, he could not articulate any concrete scenic ideas, and the design emerged through an ordeal of trial and error. In the process, though, Lee got to experiment with various textures, techniques and materials, and was able to retain one quintessentially Brechtian technique—projections. The production incorporated projected images of the Hungarian uprising of 1956—an interesting choice given that it was a populist revolt against the Communists, but Lee's fascination with Brecht did not extend to the playwright's Marxist ideology.

The play was presented at the Martin Beck Theatre, and producer Cheryl Crawford managed to rent the theatre for the rehearsal period as well, which was highly unusual. Robbins told costume designer Elizabeth Montgomery that he didn't want the usual costume plates drawn up—he just wanted lots of costumes to choose from. "He really wanted a gutsy reality rather than a design," says Lee. "The rental must have been unbelievable because half the stock of the Brooks-Van Horn costume shop was at the theatre." Lee, meanwhile, presented Robbins with an array of design ideas, most of which were soon rejected. A proposed turntable was nixed, partly because Brecht used one, but mostly because the stage was not big enough, "and the wagon would be chasing its own tail like a dog." Robbins thought he might want a raked stage, so Lee got Pete Feller to clear a section of the shop and try out a rake at various degrees, but it quickly became apparent that Anne Bancroft would not be able to pull the wagon on the rake. "We wound up with a flat floor," said Lee. "But there was no decision about the background."

When it was time to invite Crawford to the design presentation, Lee began organizing all the versions he had created. "We have a wooden floor, we have a ground cloth that looks like earth, we have four posts, we have six posts. Then we have a cyc, and we have the theatre's bare wall, or we have black. And then we have different versions of the wagon. Some look like the Brecht wagon, some look very odd. We finally made a chart and we had ninety-six versions, but Jerry insisted that we show them all! Cheryl said, 'Oh, they all look very good, it's wonderful.' Jerry said, 'Yes, we're really on our way.'" Robbins finally settled on one version, remembers Lee, but said, "I think the wheel of the wagon, instead of brown should be green."

> **So we made the change and he came back and said, "Ming, how can you be so stupid? This color green is the right approach, but the rest is wrong." I said, "Oh, well, it's not too bad, at least we have a direction." So we did a whole other version based on the green color scheme. And Jerry said, "Now we really have it. But you really have to adjust this little rooftop thing differently." We said okay. The next time he came he said, "That box is right, the rest is wrong." Meanwhile the shop was waiting for the design and all we can give the shop is a flat floor. We don't even know if it's wooden or painted planks. It was a week before the load-in and everyone was beginning to sweat.**

Somewhat panicked, Crawford wanted to call in Oliver Smith to

2

3

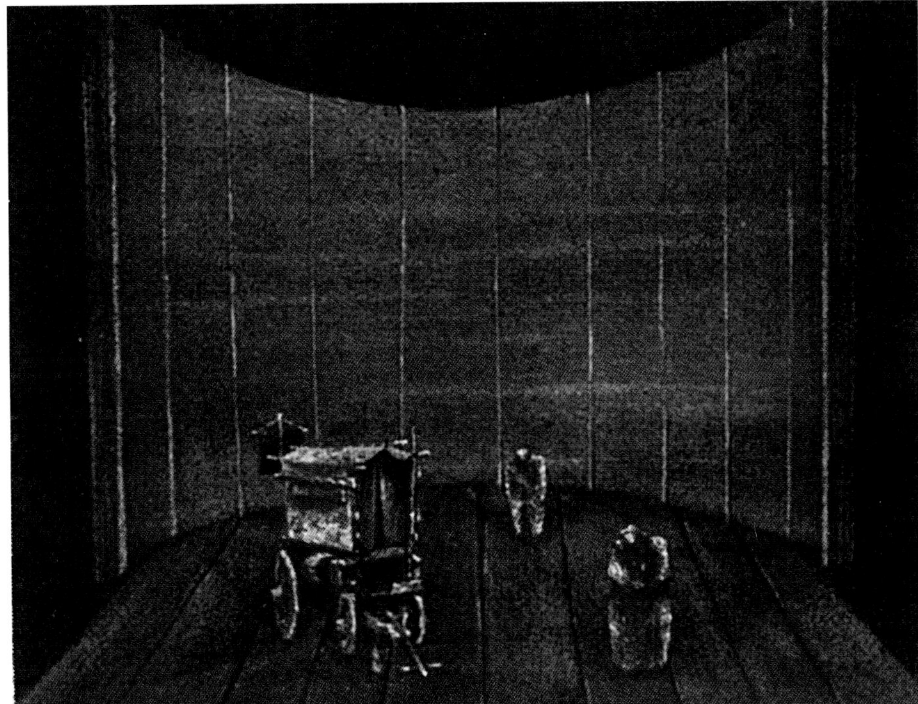

4

Mother Courage and Her Children

2, 3 Broadway, 1963, preliminary sketches.

4 Broadway, 1963, finished sketch.

5 The Acting Company, 1978, ¼" model for scene 2. "It was a good production, and Alan Schneider was trying his best to give the Acting Company the essence, the irony and the subtle humor of Brecht's writing. He said that the whole political debate in the play in essence is saying 'Capitalism is man's inhumanity to man. Communism is just the reverse.' Unfortunately, not too many of the company got it."

5

consult. Not surprisingly, Lee found this insulting, but he recalls, "Oliver called me and said, 'Ming, if you don't want me to come, I won't come, but I think I can be of some help because you're working with an impossible person. The man is sick!' That was three days before the load-in." Lee acquiesced.

> **By then we had narrowed the design down to four posts and the floor and a sky cyc that was filled with a collage of different kinds of fabric. Jerry refused to have white, so it was a rosy sunset tone. We were all sitting at the table, Jerry and Oliver on one side, Cheryl Crawford on the other, and Oliver said, "So, Jerry, what's wrong with this?" And Jerry said, "Well, what do you think?" Oliver said, "I would be very proud if I had designed this set." Jerry said, "What if it doesn't work?" And Oliver said, "Well, Jerry, you make your bed and you sleep in it." And Jerry said, "Oh. Okay." And it was approved. On the spot! All the drawings went to the shop and the shop went into overtime. I will never forget what a fantastic person Oliver Smith was. He was so unassuming.**
>
> **Then, of course, for almost every piece that came in Jerry sent it back. We set up a paint shop in the basement and used paint thinner to scrape all the texture away. [Lighting designer] Tharon Musser was having a terrible time because every time she turned on four lights Jerry would say, "That's three lights too many." Meanwhile, everyone was wearing different costumes. One day Anne Bancroft had a big animal skin thing and one day she'd blacked out two of her teeth. I mean, it was just a nightmare. And then Jerry and Anne Bancroft started having a quarrel and at one rehearsal some of the other actors started cursing at Jerry. And there I was spending day and night in the basement of the Martin Beck. I almost never got home, but the show went on. Probably the worst set *Mother Courage* has ever had.**

Not everyone agreed with Lee's self-assessment. Henry Hewes in the *Saturday Review* wrote, "Jerome Robbins has achieved a visually splendid result that is not a copy of the famous Berliner Ensemble production. And his scene designer, Ming Cho Lee, has fashioned a remarkably beautiful giant earth-colored screen broken vertically with a few irregular lines.... His supply wagon, which is slightly more angular in appearance than the original, has as much personality as any of the characters" (April 13, 1963).

Fifteen years later Lee would get another crack at *Mother Courage* for the Acting Company, and this time director Alan Schneider welcomed a very Brechtian design.

NEW YORK SHAKESPEARE FESTIVAL, 1963

Less than two weeks after the opening of *Mother Courage*, Ming and Betsy's third son, David, was born, and soon after Lee's second season with the Shakespeare Festival began. One of the realizations from the first season was how important props were in Shakespeare, particularly at a theatre like the Delacorte where the focus was inevitably on the actor and thus whatever objects the actor engaged with. In some ways they were more important than the sets themselves. (Interestingly, Brecht also felt that while decor should be minimal and presentational, props, because they were directly associated with the actors, should be very realistic.) Lee had little experience designing props (as the debacle with the Grist Mill Playhouse had demonstrated), and there was no one at the Festival dedicated to building them. So Joe Papp paid for Lee and Betsy (and infant David) to go to the Stratford Shakespeare Festival in Ontario to study how things were done there. This was the first time Lee saw the Guthrie-designed stage, and seeing it in person helped him further understand how such a stage functioned. And, crucially, he witnessed the exquisitely designed props and was amazed to learn that Stratford had a whole *department* dedicated to props. While the New York Shakespeare Festival could not replicate Stratford's resources, the attitude and approach to props changed.

The 1963 season at the Delacorte consisted of *Antony and Cleopatra*, directed by Papp, *As You Like It*, directed by Gerald Freedman, and *The Winter's Tale*, directed by Gladys Vaughan. Lee devised a new scenic configuration that would be the basic structure for all three shows, including a redesign of the floor, covering it in canvas. Working from the notion that an Elizabethan stage contained an "above" and an "inner below"—historian John Cranford Adams's model of the Globe was still the generally accepted template for most theatres that did Shakespeare—Lee created a platform upstage, about eight feet above the stage, segmented into three angular sections to mirror the front of the stage. It was reached by steps on either side, each with a landing about halfway up. While the Adams schema is now rejected by scholars as unworkable (and unnecessary) in the Globe Theatre, the design devised by Lee made great sense in the Delacorte, which was more like a Greek than an Elizabethan theatre, and so benefitted from a raised stage at the back.

The new set provided for fluid staging on two distinct levels, although it eliminated the possibility of scenic wagons rolling on and offstage, meaning that any set changes were done manually. It also provided a strong sense of enclosure for interior scenes on the stage level, solving one of the problems of the previous year. Despite the tall posts rising up behind the stage, however, the upper level tended to flatten the action below, reinforcing a horizontal visual field and subverting some of the grandeur created by the vertical elements. Papp had not quite figured out how to best exploit the fluidity that the new configuration provided. In act four, for instance, the wounded Antony is brought to Cleopatra's monument and raised up to her chamber—in this case, rather awkwardly from the stage to the upper level, which was confusing to the audience since he could easily have been carried up the stairs.

For the next production, Lee and Freedman had a better grasp on how to exploit the new configuration. *As You Like It* is a pastoral play, and the first problem to confront, as Freedman noted, was, "How do you do a forest in a park?" Again, Freedman wanted a pretty set, so Lee suggested basing it on the paintings of rococo artists Watteau and Fragonard. Lee surrounded the set with three-dimensional trees, abstract clouds and tree fragments in front of the upper level. In contrast to the rather austere sets for Lee's previous Delacorte productions, this was romantic and decorative, including a working fountain. The ornamentation helped unify the upper and lower levels, and the trees and clouds allowed the eye to flow from downstage upward toward the sky. In retrospect, Lee felt that there was not enough contrast between the court of Duke Frederick and the Forest of Arden, but overall it was quite successful and demonstrated that the Delacorte could accommodate romantic comedy as well as tragedy. If Papp hadn't yet figured out how to take advantage of the stairs, Freedman perhaps overdid it. The *New York Times* review complained that "Mr. Freedman...has his actors running up and down steps like frightened hares" (July 17, 1963).

For *The Winter's Tale*, the final show of the summer, Lee reverted to a much more basic stage with a heavy timbered, rough-hewn structure of tall posts and cross pieces, with some verticals on the front as well as the upstage side of the upper stage. It was perhaps his most overtly skeletal stage to date, although the thickness and texture of the wooden beams did not resemble the romantic skeletal structures of Mielziner, nor did it possess the industrial look that would soon be associated with Lee's designs. (The wooden posts on this and subsequent productions were actually wooden sleeves over the existing metal framework of the stage.) Although Lee had seen the play previously in Connecticut, he admits that he did not fully understand it, and Vaughan, in only her third solo outing as a director, did not provide much guidance. She was focused on the actors to the almost total exclusion of design. According to Lee, her input was merely, "'Perhaps it should be Byzantine.' So I designed some Byzantine flats." There was no major change of scenery for the shift from the court to Bohemia; it was suggested simply by actors in shepherds' costumes. This was also the first time Lee did not design the lighting. He had been asked to design a production in London—which never came to fruition—and he left the lighting entirely to Martin Aronstein.

Looking back, Lee believes that he was too complacent in that second season. He felt that after the previous year he had "figured it out," and that the pseudo-Elizabethan stage he created for the second summer would be the solution to whatever problems Shakespeare in the Park presented. While the three designs were more successful than he allows, they did not fully achieve the variety and flexibility he desired, nor did they fully address the issues of height and width presented by the Delacorte.

The year was rounded out by his first commission from the Joffrey Ballet—although it would not be realized until two years later [see chapter 6]—and two more commercial failures, the Off-Broadway *Walk in Darkness* and the pre-Broadway *Conversations in the Dark*, which never made it to New York.

JUILLIARD AND BROADWAY

Not long after Lee stopped designing in Baltimore, Peabody Conservatory director Peter Mennin succeeded William Schuman as president of the Juilliard School, which, at the time, was located near Columbia University at Claremont Avenue and 122nd Street (now the home of the Manhattan School of Music), three blocks from the Lees' apartment. One of Mennin's goals was to reinvigorate the opera program, and to that end he brought in Christopher West as director of the Juilliard Opera Theater in 1963. West had directed the *Kátya Kabanová* at the Empire State Music Festival in 1960, and now he wanted Lee to design productions at Juilliard. Lee would not design every opera as he had at Peabody, but he designed thirteen productions between 1964–83, beginning with a double bill of Puccini's *Il Tabarro* and *Gianni Schicchi*.

6

7

8

6, 7 ***As You Like It***, New York Shakespeare Festival, 1963, ½" model and production photograph of the wrestling scene (act 1, scene 2). "I didn't want to do fake foliage so I used wire mesh to create all these clouds. During daytime you just saw a silhouette against the sky, which was pretty ugly, but when it got dark you saw the rich foliage painting that made it a very beautiful set. It was actually beautiful enough that you liked to sit in the park and see the show." The foliage created a romantic look, but it is fundamentally the same set as *Antony and Cleopatra*.

8 ***Antony and Cleopatra***, New York Shakespeare Festival, 1963, ½" model [see sketch on page 69]. "I was thinking about *Antony and Cleopatra* as a very white set with inlaid mosaics, a bit like Boris Aronson's *Coriolanus*. But when you are outdoors, a white-on-white set doesn't work. Also, the painting is done from a high point of view. It looks good, but in the theatre the floor doesn't dominate in the same way. I learned a terrific lesson. Doing impressive sketches and paintings is ultimately removed from the reality of the stage. You can fool yourself. I was never so shocked by the fact that I had a different impression of the design until I saw the set."

9

10

9 ***The Winter's Tale***, New York Shakespeare Festival, 1963, ½" model.

10 ***Conversations in the Dark***, Walnut Street Theatre, Philadelphia, 1963, sketch of an apartment in the Dakota. This was Lee's first truly realistic set since college. It takes place in three locations: an apartment at the Dakota, a small apartment in Greenwich Village and a modern apartment on the Upper East Side. Since Mielziner's studio was in the Dakota, and Lee had lived in the Village, he knew two of the locales intimately, and he based the Village apartment on the one he had lived in.

11 ***Kátya Kabanová***, Juilliard Opera Theater, 1964, production photograph. "The best backdrop I have ever done."

11

Il Tabarro, with its melodramatic love story, is set on a barge on the Seine in Paris, and Lee designed a fairly realistic set that he painted himself. The traditional approach was to design the barge to be seen from the side, but Lee felt that such a ground plan forced too much lateral movement, and staged it head on with some tree branches overhead (an increasingly common motif). In contrast, *Gianni Schicchi* is a comic opera based on an incident in Dante's *Inferno*. Lee did what he referred to as "a cartoon graphic drawing style," consisting of black-and-white graphics.

This was followed by *Kátya Kabanová*. West was happy with the Empire State Music Festival design and simply asked Lee to repeat it, which he essentially did but with a much more elaborate backdrop. He and his assistant David Mitchell worked day and night painting an exquisitely evocative drop with sinuous tree trunks and branches and a serpentine river. Decades later Lee still believes "it is the best backdrop I have ever done." Lee considers *Kátya Kabanová* a breakthrough in American opera design. Now, he notes, it may look very "early sixties," with the wooden planks and abstracted realism, but it was unlike anything else that could be seen at either the Met or City Center at the time. Part Brecht, part Aronson, it referenced locale but foregrounded materials, texture and scenic iconography.

In between the two productions at Juilliard in the winter of 1964 came what appeared to be one more step in Lee's seemingly unstoppable rise to the top of the field—he was hired for his first Broadway musical, a work by Arthur Laurents and Stephen Sondheim called, at the time, *Side Show*. It was actress Angela Lansbury's first musical as well, though she would fare much better than Lee.

The design marks the first time that Lee explicitly used pipework scaffolding and scenic collage, something that would become a hallmark of his designs over the next several years. The show is set in a kind of mythical American small town that has gone bankrupt and is saved by a miraculous Lourdes-like fountain that turns out to be a hoax. "I knew exactly what it should look like," says Lee, "which was a mistake. I was very, very influenced by Ben Shahn. I wanted to do a musical that had scaffolding that was oxidized bright orange. The structure would hold up all the architecture of the small town America such as overhangs, cornices and store windows. It's all kind of collage." In fact, the model, which includes a turntable, looks like a trial run for some of Lee's subsequent shows, such as *Hair*, *Two Gents* and *Much Ado about Nothing*. "It was a beautiful set—but I was a little too confident."

One day Laurents, choreographer Herb Ross and producer Kermit Bloomgarden called a meeting and, though Lee had been given no indication there was a problem, he was fired. "After dealing with Jerry Robbins I thought: Who could be worse? Well, Arthur Laurents was worse. Herb Ross was worse." He never fully understood why he was fired, except perhaps that he was too insistent on ideas that Ross and Laurents did not like. Throughout his career, starting with his first production at Occidental, Lee had a tendency to develop strong ideas and was not afraid to express them. He is a powerful presence on a creative team, and while he has had productive relationships with many directors, he is generally not someone whose ideas evolve in a traditional collaborative approach. The rough-and-tumble world of commercial theatre does not always welcome such artists.

The show opened in April under the title *Anyone Can Whistle*, with William and Jean Eckart as the designers. Lee's only consolation was that it closed after nine performances.

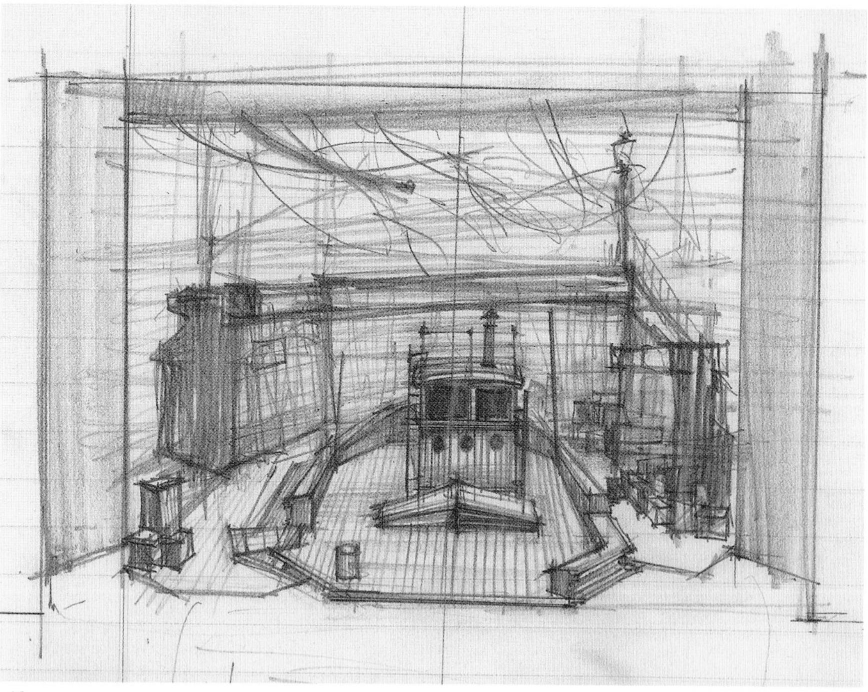

12

13

12, 13 ***Il Tabarro***, Juilliard Opera Theater, 1964, sketch and production photograph.

14 ***Gianni Schicchi***, Juilliard Opera Theater, 1964, sketch. Lee omitted the Duomo, which is central to the opera, and subsequently added a flat cutout. "That shows that I didn't read the libretto carefully."

15, 16 ***Side Show*** (***Anyone Can Whistle***), Broadway, 1964, ¼" model (top) and sketch of the bedroom. Lee was fired before the opening so these designs were never used, although it marks one of the first sets in which pipe scaffolding was a significant scenic element. As apparent in the sketch and model, the scaffolding was functional while serving as a visual and spatial framing device. *The Visit*, directed by Peter Brook on Broadway in 1958, had a floating balcony designed by Teo Otto, which left a strong impression on Lee and influenced this set.

14

15

16

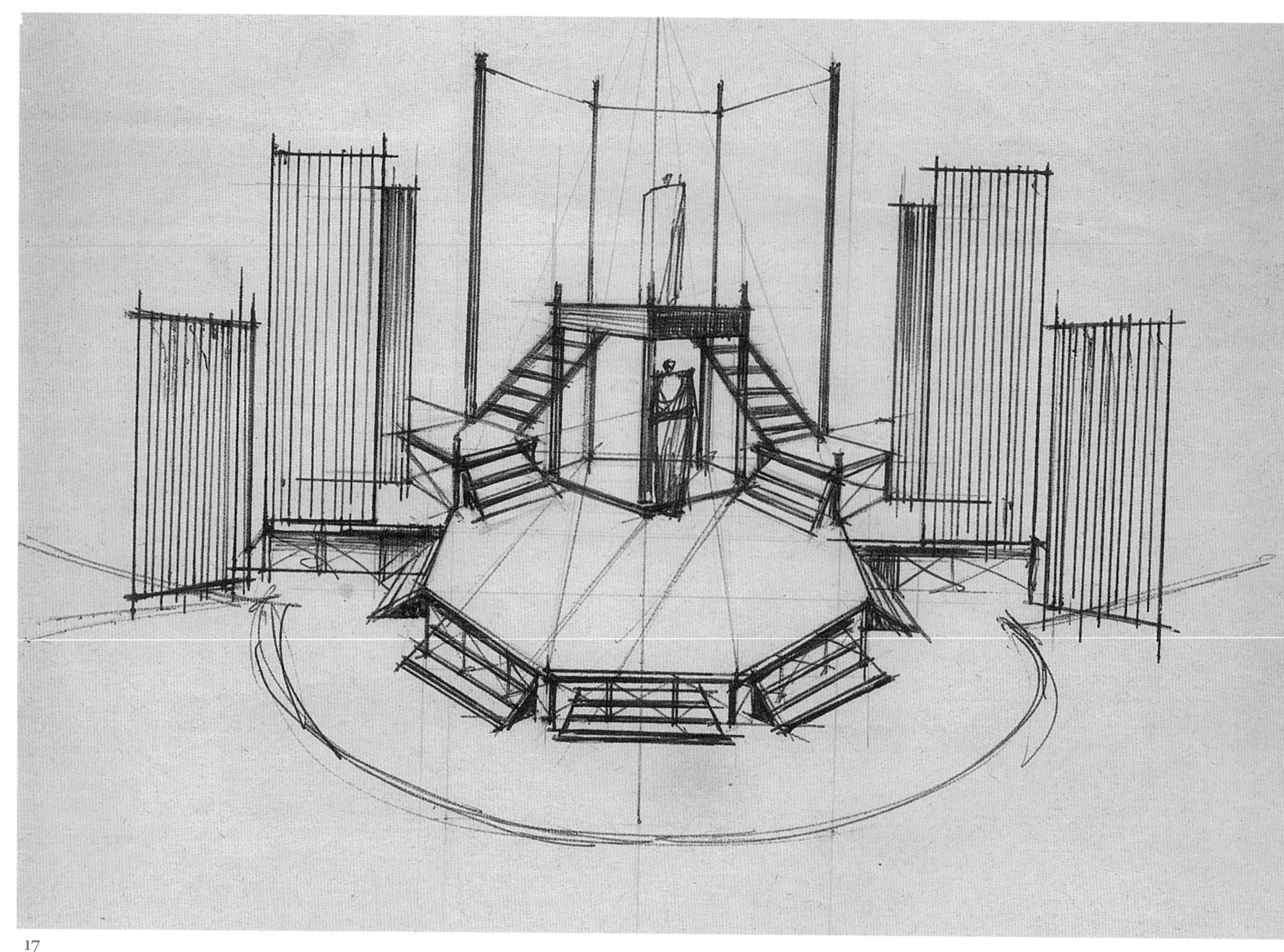

17

17–19 Mobile Unit, New York Shakespeare Festival, 1964, sketch and photographs of a performance in a playground and a rehearsal.

NEW YORK SHAKESPEARE FESTIVAL, 1964

Fortunately, Papp rescued Lee from wallowing in this failure. As Lee remembers it, Papp said, "Those schmucks don't know what they're doing. You should just stay with me. I have more things that I want to do than any of those guys. For instance, I would like to start a mobile unit and do productions that travel to the five boroughs. Since you're on my payroll, just do it." Papp was concerned that the audience that came to the park was too white and middle class, not representative of the true demographics of the city. He knew that there were large segments of the population that would never come into Manhattan from the other boroughs for any reason, let alone theatre, so he wanted to bring the theatre to them.

In the spring of 1964 Lee designed the Mobile Unit. This was not simply a matter of designing a stage—it was an exercise in engineering. Martin Aronstein assisted Lee with the design and Pete Feller oversaw the engineering and construction. Lee's assistant Richard Hay built a meticulous working model, which was used in a presentation to the mayor to solicit funds for the project. Lee devised a stage, patterned after the one at Stratford, Ontario, that would hydraulically float out of the forty-foot truck bed. There was also a control truck with a lighting bridge, that rose on pistons twelve feet above the truck; two other lighting units rolled down ramps out of the control truck, also with light bridges that rose up on pistons. There were two trailers for the actors and a truck that held units for one thousand bleacher seats and six hundred folding chairs. The stage was relatively small, only twenty feet wide and fourteen feet deep. Lee was "reacting against the Delacorte, which I thought was way too big. I felt that if you don't have many people and you have a big stage, the stage looks empty. But if you have a small stage, then ten people can look like a crowd."

The first season presented fifty-four performances of *A Midsummer Night's Dream*—with a set designed by William Ritman—at thirty-nine parks and playgrounds to an estimated seventy thousand people. Papp was well-intentioned, if perhaps a bit naïve and

18

19

20

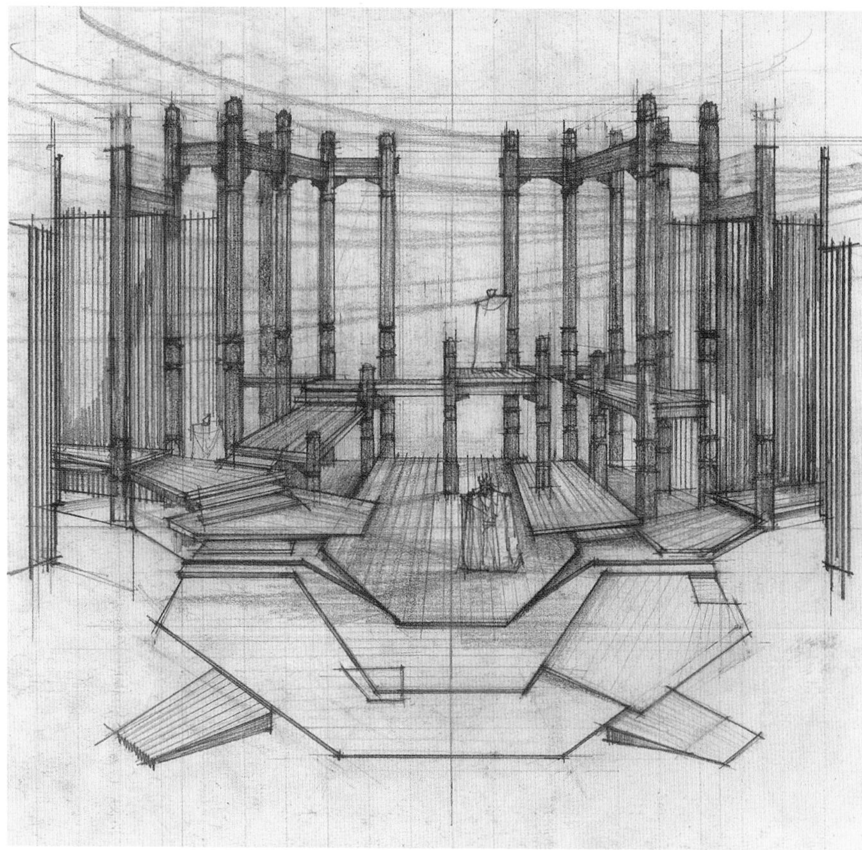

21

Hamlet

New York Shakespeare Festival, 1964

20 ½" model showing an oblique set and the slats that were not used.

21 Early sketch using strong frontal approach.

22 Production photograph with the open framework and Belvedere Castle clearly visible in background.

22

paternalistic. As Bernard Gersten later observed, "He romanticized the Mobile audience.... He didn't see what was there. It's hard enough to get *any* people into the theatre, *any* time. Joe wanted to persuade people who did not want to go to the theatre to see plays he felt they should see." Some performances were exhilarating, while others were pelted with rocks and bottles, placing the performers in serious danger. And while even the hottest nights in the park were usually tempered by a breeze from the lake, performing in a hot parking lot was something else.

With the engineering of the Mobile Unit as a sort of palate cleanser, Lee could plunge into his third season with the Festival. The three productions for the summer of 1964 were *Hamlet,* directed by Papp, *Othello,* directed by Vaughan, and Sophocles' *Electra,* the first non-Shakespeare play presented by the Festival, directed by Freedman.

At first glance *Hamlet* looks a bit like *The Winter's Tale* of the previous summer with its strong wooden posts and crossbars. But whereas the latter was rough-hewn, *Hamlet* used turned wood, richly stained, with finials capping the vertical posts—"almost like big table legs," says Lee. Lee wanted to break with the prevailing image, largely created by Laurence Olivier, of Elsinore as cold stone. The idea was to create an air of elegance. "*Hamlet* was a very different play from the previous ones," he notes. "It's not about a warrior. It's not about heroics. It's about very educated, very sophisticated people. It's a domestic tragedy. In *Winter's Tale,* using wood, you simply say, 'Oh, Shakespeare's stage was all wood.' But here the architecture becomes much more interior. I always felt that Elsinore was all about hallways and corridors. People appear unexpectedly."

The upper stage remained, but there were also multiple platforms upstage left and right in front of the upper stage, and the central platform was raked. Although the basic stage, of course, retained its shape, the set itself was asymmetrical with a strong sense of the diagonal from downstage left to upstage right—it is interesting in the preliminary sketches to see the evolution from symmetry to asymmetry. Also, most of the sketches and the model show slats—sometimes vertical—to create a greater sense of enclosure without losing the transparency. The slats were ultimately eliminated, which was probably a mistake as they provided a richness, intimacy and sense of place that was lost without them. Moreover, since the production opened in mid-June, there was natural light for at least the first hour of the performance, and the set seemed anything but dark and mysterious.

For *Othello,* starring a young James Earl Jones, Lee and Vaughan once again had difficulty communicating; her focus was on the interior psychology of the characters, and she had no strong ideas as to how to translate that into a visual environment. "All Gladys wanted was to have an archway and blue backlight on actors," claims Lee. The basic ground plan was nearly identical to that of *Hamlet,* but the background differed. Lee went through dozens of preliminary sketches trying to arrive at a solution, and many of these were quite stunning with bold splashes of red drapery or furniture and once again the slats to create a sense of enclosure. Had some version of this been realized it would have been one of the more striking sets Lee had designed for the Festival, and its verticality and sense of enclosure would have set a new paradigm for the Delacorte. Unfortunately, the final result may be one of the worst sets Lee has ever designed—a bunch of overlapping viaduct arches with some of the newel posts from *Hamlet* in the background.

The *New York Times* critic Howard Taubman was kind, noting that "Ming Cho Lee's set, with its suggestions of arches and battlements, admirably evokes the fortress of Cyprus" (July 15, 1964). In retrospect, Lee believes that part of the problem was his inability, or perhaps unwillingness, to find a better means of communicating with the director:

> **The way that we think of Shakespeare now is so different, or at least the way I'm looking at Shakespeare now. I think I would have been able to work with Gladys really well today because I think the way she was talking about acting and what was happening in the play would have been a wonderful foundation for doing something kind of real and postmodern. She may have been ahead of her time. But I was focused only on the visual aspects. I kept saying, "But Gladys, *Othello* is a play that is not metal, not wood. It's stone and plaster." I kept talking about architecture, and Gladys had no use for it.**

Given the rather disappointing designs for the first two productions that summer, there was no reason to expect much more for the final presentation of the season. Yet *Electra* turned out to be a pivotal moment in American design and Lee's career.

23

24

25

23–25 ***Othello***, New York Shakespeare Festival, 1964, ½" model and preliminary ¼" sketches. The ground plan of the model is essentially that of the second sketch, but without the slats, decorative arches and color, the power of the set was dissipated.

ELECTRA AND THE TRANSFORMATION OF AMERICAN SCENOGRAPHY

This was the first Greek tragedy for both Lee and Freedman. At this time, Greek classics were seldom produced professionally. In fact, other than a brief visit from the National Theatre of Greece in 1952, the last commercial production of a Greek tragedy had been the Judith Anderson *Medea* in 1949. Lee and Freedman quickly discovered that the spatial demands of Greek tragedy differed from those of Shakespeare. As Lee noted in a 1971 interview, "In Greek tragedy the unities are very important. Greek tragedy has unity of place and time, and, therefore, there is no problem of moving scenery to be solved—there is only one visual statement to be made." Lee eliminated the raised upper stage but kept the basic ground plan, with a raked central thrust and ramps on either side leading to an imposing central doorway (a variant of which would recur decades later in O'Neill's *Mourning Becomes Electra*). Two broad steps led up to the door. Freedman remembers that he wanted "something strong and brutal, ruins that weren't classical." He and Lee talked not so much about images as textures. Freedman found a picture in a magazine of an ancient sword that "was extremely corroded and had fantastic texture on it. I knew that the play ought to be really primitive, [not] classical Greece. That kind of rough and unfinished texture...evolved out of that sword." An impression of the sword can be seen above the doorway.

The true innovation was in the upstage scenic units. What appear to be three massive fragments of stone wall, with a roughly ten-foot-tall bronze double door in the central unit, were hung from pipe scaffolding that followed the upstage angles of the stage. Significantly, the three units floated, not touching each other, the floor or the top of the pipe structure; only the door had direct contact with the stage. As Lee remembers, this may have emerged from accidentally leaving a gap in one of the preliminary sketches. Looking at it today this does not seem that unusual, but at the time, at least in the American theatre, it was revolutionary. "Suddenly," says Lee, "they become sculptural pieces. Suddenly they become icons rather than walls." The set was surprisingly symmetrical, and any entrance through the palace doors created an ineluctable line down to the front of the central platform. This was reinforced by a red hallway behind the door with a forced perspective ceiling. However, the differing shapes of the rock units and the unequal ramps gave the impression of asymmetry. Because the stage left ramp came farther downstage than the stage right one, there was a strongly diagonal line from downstage left through the gap between the stage right and central fragments upstage. For Lee, the ground plan is a metaphorical extension of the theme and action of the play: "Electra is a daughter who wants to avenge her father. It begins with that and it never stops moving. There is this *thrust*, this tremendous *hatred* within the play, contained in a very neatly controlled classical form." The key to the success of the design is that while the rock walls might be described as "realistic" in terms of look and texture, it is really a nonliteral, nonrepresentational set. These are emblematic units that announce the stage-as-stage. As Lee later observed: "If the three panels came all the way down to the floor it would become a realistic courtyard, but by lifting it off the floor they become iconic symbols or emblems of the world of the play."

The pipe-batten scaffolding was also treated differently than before. It had been there all along at the Delacorte, as a framework for scenery and lighting, but now it was undisguised and its structure foregrounded. "Nowadays, when you think of something that is totally functional, it is metal framework," Lee explained in a 1984 interview. "Therefore, I started using metal framework on which I hung these obviously Greek, stone sculptured panels. That was the beginning." The pipework, being thinner than wooden beams, provided a strong vertical thrust in opposition to the essentially square wall units. The use of Styrofoam to carve the stone was new, perhaps the first time that material was used so extensively on a stage. Even the approach to drafting was new, "something that nobody had done before," claims Lee.

Because we were dealing with two-foot-thick, big sculptural pieces, we pretty much did it the way we did the ½" scale model. That is, I drafted it so that everything was raised—it was really a plywood box or mat board box six inches behind and then the Styrofoam on top. Then we would use Sculp-metal and modeling paste and so forth to do the set. The depth of each segment was carefully drafted out. It is six inches lower so there was six inches of foam that you do the carving on. The rest is all just scenic structure behind and then sculpture on top, rather than taking a two- or three-foot-deep block of Styrofoam and start carving.

There was one aspect of the design that was eliminated at the dress rehearsal. Lee and lighting designer Aronstein decided to use the pipe grid to hang lights "so that for once we would have backlight"—

26

it would be both scenic and functional. "During daytime it really looked great. But it got dark very early so you didn't see the lighting instruments, only the light and all the gel frames—pink, blue, amber. For the life of me, it looked like a Los Angeles used-car dealership. So we killed the back lighting.'"

Lee has always acknowledged borrowing ideas for his designs. He attributes this in part to his training in Chinese painting, where everything is copied from old masters, "so it never worried me much." He often began his design process by looking at images in books—not to copy, but as a stimulus to get the ideas flowing. In *Stage Design Throughout the World Since 1950* by René Hainaux, which was published the same year as the production of *Electra*, there was a picture of a 1959 production of *The Women of Trachis*, at the Landestheater in Darmstadt, Germany, with a design credited to Hannes Meyer, and Lee notes the obvious similarities: "It would not have fit the Delacorte, but the idea is there." Ultimately, however, it functioned more as inspiration than template. "I went through other steps before I discovered that the wall shouldn't hit the floor. It's not as if I saw the photo and said, 'Shit, I found it.'" In fact, Lee pulled together several ideas, trends and developments from various corners of the scenographic world, and put them together in a way that no one in the U.S. ever had before.

While Lee's *Electra* is now seen as one of the seminal designs of the American theatre—perhaps as significant as Robert Edmond Jones's 1915 design for *The Man Who Married a Dumb Wife* and Jo Mielziner's 1949 *Death of a Salesman*—it went largely unremarked by the critics at the time. "All these crummy designs I did got terrific reviews, and then here's *Electra* and it was hardly mentioned," laments Lee. But Aronson recognized its significance. "Boris called me and said, 'What have you done?' And I said, 'Well, the *New York Times* just said nothing.' He replied, 'Oh, what do they know! This is one of the greatest things ever.'" Whatever influence Meyer or other German designs may have had on this particular creation, Lee credits Aronson for having the most immediate impact:

> **Certainly, without Boris, *Electra* wouldn't have happened. This was my first design that had literally nothing to do with illustration. It's really dealing with the space, and also it is iconic. That was the time when Boris was doing both with a lot of his shows, like *Judith* in England. They were all sculptural, emblematic designs, like the ark in the synagogue.**

American design did not change overnight, of course, but it was now headed in a new direction, and Lee was leading the charge.

27

26, 27 ***Electra***, New York Shakespeare Festival, 1964, rehearsal photograph, left, and ½" model.

28 Hannes Meyer's design for *The Women of Trachis* at Darmstadt, 1959. A possible source of inspiration for the set.

28

The Studio

MING CHO LEE'S STUDIO—or the "Mingery," as it was dubbed by Douglas Schmidt (an assistant from 1964–66)—was one of the legendary design studios of the twentieth century, not simply for the work that was created there, but for its ambience and particularly for the way in which it intertwined with the lives of the Lee family. It left an indelible impression on everyone who entered into that remarkable realm. Zelda Fichandler summed it up by quoting a Chinese adage: "The brushstroke is the man," explaining, "If I never understood on the deepest level what that meant, I got it the day I first walked into Ming and Betsy's apartment! The unity of life and art, of dailiness and the act of creation, and—may I say it?—the mess, the confusion, made by this wonderful comingling became entirely clear to me."[1]

The studio was part of the Lees' apartment on East Eighty-Seventh Street in Manhattan, near Fifth Avenue and Central Park, within blocks of the Guggenheim Museum and the Metropolitan Museum of Art. It was also a fifteen-minute walk or even shorter bike ride from the Delacorte Theater. In New York, where space is at a premium, it is not unusual for designers to work out of their apartments, but few who do so also raise a large family, maintain as many as four or five assistants at a time and throw famous Christmas parties for more than two hundred people. The four-room apartment—bedroom, dining room, living room and study (the latter two connected by a wide archway)—was reasonably large by New York standards, and its high ceilings created a sense of spaciousness. But there was only one bath and a tiny kitchen. The study, with wood paneling and bookcases, functioned as the studio, with drafting tables and all the other accoutrements, materials and detritus of a working studio. But it also contained something that probably no other design studio has ever had—a double bed. For some twenty years, as they were growing up, the three boys shared the one bedroom while Ming and Betsy slept in the studio. During the day the materials and tools of design would be piled on the bed, and at night the bed would be cleared off to sleep. Marjorie Bradley Kellogg, an assistant in the mid to late sixties, observes that "at first you had the sense that you were trespassing on private space, yet very soon you accepted it. That was their space, and there were two languages in that space: There was the language of creation and the language of domestic life, and they were separate, even though the bed was right next to your drafting table. Somehow you made that separation, and once you did there wasn't a problem."

When asked about this arrangement, long after the boys were grown and Lee and Betsy had reclaimed their bedroom, Lee says, simply, "It was terrible." Yet he would not have had an outside studio even if he could have afforded one.

1

I'm not keen having to go elsewhere to work, to another place that has no connection with Betsy or, at that time, with the kids. Sleeping in the studio was not good, but it was better than picking up the phone and saying, "We're working late and I won't be home for dinner," and before you know it my life is split into different segments. In some way when you are working at home there is a natural time when you have to stop. Especially when I was with the Shakespeare Festival, there was usually some point when people began to feel exhausted, and we'd break out the scotch and then everyone went home. I never regretted it. I felt in some way it was good for the kids because they all knew my assistants. They were part of the family.

For Kellogg, "The boys were like cousins to me because our lives were so interlaced with the family. It was not just the proximity—you were welcomed into it. In Ming's studio you couldn't avoid it. It became a part of you." The arrangement served as a model for former assistant Chris Barreca: "When I started my family I moved my studio back into my house because I could see the profound effect we assistants had on Ming's children. My children say often that my students/assistants are some of their closest friends, and I see how that community has nurtured them."[2] Many of the former assistants

1 Lee in his first studio in his apartment on 121st Street in Manhattan, c. 1962.

2 Christmas card designed by Lee in the style of Ben Shahn, with a sketch of Betsy and their basset hound Susie, c. 1959.

were guests at a dinner honoring Ming and Betsy's fiftieth anniversary in 2008, and Richard, the oldest son, acknowledged them in a toast, referring, a bit tongue in cheek, to Kellogg as his older sister and to Leiko Fuseya, one of the later assistants, as his baby sister. He explains family this way:

> **A Chinese family goes like this [making a broad horizontal gesture], extended in all directions. So family meant this large number of people—we would have thirty people at Thanksgiving. So how do you distinguish between the people you're eating meals with every day, and "the family," which you may see less often but that also revolves around the table? There certainly was a remarkable degree of intimacy, or just general physical comfort being around the assistants, and I suppose that's as good a sense of family as anything.**

The apartment itself had a fascinating history. When Lee's mother and stepfather, H.L. Yung, came to New York in 1947, it was to work for C.V. Starr, and initially they stayed at Starr's Fifth Avenue apartment. Another Starr employee had been renting the Eighty-Seventh Street apartment, outfitting it with furniture and art from Starr with the intention of moving in with her husband following their marriage. But something happened and they never came back to the apartment, so Lee's mother and stepfather moved in and the previous tenant simply sold them the contents. To this day there are still C.V. Starr remnants in the apartment.

Yung died in 1961, leaving Ing Tang with an apartment that was generous for one person. In 1963 a smaller adjacent apartment became available, and it seemed to make sense for Ming and Betsy with their three boys (David was born in April that year) to take over the large, rent-controlled apartment, while Lee's mother moved next door. The local grade school was very good, so it was ideal for the boys, as was having their grandmother—whom they called *hawbu*, a Shanghai dialect name for grandmother—next door. Thus, the apartment has been in the Lee family since 1947. It was Lee's home on his vacations from college and a place to bring his friends for a home-cooked Chinese dinner during his early years living in the city.

The studio contained three drafting tables—two for the assistants and one for Lee (plus a collapsible one when an extra was needed)—flat files and a work table covered with paints, brushes, books, supplies and, as several assistants remember, numerous Mongol No. 2 and 3 pencil stubs. In 1954 Lee bought a three-by-two-foot wooden drafting table for twelve dollars, which he held onto until 1966.[3] It wobbled but he would not throw it out. Schmidt claims that when asked why, Lee would respond, not entirely facetiously, that he was afraid that if he got rid of it he would never get another job. That superstition also accounted for the ancient triangle and architect's rule. "He did not use the ½" or ¼" scales, only the actual inch side," recalls former assistant Ralph Funicello. "He could convert actual inches to any scale in his head. In fact, I am not sure that he even needed the ruler, as he could estimate scaled distances on a drawing with great accuracy."

Every description evokes chaos. An article from the 1980s noted that "every other surface teeters with books, papers and [phonograph] records.... Among piles of art supplies and research materials reside the drawing tables and a gigantic model stand which looms at the foot of the double bed. Tucked into crannies, sometimes balanced in leaning towers, are...the famous Ming set models."[4] Until the neighbors began to complain, the air could be toxic, filled with fumes from soldering flux, spray paint, spray adhesives and fixatives, and Styrofoam. Kellogg concurs that "it was always a mess and we were always looking for things and trying desperately to find space for your own stuff and yourself in that mess. The greatest miracle was that such order and beauty came out of such a small, cramped, chaotic space."

The walls were surprisingly bare. Through the mid-seventies they were adorned, as one might expect, with sketches and photos of Lee's work. But when they were removed to repaint the apartment, explains Lee, "the room looked so much better that we

2

3

never put anything up again, with exception of a painting by Katie, our granddaughter." There is, however a large Chinese rubbing of a horse dominating the dining room, still left from the original C.V. Starr furnishings.

There may have been physical chaos, but there was structure. The studio operated six days a week. The workday began at 10 A.M. and, except on rare occasions, ended at 7 P.M.—although, as Funicello remembers, "the last hour was more of a social/cocktail hour, cleaning up, listening to opera and recapping the day's progress." At 1 P.M. everyone broke for lunch, which was always prepared by Betsy with occasional contributions from Ing Tang. Funicello says he still associates the creative process with matzo ball soup and sliced cucumber sandwiches. The Lee boys would generally come home from school for lunch, and this lunchtime routine, filled with conversation, further reinforced the sense of family.

The intimacy of the studio also meant that any conversations Lee had with directors or writers about a production were heard. Perhaps remembering his experience with Boris Aronson, who kept his assistants out of the loop, Lee never took the director into another part of the apartment for a private conversation. (Also, Lee hated using the living room. "How do you converse in the living room?" he asks. "It is formal, everyone is polite, the furniture is too far apart.") Over the years notables ranging from Tennessee Williams to George C. Scott to Jerome Robbins visited the studio. Because the assistants were privy to the creative conversations, they understood why they were doing what was asked of them. Assistants could see a show develop from reading the script (frequently Betsy would read the play first and give Lee a sense of what it was about), to rough sketches, to models and drafting. The assistants would build the ⅛", then ¼", then ½" models to Lee's exacting specifications, with Lee "redesigning, refining and perfecting as he went," in the words of Schmidt. Lee would generally paint the models himself.

There was little or no casual conversation in the studio during working hours, but it was often filled with music. When Lee was designing an opera, it would be the soundtrack of the studio. At other times, though, opera wasn't played during working hours. "Ming said that he loved opera so much," recalls Funicello, "that he could not play it during the actual workday, as he would stop working to listen to it and get nothing done." The music that filled the apartment had an influence on Richard Lee, who became a composer. In fact, all the sons went into the arts: Christopher builds scenery for movies and television in Los Angeles, and David is a gaffer in the movie and television industry. "The three of us embraced rather than rejected our parents' life in the arts," remarks Christopher, "despite my father's frequent admonition that this was not the place to work if you wanted to get rich. He was right about that, but he also provided an example for us of a man whose profession was also his love, the key to his longevity." Lee impressed this on his assistants as well. "Ming never tried to dissuade anyone from a life in the theatre," says Barreca. "But he would say that you better love your work because you will spend most of your time doing it. He was pretty sure that if you loved theatre, in the long run you would succeed."

Betsy, of course, did more than prepare lunches. She essentially managed the studio—she had a desk in the living room (though

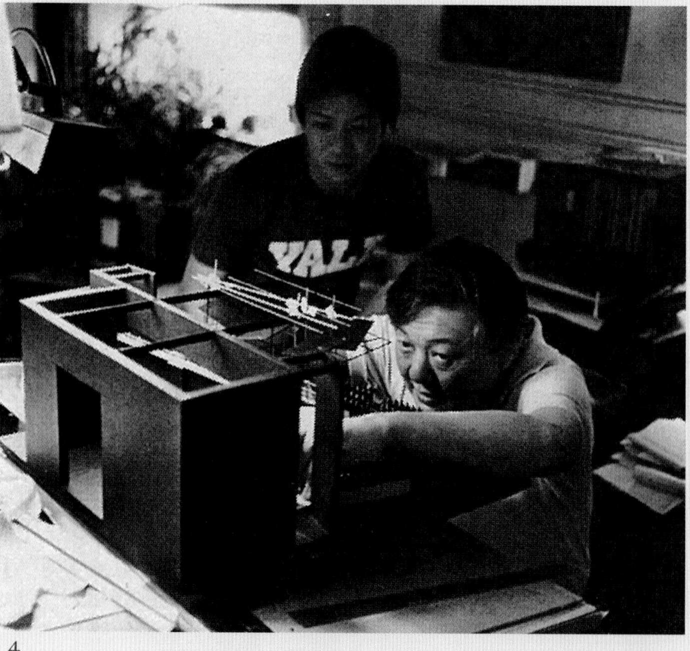

4

3 Lee in the studio, as pictured on the cover of *Theatre Crafts*, 1984.
4 Lee with an assistant working on a model.
5 Lee listening to opera in the studio, c. 2000.

when she got a computer she moved to the dining room)—and almost all aspects of Lee's career. She was his agent, manager, accountant, secretary and assistant. As Lee told James Leverett in a 1989 interview, "It is a great marriage. I'm very selfish. I don't know what I'd do if she wasn't there. I don't drive, I don't know about bank accounts or dealing with the IRS. She manages the business end. I can't negotiate so she handles all that."[5] (While Betsy did, in fact, handle the straightforward contracts in the early days, for much of his career Lee used the well-known agent, Helen Merrill, and later Patrick Herold, senior vice president for theatre at ICM.) At the conclusion of his acceptance speech for his Tony Award for *K2*, Lee said, "I know my wife, Betsy, is going to kill me, but she is really the backbone of it all." When he received the Lifetime Achievement Tony in 2013, he spent a significant part of his comments praising Betsy even more for "tenaciously staying with me, mistakes or winners" and for "always making the right judgment when I strayed." This was not *pro forma* praise for a spouse. Lee could not have had his career without her. Everyone who has ever had any dealings with Lee, professional or personal, talks about Betsy as the person who welcomed them into the home/studio, fed them and dealt with every detail of getting a project done.

Betsy had been working in theatre when they met, but she stopped during her first pregnancy. Once all the boys were in school, however, she was eager to be more active in the studio. Lee was designing *Boris Godunov* at the Met at the time, and asked one of his assistants, Miguel Romero, "What can Betsy do?" Although she says she had "never built a model in my life," Romero suggested she build the model for the very complicated inn scene. She turned out to have a talent for model building and continued to work in the studio for many years, though—as she is quick to point out—never as the first assistant. She also discovered an "affinity for brass," and often did the metal work on models.

Betsy never publicly takes credit for her contributions, though she described the relationship in a note to Lee's cousin, Billy Ming Sing Lee, as part of the tribute for their fiftieth anniversary:

> **Ming and I have always been partners. In work, he is the DESIGNER, and I am the MANAGER, but without either of us, his work could not take place. Certainly he asks what I think about a certain look, but in the end he makes the final decisions. Questions on which show to take, how to handle a difficult situation, whom to hire as assistants—these are discussed and we arrive at an agreement. Ming tends to leave [household things] to me, but if there's a question, there's a discussion. Ming is always there, and we work it out together.**

For years the apartment was the site of one of the more famous Christmas parties in New York. It began in the early 1970s when Lee took over Donald Oenslager's position at Yale. Oenslager had always hosted a holiday party for his Yale students at his Fifth Avenue apartment, so as Lee assumed Oenslager's role he, too, threw a party. The first year, in addition to his students, he invited Jo Mielziner, as well as his current and former assistants. The party expanded rapidly over the next couple of years to include Yale colleagues, former students and directors and designers with whom Lee had worked. Once invited to one party, you were permanently on the guest list. Although Betsy called many people individually to let them know the date, the information spread

5

by word of mouth. At its peak as many as 250 people streamed in and out over the course of the evening, and it was almost impossible to move. Ample quantities of Chinese hors d'oeuvres would emerge from the tiny kitchen, prepared by Betsy or purchased in Chinatown. But at some point in the early nineties, the size and notoriety of the party became too much for the building residents and the Lees received a "cease and desist" order from the co-op board lawyer, citing city fire regulations.

When Lee retired from design in 2005, the studio was somewhat dismantled—the thought of a design studio with no work was inconceivable. The flat files and all but Lee's personal drafting table were disposed of. For a brief period it was transformed into a watercolor painting studio and subsequently devolved into a de facto storage area for models, sketches, paintings and the like. Artifacts of Lee's career are tucked into seemingly every nook and cranny of the apartment. All meetings and discussions now take place at the dining room table—including the more that 150 hours of interviews for this book.

CHAPTER 6

Explorations in Opera and Dance 1965–68

1

1 ***Bomarzo***, Opera Society of Washington, 1967, and New York City Opera, 1968, ½" model.

BY THE MIDDLE OF THE 1960S Lee's career had begun to follow a trajectory more typical of European designers than those in the American commercial theatre. With only a few notable exceptions, Lee's work was focused on classical theatre at institutional venues, opera and dance. In fact, 1965—a very busy year with eleven productions—included no commercial theatre whatsoever. Dance designs for Martha Graham, the Joffrey Ballet and Alvin Ailey allowed him to further explore stage space, sculptural objects and new materials. His rapidly expanding career in opera design at the Juilliard Opera Theater and New York City Opera let him expand upon sculptural and emblematic scenography and to imprint it on American opera. These changes were as transformative as they had been for theatre.

THE JOFFREY BALLET AND ALVIN AILEY

While working at the Delacorte in 1963 Lee had received a call from the Joffrey Ballet. The company had been founded in 1956 by Robert Joffrey and Gerald Arpino as a small itinerant troupe. By 1963, with support from Rebekah Harkness, it had begun to establish a reputation, but had performed in New York City only twice—at the 92nd Street Y in 1961 and at the Fashion Institute of Technology in 1962—and was completely unknown to Lee. The caller invited Lee to come to Harkness's mansion in Watch Hill, Rhode Island, to discuss designing a dance for them. Arpino met Lee and introduced him to Mrs. Harkness. "We went to her private dance studio where she was taking a lesson. It was the middle of summer and the heat in the room was stifling." Lee and Arpino went to a coffee shop for lunch where Arpino explained that the dance used the second movement of Maurice Ravel's Piano Concerto in G. "Jerry said, 'I have a very definite idea of what I want.' He opened up a book and pointed to a picture. 'I would like a piece that looks like this.' And I said, 'Well that's not too difficult because I designed it!' It was *A Look at Lightning*."

Of course Lee's set was not a copy of the Graham piece. The ballet, which became *Sea Shadow*, is set on a beach, where a young man is seduced by a sea nymph. Lee created a beach of boulders, some vertical poles and a large cantilevered rock stage left that rose at a slight angle toward the center of the stage. At a climactic moment, the nymph ran up the rock and dove into the arms of the young man. The backdrop of loose-woven burlap and scrim netting was very textural, more similar to *The Moon Besieged* than to *A Look at Lightning*. This was one of Lee's earliest uses of the rough-textured industrial materials that would play an increasingly important role in his designs—and through his influence soon became pervasive in American scenography.

Lee went on to design six more pieces for the Joffrey through 1969—*Olympics, Nightwings, Elegy, Secret Places, A Light Fantastic, Animus* and *The Poppet*—as well as a sort of valedictory in 2003, *I/DNA*. In a 1976 interview Lee said of Joffrey and Arpino, "They're not ashamed of doing a little bit of show-off.... They're very human.... A good deal of it was Jerry Arpino, because he was fantastic at showing off the dancing. He was easy to work with.... He had tremendous energy. And the company was close-knit. Everyone enjoyed working with each other. They were not establishment."[1]

But from that initial meeting with Arpino it was more than two years before *Sea Shadow* was actually performed with Lee's set. In 1964 there was a split between Joffrey and Harkness that almost resulted in the company's demise, and it did not perform for over a year. In August 1965 a newly reconstituted Joffrey Ballet performed at Jacob's Pillow, followed by a weeklong engagement at the Delacorte. These performances included the formal premiere of *Sea Shadow*, but not yet featuring Lee's design. That would have to wait until the company's debut at the New York City Center in March 1966.[2]

Instead, Lee's first dance of the 1965 season was *Ariadne* for choreographer Alvin Ailey, who developed the piece for the newly created Harkness Ballet. Based on the Greek legend of Ariadne, Theseus and the Minotaur and set to music by André Jolivet, the dance was a critical triumph and Lee's set received raves. The curtain rose on a striking ten-foot-tall statue of Pasiphae, the Minotaur's mother (surprisingly, Lee has no memory of this image and wonders if it was created by costume designer Theoni Aldredge). The basic set, however, was in essence a metallic version of *Sea Shadow*. Ailey described it as "all brass poles and enormous pieces of shattered rock."[3] *Ariadne* premiered at the Opéra Comique, and Lee went to Paris for the load-in where he clashed with the Harkness technical director. Lee wanted to move each pair of stage legs a few inches farther offstage as they receded upstage, so that the stage would seem to flare out. The tech director had created a repertory arrangement for the masking and refused to change it to accommodate one dance. Furthermore, Lee was not enjoying Paris: "I don't speak French. The hotel was not that good. I tried to talk to the concierge about where I should have dinner and I was directed to a Russian restaurant. Why should I have Russian food in Paris?" He changed his airline ticket and returned home before opening night, something he still regrets. "It's one of those few things that I eventually told myself I shouldn't do. It's like resigning from *Crucible*. That was really stupid."

Although Lee still had limited experience with contemporary dance at this point, he had an almost instinctual understanding of the abstraction it demanded. "I loved designing dance because you can't talk about it." Speaking now about *Olympics* and *Nightwings*, the pieces he designed for the Joffrey's 1965–66 season, he says, "I think I didn't really take those dances too seriously because the designs came very quickly. Jerry would say, 'Oh, it looks great.' Rehearsals went by very fast. Then I'd go and take a curtain call and call it a day." He felt that he was falling into an easy routine of abstract and sculptural design, relying on his self-admitted "signature" of "structural pipe with emblematic pieces." The process may have felt too effortless to Lee—and no doubt the demands of a ten- or fifteen-minute dance are not the same as a three-hour multi-scene opera or five-act Shakespearean tragedy. Yet the task of creating an image that captures the mood, tone and spirit of a dance, while providing the necessary physical environment for the dancers, is not a simple one. The fact that it came so easily suggests, in fact, how well suited Lee was for this kind of dance; almost no other designer from the world of theatre and opera was doing this. Furthermore, the brevity of the works and the need to allow the dancers to emerge as the dominant visual image allowed him to use dance as a laboratory to experiment with new ideas and materials.

MARTHA GRAHAM

Toward the end of 1965 Lee did his second design for Martha Graham, *The Witch of Endor*, with music by William Schuman. The story was taken from the first book of Samuel in the Old Testament, in which the Witch of Endor conjures the spirit of the prophet Samuel to reveal to King Saul his fate at the hands of David. The seventy-one-year-old Graham danced the role of the Witch. Despite all the settings created for Graham by Isamu Noguchi—designs which profoundly influenced Lee—the set for *The Witch of Endor* remains one of the most iconic in the Graham repertoire.

As with *Ariadne* Lee's design captured the attention of critics, particularly the transformation that occurred for the revelation of Samuel. Lee took his cue not only from the rehearsals he watched that made clear the necessity of the vertical elements, but from the percussive quality of the music, which to him suggested corroded metal. In an essay on opera in *Contemporary Stage Design U.S.A.*, but equally applicable to dance, Lee discussed the relationship of materials to music: "Different materials also suggest different qualities, reflecting even the sound of the orchestration. Stone suggests the bass instruments; metal a percussiveness and sharpness; wood is closer to the lighter warmth of the lower strings, whose tones do indeed emerge from a wooden sound box."[4] Lee refers to *The Witch of Endor*'s rectangular floating pieces with holes as "jewelry store sculpture" and believes that now "people would laugh at it because it's so fake. It's not real metal. It's cutout plywood with Sculp-metal applied and then painted to look like corroded metal." Clearly *Saturday Review* critic John Martin did not find it laughable at the time:

> **Within the dimensions of elegant design, [Lee] has produced a rough and primitive surface, largely by superimposing over the face of his central unit a series of varied smaller surfaces, almost like crude laminae, spiked onto the structure. The great episode of the work...begins with the ominous lowering of Mr. Lee's centerpiece like an armored drawbridge over a moat separating the natural world from the supernatural. Behind it is revealed the white figure of the ghost of Samuel...swaying atop a white column out of which he seems to grow integrally. In the slow motion of his prophecy we are shown David defending himself from the murderous designs of Saul in a duel to the death on the ramp of the "bridge"** (December 11, 1965).

Lee designed four more dances for Graham: *The Lady of the House of Sleep* (1968), *Myth of a Voyage* (1973), *The Owl and the Pussycat* (1978) and *Tangled Night* (1986) [see chapter 13 for a discussion of the last two]. *Myth of a Voyage*, based on the tale of Odysseus, featured a visually striking, almost macramé-like setting, made of rope held taut by tension connectors. Though somewhat abstract, the idea evolved from the image of Penelope's loom—and, as the *Village Voice*'s Deborah Jowitt enthusiastically declared, "suggests rigging, the cosmos, a web, Penelope's loom, you name it" (May 17, 1973).

While many of Lee's dance designs were singled out by critics, and even given credit for the success of some productions, Lee did not have quite the same impact here as in opera and theatre. This was in part the nature of modern dance itself, which was first and foremost about

2

3

2 ***The Witch of Endor,*** Martha Graham, 1965, ½" model. The final set did not have the floating ceiling pieces seen here. Because they were free-hanging, it was difficult to trim them properly during the short scene change between dances. More important, despite Graham's emphasis on gravity and earthbound movement, the ceiling seemed oppressive and claustrophobic in a way that was antithetical to the spirit of the work.

3 ***Myth of a Voyage,*** Martha Graham, 1973, ½" model.

LEE ON MARTHA GRAHAM

With Martha Graham, you bow yourself in, you bow yourself out. That's the way she treats her designers. She'd say, "Ming, come and take a look at rehearsal." If there was another dance going on, you'd wait outside the rehearsal studio. She would open the door and take my arm and I'd walk awkwardly into the room, and there would be all the dancers. And she would say, "Of course all of you know Mr. Lee." And they would say hello and so forth. You would sit with her on the one side of the wall against the mirror. Then she would apologize and say, "This is very rough. We are poor. The ceiling is only twelve feet, so we can't do the jump." After the dance you'd say, "Oh, Martha, what a great dance." And you'd bow yourself out and you'd go home and work. I actually got to know her fairly well and once or twice she invited me to her apartment where we would talk about dance. You know, she is one of those dancers who spoke so amazingly. It's a little like Zelda [Fichandler]. You listen to her speak and suddenly the world is different.

4

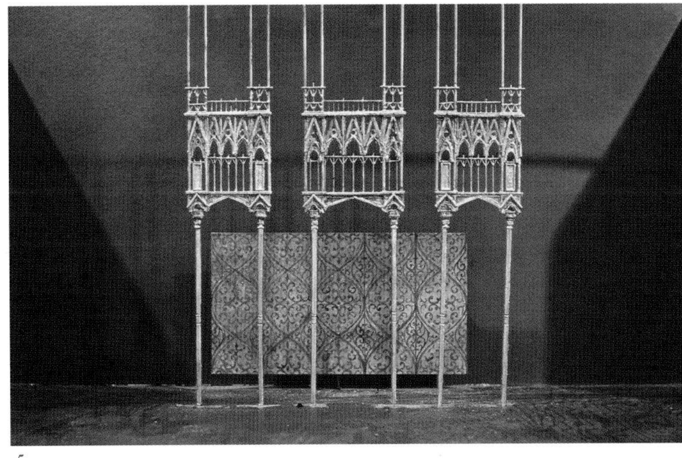

5

6

7

4 ***Sea Shadow***, Joffrey Ballet, 1965, ½" model.

5 ***A Light Fantastic***, Joffrey Ballet, 1968, ½" model. The delicacy of the architectural setting—gold-painted Tudor-Gothic structures in front of a red panel—is at once an example of Lee's "routine" designs and a demonstration of how he evoked precise tone and atmosphere through simplicity.

6 ***Animus***, Joffrey Ballet, 1969, photograph. This was an early use of Mylar, an industrial material popularized on the stage by Czech designer Joseph Svoboda—so new that the baffled *New Yorker* critic described the set as "an arrangement of pipes before a curious mirror-like backdrop, apparently of something like aluminum foil, which reflects the movements in front of it in a hazy sort of way" (March 15, 1969). Clive Barnes in the *New York Times*, while equally unsure of the material, was quite aware of the effect: The set "is dominated by a metallic, angled mirror, which reflects the dancers, but strangely in miniature. As a result, you see a ballet in the foreground and also the effect of another ballet—far off in the distance, only dimly seen. It is a fascinating effect" (March 23, 1969).

7 ***Ariadne***, Harkness Ballet, 1965, ½" model.

8

9

8, 9 ***Madama Butterfly***, Met National Company, 1965, production photographs of the opening scene (top) and the wedding. Although the opera contains both interior and exterior scenes, Lee designed it as a single-set show for touring. The bamboo blinds allowed Cio-Cio-San to look downstage while waiting for Pinkerton's boat.

10 ***Fidelio***, Juilliard Opera Theater, 1965, sketch.

11 Sketch made in 2013 showing *Fidelio*'s second-act set with catwalk removed and stairs added.

10

11

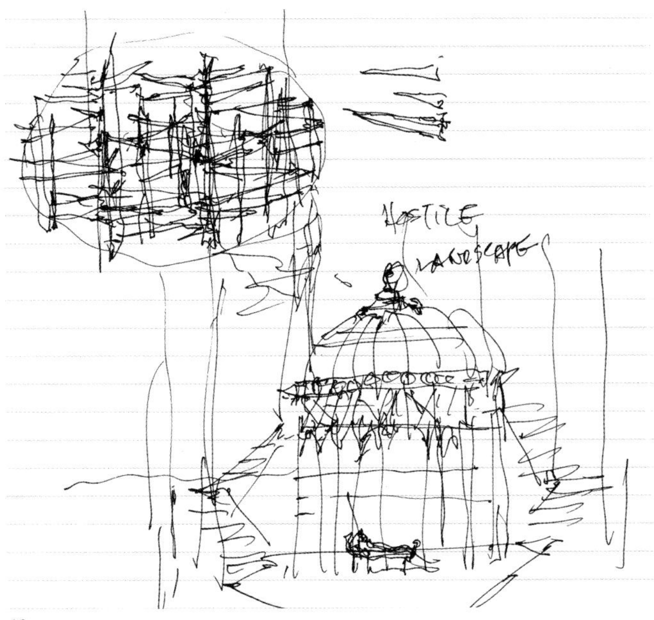

12

13

14

15

12 The original artwork for ***The Magic Flute*** is lost. In 2011 Lee sketched out some of the scenes: a thorny tree for the "hostile landscape" and Pamina's cage made of metal rods welded together.

13 ***The Trial of Lucullus***, Juilliard Opera Theater, 1966, production photograph. Irving Kolodin, the music critic of the *Saturday Review*, began his review by heaping praise on Lee: "Whatever else may be said of the double bill . . . it left one indelible impression. That is, that the young man called Ming Cho Lee is the most original new designer for the musical stage to come to prominence here in some time. Match him with Beni Montressor, and the field of new talent in this area, locally, is about swept clean" (June 4, 1966).

14 ***The Rape of Lucretia***, Juilliard Opera Theater, 1967, ¼" model. It has many of Lee's signature elements from the period—pipe scaffolding, stylized trees and a textured backdrop.

15 ***The Barber of Seville***, Juilliard Opera Theater, 1968, ¼" model for act 1. "*The Barber of Seville* is a very difficult opera to design. My design for the first act was more successful than those for the second and third acts. Unfortunately, the second and third acts of the opera are much more literal than the first; you have to know where the hell Rosina is, why she is there, and then arrange a screen and tables with the understanding that at some point everyone has to hide. . . . I wanted to give the opera a certain amount of formal framework, because Rossini was still carrying on the Italian opera tradition which required a duet here and a trio there. I made the balcony and the door into a formal framework, with pipes supporting a very Italian, distorted, fat piece of header that frames the action. I also had a little raked platform and a fountain with the commandatori with a pigeon sitting on his head, augmented by simple pieces, hanging fragmented pieces, saying 'Seville.'"[5]

16 From left, Marsha Eck, unidentified assistant, Lee and director Tito Capobianco painting scenery.

17 From left, Lee, Juilliard president Peter Mennin and Capobianco at a rehearsal. Christopher West, director of the Juilliard Opera Theater, died in 1967. When Juilliard's American Opera Center was established in 1968, Tito Capobianco was appointed director. Capobianco had first worked with Lee on the New York City Opera's production of *Don Rodrigo* in 1966 [see page 104], and it was partly this collaboration that led to his appointment at Juilliard. In addition to the productions at the New York City Opera, Lee and Capobianco did four productions together at Juilliard.

16

17

movement in space. The role of the decor was to set a mood and create an environment for the dance; it was rarely as integral to the work as it was in theatre and opera. In most cases, the scenography was created in response to an already choreographed work; it was the job of the designer to fit the design to the movement. It also had to do with the companies Lee was working with: Graham had a distinctive style that had been defined by Noguchi for decades. The Joffrey's Arpino, on the other hand, had no single style—every new dance was different and thus did not allow for a distinctive scenographic style to emerge. Also, an evening of dance was usually composed of several pieces from the repertoire, each with its own designer. Nonetheless, Lee felt that he "was doing something different, because aside from Noguchi or Rouben Ter-Arutunian, no one in America was doing those things."

THE METROPOLITAN OPERA NATIONAL COMPANY AND JUILLIARD OPERA THEATER

In 1965 the Metropolitan Opera established a touring company that would employ younger singers and have a more contemporary look. Its inaugural season, under the direction of Risë Stevens and Michael Manuel, consisted of *Susannah*, *Carmen*, *La Cenerentola* and *Madama Butterfly*. Director Yoshio Aoyama was hired to recreate the 1958 Met production that Lee had worked on as costume supervisor. The original set designer, Motohiro Nagasaka, was unavailable, so Lee was asked to recreate the sets. But in the intervening seven years, of course, Lee had emerged as one of the leading American designers, whose résumé included eighteen operas at Peabody, Juilliard and elsewhere; recreating someone else's design was not appealing. Manuel agreed that Lee could use his own *Butterfly* design for Sarah Caldwell as the basis, as long as it included cherry blossoms. Lee reversed the ground plan and, along with the blossoms, added pine trees; the foliage created a distinctly different feel. Instead of the usual two sets—first act exterior, second act interior—Lee designed it as a one-set show, partly to accommodate touring. He wasn't too concerned about essentially copying himself because he assumed the Caldwell *Butterfly* would never be seen again, not imagining that Caldwell would tour it for more than thirty years. The costumes were from the Met production, including those Lee had designed for Pinkerton, Sharpless and Kate Pinkerton.

Lee also took over the design on *Carmen* that season after Bernard Daydé quit (he and Stevens squabbled over white stockings versus bare legs for the chorus), and designed the following season's *The Marriage of Figaro*, more or less in the style of Oliver Messel. Despite the apparent popularity of the productions, the Met reduced its support and the National Company died after two seasons.

Juilliard Opera Theater productions bookended 1965, with *Fidelio* in January and *The Magic Flute* in December. *Fidelio*, Beethoven's only opera, has two locales: the courtyard of Don Pizarro's prison fortress and the dungeon in which Florestan is held captive. Productions generally opted for the theatricalized realism of Gothic prisons, but Lee rejected such specificity. "A realistic Spanish prison of the period, however masterfully designed, simply won't do," he declared in the opera design essay. "Ultimately *Fidelio* has little to do with things Spanish or with any particular prison. It is about all prisons. It deals with the very essence of tyranny and despair, and finally of hope and the human spirit itself. The design concept can be nothing less."[6] This is noteworthy for Lee's use of the word concept, a term he normally rejects. His design for *Fidelio* was more about the *idea* of a prison than an embodiment of an actual place. Clearly informed by his work for Shakespeare in the Park, the fundamental design was comprised of a surround of pipe-grid scaffolding on which were mounted three heavily textured panels along with a catwalk at the back. The catwalk was removed for the second act and replaced

18

19

20

21

The Rake's Progress

Juilliard American Opera

18 Dress rehearsal photograph, 10 the garden of Anne Trulove's 1, This production opened the ne theatre at the Lincoln Center ca se. W.H. Auden and Chester Kallma was loosely based on William Hog engravings, and director Tito Capo asked for a simple platform and peria with the Hogarth etchings. The three- flats revolved to present a different imag for each scene. Once again, a pipe grid provided the overall framework.

19 Sketch for act 1, scene 2, Mother Goose's brothel.

20 Dress rehearsal photograph, act 2, scene 1, outside Tom Rakewell's house. Note that the upstage right periaktoi is not yet complete.

21 Sketch for act 3, scene 3, Bedlam. The jail-like structure was essentially a copy of *Invitation to a Beheading* at the Public Theater the previous year.

22

23

24

Il Giuramento

Juilliard American Opera Center, 1970

22, 23 Sketches. Composed by Saverio Mercadante in 1837, the opera is set in fourteenth-century Syracuse. Lee feels that Capobianco was more comfortable with nineteenth-century romantic opera than with modernist works such as *The Rake's Progress*, and this was reflected in the designs. Capobianco suggested two platforms converging in the middle instead of a single raked platform as usual. "I did some research on Sicily and we did it in a kind of Renaissance Italian Gothic, with a touch of Sicily.... It actually ended up very realistic, somewhat Eugene Berman–like. Raked platforms, heavy perspective."

24 Photograph. The set "without people looked great!" remarks Lee. But he did not compensate for the performers in the perspective, so the scale is wrong.

by a long metal staircase. The elements of "Ming Cho Lee style" really coalesce in this design: the scaffolding, the disjointed three-panel surround, the use of texture, including the wooden planks of the extended thrust, the realistic details in an essentially abstract environment, the upper level and the stairs. The verticality of the three walls encloses the performers, typical of East German scenography at the time, while the raked central platform literally thrusts the performance into the audience.

The ground plan for Mozart's *The Magic Flute* was based on the stage at Stratford, Ontario—"When in doubt, you do your Stratford thing, and before you know it the set is designed," declares Lee. His initial impulse was to angle the set off the centerline, "as I loved to do at the time," but director Christopher West insisted this would be inappropriate because the opera is based entirely on symmetry and balance. For the "hostile landscape" of the first scene Lee, building upon his approach in *Tristan und Isolde* in Baltimore, created trees with large thorny protrusions radiating out—"what I call, 'German art gallery modern.' That's the first time, I think, that people had seen something like that on the stage. This is such naïve sculpture that Noguchi wouldn't dream of doing it, but it was very well received because it was something new." As in the designs at the Delacorte, Lee created a versatile unit set that could be transformed by visually arresting scenic pieces.

Juilliard's spring 1966 season included Roger Sessions's *The Trial of Lucullus*, a one-act opera based on a didactic 1939 radio play by Brecht (not to be confused with Paul Dessau's 1951 opera adaptation, *The Condemnation of Lucullus*). This was Lee's first opportunity to work with true Brechtian material since *Mother Courage*, and he employed some standard techniques, such as projected legends and a half curtain. For many of the scenes he used photomontage backdrops of triumphal arches, marching troops and a sea of faces.

Lee continued his work at Juilliard through 1983, designing *The Rape of Lucretia*, *Ormindo*, *The Barber of Seville*, *The Rake's Progress* (which inaugurated the new Lincoln Center campus), *Il Giuramento*, *La Bohème* [see chapter 10], *Montezuma* and *I Capuleti e i Montecchi* [see chapter 12]. Though Lee is often critical or dismissive of his past work he declares that he was "very proud of those productions at Juilliard. Now they look so old-fashioned, but at the time it was emblematic and definitely not literally realistic. The Met certainly wasn't doing things like that. City Center Opera was not doing things like that. My work with Juilliard was essentially establishing a new look for opera. I carried it through to City Opera, but it began at Juilliard."

NEW YORK CITY OPERA

As with American theatre design, American opera scenography at the time was largely typified by poetic or romantic realism, even in much of the work of European designers at the Met. Lee's work at Juilliard had begun to challenge that aesthetic, and his design for the New York City Opera's *Don Rodrigo* in 1966 would be almost as transformative for the world of opera as *Electra* had been in the world of theatre while establishing him as one of the major opera designers in the U.S.

City Opera chose the American premiere of this serial opera by Argentinian composer Alberto Ginastera to inaugurate its new home, the luxurious New York State Theater at Lincoln Center, on February 22, 1966. It was a production of epic proportions with 119 performers and an orchestra of more than 80, and it catapulted the relatively unknown Plácido Domingo to stardom. Will Steven Armstrong had been the primary designer for the City Opera during the early 1960s at City Center, but Argentine-born director Tito Capobianco had seen Lee's work and specifically asked for him—launching one of Lee's most productive artistic relationships.

The opera is set in early eighth-century Spain and tells the story of the downfall of Rodrigo, the last Visigothic king before the Moorish conquest. Lee, however, felt that the Romanesque architecture of the eleventh century was a better fit for the sensibility of this opera. "This is a contemporary opera on a historical theme, so what difference does two or three centuries make?" he asks. Although he had never been to Spain, he had very strong ideas: "My sense about Spanish architecture, especially the Romanesque, before it gets overly complicated, was that it is very, very white and plain, and that was what I was going for, except in the center where it has all kinds of ornaments and heraldry that are very complex and detailed. And I kept feeling it should be played against a gold sky."

Upstage there was a massive, sculptural emblematic piece that remained until the final scene of the three-act opera, and four very tall, thin gold poles on either side of the flared, raked platform. Four lean figures, two on each side, were mounted high up on the poles, "languid saints [who] brooded throughout the opera's nine scenes" as described by critic Robert Kotlowitz (*Harper's Magazine*, June 1966). (The floating figures would reappear in several theatre and opera productions.) For some scenes the stage was enclosed by white carved stone walls with catwalks above, and there were circular iron chandeliers above the stage. Lee was breaking with the typical practice of the time of painted drops and two-dimensional scenery. And he created a unit set that he believed did not neutralize the space the way he felt Mielziner's unit sets often did: "I think *Rodrigo* was the first of the opera productions here that did not become characterless and still managed to have a unity that went through the whole performance.... At the time, at least, I thought it was relatively groundbreaking."[7]

For anyone who had been paying attention to Lee's work at the Delacorte, there was much in this design that might seem familiar. "All the hanging statues, the structural poles and so forth came from the structure of the Delacorte," Lee notes. "It was time to bring it indoors for this opera." But the scale was far grander than anything Lee had done before, and the vocabulary he had developed coalesced into a bold statement. While he had begun to experiment with some aspects of this work at Juilliard, this was really the first time that the larger American opera world had been exposed to this somewhat German-inflected structural and sculptural design. Going forward, historical realism in opera decor would become decidedly old-fashioned. Strangely, as with *Electra*, few critics seemed to recognize the import of the design at the time. Nonetheless, Lee had created a look for the New York City Opera in its new home, and he would be one of its primary designers for the next several years.

City Opera opened its fall 1966 season with Handel's *Giulio Cesare*. The production, directed again by Capobianco, made soprano Beverly Sills a star and was partly responsible for the renewed interest in baroque opera, which at the time was still a rarity on American opera house stages. The costumes by Jose Varona were period—a sort of eighteenth-century version of Roman—and Capobianco's direction was, to quote critic Harold Schonberg, "stately and old-fashioned" so as to "resurrect the feeling of Handel opera as it was done in the early eighteenth century" (*New York Times*, September 28, 1966). Lee feels that the achievement of this production was to give the opera "a heroic scale without losing its inherent sense of humor." Looking back, though, he finds it "really dated" and wishes it could have been as boldly conceived as Peter Sellars's 1985 production in which Caesar was envisioned as an American president, but postmodern interpretations of opera were not yet in vogue in 1966. Despite Lee's regrets, his set was, in fact, almost postmodern, particularly in its quotation of classical and baroque motifs. The design was perfectly symmetrical with two skeletal towers flanking the stage with a platform in each tower about fifteen feet above the floor. Classical columns were sleeved over the pipework scaffolding, but, significantly, these sculptural elements did not cover the pipes completely—there were gaps between sections of the columns revealing the pipes. Detached capitals floated above the lower columns, but the upper columns seemed more like abstract verticals—echoing earlier Lee motifs—suggesting a stark modernism. But, unlike *Electra*, in which floating pieces foregrounded the theatricality of the scenery, this scenic device foregrounded the structural elements, which emphasized the artificiality of the stage. A pair of stairs led to an upstage center platform from which another pair of stairs led up to the higher platforms of the towers creating an X-like pattern. Far upstage were three towers that rotated to create different scenes. Handkerchief drops with painted scenes flew in either in front of or behind the central platform. It was these drops in particular that created the postmodern sense of scenic quotation. When the opera was restaged in Hamburg, Germany, three years later Lee used essentially the same design, but it became more decorative.

Bomarzo, another twelve-tone opera by Ginastera, again directed by Capobianco, premiered at the Opera Society of Washington in May 1967 and transferred, essentially unchanged, to the New York State Theater a year later. While architecturally the design utilized Lee's established scenic vocabulary—what he calls his "usual Renaissance structure" consisting of stair units on either side of a high raised upstage platform—visually it was a significant departure, marking a new direction. It was probably the most complex production he had done. The fifteen-scene opera tells the story of the sixteenth-century Italian duke Pier Francesco Orsini through flashbacks as he is dying. The title comes from the province where Orsini built the "Park of Monsters," containing large, grotesque sculptures, several of which were reproduced or referenced within Lee's design. While most of the Shakespeare plays, of course, contain a greater number of scenes, Lee had always employed unit sets. For *Bomarzo*, however, each scene had a different configuration. More important, the structure was disguised by an elaborate scenic decor inspired by the paintings of the Argentine-Italian painter Leonor Fini whose often erotic work shows influences of Klimt and expressionism—some of her paintings include images of hands with rotting skin exposing underlying nerves and veins—imagery that Lee incorporated into the set with its gruesome decomposing faces on the rear wall and on the tapestry on Orsini's bed. Lee also borrowed from the Netherlandish painters Hieronymus Bosch and Pieter Bruegel. The result was a set that seemed to be decaying, melting, eaten away. There was some similarity to *The Tempest*, but while that design suggested fantasy, this production was overwhelmingly grotesque. "People who worked on the show thought I had had a horrible nightmare," exclaimed Lee.[8] This set was not primarily structural, certainly not industrial; it was a truly imagistic design.

The complexity of the scene changes overwhelmed the limited stage crew in Washington and Lee and Capobianco were backstage moving scenery, a task which they were spared in New York. The production was subsequently done at the Teatro Colón in Buenos Aires in 1972.

Nikolai Rimsky-Korsakov's 1907 opera, *Le Coq d'Or*, also known as *The Golden Cockerel*, was produced by the City Opera before the New York presentation of *Bomarzo* and continued Lee's collaboration with Capobianco. Capobianco wanted something in the style of Russian artist Natalia Goncharova, who had designed the Ballets Russes production in 1914, but Lee was more interested in Paul Klee and the way that artist divided space. The result, while semiabstract, was more painterly, more concerned with flat planes, than his predominantly sculptural work of the period.

Lee's next work for City Opera was Charles Gounod's *Faust*. Lee had seen Peter Brook's production at the Met, designed by Rolf Gérard, when he first moved to New York in 1954: "There are images that I will never forget. I can still draw it." He had read—or attempted to read—the Goethe play as a student at Occidental and was fascinated by the philosophy and morality of the work. "*Faust* for me is one of the key works in the transition from the Age of Reason to Romanticism. Gounod, of course, puts this complicated, dense, philosophical interpretation of the world into an easy-to-understand melodic score. I think Gounod's *Faust* is so human."

Getting to the finished design was a struggle. The director, Frank Corsaro, wanted a fantastical *Faust* with the sort of effects that "as a Brechtian you just go, 'eww.'" But Lee and costume designer Varona convinced Corsaro to focus on the humanity of the characters. Faust's study was designed a bit like Dr. Frankenstein's laboratory, with scientific instruments and cadavers, one of which came to life as Mephistopheles. The kermesse scene included a small hell mouth, inspired by *Bomarzo*. But the scenery, though theatrically striking, wound up a messy amalgam of Brecht (including a *Mother Courage*–like wagon) and pictorialism.

25

Don Rodrigo

New York City Opera, 1966

25, 26 Production photographs of the coronation scene and scene 1 (opposite).

27, 28 ½" models of scenes 2 and 8.

29 Production photograph of scene 9, with the stage stripped to only a cyclorama and a single floating figure.

26

27

28

29

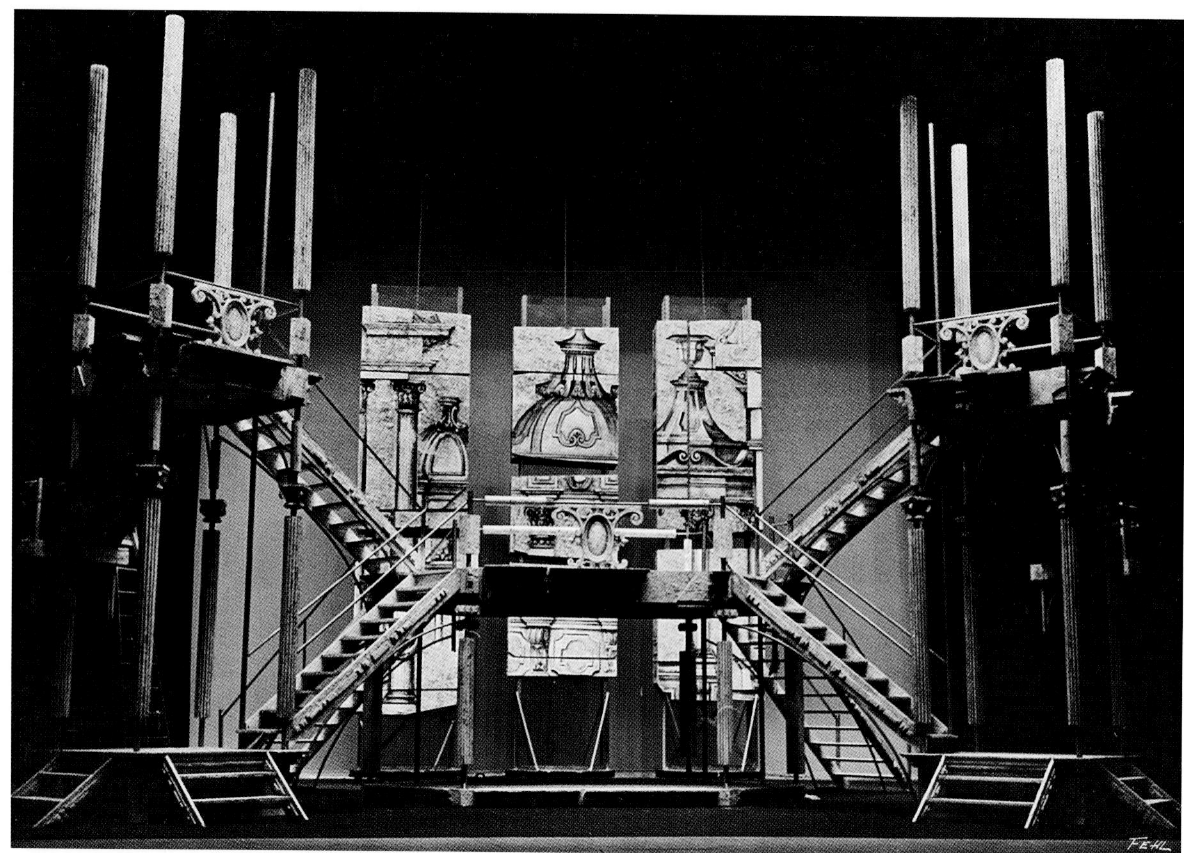

30

31

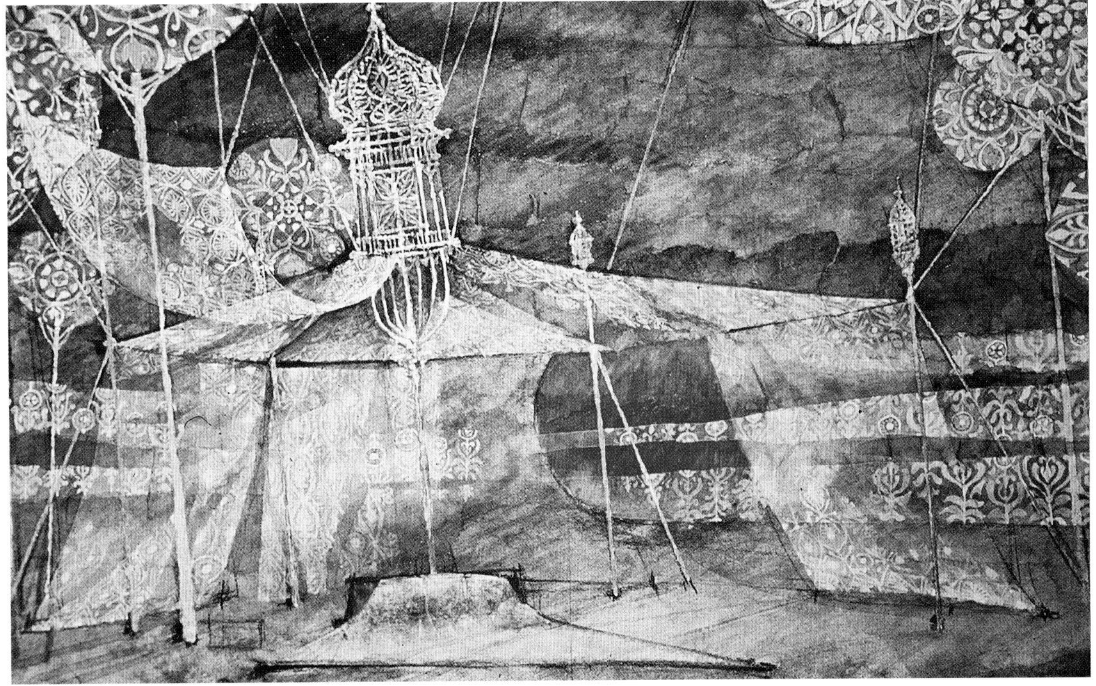

32

33

30, 31 ***Giulio Cesare***, New York City Opera, 1966, photographs. The use of a drop in front of the structure platform, with its cartoonish quotation of scenery, anticipates postmodernist techniques by nearly a decade.

32, 33 ***Le Coq d'Or***, New York City Opera, 1967, sketch and photograph. Lee was beginning to use color more boldly than ever before. A couple of months earlier *The Comedy of Errors* at the Delacorte marked an infusion of color into his Shakespearean sets. For the opera Lee used a backdrop that, as he described in a *New York Times* interview, was "*really* red—in fact, it must be the reddest drop ever, and a gold show curtain that is really gold" (September 24, 1967).

34

35

36

37

Bomarzo

Opera Society of Washington, 1967;
New York City Opera, 1968

34, 35 Research photo of hell mouth from Orsini's "Park of Monsters" and production photograph with it incorporated into the set.

36 Preliminary sketch. Lee started with a long perspective hall and celling, but it was not used.

37 Production photograph. The faces in the wall were inspired by the paintings of Leonor Fini.

38, 39 Production photographs, garden scene (top) and Orsini's bedroom.

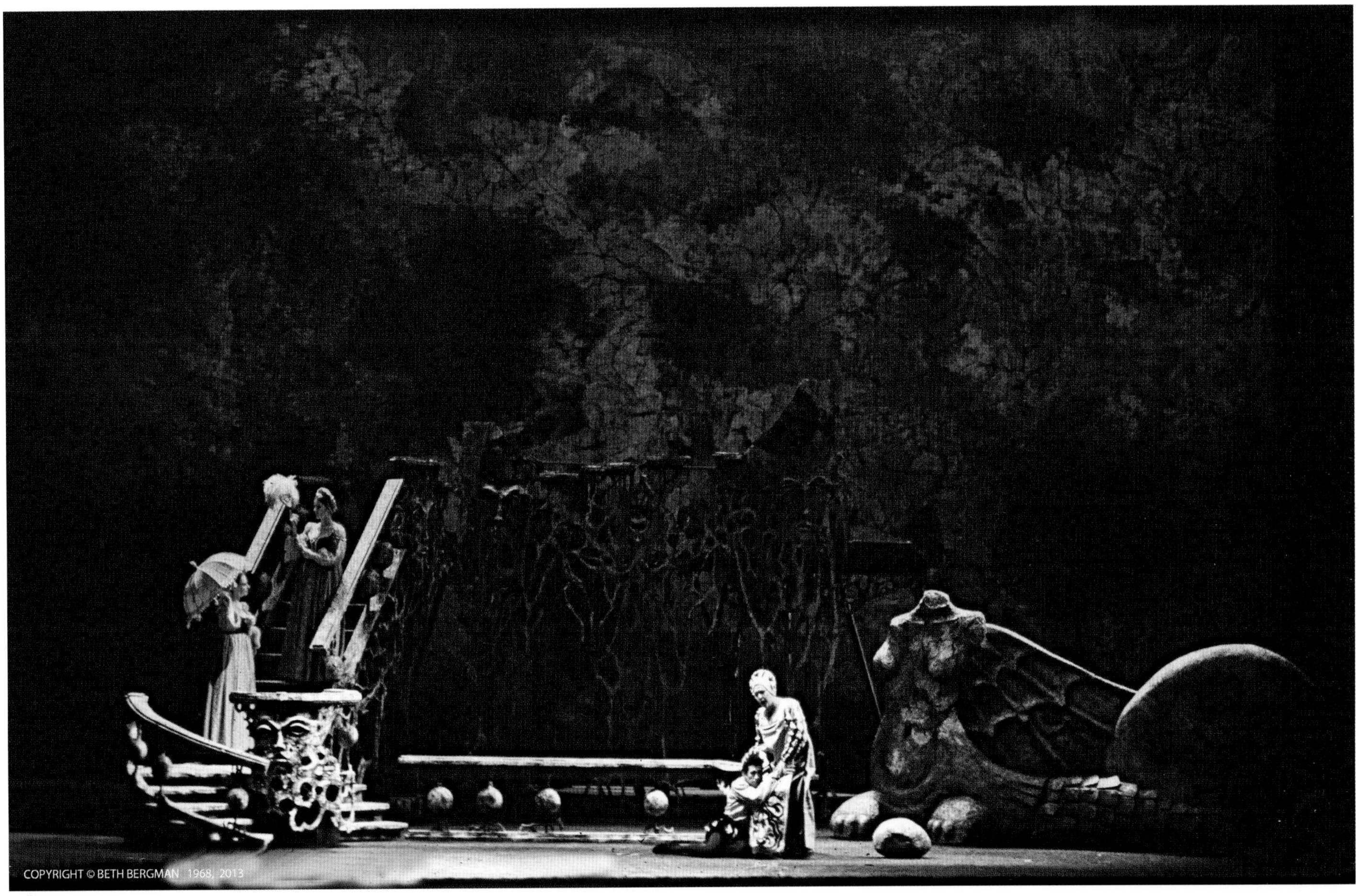
COPYRIGHT © BETH BERGMAN 1968, 2013

38

COPYRIGHT ©BETH BERGMAN 1968, 2013

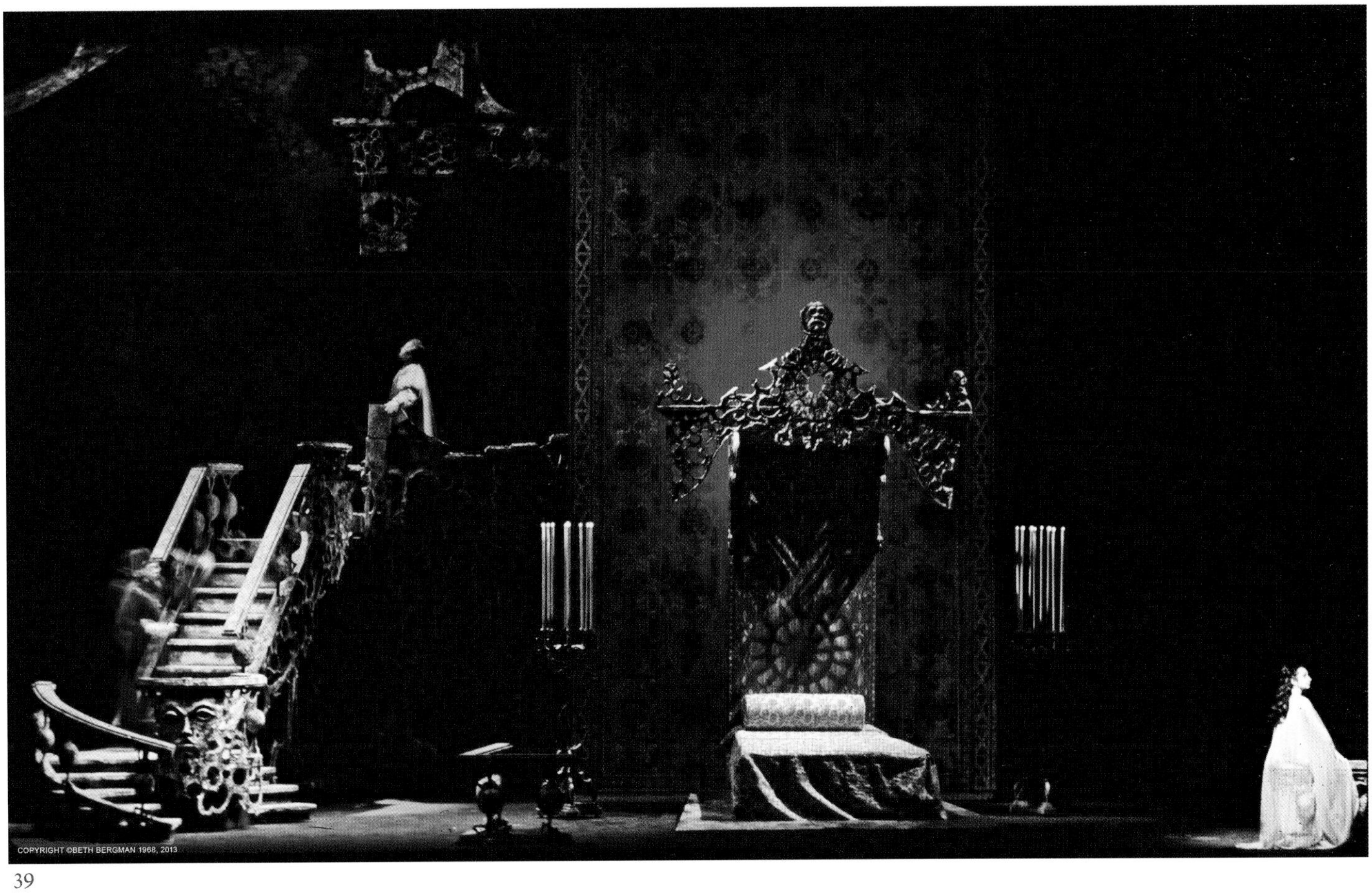

39

40

Faust

New York City Opera, 1968

40 Sketch of scene 1. The cadaver in the center of the Dr. Frankenstein–like laboratory rose up as Mephistopheles.

41, 42 Model and production photograph of the kermesse scene. "If I had just designed a German town it would've been much better. Instead of having the tavern where blood comes out of the wine casket, we had a fountain with a crucifix mounted on top. Mephistopheles went, 'Whoosh,' and the wine came out of the wound, which we thought was fantastic. I was actually trying to reproduce the feeling from a scene in the movie *The Red Shoes* where there's a ballet that has a yellow sky and white newspapers floating down. But by having scaffolding and wooden posts going up, I destroyed it."

41

42

43

43 ***Titus Andronicus***, New York Shakespeare Festival, 1967, ½" model. The actual set was not as effective as the model. Lee had expected the shop to build the set similar to the way they constructed *Electra* with six inches of Styrofoam on top of a frame so that he could then carve it with acid. But instead they used spray foam on top of wire mesh and the effects had to come through painting.

44 ***Henry IV, Parts 1 and 2***, New York Shakespeare Festival, 1968, ½" model. Gerald Freedman referred to it as an "architectural sculpture." This was Lee's first Delacorte production that did not employ a structural background or surround.

FROM OPERA BACK TO SHAKESPEARE: *TITUS*, *HENRY* AND *LEAR*

Just as Lee's creations at Juilliard and the New York City Opera drew upon the earlier emblematic, iconic and sculptural designs at the Delacorte, his subsequent Shakespearean designs now began to incorporate his scenographic explorations in opera and dance. Three productions are of particular note: *Titus Andronicus* (1967), *Henry IV, Parts 1 and 2* (1968) and *King Lear* (1968).

For *Titus*, at New York Shakespeare Festival, Gerald Freedman was looking for an abstract representation of violence and decay. The result, inspired by an aerial view of the Coliseum in Rome, contained echoes of *The Witch of Endor* and *Ariadne*—a corroded metallic world eaten away by acid. As mounted on the pipe grid the background had structural echoes of *Electra,* and the sense of decay, especially the fractured circles, was reminiscent of the recent *Bomarzo*. It was the most abstract design Lee created at the Shakespeare Festival.

Henry IV, Parts 1 and 2, also at the Delacorte, utilized the same set. The three iconic figures—warrior kings—were an obvious echo of the floating saints of *Don Rodrigo* ("I thought I had to have *something* that's emblematic"), but of even greater significance was the ground plan. Until this production, all the designs in the park consisted of a platform and a structural background or surround, but for *Henry IV*, there was a large platform with a scenic unit in the middle. The structure, with its nooks and crannies, multiple levels, doors and stairs, provided for every aspect of the world of Prince Hal/King Henry. (Lee was inspired by Douglas Schmidt's design for *King John* the previous season which used a revolving unit in the midst of the stage.)

In 1968 Gerald Freedman was asked by Jules Irving, artistic director of the Repertory Theater of Lincoln Center, to direct *King Lear* at the Vivian Beaumont Theater with Lee J. Cobb as Lear. It, too, seemed to reflect motifs that had been emerging in Lee's opera designs and bore some striking resemblances to *Don Rodrigo*. (It opened just a few weeks after *Faust*, and Lee found himself going back and forth

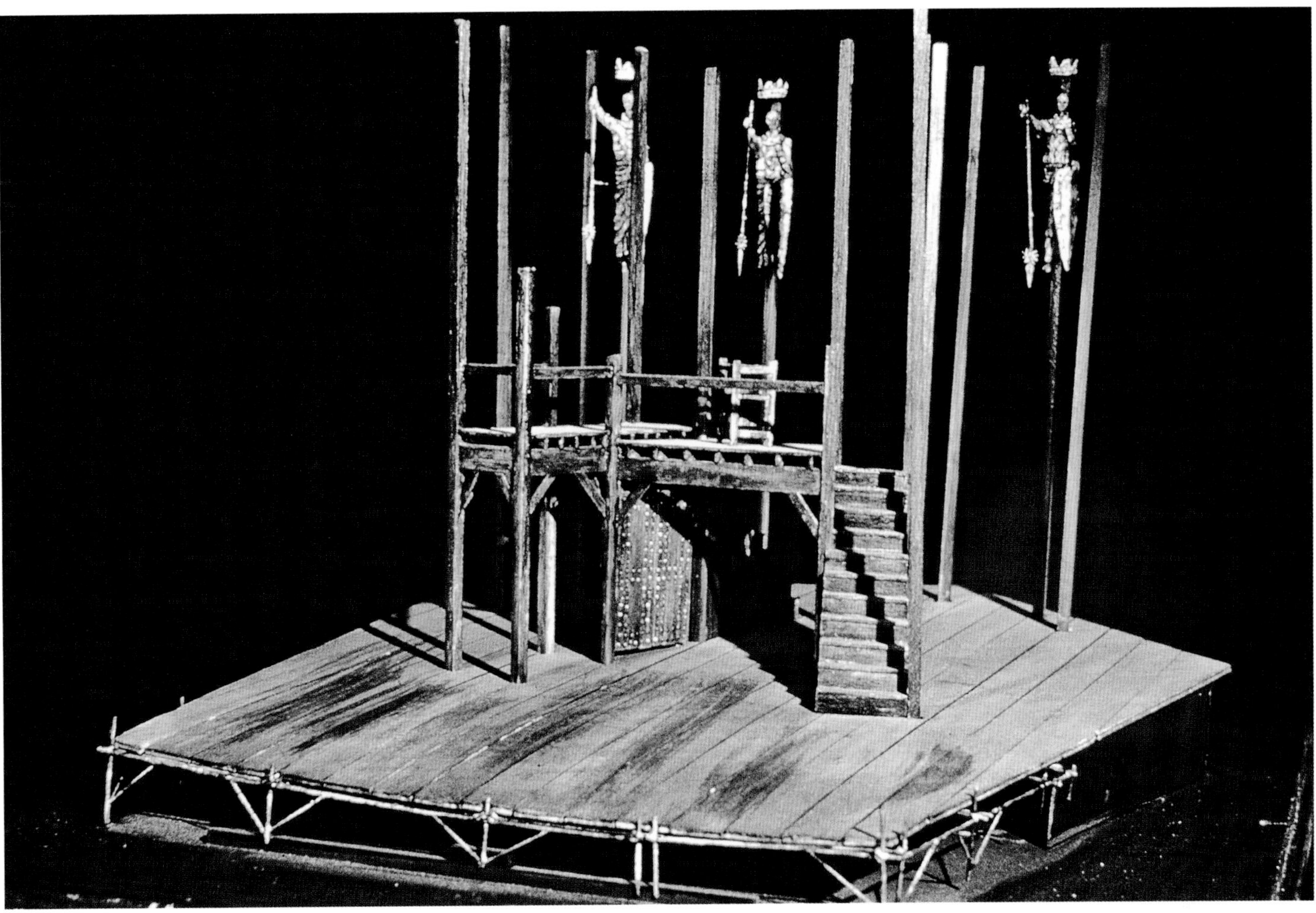

44

between the two theatres. "At the time Lincoln Center was still fairly new and you felt like you owned the whole of New York theatre just walking across the plaza.") Freedman's concept was that as Lear lost the trappings of power and humanity, the set would be stripped away as well, leaving an almost bare stage by the end. He also wanted a somewhat rough and primitive feel which Lee achieved through the use of a wooden platform, wooden superstructure and erosion cloth.

Critical response to the production as a whole was mixed, and Lee's set fared no better. This is somewhat surprising given that the sketches and model suggest a powerful set that seems to embody Lear's disintegrating world. Lee attributes the failure, in part, to the notorious problems of the Beaumont itself—although he readily acknowledges it was his own fault for not grasping the issues until it was too late. The theatre, co-designed by Jo Mielziner with architect Eero Saarinen, tried rather unsuccessfully to combine a proscenium with a thrust. A proscenium theatre is what Lee refers to as a "theatre with two roofs"—the audience and the stage occupy separate architectural spaces; a thrust is a "theatre with one roof"—crucially, the mechanics of the stage cover spectators and stage alike. But while the seating of the Beaumont enveloped the stage, Mielziner hid the lighting equipment and made the walls black, in essence creating a "two roof" environment within a "one roof" space. The proscenium opening was flexible and Lee wanted it as wide as possible so as to fully utilize the great depth of the stage. It looked fine during rehearsals under work lights, but when the house lights were turned off "it felt like you were looking into a cavernous space. We kept making the proscenium opening smaller and smaller, but then the auditorium felt too big. At one point I threatened Jules Irving. I said, 'One night I'm going to come in with a whole bunch of house painters and paint the whole theatre white. Then you'll have a working theatre.' Of course I never did."

In a strange way, the lukewarm response to the *Lear* set was indicative of how far Lee had transformed design in such a short time. As recently as 1964 the emblematic and iconic was a rarity on the American stage. Now, thanks largely to Lee's efforts, it was an almost too familiar style.

45

King Lear

Vivian Beaumont Theater, Lincoln Center, 1968

45 ½" model for act 1, scene 1, Lear's court. "I did a rough sketch that's just structure, copying my *Crucible* at Arena Stage [see Chapter 8] with a ring like a crown of thorns. Then I added some pieces flying in and so forth. Kind of copy of Wieland Wagner's *Ring*, then a floating sculptural piece and a bit of *Don Rodrigo* platform on the side."

46–48 ¼" sketches for, from top, Gloucester's castle, the heath and the storm. As Lear's world disintegrated, so did the set. For the storm scene everything was flown out except for four posts. Lee wanted the storm to be a kind of whiteout. "Of course we never achieved the whiteout because it's easy to put a lot of gesso on the sketch but what does that mean in lighting terms?"

46

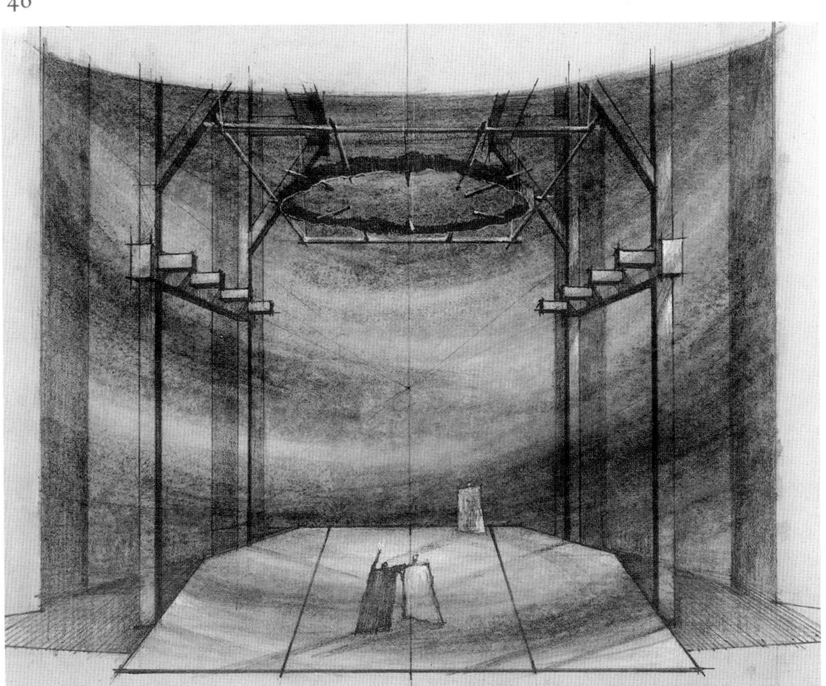

47

48

CHAPTER 7

Verticals, Scaffolds and Collage 1965–72

1 ***Ergo***, Public Theater, 1968, sketch. Jakov Lind's play had to contain two worlds simultaneously: the stark white room of the Prussian character stage left, and the cluttered world of the Austrian character stage right, depicted by a scenic drop of pages torn from books and newspapers, with papers spilling out onto the stage. The design won a Maharam Award.

1

2 ***The Mutilated***, Broadway, 1966, ½" model.

3 ***The Gnadiges Fraulein***, Broadway, 1966, ½" model. Due to budget constraints, the swirling background was replaced by a simple drop and black wings on either side. Note the multiple perspective angles juxtaposed within the single image.

"**MING CHO LEE**... has given scaffolding a new chic"—so declared Lee's ardent supporter, *New York Times* critic Clive Barnes (December 2, 1971). By the mid-1960s, metal pipe grids and scaffolding had become the most iconic aspect of Lee's work. Initially developed as an efficient and economical solution to practical scenic problems, it soon evolved into a fundamental attribute of Lee's scenographic vocabulary. Soprano Beverly Sills, referring to a City Opera production, even quipped, "Between Ming's pipes and mine, we'll be okay." But unlike the ethereal skeletal structures of his mentor Jo Mielziner, Lee's architecture was closer in spirit to the Russian constructivists and possessed a gritty, industrial look.

The first hints of this technique were seen in the early 1960s designs for *The Fall of the City* and *The Pearl Fishers* at Peabody Conservatory, but scaffolding came into its own at the Delacorte as the underlying structure of Lee's neo-Elizabethan stage. With the ill-fated *Side Show* in 1964 the pipe grid emerged as a unique scenic motif, and was fully incorporated into scaffolding with *Fidelio* at Juilliard Opera the following year. The pipe grid served to segment space and to emphasize and enhance the volume of the stage, creating sculptural area rather than the more common two-dimensional terrain of the pictorial stage. Perhaps most important, it added a strong vertical thrust to the decor, drawing the eyes of the audience upward, foregrounding that oft-ignored dimension of the stage. Lee studied construction scaffolding wherever he went, observing that "scaffolding here [in the U.S.] is all pre-made frames.... In Europe, it looks like they just have a lot of pipes and clamps and there's an improvised look. Then you go to Hong Kong and it's all bamboo lashed together and you wonder how they can build skyscrapers. Lines cutting across planes are interesting for me."

SLAPSTICK TRAGEDY

With Tennessee Williams's *The Mutilated* in 1966 Lee's scaffolding became a bold scenographic statement. The one-act play, presented on Broadway as part of a double bill with *The Gnadiges Fraulein* under the collective title *Slapstick Tragedy*, is set in a fleabag residence in the French Quarter of New Orleans. Williams called for sets "as delicate as Japanese line-drawings...so abstract, so spidery, with the exception of Trinket Dugan's bedroom, that the audience will accept the nonrealistic style of the play." Lee's design was hardly delicate—with a riot of platforms, railings, balconies, vertical pipes and louvered doors and shutters creating a gritty, if bizarre, reality—but it nonetheless captured an aspect of Williams's play. Only the backdrop offered the ethereal quality Williams had asked for.

The producers sent Lee to New Orleans and Key West to research. His response to the French Quarter was "the feeling that I was standing in a sea of vertical pipes and balconies. When I came back, instead of designing the set I did an impression of what I remembered of New Orleans, and that actually ended up being the background—a kind of an abstract impression of New Orleans. That took me away from Mielziner's *Streetcar*." This was also an early example of Lee combining painted and structural scenery.

The Gnadiges Fraulein, on the other hand, was set in a surreal boarding house in the Florida Keys, described in the stage directions as "a totally unrealistic arrangement of porch, steps, yard, and picket fence...I mean like Picasso designed it.... Everything is in the subtle variety of greys and greyish whites that you see in pelican feathers and clouds. Even the sun is a greyish white disk over the lustreless grey zinc roof that sits at the angle of Charlie Chaplin's derby on the house." Lee captured this imagery with brilliant artistry. Inspired by his impressions of Key West, he designed a decidedly expressionistic house set within a surrealist landscape. "The architecture in Key West is strangely like New England," he observed, "except that all the roofs are silvered against the sun. The set was extremely grotesque, with the house leaning and the perspective distorted in an attempt to reflect the distortions in the characters themselves." Of particular note were the mysterious vertical posts around the house—were they trees? Utility poles? Fragments of scaffolding? "Nowadays I certainly would not have those pipes going up, but at that time I wouldn't do anything without being emblematic. So here are those pipes going nowhere." Yet the pipes seem integral to the architecture, somehow supporting the dangerously leaning structure while situating it in an otherworldly landscape. Once again, the sets received positive reviews while the plays were generally savaged.

This was the most visually captivating set Lee had yet designed, a unique and arresting image that remains one of his most famous. It evoked the Southern Gothic of Williams's world, with echoes of Mielziner's painterly style, though distorted so that the romanticism of his mentor was replaced by expressionistic horror. *Saturday Review* critic Henry Hewes planned to nominate it for a Joseph Maharam

2

3

4

4 ***Measure for Measure***, New York Shakespeare Festival, 1966, ½" model.

Award that season, an annual design award he had established (now the Henry Hewes Design Awards). Lee, in fact, had won the very first Maharam Award in 1965 for *Electra*. But when Hewes called to tell him of his intention, Lee demurred, protesting with typical self-deprecation that it was not a very good set. Hewes responded, "Well then, I don't want to give you an award if you don't like the set." And he didn't. (Lee admits that his frequent belittling of his own work comes from a characteristically Chinese tendency to deflect compliments and minimize accomplishments. As this incident demonstrated, it could backfire.)

VERTICAL SHAKESPEARE

Lee, perhaps better than any of his peers, understood the stage in geometric terms, and this, too, marked a radical shift in American set design. This is remarkably apparent placing the three productions of the 1965 Shakespeare Festival side by side: *Love's Labor's Lost*, *Coriolanus* and *Troilus and Cressida* are all dominated by strong vertical lines.

But it was the middle show of the 1966 Shakespeare Festival season, *Measure for Measure*, that finally brought true verticality and industrial scaffolding to the Delacorte. The set was something radically different, for both the Shakespeare Festival and Lee: a very frontal white brick façade with a kind of fire escape structure and steep industrial stairs leading up from either side. Director Michael Kahn, who came from the Off-Off Broadway world, wanted neither abstraction nor a historically accurate Vienna. He told Lee that he wanted it to look like New York City's meat market district, at the time an area of low-rise brick tenements and warehouses. "He wanted Ninth Avenue, so I gave him Ninth Avenue," says Lee. This was not intended to be an illusionistic set—essentially it was a fragment, a quotation of the neighborhood. The pipework's verticality counteracted the potential squatness of the building, and the metal structure provided the upper stage area that Lee had incorporated into most of the previous Delacorte sets—but now it was an integral part of the architecture. The fire escape even created an "inner below" that could become the setting for the jail scenes by placing a construction of metal bars below the balcony. For all his rejection of the pictorial and painterly up to that point, Lee had never created a setting so hard, cold and disturbing in its brutality.

The other two shows from that season echoed earlier productions. *All's Well That Ends Well*'s frontal rectangular architecture and broad balcony gave the set a horizontality that the randomly placed barren trees, adapted from the previous season's *Love's Labor's Lost*, did little to offset. On closer examination the façade bears a striking similarity to *Coriolanus*. *Richard III*, directed by Gerald Freedman, at first glance seems a reprise of *Electra*, with sculpted heraldic slabs mounted on vertical poles that did not touch the floor. But instead of stone these were intended to look like corroded copper, the chaotic detritus of war hanging in vertical strips, reinforced by the steep stairs. The effect was somewhat collage-like, a harbinger of that soon-to-emerge technique.

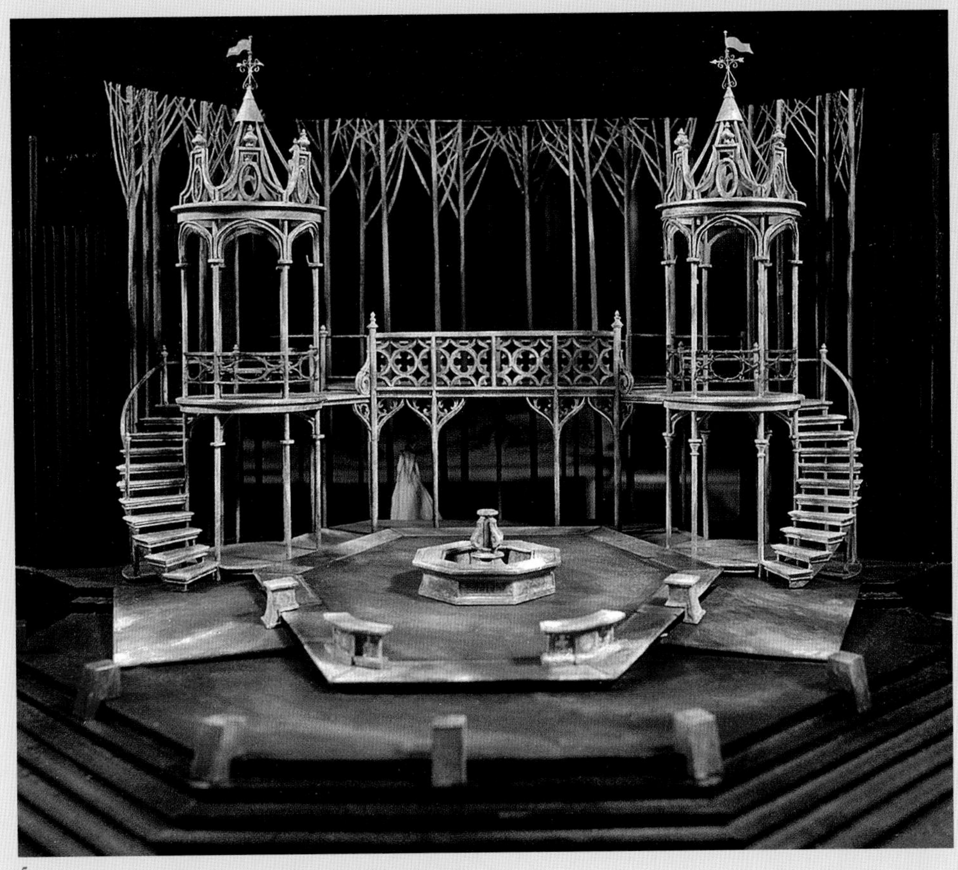

5

6

LEE ON *LOVE'S LABOR'S LOST*

I have always thought that *Love's Labor's Lost* is a very French play. I found Shakespeare to be remarkable, whether he traveled to Europe during that missing twelve years or not, he had such a grasp of all the locations. His plays in Italy are unmistakably Italian. In *Romeo and Juliet*, you read the play you feel as if you've been to Verona. *Merchant of Venice*—it's as if you have been to Venice. And the few things that he set in France, like *As You Like It* and *Love's Labor's Lost*, are really very French. And I always am absolutely amazed by the fact that the one play he wrote that is set in Vienna...it's the most German play I've ever read! And that's *Measure for Measure.*

5, 6 ***Love's Labor's Lost***, New York Shakespeare Festival, 1965, ½" model (top) and production photograph. Lee designed a whimsical set that resembled a French garden pavilion (Bernard Gersten thought that it should be donated to the park as a playground). The symmetry of the set and the graceful curves of the gazebos and stairs were offset by a colonnade of irregularly spaced, stylized trees in the form of slender vertical posts and angled "branches" sliced off in straight line across the top. The trees brought the vertical thrust of the set up to twenty-eight feet, greater than any previous design. Lee did meticulous period research for the quatrefoils before discovering that the patterns could be found on the bridge railings in Central Park. "When the damn set was going up I was riding my bicycle back home and realized, 'Oh! It's right there!'"

7

8

7 ***Coriolanus***, New York Shakespeare Festival, 1965, ½" model. The two tiers of arches suggested fragments of the Coliseum or perhaps a Roman aqueduct. The dominant scenic element in many *Coriolanus* productions is a gate—it was a massive element, for instance, in Boris Aronson's design for Stratford on which Lee had assisted. But the upper stage of the Delacorte limited the height of the gate to some eight feet, resulting in a triumphal arch that Lee declares "insignificant, piddling. I was still thinking too much of sculpture and stone, and I didn't really have a sense about Rome." Lee thinks the design was caught between abstract and "not so abstract," and even then felt old-fashioned.

8 ***Troilus and Cressida***, New York Shakespeare Festival, 1965, production photograph. Literally *Coriolanus*'s set reduced to only the vertical posts—Lee simply removed the cross pieces from the arches (the markings are still visible). For the battle scene toward the end, soldiers carried more beams onstage, placing them irregularly to create a sense of a destroyed terrain.

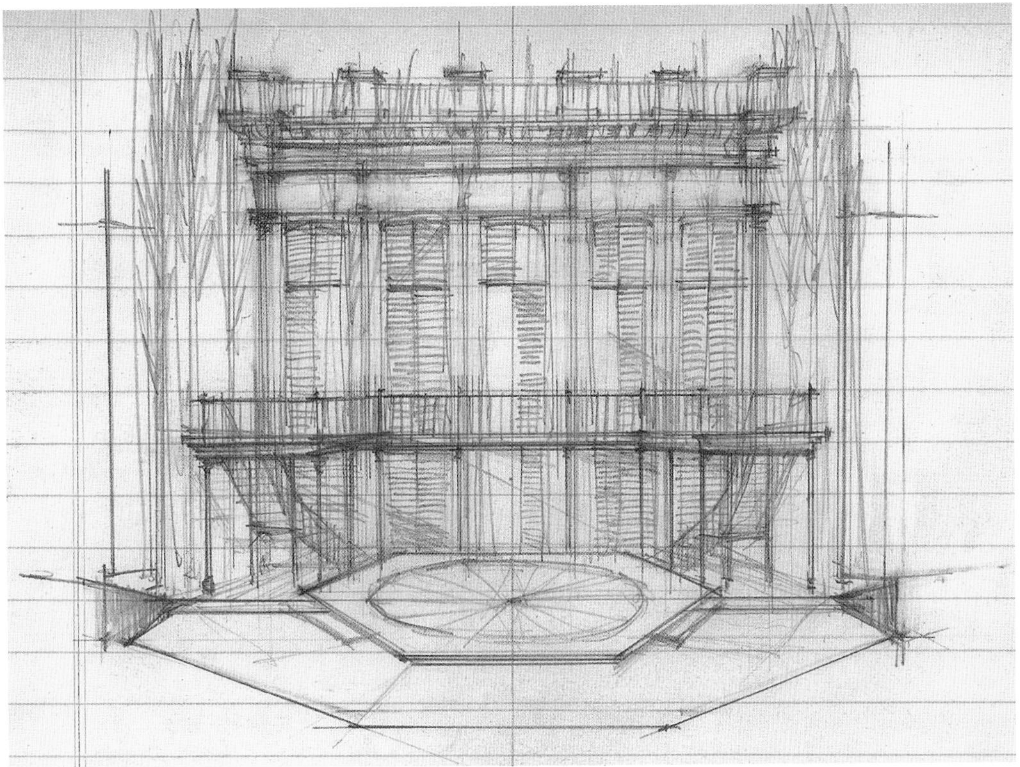
9

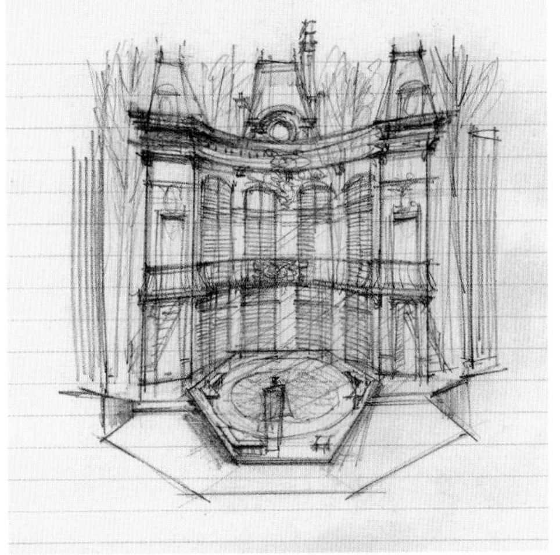
10

9, 10 ***All's Well That Ends Well***, New York Shakespeare Festival, 1966, sketches. Lee wanted a neoclassical French sensibility, "something that looked like the façade of the Frick museum," and early sketches suggested a Mansard-style house, but it evolved into something more linear and frontal. The camp scenes became problematic in this design. Tents were erected in front of the façade, but that simply became confusing; the solidity and specificity of the wall created a realism that resisted transformation of locale. "I don't think Joe [Papp] really knew how to use this set," says Lee.

11 ***Richard III***, New York Shakespeare Festival, 1966, ½" model.

11

Hair
Public Theater, 1967

12 Collage. Note pillars onstage.
13 Production photograph.
14 View of the Anspacher Theater.

HAIR AND THE PUBLIC THEATER

For some time Joe Papp had been looking for a winter home for the Shakespeare Festival. After considering several sites his team settled on the former Astor Library on Lafayette Street, just south of Astor Place. The building had been built in three sections between 1853 and 1881, but by 1965 it was largely abandoned and under threat of demolition. Partly through Papp's efforts—to prevent real estate developers from purchasing the building—it became one of the first buildings landmarked under the city's newly formed Landmarks Preservation Commission. Despite reservations by most of the Festival staff, who worried about how to finance the building and thought that the 54,000 square feet was far more than they needed, Papp pushed ahead. Lee was among the doubters: "I was still thinking that the Delacorte was the main event and the winter home would be the workshop that fed the summer theatre. What did we need the Astor Library for?"

Lee was responsible for designing the theatres in the new space. He wanted to bring his architect friend Hugh Hardy on board, but Papp hired Giorgio Cavaglieri, a Venetian-born architect with a track record as a preservationist, though he had never designed a theatre. Not surprisingly, he and Lee had some heated arguments as the renovations moved forward. Papp's original plan was to gut the building and create an 850-seat theatre, but the tripartite structure—each section separated by four-foot-thick walls—posed problems (as did, ironically, its new landmark status). Eventually they all agreed upon a plan for several 300-seat theatres, beginning with what became known as the Anspacher in the former reading room of the library on the second floor of the middle section.

The room was two stories high with a balustrade gallery and a translucent dome above, which created an atrium-like effect. While allowing for the height and volume that Lee desired, it was also well suited for an intimate thrust stage. Lee designed a rectangular thrust surrounded on three sides by a steeply raked auditorium with 275 seats. He liked the idea that the severe thrust stage created a tension with the ornamental neoclassical room. The audience entered at the top of the auditorium by climbing stairs on either side from the second-floor landing. "At the time I loved staircases. I loved people going up and down staircases, as if there's a theatrical sense of engaging with the architecture," declares Lee. These were the days before much consideration of people with disabilities. Decades later, as Lee developed mobility problems himself, he became acutely aware of the accessibility issues that stairs create. A major architectural issue in the renovation were the sixteen wood-encased cast-iron Corinthian columns that supported the upper gallery. This was the source of Lee and Cavaglieri's most intense fights, particularly because two of the columns would be at the upper corners of the stage. Cavaglieri wanted to preserve them, Lee wanted them gone. But the columns were weight-bearing and could not be eliminated, so they compromised by stripping the onstage columns down to the cast iron and removing the balustrade and gallery above the stage. That meant that, henceforward, all productions had to work around the columns.

From the start the Public was intended as a home for new plays, but even so the selection of the rock musical *Hair* as the opening event in October 1967 was surprising to just about everyone. It was directed by Freedman but was unlike anything he and Lee had previously worked on. Both of them conceived of *Hair* as a "collage musical"—there was no real narrative, just a pastiche of scenes, which made it difficult for Lee to find a way into the design. "There was no script," recalls Lee.

> **So I asked Jerry, "How are you going to direct it? What do you do in the first rehearsal? "Well," he said, "we have songs, and then we'll improvise into it"—it was all terribly sixties—and I said, "I don't know how to improvise into a set. At least tell me a story." Eventually I got a script. When we got to the song "Hair," the page read, "hair hair hair hair hair hair," and the next page, "hair hair hair hair hair," and it went on for four pages. And I said, "I don't know what's going on." I asked, "Do we want to make it a protest design about the Vietnam War? Or are we talking about the flower children, the peace movement?" Jerry said it was not just antiwar. "It's a very upbeat musical."**

To provide perspective, Freedman and the writers, James Rado and Gerome Ragni, took Lee on a tour of nearby St. Mark's Place in the East Village, the "main street" of the New York hippie scene. They visited the Electric Circus and head shops and soaked in the atmosphere. "I pointed out the excitement, the color, the psychedelic influences, the posters," Freedman remembers. "Ming took this information not any differently from how we talked about Shakespeare, and made a coherent design out of the politics around St. Mark's Place. He understood that it needed an environment, not a specific locale, which again was no different than the things we were doing in the park. They weren't site-specific, they were about environment, which you have to do on a thrust stage."

12

13

14

15

16

Ultimately, Lee's solution was simple—the two onstage pillars provided a kind of built in frame for scaffolding which extended to the sides and upstage of the pillars. Now, however, the scaffold served not as a framework for emblematic scenic pieces, but for a collage of images reflecting contemporary culture. As part of his research Lee had taken images from a *Life* magazine article on hippies and began cutting them up into a collage, and this led to the idea of images mounted on and around the scaffold. This was the most complete use of collage that Lee had yet employed—but it also went back to his work with Boris Aronson, particularly on *Do Re Mi*. "Boris said the whole American look is really collage. Americans can never leave anything alone, it's all patchwork. Even if we patch a jacket, it's never with the same material." The orchestra was also placed on an upper level of the scaffolding.

Getting to opening night, however, was not easy. Ragni, Rado and choreographer Anna Sokolow got Freedman fired and Sokolow took over. Then the United Scenic Artists were about to strike against the scenic suppliers. As Lee recalls,

Pete Feller told me, "The minute they put up the picket line, all your scenery will be locked in my shop and you won't be able to open the show until the strike is over." So we hired a truck and smuggled all the scenery out of the scenic studio at midnight and took it to the Public Theater and loaded it into the south building's third floor, LuEsther Hall, that was still an empty place. We set up some sawhorses in order to paint it ourselves. The union was furious, saying I was sabotaging the strike. We said, "Well, we are nonunion. We have no contract with you. We're building our own scenery." They wanted to bring me up on charges. We finally agreed to hire a union charge person plus a union scenic artist.

Meanwhile, recalls Lee, Sokolow was downstairs doing modern dance. "We went to see a rehearsal and it was terrible. It was a rock musical with 1930s modern dance." Two days before the first preview, Lee and several others went to Papp to intervene. Papp fired Sokolow and rehired Freedman. The show began to take shape. "The first act was amazing! We had never seen anything like it. A collage musical, no story. At the final dress we had half the set; at the first preview, three quarters of the set was up. Then Jerry rehearsed the second act and finally the whole show pulled together and we got the set up. It was a terrific show, very moving."

Although it was a hit, the Anspacher was scheduled for Papp's new production of *Hamlet*, and not even Papp recognized *Hair*'s commercial potential. An investor named Michael Butler came on board as a co-producer and wanted to move it to Broadway, but the creative staff, gripped by a kind of 1960s idealism, was not interested in "selling out." It moved to a discotheque called Cheetah, but that was the completely wrong environment, and the show soon closed. With no one else interested, Butler moved it to Broadway—without any of the

17

15 ***Cities in Bezique***, Public Theater, 1969, sketch. This was a double bill of poetic, dreamlike one-acts by Adrienne Kennedy: *The Owl Answers* and *A Beast's Story*. The pipework this time encompassed the entire stage, supporting the plays' underlying cage metaphors.

16 ***Invitation to a Beheading***, Public Theater, 1969, sketch. Based on the novel by Vladimir Nabokov, the play was set in a prison with the audience watching through the bars. "A prison cell that manages to be romantic without being sentimental," wrote Clive Barnes, "A prison cell in which you die…and with some of the most stylish graffiti in New York" (*New York Times*, March 18, 1969). The backdrop was a photo collage of watching faces.

17 ***The Tale of Cymbeline***, New York Shakespeare Festival, 1971, sketch. The young director A.J. Antoon had done a highly successful production of *Subject to Fits* at the Public earlier that year, leading Papp to offer him a Delacorte slot. Antoon was happy with the scaffolding but wanted it to look like an office building, so Lee added black Plexiglas panels and made the stage floor shiny black. "It looked like nothing I'd ever done before," Lee marvels. The reflective panels, in turn, inspired the actor Sam Waterston, who played Cloten, to develop an ongoing comic routine about catching his own reflection.

18

18 ***Peer Gynt***, New York Shakespeare Festival, 1969, ½" model.

19 ***The Wars of the Roses***, New York Shakespeare Festival, 1970, ½" model.

20 ***Timon of Athens***, New York Shakespeare Festival, 1971, production photograph. The design process was plagued by miscommunication. Director Freedman feels the production was "my one real failure. I wanted some abstract environment, but whatever terms I was using to communicate, neither Ming nor Theoni [Aldredge, the costume designer] came up with something that was visually appropriate to my vision. Ming kept on wanting to give it some literal Athenian placement. So he hung pediments and fragments of Greek architecture around. That isn't what I meant at all." Lee's understanding was very different: "Jerry thought it should be Byzantine because that's a period that was ornamental. I had these Byzantine things on the catwalk and a Byzantine kind of floor."

Public's team. Tom O'Horgan was brought in as director and Robin Wagner, Lee's former assistant, designed the set. The show, of course, went on to become a huge commercial success.

The spatial configuration of the Anspacher, particularly the height in relation to the area of the stage, dictated, in Lee's mind, a vertical approach to design. Thrust stages were still a relatively new phenomenon, and because the stage occupied the same architectural space as the auditorium Lee felt it was crucial to create a vertical framework that would not only engage the visual field of the spectator from any location in the seating area but would also emphasize the implicit cubic volume of the stage space. Over the next few years Lee designed *Ergo* (1968), *Cities in Bezique* and *Invitation to a Beheading* (both 1969) in the Anspacher, utilizing some variation of scaffolding and a certain similarity began to emerge in the designs, not unlike what happened at the Delacorte.

FINAL SEASONS WITH THE SHAKESPEARE FESTIVAL

Following the experiments with scaffolding and collage that began with *Hair*, those techniques emerged as a dominant motif at the Delacorte with *Peer Gynt* (1969) and *Timon of Athens* (1971), reaching an apotheosis with *Two Gentlemen of Verona* (1971) and *Much Ado about Nothing* (1972). For some, it was already becoming cliché. Writing in the *New York Times* of July 9, 1972, Julius Novick pointed out "how very conventional most of Joseph Papp's Shakespeare productions have been...much of the time it has been a matter of finding an appropriate period for the costumes, getting Ming Cho Lee to design another of his scaffoldy settings, and very straightforwardly getting the thing on."

For Lee, *Peer Gynt* was a chance to revisit the play that gave him his first acting role at Occidental College. What had stuck with him from that time was Peer's famous act five "onion monologue." "I was able to grab onto the fact that Peer somehow doesn't have the core of a person. It's all layers and there was no positive philosophical commitment to anything. Therefore it's a life of running around in a circle. He never got anywhere." Lee began to envision Peer's life as a roller-coaster ride with its the ups and downs and circular movement. Aspects of the play also struck him as essentially like musical comedy. He wanted "the set to have something fun, a sense of a carnival." Meanwhile, Freedman had been in Hong Kong the previous year and had seen bamboo scaffolding and hoped to incorporate that, although he had no specific idea of how to do so. Lee devised a rickety, constructivist spiral of wooden posts, "tapered so it looked like bare trees." The structure was placed on a turntable so that it became a dynamic, ever-changing environment through which the actors could move—and it did resemble bamboo scaffolding.

Largely because of all the work at the Public Theater, Lee was beginning to cut down on his Festival commitment, and *Peer Gynt* was his only production that summer. (Already he had given 1967's *King John* to his assistant Douglas Schmidt.) The 1970 season, imperiled by severe financial problems, was given over entirely to a single, though ambitious, undertaking: the three *Henry VI* plays plus *Richard III*, under the umbrella title *The Wars of the Roses*—all done on a single set. Unlike the 1963 tetralogy by England's Royal Shakespeare Company, the Festival's text was largely uncut. The four plays were presented over three evenings.

19

20

Initially, Lee felt that director Stuart Vaughan had limited him scenographically. "All he wanted was a typical Shakespearean thrust stage—a machine that could propel the play. I did my typical Louise Nevelson boxes with heraldry, statues and so forth." But as they got into technical rehearsals Lee admitted that Vaughan was "a very clever and knowledgeable director," and he praised the clarity Vaughan brought to the text. The "neutral stage," allowed the audience to concentrate on the words, ideas and action in this complex play.

The result was a by-now-familiar symmetrical design with staircases, platforms, soaring wooden poles and horizontal beams, and a central façade with emblematic decor and openings above and below that could be plugged with scenery or left clear to expose the Belvedere Castle across the pond. Lee designed it all in polished dark wood, which achieved the desired neutrality while giving it a certain elegance. But beneath the medieval surface was the equally familiar scaffolding structure. Clive Barnes enthusiastically declared it a "set for all seasons" (*New York Times*, July 2, 1970). Ultimately Lee was captivated by the enormous sweep and scope of the production and felt that "to see this whole history just unfold in front of you" made it one of the most exciting events produced by the Shakespeare Festival—particularly the one all-night marathon. Papp presented the entire sequence on June 27, beginning at 7:30 at night and ending at 6:45 the next morning, when the cast of *Hair* came onstage to sing "Let the Sunshine In." This was three years before Robert Wilson staged an all-night marathon with *The Life and Times of Joseph Stalin*, and a decade prior to the Royal Shakespeare Company's eight-and-a-half-hour *The Life and Adventures of Nicholas Nickleby* that really began the fad of marathon productions. Not only was the event precedent-setting, it kept three thousand spectators in their seats outdoors throughout a damp and chilly night. For Lee, theatre couldn't get much better than that.

In 1971 the Delacorte underwent some renovations as part of Papp's attempt to create a more fluid interaction between the stage and auditorium. A few rows of seats were removed to move the stage closer to the audience, and vomitories—tunnels opening onto the stage from under the seats—were added. For the season, consisting of *Timon of Athens*, *Two Gentlemen of Verona* and *The Tale of Cymbeline*, Lee created an elaborate jungle gym of pipework scaffolding—"the pipe thing," as Lee called it—intended to serve each play with minor adjustments.

The major event of that summer was the middle production, *Two Gentlemen of Verona*, reconceived as a rock musical by downtown director Mel Shapiro, with music by *Hair* composer Galt MacDermot and the book adapted by playwright John Guare whose Off-Broadway hit, *The House of Blue Leaves*, had opened earlier that year. The inventive, celebratory and—significantly—multiracial adaptation, fondly dubbed *Two Gents*, was a huge success. Having learned his lesson from *Hair*, and sensing another hit, Papp moved it to Broadway.

Shapiro was not initially happy about the scaffolding, insisting that musicals were horizontal, not vertical. Lee painted the pipes orange and red—that alone was a striking change from the typical monochrome of the Delacorte—and added architectural elements such as window cornices and fire escape–like balconies that evoked both New York and Italy. To allow for the change from Verona to Milan, there were venetian blinds with images of Verona painted on one side, and Milan on the other. Since modern Milan is filled with billboards, Lee employed advertising graphics. The overall effect was

21

22

23

21 ***Two Gentlemen of Verona***, New York Shakespeare Festival, 1971, ½" model.

22 ***Two Gentlemen of Verona***, Broadway, 1971, ½" model.

23 ***Much Ado about Nothing***, New York Shakespeare Festival, 1972, ½" model. "I have not seen another *Much Ado* that really topped it," declares Lee.

24 ***Hamlet***, New York Shakespeare Festival, 1972, ½" model.

24

not unlike the collage for *Hair,* though less dense. There was a much greater sense of space breathing through the whole structure.

The move to Broadway was not smooth on any level. Weaknesses in the script and production that were easily overlooked in the festive atmosphere of summertime in the park became exacerbated on Broadway. There were some cast changes that did not work. The commercial pressures made everyone tense. Lee assumed that Shapiro would want a more horizontal set, but the director had actually grown to like the verticality, so Lee took the scaffolding to three levels to fill the entire proscenium opening of the St. James Theatre, although the forty foot width meant condensing the footprint from the Delacorte. Initially the orchestra was placed at the back against the bare brick wall of the theatre, but the acoustics were wrong; Broadway theatres are designed for an orchestra in the pit in front of the stage. So the orchestra was moved to the front and Lee expanded the apron with an orange-painted metallic runway that covered part of the pit so that actors could perform on top. With the orchestra no longer at the rear, Lee felt the bare brick wall was not appropriate, and painted it overnight with blue sky and white clouds. This was all done during previews.

"By then I must confess I was sick of Broadway," says Lee. "Nobody plays straight. Just too much politics and gambling; you're forever playing Russian roulette. The tension is huge. *Two Gents* became a hard-pushing Broadway show and I don't think it had the charm it had in the park." Nonetheless, the show won the Tony that year for best musical, although the sets weren't even nominated, and at 614 performances it would be Lee's longest run on Broadway. There was also a successful London production using a nearly identical set.

Lee did one final season in the park the next summer designing two shows, *Hamlet,* directed by Freedman, and *Much Ado about Nothing,* directed by A.J. Antoon. The *Hamlet* set looked a bit like a sleek version of *Peer Gynt* with curving crisscrossing staircases, a sea of vertical poles and two turntables, intended to suggest a maze of hallways with platforms on multiple levels. While this was not what Freedman originally had in mind—he had wanted something along the lines of a Richard Lippold sculpture with its geometrical complex of wires—it actually inspired him. The uppermost platform became the locale for the Claudius prayer scene. "I put him up high, close to Heaven," Freedman recalls, "There was Jimmy [James Earl] Jones isolated against the sky on this high platform. And it was along a path that Hamlet took to the closet scene. So he went up and down, stopped there, then continued on. It looked like a journey through a labyrinth."

The double revolving stage meant that the angles and perspective changed continuously throughout the nearly four-hour production, emphasizing the constantly shifting world of Elsinore. Clive Barnes credited Lee with the fluidity of the production: "Ming Cho Lee has designed...a glittering revolving set, which with its staircases and rostrums can literally keep the play on the move. And it is this sense of movement that is the production's sovereign virtue" (*New York Times,* June 30, 1972). Whether or not inspired by Lippold, the model, at least, looks like a piece of modernist sculpture. Lee once again dismisses the set as "very old-fashioned," though his self-criticism may have more to do with a feeling of having run out of ideas for designing at the Delacorte and the constant substitution of pragmatism for vision.

Much Ado about Nothing, like *Two Gents,* moved to Broadway in the fall, and it was a genuinely happy experience for Lee. Although it was fundamentally another scaffold-and-collage set—some of the structure and complex staircase pattern, in fact, came from *Hamlet*—it was really a celebratory decorative design. Antoon situated the action in 1912, in what Lee called America's "age of confidence," and the atmosphere was that of a summer evening in a small town. "No great social comment, nothing Brechtian," says Lee. "Just do it and the play itself will say all the things that are pretty horrendous." Scott Joplin's ragtime music provided the soundtrack; Dogberry and company were played as Keystone Kops; canoes floated into view on a turntable, as did a Model T Ford. Lee's first impulse was to have the scenery floating off the floor as he had done several times since *Electra,* but Antoon wanted billboards, so Lee designed a background collage of advertising images and photogravure blowups of Teddy Roosevelt and others, firmly planted on the ground. A thoroughly enchanted Clive Barnes, describing the essentially identical Broadway set at the Winter Garden Theatre, praised "Ming Cho Lee's vast, white and brilliant setting. This is a lovely wooden construction of complex terraces, platforms, catwalks and alcoves that remarkably gives the mood and style of early twentieth-century American architecture.... The total effect is startling and yet beguilingly attractive" (*New York Times,* November 13, 1972). Lee acknowledges that "I was breaking all the rules I had set up for the park. It was deliberately decorative and it was realistic, but because of the collage the look was not *real* realism. It was filled with wonderful touches, as if you were right in the midst of 1912, living with these people." As with *Cymbeline,* Antoon

25

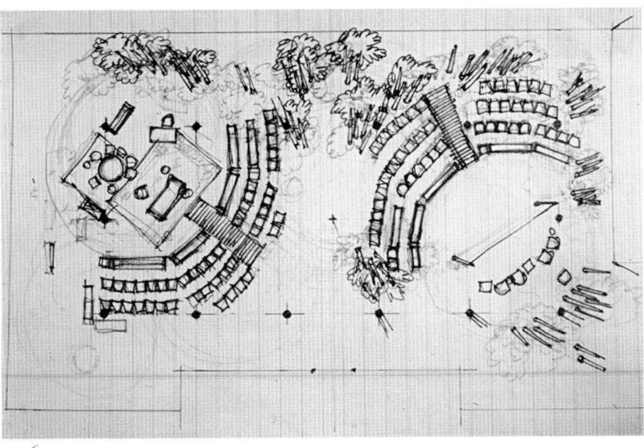

26

25 ***Wedding Band***, Public Theater, 1972, sketch. Lee created an uncharacteristically naturalistic set of wooden and brick apartments around a courtyard, with an apartment as a cutaway so that the interior was visible. Lee wanted the quality of magic realism he had seen in some of Santo Loquasto's sets. However, he says, "I didn't know how to do a real dirt floor. I think today I would have done a packed dirt floor or some grass mats or whatever so that it doesn't feel as if these very real houses are just sitting on a stage floor painted to look like dirt." The model is lost.

26 ***The Seagull***, Public Theater (Manhattan Project), 1974, sketch of ground plan showing seating for all four acts. "It was an attempt to make Martinson Hall more like a country estate than a room filled with theatre people." In actuality for the first half the seats were in the section on the left of the plan and were moved to the other part of the space during intermission which, remembers Lee, "became impossibly confusing, chaotic and cumbersome."

succeeded in getting Lee to think outside of his more usual patterns.

The show moved to Broadway with outstanding reviews and good box office. At the same time Papp had worked out a deal with CBS to produce thirteen Shakespeare and contemporary plays for television with *Much Ado* as the initial offering. Lee had no interest in designing for TV, so Tom H. John was hired as art director—essentially co-designer—and he transformed Lee's design into a realistic setting. As Lee rightly notes, "The charm of the whole thing on the stage is that everything is real, but it's not *realistic*; it is not a realistic small town. It is a collage and you add all the pieces together and it has the life of a summer evening in a small town." This charm evaporated on television. Ironically, once the play was broadcast, no one wanted to pay to see it on Broadway; ticket sales plummeted and the show closed one week later.

Lee's increasingly time-consuming career in opera, as well as Papp's demands and expectations at the Public Theater, took a toll on their relationship. Papp, Lee felt, had lost interest in the Delacorte and became more focused on new plays. This might have had some appeal for Lee if there had been some underlying philosophy to the choices, but in his view, "the new things, typical of Joe, had no preconceived goal or conception or aesthetics." At some point over the winter Papp informed him that he would not be the designer for the coming summer season. "I went home and I was a little bit hurt. But I was actually very relieved. Suddenly on summer nights I wouldn't be rushing dinner and riding a bike to the park, seeing a show and coming back late at night. My evenings would be free, and free of all the bugs! I hate bugs."

From 1962 to 1972 Lee had designed twenty-six productions in the park (counting the two parts of *Henry IV* and *The Wars of the Roses* each as a single production). Of the three productions he did not design, two were done by his former assistant, Douglas Schmidt. (Several other assistants who learned their craft in the park would go on to major careers, including Marjorie Bradley Kellogg, David Mitchell and Ralph Funicello.) Despite the pleasure of *Much Ado*, however, Lee had lost interest and fallen into a pattern. After *Hamlet* even Mielziner sent a note saying that he was repeating himself. Lee was so locked into his approach that could not conceive of anything that did not resemble a version of a so-called Shakespearean stage, and while he was rightly concerned with the issue of maintaining focus on the stage in the midst of Central Park, his primary solution was verticality.

27

28

27 ***Jack MacGowran in the Works of Samuel Beckett***, Public Theater, 1970, ¼" model. This one-man show had originally been done in England with a set by Sean Kenny, but the set never arrived for the New York production and Papp asked Lee to design it. It also needed to be easy to tour. Lee's set consisted of a drop and two cloth side pieces sewn to a ground cloth. It was painted in sand colors like edgeless desert. There was a rock to sit on and give focus to the space. "For awhile I thought it was my best design," Lee says. At some point during the tour, Kenny's set arrived, and both designers' sets were used interchangeably—with Kenny getting credit for both.

28 ***Older People***, Public Theater, 1972, ¼" model. John Ford Noonan's play consists of fifteen mostly comic scenes about aging. Lee thought the best imagery for waiting—a recurrent theme in the play—was captured by Edward Hopper, so he created a kind of installation piece of a Hopper landscape in the framework above the stage. "I'm proud of *Older People*," states Lee. "I was trying something new and I think the design is a little ahead of its time. Less emblematic and more imagistic."

Since that time, of course, dozens of directors and designers have made the Delacorte a showcase for virtually every genre and style of scenography imaginable. This was possible because Lee had spent ten years shattering American preconceptions about Shakespeare and design in general, paving the way for new approaches.

POSTSCRIPT

Lee designed the Newman Theater at the Public, which opened in 1970 (Martinson Hall, which he did not design, had opened in 1968). It was in the south part of the building, and as opposed to the intimate thrust stage of the Anspacher, this was a starkly frontal arrangement with an end stage and a long, relatively narrow auditorium. Once again, construction required removing some columns. The stage was raised only two feet which, in retrospect, created sightline problems from some locations in the house. Lee wanted continental seating (no central aisle), but New York City codes require forty-two-inch rows (as opposed to thirty-six) if there are more than seven seats between a spectator and an aisle. This creates more legroom to aid egress, but it also means that the rows farther back can begin to feel distant. Lee feels that the simultaneous increase of the rake of the auditorium and the space between rows created an acute sense of remoteness around the eleventh and twelfth rows. "It's very obvious to me," notes Lee, "but I haven't heard many complaints." He designed the second show to be produced in the Newman, *Jack MacGowran in the Works of Samuel Beckett* in 1970, and he went on to design two more shows for the Anspacher, John Ford Noonan's *Older People* and Alice Childress's *Wedding Band*, both in 1972.

Papp had been pressuring Lee to move his studio into the Public as Theoni Aldredge had already done. But Lee liked working at home, and he couldn't see how he could continue to do his opera work from downtown. If Lee needed any further convincing that this would not be the right environment, it came one night after a late rehearsal of *Older People*: "I discovered that there were quite a few mice. I'm deadly afraid of mice. So I said, 'That's it.' I just left and went home." The feeling of the Shakespeare Festival as a family was gone. "It became very much like any other commercial house; it grew so big, I felt I was working in a corporation. I was never very comfortable at the Public."

As it turned out, Lee did design one more show at the Public—what he refers to as his "secret return." In the midst of *Boris Godunov* at the Metropolitan Opera in the fall of 1974, director Andre Gregory contacted him about a production of Chekhov's *The Seagull* in Martinson Hall. At the time, Gregory had a well-established reputation for experimental work developed over long rehearsal periods. Gregory had worked closely with designer Eugene Lee, often creating environmental designs. Lee does not know why Gregory asked him to work on this project. He had never done Chekhov before, and he was a very different designer than his namesake. Papp had nothing to do with choosing him, and it is not clear that he was even aware that Lee was designing ("I kept going to the third floor, skipping the second floor, so that I didn't need to say hello to Joe"). But Lee loved talking with Gregory, a charismatic polymath. They discussed Chekhov and all aspects of the play and Gregory described a production that had been done at an estate in Rhode Island with the audience moving around the grounds and through the house—he wanted something analogous at the Public. At the time Martinson Hall was simply an open space painted black. Lee proposed renting a lot of trees and using them to divide the theatre into a tripartite area with moveable seats. The audience would move from one section to another over the course of the play. This scheme could work with an audience of about fifty, which would have suited Gregory in his Off-Off Broadway productions, but here he needed one hundred in order to make it financially viable. The attempt to accommodate this greater number destroyed the intimacy and fluidity of the production. Even so, the experience led Lee to truly appreciate Chekhov: "I'd always had trouble with Chekov. It just seemed so boring, and what was so funny about any of it? But when I was forced to do it, it suddenly became clear."

During this period Lee experienced the exhilarating dichotomy of straddling the two radically different worlds of downtown experimental theatre and institutional high art as he commuted almost daily by subway between the Public and the Met. It is a bit surprising how easily and thoroughly Lee threw himself into such a nontraditional design. Had he been able to, he would have transformed the entire space into a theatrical environment. It makes one wonder what the implications for Lee's design—and experimental theatre—would have been had he done more such work. But Gregory's endeavors moved in other directions and the opportunity to work with him never arose again.

CHAPTER 8

Regional Theatre

1

1 ***The Iceman Cometh***, Arena Stage, 1968, sketch.

IN THE EARLY TWENTIETH CENTURY the Little Theatre Movement spawned several professional theatres outside of New York City, such as Cleveland Play House, the Pasadena Playhouse, Goodman Theatre in Chicago and the Old Globe in San Diego. But the origins of the modern resident professional theatre movement really began in 1947 with Margo Jones's Theatre '47 in Dallas. Among the first theatres to emerge in the wake of Jones's enterprise was Arena Stage in Washington, D.C., co-founded by Zelda and Thomas Fichandler and Edward Magnum in 1950 (Zelda became sole artistic director in 1952), and to this day it remains one of the preeminent theatres in the country. Over the first postwar decades these organizations endeavored to forge identities distinct from the theatre industry of New York, and even in the mid-1960s it was not yet common for established New York designers to work in them. Lee's involvement with Arena Stage, beginning in 1967, was unusual.

ARENA STAGE

Lee first learned about Arena through his former assistant Karl Eigsti, who was designing there, and the theatre intrigued him. In 1966 Lee was in Washington for a cousin's wedding, and he contacted another former assistant, Robin Wagner, who was also designing extensively at Arena. Wagner gave him a tour of the theatre, and shortly thereafter Lee was hired to design *The Crucible*, directed by Milton Katselas. "Washington, D.C., was definitely not New York," Lee admits, "although they paid somewhat better than Joe Papp. I think I was very anxious to have an outlet other than New York Shakespeare Festival. I never really expected that Arena Stage would have gotten so much attention from the New York press, but it got a sufficient amount that it made working at Arena Stage not feel like slumming." Ironically, Wagner returned to New York where, in 1968, he would design the Broadway production of *Hair* that had slipped through Lee's fingers, launching a successful Broadway musical career, while Lee was taking a first step toward a theatre life outside the city. But in 1967 Lee never anticipated that Arena would become a second home where he would ultimately design a total of twenty-one productions through 1998.

Part of the appeal was the space itself. The theatre took its name from the stage configuration it used, a theatre-in-the-round, also known as an arena stage. (Jones's theatre in Dallas was also in-the-round, which was increasingly popular in the decades after World War II.) Despite the name, Arena's stage was not circular but rectangular, surrounded on four sides by steeply banked seating risers—Fichandler referred to it as a gladiator ring. Designing for the round imposes peculiar demands. It is not possible, for instance, to have standard walls because they block sightlines for some part of the audience; entrances are generally made through the vomitories, passageways to the stage from under the seats. The most important scenic element tends to be the floor. At the same time, the stage must be envisioned as a cube with the vertical space crucial for establishing the stage as a distinct locale within the auditorium. Lee was eager to take on such a challenge.

Lee seemed to have an instinctive feel for the space. "I have a real understanding of working in a theatre where the audience and performers are under one roof," he observes. "I always thought in terms of floor and scenic elements and icons. When you approached things at Arena Stage with the greatest of simplicity, the play being in the middle of the audience, and you were not distracted by pictures, it could be so potent, you can't imagine." His deceptively simple set for *The Crucible* was so effective that the *Washington Post* review began by praising the "platform of rough-hewn, unpainted planks, constructed in the figure of a square. Ming Cho Lee's set... is sharp-edged and angular, with high-rising frames lending a sense of confinement to the deadening oppression of the Puritan society being portrayed" (January 19, 1967). This was precisely what Lee was striving for, believing that the play happened in "a very structured world. There is the right behavior and the wrong behavior, but what's underneath is bursting through. I just designed the structure and let everything else happen within it." The stage floor, made of wide wooden planks, appeared to float, and at each corner were wooden posts rising to the grid. (Despite reviewer's description, the planks were actually painted dark, then sanded and whitewashed.) Textured wood planking would soon become a dominant motif in American theatre and, as with erosion cloth, it was largely Lee's innovation. Although the design was different, of course, than his original design for the Off-Broadway *Crucible* in 1958, Lee nonetheless feels that "it was very much like having my original vision for the play come true."

The following season Lee returned to design Paddy Chayefsky's *The Tenth Man* and the 1930s farce *Room Service* in rep, followed

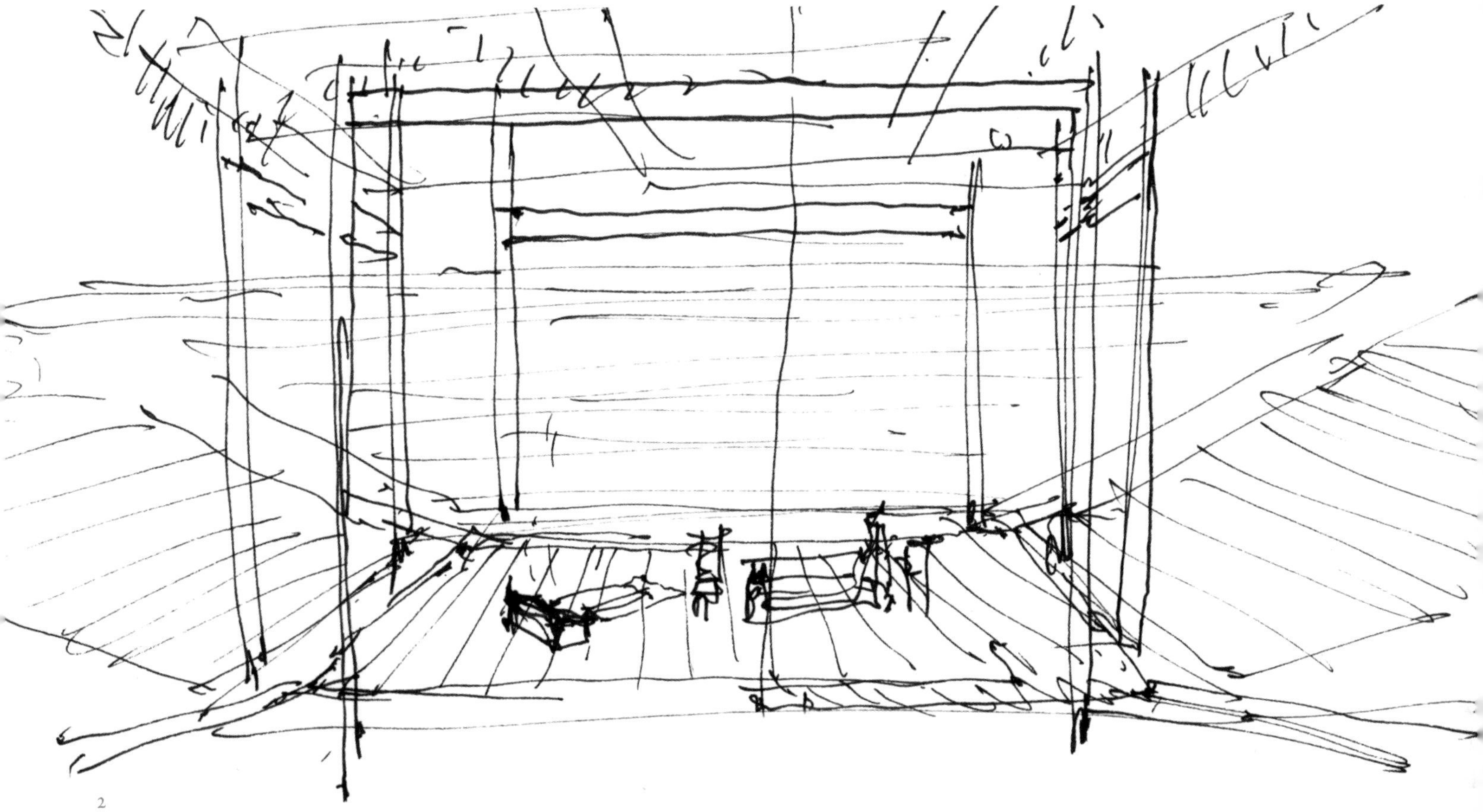

2

3

The Crucible

Arena Stage, 1967

2 Sketch made in 2010 showing three of the four banks of seating risers and the posts that established the volume of the stage.

3 Production photograph of Giles Corey sitting in John Proctor's house.

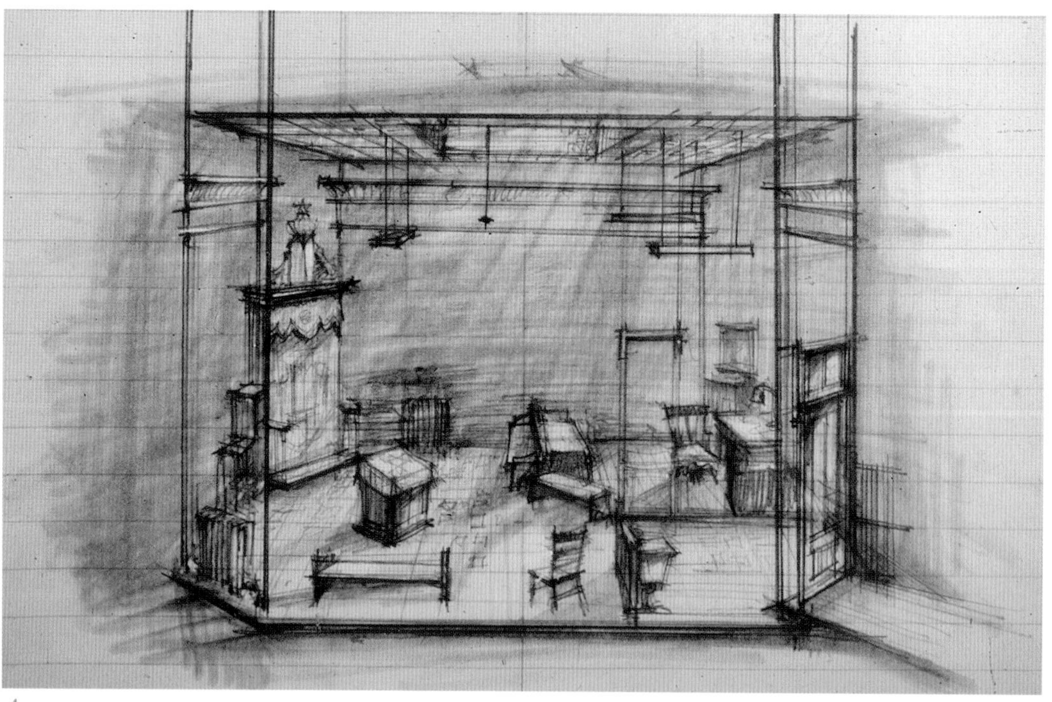

4

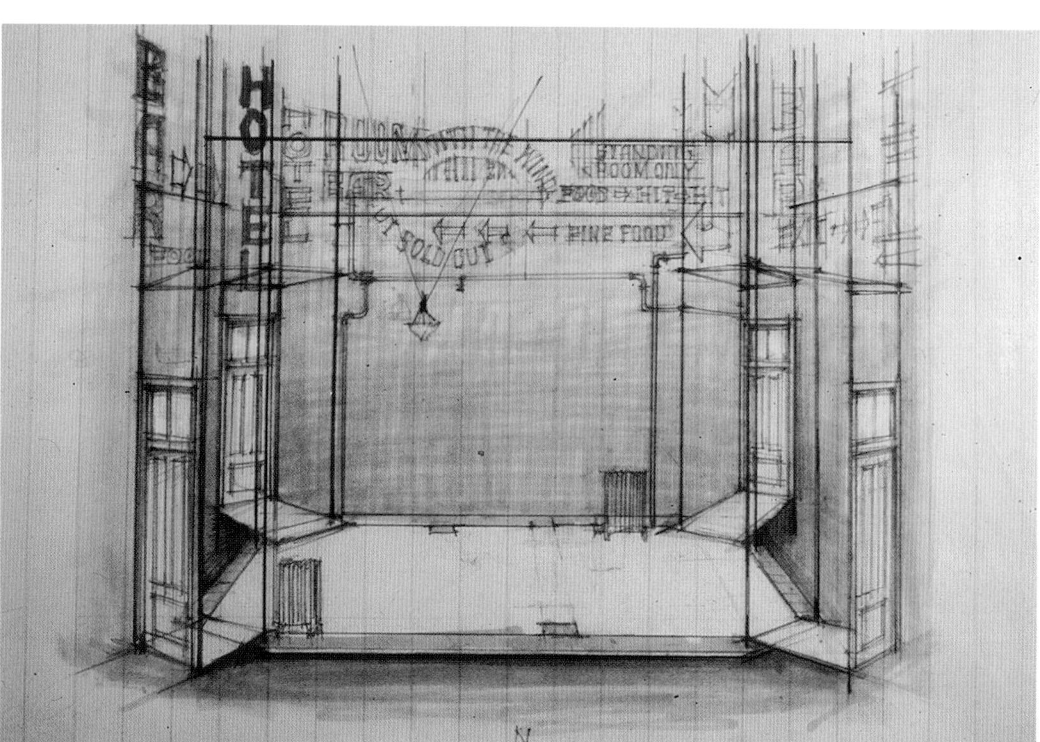

5

6

4 ***The Tenth Man***, Arena Stage, 1968, sketch. The ark is seen at the entrance to the up left vomitory, but this would have blocked sightlines. Lee tried pushing it farther back into the vom, but that made it seem detached from the rest of the set so that the performers appeared to be exiting when they went to the ark. The solution was to make the ark out of wire mesh so it would be transparent.

5, 6 ***Room Service***, Arena Stage, 1968, sketch and production photograph. The pipe structure framework is identical to *The Tenth Man*. Ten phosphorescent-painted signs hung above the audience and stage, reading "Hotel," "Standing Room Only," "Pepsi-Cola," "Cocktails," etc., intended to evoke Times Square.

by Eugene O'Neill's *The Iceman Cometh*. It was decided to have a single deck (stage) for all three shows. A great deal of time was spent determining the proper height for the deck, down to the quarter inch. Too low and the definition of place is lost; too high and the furniture blocks sightlines for the first rows of seats. One inch could make a great difference, Lee discovered. He also created a framework of pipes and floating cornices to serve all three plays. But unlike the pipework that created an industrial feel and functioned as a framework for emblematic scenic elements in his other designs of the time, these were a kind of fragmented realism. The pipes created the structure that gave the stage unity, but also could be seen as practical elements, such as steam pipes, within the context of the plays.

Each of the plays presented problems peculiar to staging in the round. *The Tenth Man* takes place in a small, rundown Orthodox synagogue—as part of his research Lee visited an old synagogue on the Lower East Side and another near Harlem—but requires a separate office for the rabbi. The office was indicated by a small, slightly raised platform, a fluorescent light and a door frame. *Washington Post* critic Richard Coe noted that the "use of a skylight and a bare lightbulb indicate how powerful the choice of precisely the right physical props can be to arena staging. There is, to be sure, much more to her [sic] setting, but these are at an eye-level of exceptional astuteness" (February 15, 1968).

Room Service, as a farce, was all about doors, but since walls or solid doors are not possible in the round it became difficult for characters to hide or make sudden entrances. The problem was never fully solved and Lee believes that "it was a stupid idea to do *Room Service* at Arena Stage, and it was not very funny." But critics were impressed by how completely the clutter of hotel furniture and the addition of neon signs above the spectators transformed the environment scenographically from *The Tenth Man*.

The Iceman Cometh retained the pipe structure, one radiator and a hanging shaded light over the stage. Lee placed the bar in one corner coming out of a vom and the stage was crowded with a chaotic array of bentwood chairs and small tables for the bar patrons. For all three plays, the pipe structure was essential in defining the stage, emphasizing the verticality or cubic structure of the space. One does not normally associate arena staging with verticality, but here Lee's penchant for that dimension allowed him to distinctly demarcate the stage space and create a strong dramatic structure.

MARK TAPER FORUM

Lee did no regional theatre in 1969. In the fall of 1970 he designed another show at Arena, *The Night Thoreau Spent in Jail*, and then his first production in Los Angeles, Mart Crowley's *Remote Asylum* at the Ahmanson Theatre. This led to the Mark Taper Forum a year later and to an ongoing collaboration with artistic director Gordon Davidson (they had first met when Davidson was a stage manager at Dallas Civic Opera and Lee came through with *Lucia di Lammermoor* in 1961).

The Mark Taper Forum, opened in 1967, is a circular building in the midst of the rectangular campus of the Music Center, which also houses the Ahmanson. The buildings were designed by architect Welton Becket, but the theatre itself was designed by Jo Mielziner, who had also designed the Vivian Beaumont Theater at Lincoln Center in New York. The stage is a thrust surrounded by a semicircular amphitheatre. Davidson says that as a director he has always been interested in the three-dimensionality of the thrust, in particular the intersection of stage and audience. "I never had to explain that to Ming," he remarks. "He thrived on it. He was very sensitive to how the set lived within the larger place. It was one entity."

Davidson proposed staging Ben Jonson's *Volpone* and Shakespeare's *Henry IV, Part 1* in sequence using the same set, since historically they would have been produced on the same stage. This idea was ultimately abandoned and Lee designed two distinct sets. *Volpone* was a purely frontal, two-level façade based on the "Shakespearean" setting employed so often at the Delacorte. The time and locale of the play had been transposed to San Francisco in the 1870s and that, says Lee, "worked right into what I love—West Coast Victorian buildings." To emphasize the themes of greed and corruption, he took etchings of figures associated with Tammany Hall in New York, blew them up, and placed them over the façade, a bit reminiscent of *Two Gentlemen of Verona*.

Henry IV, Part 1, directed by Davidson, was neither frontal nor symmetrical. The thrust was now made of the familiar wooden planks, and while essentially rectangular, it had extensions, a lower level in the front, angled stairs and—importantly—was set at an angle to the back wall. The towering set was fronted by massive wooden beams and a façade that combined emblematic elements and stonework—"an outer surround that represented the

7

8

7 ***Volpone***, Mark Taper Forum, 1972, photograph.

8 ***Henry IV, Part 1***, Mark Taper Forum, 1972, photograph.

world of the political struggle"—reminiscent of *Richard III* at the Delacorte. But perhaps most intriguing, in opposition to the stark frontality of *Volpone,* the centerline was set at a diagonal that created a subconscious disorientation for the audience. Lee believed that one of the things that distinguished *Henry IV, Part 1* from the other Shakespearean histories was the focus on private life in juxtaposition to public display. The asymmetry of the set allowed for alcoves and niches—private spaces within the architecture of power. "He was able to create a universe," Davidson declares. "On the one hand a version of the Shakespearean stage, the wooden O. But also the multiplicity of place without the movement of scenery. A sense of height and grandeur, and a sense of immediacy."

TAKING ARENA TO THE U.S.S.R.

At the end of 1972 Lee returned to Arena Stage to design *Our Town.* When director Alan Schneider first approached him, Lee was reluctant. The play was traditionally done on an empty stage, which would not work well in the round. "If you expose the back wall of a proscenium theatre, there is an aura of the backstage: the brick wall, the radiator pipes, the fly lines, the grid," Lee explains. "But the empty Arena Stage without anything was a very uncomfortable space. There was a crummy floor and a catwalk above. Nothing. It's not a place." Furthermore, Lee thought of the play as sentimental and filled with "naïve theatrics." He was also disturbed that it ignored the people "on the other side of the tracks." But Schneider convinced him that the people on "this side of the tracks" were also worthy of consideration. Schneider also pointed out, Lee recalls, that the play was set in a time when "the things you used were still being handmade, weren't mass produced. There was a love for the things you used and touched and lived with." This, not surprisingly, appealed to Lee's aesthetics. He reread the play and while he still found the first act problematic, "I absolutely fell in love with the soda fountain scene. I couldn't keep myself from crying for the wedding, and the last act absolutely wiped me out. What a fantastic play. Sentimentality be damned! It was so moving."

Lee covered the stage floor with highly polished, stained planking and designed carefully crafted furniture. Tree branches with leaves hung above the stage, replaced in the third act cemetery scene by bare branches. He designed an elaborate marble and chrome soda fountain for his favorite scene.

In the fall of 1973, under the auspices of the State Department, Arena Stage became the first American theatre company invited to the Soviet Union, to present *Our Town* and *Inherit the Wind* in Moscow and Leningrad. The latter, directed by Fichandler, was produced specifically for the tour. *Our Town* needed to be adapted for a proscenium stage, and Lee created a hanging collage of objects from Grover's Corners for the background. For *Inherit the Wind,* he traveled with Betsy to Dayton, Tennessee, the actual location of the Scopes trial that was the basis for the play. In Peter Larkin's original Broadway design in 1955, the buildings were all clapboard, so Lee was surprised to discover that in reality the old buildings were all brick. He created a façade of two- and three-story buildings on three sides of the stage that suggested the town square in Dayton (called Hillsboro in the play), but that could also transform into the courtroom with

LEE ON EAST VS. WEST

I discovered that West Coast and East Coast actors were very different. The pace in the West is more relaxed. I felt the same thing when I went to the Rose Bowl to see a football game when I was at Oxy. The Big Ten, which are all Midwestern schools, came from very cold weather and of course the West Coast players didn't have cold weather. When the game began, the Big Ten would usually score immediately. They overran the Californians who were still getting ready. It was three quarters before USC began to get themselves together. Very often the West Coast would win, but at the beginning you'd say, "My god!" I felt the same way when I sat in the rehearsal at the Taper—the way people talked and the atmosphere. Gordon's pace was not as intense as Jerry's [Freedman], and certainly never as intense as Joe Papp.

9

people watching from balconies. Though filled with architectural and historically accurate detail, the scenic units did not touch the stage floor, which had the effect of isolating, thus theatricalizing, the naturalistic detail.

It is interesting that when Lee was confronted with plays grounded in a particular reality he needed to start from historical or site-specific research, as he had done with *Slapstick Tragedy*. One might ask, for a play that claims to be fictionalized, does it matter—from the point of accuracy—if the buildings are brick or clapboard? But for Lee, the materials and textures are inextricably bound up with the narrative, and this is derived from his Brechtian thinking. "I always thought very seriously about the difference between how you create a set that has reality and is yet abstract, and how you avoid creating set that is an illustration of a place, so that you are able to zero in on the essence or the core environment of the play." He believes that Larkin's clapboard buildings made the play too folksy, almost like musical comedy, whereas brick gave it a certain urbanity and seriousness. But he might never have thought to make it brick if he had not seen the original town.

The productions were well received in the Soviet Union, though not without some glitches, particularly for the design and technical crew. It turned out that the theatres did not have ladders! The general practice for hanging lights was to lower the battens, aim the lights, tighten the clamps, and raise them back up. If something needed to be refocused the pipe batten would be lowered again. Trying to explain how the scenery was to be flown was complicated by the lack of a translator with knowledge of theatre terms—for instance, no understanding of what "flying" meant in regard to scenery. Load-in and tech rehearsals took at least twice as long as they should have. After returning from the Soviet Union, both shows reopened in Washington, but with a twist. *Our Town* now moved into the Kreeger Theatre, Arena's end-stage space that had opened the year before, while *Inherit the Wind* played in the round, requiring that set to be adapted from its proscenium configuration.

In 1975 Lee did two more productions for Arena Stage: *Julius Caesar,* directed by Carl Weber, who had been Brecht's last dramaturg, and *The Ascent of Mt. Fuji,* a Kazakh play that had been discovered by Fichandler and Schneider during the Soviet trip. *Caesar* held a special place in Lee's heart because, as the play his English tutor in Hong Kong had him read, it had been his first encounter with Shakespeare. "It was [in Hong Kong] that I began to understand that Shakespeare isn't about heroes and so forth, or like Hollywood movies. You would think that Julius Caesar would be the leading man, instead it's Brutus and Cassius and Antony. You'd think that he would favor Antony's side, but no. And Brutus is not effective. All those aspects that are very humanistic and complex." With several Arena productions under his belt Lee wanted to try something new in terms of space and texture. Instead of utilizing the central square of the stage, he created a more linear space by having the set extend in a long diagonal from one vom to another. "There are a lot of scenes in the public square," he notes. "But I also had a sense that they were always on the road from one forum to another, from public place to private place. They were always on the street." This ground plan was intended to emphasize that sense of movement.

On one side there were steep steps going up above the vom so that the characters had to descend into the forum. The path then crossed the stage and descended into another vom. During the intermission the steps and the path were removed (this was more cumbersome than Lee anticipated) revealing what appeared to be a mound of earth—an uneven surface with actual dirt spread over it—that was the setting for the battle at Philippi. Thus Lee succeeded in creating two distinct spatial dynamics with the space: the linear diagonal path of descent for part one, described in the *Washington Post* as "all marble, several levels and one headlong staircase of twenty steps" (February 27, 1975), and the mud-pit-like environment for the second half of the play.

The plot of *The Ascent of Mt. Fuji* is simple: A group of acquaintances make a trip to a mountaintop to picnic and stay overnight during which time their conversations reveal details of their pasts. Thematically it deals with individual moral responsibility and conscience, and was thus seen as a critique of individual responses to Stalinism. Scenographically, *Mt. Fuji* picked up where *Julius Caesar* left off. Lee created a craggy mountaintop covered with grass, flowers and a few windswept trees—a surprising turn to superrealism from someone known as a Brechtian, minimalist and emblematic artist. At the turn of the twentieth century, directors such as David Belasco created "realistic" surfaces for outdoor scenes, but this was one of the first examples of a sculpted stage floor in modern American theatre. Other designers would pick up on this superrealistic approach, notably Michael Yeargan in his set for a 1984 production of *Tobacco Road,* and Lee would go on to perfect the style a few years later with *Traveler in the Dark* at the Taper [see chapter 12].

9 ***Our Town***, Arena Stage, 1972, production photograph. Lee designed carefully crafted library ladders for the scene between Emily and George in act 1.

10, 11 ***Inherit the Wind***, Arena Stage, 1973, sketch for production in the round (right) and ¼" model for end-stage configuration in the Soviet Union production.

12, 13 ***Julius Caesar***, Arena Stage, 1975, sketch for first part, the Forum (left) and ¼" model for second part, Philippi.

10

11

12

13

14

CIRCLE IN THE SQUARE

In the context of arena staging it is worth considering two productions Lee did with Circle in the Square in 1975: Eugene O'Neill's *All God's Chillun Got Wings* and Tennessee Williams's *The Glass Menagerie*. Circle in the Square, established in 1951, was one of the first Off-Broadway theatres. Begun in a converted nightclub in Sheridan Square in Greenwich Village, it used a stage generally described as three-quarter round—an arena-like stage, but with the audience on three sides rather than four. When the company moved to a new space on Bleecker Street in 1960 it retained the distinctive configuration, as it did when it opened its Broadway home on West Fiftieth Street in 1972. Although the uptown theatre has the capability of converting to a full-round theatre, it most often worked alley-like, with most of the audience on either side of the long narrow stage.

All God's Chillun, which investigates issues of interracial tensions and miscegenation, is dramaturgically awkward, spanning some seventeen years through seven scenes divided into two acts. The first act occurs on a street where a white and black neighborhood converge, while all the scenes of the second act are indoors. Lee took advantage of the alley configuration to create a street as the setting for act one. This was Lee again as theatrical realist. The street had a cobblestone texture and even storm drains and manholes, stoops and trashcans lined the street, and fire escapes hung above the heads of the audience. The façade of a tenement covered the upstage end of the stage. For act two, the street surface was removed and a carpet laid down, a chandelier dropped in, and a radiator and steam pipe added, along with furniture. The tenement façade could still be seen through the transparent upstage wall of the apartment. The stage was essentially an arena, but the upstage wall anchored the design in a specific reality, as well as providing for entrances and exits through an illusionistic locale.

The same configuration worked to create a railroad apartment for *The Glass Menagerie*. "I did essentially a Mielziner set on a thrust without having the pictorial thing. And I didn't need to have all the scrim." The living room was on the raised thrust, with the dining room and kitchen upstage. There was an area around the thrust that functioned as the street for Tom's narrative speeches. As with the previous play, the details were very realistic—not only the fire escapes above, but real linoleum on the floor, faux brick walls upstage, detailed door frames. But the realism seemed at odds with the play's atmosphere of dream and memory; the ethereal quality of Mielziner's scrims for the original Broadway production was lost. There were other issues: Lee had designed a gently raked platform which would have counterbalanced the realism a bit. But Maureen Stapleton, who played Amanda, stipulated in her contract that she would not perform on a raked stage. Lee even had her come to the shop to try out the rake, but ultimately her agent said no. So the floor was flat and an extra step was added to reach the dining room upstage. It seemed like a minor adjustment but "it changed the whole look of the set," says Lee. "There just wasn't a flow." When Nikos Psacharopoulos, artistic director of Williamstown Theatre Festival, saw the production he told Lee he was missing the sensibility, even the sound, of tinkling glass, a criticism Lee would take to heart for his next production of the play [see chapter 14]. For now, his attempt to mix realism and symbolism within the rather odd configuration of the Circle in the Square was an important experiment, but not wholly successful.

14 ***The Ascent of Mt. Fuji***, Arena Stage, 1975, ½" model. The set was carved from Styrofoam. As the actors determined where they needed to sit, those areas were smoothed out while trying to maintain a natural look. The cyclorama behind the mound was in the style of Chinese landscape painting. The mound sat a bit like an island on the stage. From the orchestra level the effect could be very realistic, but from the balcony the audience could see over the top and see the bare stage between the mound and the cyc.

15, 16 ***All God's Chillun Got Wings***, Circle in the Square, 1975, ½" sketches for acts 1 (below) and 2 (right).

15

16

17

18

17 ***Hamlet***, Arena Stage, 1978, production photograph.

18, 19 ***Don Juan***, Arena Stage, 1979, production photograph (left) and detail of the lower stage.

19

LIVIU CIULEI

Lee designed only two productions at Arena with Romanian director Liviu Ciulei: *Hamlet* in 1978 and Molière's *Don Juan* in 1979—but they fundamentally changed his way of working and had a profound effect on much of his subsequent work. It also resulted in two remarkable sets.

Ciulei was well established as a theatre and film director in Romania and elsewhere in Europe—he won the best director award at the 1965 Cannes Film Festival and was artistic director of the Bulandra Theatre in Bucharest—when he made his American debut at Arena in 1974 with Georg Büchner's *Leonce and Lena*. A strongly visual director, he often designed his own productions, which caused Lee some apprehension, but they developed a very easy rapport. Looking back on this experience more than thirty years later Lee still gets visibly excited. "*Hamlet* changed my whole way of talking about the play almost instantly. Now I can't *wait* to talk about what period you are going to put it in. What are they wearing? I'm suddenly more interested in the clothes and more interested in getting a portrait of the people than about the material of the set, thinking about whether it is wood, is it metal."

Ciulei initially suggested using mirrors in some way—"to hold as 'twere the mirror up to nature," as Hamlet tells the Players—but Lee feared he would "just do fourth-rate Svoboda" (the renowned Czech designer's use of mirrored surfaces at the time was as ubiquitous as Lee's scaffolding had been a decade earlier). As for period, Ciulei suggested late nineteenth-century Germany under Bismarck, partly inspired by a series of photographs of European royalty he remembered from his childhood, as well as family photos of his own grandparents. (Ciulei believed that photographs capture something about the lives of their subjects, whereas a painting really tells you more about the artist.) There was discussion of the sort of music that might be used to create mood. "By doing it at the turn of the century, it's liberating," Lee declares. "You can use any kind of music. You can use Tchaikovsky without a problem!" This sort of engagement with a director was what Lee had been craving—someone who wanted to examine the world of the play.

Lee had been intrigued by a production Santo Loquasto had designed for Arena in which he had taken out a section of the stage floor to reveal the basement below. Lee proposed taking out the whole floor, then raising the playing space higher, allowing the audience to see beneath the stage. (Fichandler places Lee's Arena productions in three categories: mountain plays, platform plays and pit plays. This was an example of the latter.) Lee designed a floor of dark polished wood, inspired by a church he had seen in England, and beneath it was visible the brick vaulting and foundations, "so that underneath is rotten but on top it is very, very clean and polished." The raised stage was framed by low benches but was otherwise barren—save for the occasional piece of furniture such as a tangerine-colored desk for Polonius, a gold chaise for Gertrude and a dinner table where Ophelia went mad—so that actors were isolated in a kind of theatrical void. Entrances and exits were made through the labyrinth of this ominous, vaulted underworld—the ghost, Hamlet on his way to confront the praying King. Polonius was murdered there and Laertes burst from below to avenge Ophelia. Almost accidentally, Lee had discovered a way to indulge his penchant for verticality in reverse. Instead of poles ascending above the stage, there was seemingly unfathomable depth beneath the stage; the audience was witnessing only what transpired at the pinnacle of this subterranean structure. This was a *Hamlet* revealed through architecture. And while there were no mirrors, the pit was lined with Plexiglas that created a reflective surface providing the audience with views of the underside of the stage and parts of the walls not otherwise visible to them, as well as extended and sometimes distorted glimpses of characters coming and going.

Molière's *Don Juan* (in Richard Nelson's translation) was done a year later. Once again, the stage was removed and the playing area raised up. But this time, instead of the stark, brutish, rectangular decor, there was a light, open, airy circular space. Ciulei chose to set the play in La Belle Époque. The supporting ribs—resembling an angular spider web or perhaps a mandala—of the circular raised stage were visible through a Plexiglas floor and sat atop a fully appointed art nouveau glass gazebo or solarium, partially sunken below the floor level of the theatre. This below-stage room was remarkable for its intricate detail—architectural supporting columns, glass French doors, faux tile floor, period furniture and a great deal of foliage. In terms of architectural space it was the most realistically detailed of anything Lee had done to that time, and it was also the most curvilinear set Lee had ever designed, with hardly a straight line to be found. This stunning setting, however, did not fit every scene of the play. The lower level worked spectacularly well as part of the palace, or as the entryway to Don Juan's home, even the Commander's tomb, but, as Lee asked Ciulei, what about the beach of act two? Ciulei, who

20

20 ***Twelfth Night***, American Shakespeare Theatre, 1978, ½" model.

was going through a divorce at the time and was a bit distracted, had not fully thought through the show and did not have an immediate answer. The beach was solved by a mound of sand—a structure resembling a sand dune coated with sand that was brought out for the scene and placed on the upper stage—and somehow the seeming absurdity of sand atop the glass floor worked and went unremarked by critics. The notion of observing the action as if in a kind of fishbowl, as one scholar astutely described it, could have worked well, but the critical response suggested that Ciulei's conception—or perhaps lack of a coherent one—did not serve the play well.

Only a few months after *Hamlet*, Lee designed a production of *Twelfth Night* for Gerald Freedman, who had recently been appointed artistic director of the American Shakespeare Theatre in Connecticut—and the experience served to demonstrate the difference between the two directors. Freedman came in with a predetermined idea of a play-within-a-play—"I conceived of it as a grand house," says Freedman, "and the people within it were doing an entertainment. They were getting into costume and creating a Shakespeare play, *Twelfth Night*"—that allowed little room for the sort of give-and-take Lee had just had with Ciulei. He designed what everyone agreed was a striking set, a rather stark, symmetrical interior of a two-story Georgian mansion which could be transformed as necessary by sliding units, but it was not a rewarding experience.

The following year, right after *Don Juan*, Lee designed *The Tempest* for Freedman, which had been their first collaboration at the Delacorte. Without knowing it at the time, this production would also be their last. It demonstrates how far apart they had drifted in their ability to communicate. "Jerry still went on his own way, while I had kind of secretly changed, and he never really knew it," says Lee. Freedman, as he often did, came in with art as inspiration, in this case the work of a sculptor who created kite-like forms. He admits, however, that he was unable to convey to Lee what he wanted from these sculptures. "I wanted a very minimal set. A disc that was the island and these overhanging [fabrics] that would suggest sky, wind, the elements, Ariel's elements. Ming didn't glom onto the images I was using and did something else that was fun and used contemporary materials—plastic material that people could slide on. So it was fun but it wasn't our best." From Lee's perspective, it was a question of talking about images rather than substance. "He showed me some abstract sculptures that had a sail-looking thing. That didn't tell me a thing. Was I supposed to just copy that sculpture? Jerry is so knowledgeable about art and abstraction and we talked a great deal about the visuals, but we never really talked about the play."

They had done twenty-three productions together, including the landmark *Electra*. Lee refers to Freedman as his mentor and credits him with teaching him to understand Shakespeare. In a commencement address at the University of North Carolina School of the Arts when Freedman was dean, Lee declared, "Without Jerry, I think I would still be in the woods." But it was time to move on.

ASTOR COURT AT THE METROPOLITAN MUSEUM OF ART

In the early 1970s, as the Metropolitan Museum of Art was expanding its Far East Asia collections, Mrs. Vincent Astor, a trustee of the museum who had grown up in China, proposed building a Chinese garden court that would adjoin a room displaying Ming Dynasty furniture from the museum's collection. The architect I.M. Pei was approached to design it, but he told the Met that they would be better off working with a set designer and proposed Lee. Lee's initial plan was an amalgam of several kinds of Chinese garden plans and resulted in what the project director Wen Fong, a Chinese-born Princeton art historian, described as a theme park.

In 1977 Fong visited the ancient town of Suzhou, near Shanghai, renowned for its canals and gardens, together with professor Chen Congzhou of Tongji University, and decided that the Garden of the Master of the Fishing Nets, an eighteenth-century scholar's garden, would be the ideal model, in part because its small size, especially its use of the half-pavilion, allowed it to fit within the available space at the Met with little compromise, and because the half-pavilion also created a sense of intimacy. Fong provided Lee with photos and a sketch made by Chen and asked if he would still be interested, given that it would be more of a reproduction than an original design. But this rare opportunity to work on something authentically Chinese was enormously appealing and besides, as Lee noted, "I didn't have sufficient knowledge of garden architecture to invent anything better." Moreover, he looked forward to producing something that had a sense of permanence. He then built a 1⁄48 scale model for preliminary approval, followed by a 1⁄24 scale model which was photographed at I.M. Pei's studio so that architectural cameras could take photos from inside the model.

In June 1978 Lee accompanied Fong to China, bringing the photos of the model. It was his first trip back since leaving in 1949, marred only by the fact that he could not take Betsy. The visit began in Beijing, where Lee had never been, and then to Suzhou to study the garden architecture firsthand. The final plan was not a simple copy; it incorporated details from several gardens, and of course had to fit within the given space at the Met (including masking the air-conditioning units). And because the furniture at the Met was court furniture, it would not have fit aesthetically in a purely scholar's garden, so there were compromises. The materials were all made in Suzhou, built to plans drafted by Lee. A full-scale model of Lee's design was built in Suzhou with cheaper materials to test it out and then all the parts of the actual garden were prefabricated there including tiles made in a restored eighteenth-century kiln and nan wood for the fifty pillars. Chinese workers came to New York to build it.

Lee found that designing the garden was not all that different from set design. He discovered, however, that he was more comfortable with the architectural elements than with the rocks and plants and was happy that Fong—a scholarly authority—assumed responsibility for the landscaping, giving the space a sense of authenticity. Lee and Fong, however, never got along well, so the process was not always a happy one—Lee did not even get to see the Astor Court until construction was nearly complete in 1981—but, he says, it gave him "a kind of satisfaction I had never experienced before. First, it's a very beautiful garden. It has a quiet dignity and a sense of repose, and most importantly, the garden will last as long as the Met. That is different from theatre."

21

21 The Astor Court at the Metropolitan Museum of Art.

CHAPTER 9

The Curse of Broadway

1 ***Angel***, Broadway, 1978, sketch.

1

THROUGH THE MIDDLE OF THE TWENTIETH CENTURY, American theatre and Broadway were essentially synonymous. The Little Theatre Movement began in the teens and twenties and by the thirties there was enough production beyond Broadway's boundaries that critic Burns Mantle would coin the term "Off Broadway." Nonetheless, success in the theatre meant one thing: Broadway. When Lee began his professional career, Broadway scenic design was dominated by a small group of people: his mentors Jo Mielziner and Boris Aronson, Oliver Smith, Donald Oenslager, Howard Bay, William and Jean Eckart and a few others. By the 1960s, however, shifting economics and demographics led to a precipitous decline in the number of Broadway productions, while the number of designers was increasing as a consequence of university training programs. In the surprisingly compartmentalized world of theatre, Lee's opera work and even his New York Shakespeare Festival work was largely unseen by Broadway producers. His earliest Broadway ventures had been critical failures, even as his sets got good reviews, so it was hard to gain a foothold in the commercial world. He had been fired from his first musical, and the show that might have changed the trajectory of his career, *Hair*, was a lost opportunity. Nonetheless, he did a respectable twenty-two productions on Broadway between 1962 and 1986, including seven musicals. But with the exception of *Two Gents*, which was a Shakespeare Festival transfer, the musicals were all flops—and some were unmitigated disasters of epic proportions (three closed after a single performance).

In 1966, when director Gerald Freedman conceived the musical *A Time for Singing*, based on Richard Llewellyn's 1939 novel *How Green Was My Valley*, he naturally turned to his Shakespeare Festival collaborators Lee and costume designer Theoni Aldredge. (Instead of Martin Aronstein, however, Jean Rosenthal designed the lights.) The novel, which had been made into a successful movie in 1941, is set in a Welsh mining town in the late nineteenth century and concerns the formation of a miner's union and its impact on one family. Freedman co-wrote the book and lyrics with John Morris and also directed.

It was a complex, multi-scene show in which Freedman attempted a cinematic continuity that required an effortless transition between scenes. This posed a challenge for Lee whose experience to this point had been mostly with unit sets at the Delacorte, Peabody and Juilliard. In one twenty-minute musical sequence, for example, the location went from the Welsh countryside, to the interior of a coal mine, to the interior of the Morgan family house. When faced with challenging problems, Lee says, he "thinks with a pencil." Using photographs Freedman had brought back from a trip to Wales, Lee produced a large number of sketches, many of which depicted floating white houses—never used in this show, though the motif would recur in a few subsequent designs—and a mineshaft tower, all suffused in shades of green ("*Brigadoon* with a mineshaft," jokes Lee). Ultimately he devised a set of overlapping stretched scrim units of varying shapes representing the hills and valley in the distance—an almost Cezanne-like landscape—with fragmentary but realistic interiors filled with carefully selected detail and exteriors of stone architecture. Some scenes also included Lee's increasingly common floating branches that seemed to descend from a tree hovering outside the confines of the stage. The branches served as a framing device that could be either romantic or stark, enhanced the sculptural quality by adding layers of depth, and connected the visible set to a larger world beyond. Mechanically, the sets were a combination of units on a turntable and wagons and flying pieces.

The critics were not kind to the show, pronouncing it a lesser version of both the novel and the film, and dismissing the music as derivative. Lee's sets were largely ignored, which was rare, especially given how lovely and atmospheric they were. But it was not an embarrassing failure and managed to run for forty-one performances.

Lee's next Broadway venture, one year later, was *Little Murders*, an absurdist black comedy written by the *Village Voice* cartoonist Jules Feiffer. Set in an Upper West Side New York apartment surrounded by random violence and constant assaults on the dignity of daily life, it was a rather prescient, if exaggerated, view of where the city would be headed in the 1970s. The balance of the comic and grotesque, however, never quite worked for Broadway audiences or critics, who were nonplussed or put off. The show lasted only a week (though it did have a successful Off-Broadway run two years later with a different creative team). Lee used his former West End Avenue apartment for inspiration. The interior was a superb rendition of a pre-war apartment, done in fairly straightforward Broadway realism, with faux plaster walls and crown moldings, detailed trim, practical windows and the like. A few years later Lee told an interviewer that he did not enjoy designing for this kind of show: "I can't imagine the boredom one has to go through designing *Red Hot Lovers*. You've got to have the icebox in a certain place and the bourbon has to be

2

3

2 ***Little Murders***, Broadway, 1967, ½" model. It appears as if the surrounding buildings loom over the apartment, but this is somewhat misleading as much of the surround was above sightlines for the majority of the audience. Lee wanted the height to eliminate the need for black borders for masking.

3, 4 ***A Time for Singing***, Broadway, 1966, sketches for Angharad's bedroom and the Morgan home.

4

5

6

Here's Where I Belong

Broadway, 1968

5, 6 Sketches of Trask house (top) and barn. An example of Mielziner-like romantic realism.

7 Sketch of a willow tree.

7

bourbon, otherwise the play falls apart. Set designing is reduced to problem-solving, and that is boring."[1] Box sets at this time still tended to have ceilings, but Lee was trying to resist total realism and floated the ceiling over the set so that the backdrop could be seen between it and the top of the walls. Given the reality of the rest of the apartment, though, the floating ceiling didn't quite make sense. The background was somewhat reminiscent of the apartments seen behind the Loman house in Mielziner's *Death of a Salesman*, which Lee acknowledges: "I think Mielziner's design is always in the mind of any designer dealing with New York." But Mielziner's buildings were on scrim, giving it a hazy, dreamlike effect. Lee's backdrop consisted of photo blowups that created a hard-edged reality that the play demanded.

Despite the lack of a hit, Lee was now designing a Broadway show every year, and in spring 1968 there was another musical, *Here's Where I Belong*, based on John Steinbeck's *East of Eden*, set in the farmland of California's Salinas Valley. It reunited Lee with director Michael Kahn. The show was plagued with problems from the beginning and Kahn believes that everyone involved, himself included, "were all way too young." This was the first Broadway project for co-writer Terrence McNally, who had established an Off-Off Broadway reputation, but he had his name removed from the credits after the producers inserted material without consulting him. James Coco, a Caucasian actor, played the Chinese houseboy, provoking Chinese actors to picket the theatre. "I didn't know whether to respect the picket line or sneak in to deal with my set," says Lee "It was a mess." (He sneaked in.) Lee had the sense that Coco was studying him to learn how to play the part.

Lee was familiar with Salinas, which is evident in the Victorian-style houses he designed. There is a loving quality to the sketches that are bathed in a soft romantic light and perhaps a touch of nostalgia. Once again there were floating branches protruding from the proscenium. Lee had grown more sophisticated with the use of stage wagons to effect scene changes and there were wagons coming in from stage left and right and upstage. In a scenic coup de théâtre two scenic units rolled in at diagonals from upstage and met at the center to form the brothel with Kate standing on the porch in front. The transition seemed magical and inevitably got applause. Lee, who had always been adamant that sets should not be applauded, was nonetheless seduced. "The hell with this idea of no applause for sets!" he says, only a bit facetiously. For another scene, a tree-trunk unit glided onstage as "tons of willow branches" flew in from above, also eliciting applause. Forty-five years later the willow tree was still Kahn's most vivid memory of the show. The design's romantic pictorialism—soft earth tones, watercolor washes in the sketches, the sensual curves of the tree branches—was unlike almost anything else Lee was doing at the time. It seemed closer to Mielziner than his work had been for years. Had the show itself been a success, this might have been the start of a musical theatre career for Lee, but it was not to be. The reviews were scathing—singling out only Lee's design for praise. Clive Barnes's *New York Times* review famously began, "The most distinguished aspect of *Here's Where I Belong*...is the scenery by Ming Cho Lee. But no one ever walked out of a theatre humming the scenery" (March 4, 1968). Barnes did not coin that phrase—it seems to have been an old joke in the theatre business—but it is the first time that it appeared in a *Times* review, thus elevating it to classic status. The show closed on opening night.

A year later Lee designed *Billy*, a folk-rock musical based on Herman Melville's *Billy Budd*. The novella's plot is secondary to its allegorical themes and haunting atmosphere, but the writers and composers—none of whom had ever done a Broadway musical—pretty much jettisoned everything but the superficial aspects of the narrative and turned it into an almost campy show about sailors on a ship. Not surprisingly, *Billy*, too, closed in one night, though the sets received a Tony nomination. The basic set—the "success of the occasion," per Brendan Gill of the *New Yorker*—depicted "the deck, fo'c'sle and captain's quarters of an eighteenth-century man-of-war, with a great mast and its accompanying cat's cradle of ratlines leaping heavenward, and, during a battle scene, authentic-looking cannon firing away at an invisible enemy" (March 29, 1969). Lee had researched ships at Mystic Seaport in Connecticut.

With hydraulics, the below-deck section of the ship could rise from beneath the stage floor; the crow's nest could fly out. *Daily News* critic John Chapman wrote that the complex show "worked like a Swiss watch" (March 24, 1969)—but getting to that point was a technical nightmare. The work should have gone to Pete Feller, whose shop was the most experienced in the city at building with steel and using hydraulics, but the producer instead hired Richard Wright, who wanted to break into the theatre business, though his prior experience was building swimming pools. A blizzard delayed the delivery of the hydraulic units, so the load-in was incomplete,

8

9

10

11

8 ***Billy***, Broadway, 1969, sketch. Because the shop went bankrupt, most of the sketches and plans were lost. Clive Barnes concluded his review with the suggestion that the sets be donated to the New York City Opera so they could finally premiere Benjamin Britten's opera *Billy Budd*. "I think it is a duty these producers owe to the memory of Melville" (March 24, 1969).

9–11 ***La Strada***, Broadway, 1969, ½" models of, from top, the village square, farmhouse yard and Alberti Circus grounds.

12 ***Lolita, My Love***, 1971, ½" sketch of Lolita's mother's house in Vermont. "The wallpaper is really a Jo Mielziner version of Boris Aronson," says Lee. "The house had pieces of fabric with windows. And the tree branches were all on panels that were just disjointed enough. All the doors were painted in great detail and then arbitrarily cut up. It's all very broken up."

leaving a huge hole in the stage floor. As the crew raised the crow's nest into the fly space, something went wrong; it hit the grid, snapped all the lines and crashed through the opening in the stage floor into the basement. As Lee remembers, "It was hugely depressing to be there. A big hole in the middle of the stage, steel lying all over. Thank god nobody got killed!" This meant a one-week delay—the first of several. While waiting for the hydraulics to arrive Wright and his foreman took on another show, *The Dozens*, designed by Rouben Ter-Arutunian, which became more complicated than anticipated and ultimately drove Wright into bankruptcy. "Meanwhile we had a hole in the ground!" exclaims Lee with amazement.

When the hydraulics finally arrived, Lee remembers, Feller came by the theatre.

> **He whispered to me, "They got the wrong hydraulic. It's not powerful enough." The crew installed it and pushed the button and it went "zzzzz, stop, zzzzz, stop." I said to Wright's foreman, "You've got to call the hydraulic firm." He said, "It's nine o'clock at night, we can't get him." "Well you better get him," I said. Then by midnight he still hadn't called. I got so angry. I went and picked up a fire axe and said, "I am going to axe you." They held me back. Of course, I probably wouldn't have done it.**

The technician arrived at eight the next morning and confirmed that it was the wrong machine, leading to yet another delay. Meanwhile, Wright sold his studio to Feller, who came in, replaced all the hydraulics and got a welder from the Metropolitan Opera to finish the metal work. When previews finally began, Lee's set garnered

12

applause when the curtain went up, and more applause during a scene shift in which two scenic units tracked downstage as the hydraulic lift came up with the sailors.

La Strada, at the end of 1969, was yet another disaster of a musical, based on the 1954 Fellini film, with music and lyrics by Lionel Bart and book by Charles K. Peck Jr. Lyricist Martin Charnin was brought in at the last minute to try to salvage the show. The music and lyrics took the brunt of the criticism, though Lee himself questioned the suitability of director Alan Schneider and choreographer Alvin Ailey for musical theatre. The musical, like the film, tells the story of a street performer who purchases an innocent young girl from her mother to be his assistant, and together they travel throughout Italy. Lee was able to bring to his designs something that he had not been able to bring to all the prior Italian settings of Shakespeare's plays—direct research. He and Betsy had been planning a six-to-eight-week round-the-world vacation, but ultimately his schedule only allowed for less than three weeks. They traveled to London, Paris, Hamburg—where he was doing *Giulio Cesare* with the Staatsoper—Italy and finally Hong Kong and Los Angeles. Around the world in twenty days. The longest stretch was devoted to Italy, with a little over a week in Venice, Florence and Rome, sketching constantly. "While I didn't totally change my view of Italy, I actually began to have a real sense of the texture, the walls, the shapes, what the cafés looked like," says Lee. "Just the life in Italy."

At the core of the design was a turntable and all the scenes were mounted on it, like an island in the midst of the stage that was otherwise masked with burlap panels and applique clouds. "What happened on the turntable was very, very real; real travel through Italy," he said. Barnes (who had become Lee's biggest fan) praised the design: "atmospheric, dusty, brilliantly conveying the sense of Fellini's Italy, and theatrically adroit in the way various components turn inside out on one another, always maintaining a sense of movement in the show" (December 15, 1969). In many ways this was Lee's most successful Brechtian design. The detailed naturalism of the set pieces, particularly the *Mother Courage*–like wagon, isolated on the stage against a textured, evocative, but obviously scenic background looked strikingly like some of Teo Otto's Berliner Ensemble designs. The perceptive critic of *Women's Wear Daily*, Martin Gottfried, praised Lee as "one of the few people involved with the show to seriously try to solve its problems"—but felt that even Lee could not overcome "the big, high stage of a Broadway theatre [which] is probably the world's worst place for an outdoor setting" (December 15, 1969). Once again, the show closed on opening night.

Although Lee had no Broadway shows in 1970, he maintained his streak with the Off-Broadway *Gandhi*, which closed on opening night, though once again Barnes praised the "splendid all-purpose... skeletal staircases and monkeywalks" (October 21, 1970). This was followed a year later by a musical adaptation, of Vladimir Nabokov's novel *Lolita*, entitled *Lolita, My Love*. It is hard to imagine why anyone thought this would be a good idea. Nabokov had always resisted a stage adaptation because he understood that an actual adolescent, live onstage, being seduced by an older man would be disturbing in a way that it is not on the page, or even in Stanley Kubrick's film, where the medium

13

14

15

13 ***Romeo and Juliet***, Circle in the Square, 1977, ½" model. "I got stuck, architecturally," says Lee, "and didn't know how to finish the balcony. I should have just taken the thing up to the grid, but I decided to have a little roof. That was a big mistake. If I didn't have the roof, if I had the balcony cantilever out, it would have been a very beautiful set."

14 ***for colored girls who have considered suicide/ when the rainbow is enuf***, Broadway, 1976, production photograph. Jennifer Tipton won a Drama Desk Award for her lighting.

15, 16 ***The Shadow Box***, 1977, ½" models for the Long Wharf Theatre, left, and Broadway productions.

17 ***Angel***, Broadway, 1978, ½" model. The house was mounted on a turntable.

16

17

provides a crucial distance. But with Alan Jay Lerner, the lyricist of *My Fair Lady* and *Camelot*, writing the book and lyrics, he consented. The music was by film composer John Barry. The choice of director was surprising—Tito Capobianco with whom Lee had previously done nine operas. (In fact, they were working on a *Lucia di Lammermoor* for the Hamburg State Opera in Germany at the time, though both ended up resigning from that production to work on *Lolita*—a rather unprofessional move.)

Moments of cultural misunderstanding hampered the design process. At the end of the play, Lolita is living in a trailer park and Lee designed a suitably trashy American trailer that baffled Capobianco. "In Argentina," he said, "a trailer park is very luxurious." Lee, too, misread the script and thought that Humbert Humbert's den was in New York, and designed a very modern apartment with the latest hi-fi equipment. Lerner said it was supposed to be an Arizona hacienda—Lee adjusted accordingly. Capobianco initially wanted to use projections. "He had no idea how that fit in," says Lee, "he just wanted to be the most up-to-date musical director of the time." Eventually an approach evolved that was a kind of abstraction with fragmentary scenic pieces fitting together into a sort of collage. There were scrim panels with photo blowups.

After the out-of-town tryout in Philadelphia, Capobianco was fired, the girl playing Lolita was replaced and a significantly reworked version opened in Boston under the direction of Noel Willman. It closed there, never reaching New York.

Such a string of spectacular failures could have put an end to Lee's Broadway career despite, or perhaps especially because of, the good notices his sets received. His reputation was rescued at the end of the year, however, with *Two Gents*—as close to a hit musical as Lee would ever have—and a year later with *Much Ado about Nothing*, both Shakespeare Festival productions that had already demonstrated their popular and critical appeal. After *Much Ado* it would be three years before Lee returned to Broadway.

In the early summer of 1976 Joe Papp called out of the blue and asked Lee to come down to the Public to see Ntozake Shange's *for colored girls who have considered suicide/when the rainbow is enuf*, a collection of dramatic poems telling stories of African American women through the voices of seven female performers. As staged at the Public by Oz Scott, there was a very simple setting designed by Shange's sister, Ifa Iyaun, of a white flower cut out of plywood. Papp wanted to move the show to Broadway and knew that it needed something more sophisticated. He must have realized that Lee was the right designer to create the necessary grandeur to support the poetry while retaining a simplicity that would not overwhelm the delicacy of the text. Lee recognized that the fundamental impulse behind the existing design was right—a single emblematic image—but for Broadway the show would need a more encompassing environment. The image remained a flower, but now it would be a large blood-red rose. Moreover, it would be a three-dimensional soft sculpture, rather than a flat painted backdrop.

In the process of making the model Lee discovered that he had no idea how to make the flower, but Betsy came to the rescue, making a ¼" scale flower out of strips of organza sprayed black. She joked that she could do it because it was "women's work"—but having begun her own career working in a costume shop, she had a better understanding of fabric. The actual set piece was created from buckram on a wire frame and strips of scrim hanging in front of a black, pleated soft curtain. Otherwise the stage was bare, with the floor suggesting large tiles. The play was an enormous success, though Lee's design went largely unmentioned in reviews—appropriate since the aim was to provide a framework and texture for the powerful and emotional language.

The following year, 1977, was one of the stranger ones of Lee's career. He did only four productions, but three were on Broadway, the most he had ever done in a single year. (The fourth show was a remounting of *for colored girls* at the Mark Taper Forum in Los Angeles.) Ironically, unlike the musicals in which his designs were usually praised regardless of the fate of the show, none of his work fared particularly well with critics this time, even with the one hit, *The Shadow Box*. (In my discussions with Ming, when we came to 1977 his first response was, "Oh, oh, oh, oh...1977. A bad year.")

First up was a production of George Bernard Shaw's *Caesar and Cleopatra* starring Rex Harrison and Elizabeth Ashley. Noel Willman, the director who had replaced Capobianco on *Lolita, My Love*, was to direct and asked Lee to design. Despite misgivings—Lee could see the combination of personalities was a recipe for disaster—he agreed, in part because he had fond memories of seeing Laurence Olivier and Vivien Leigh in the play during one of his early visits to New York. Willman, who had successfully directed *A Man for All Seasons* and *The Lion in Winter* on Broadway, saw this as another historical drama with visual possibilities for period details and splendor. But while the play has the trappings of historical spectacle, it is really an intimate drama of two people grappling with intertwined aspects of politics and romance. Lee tried to strike a balance between the personal and spectacular by creating a more skeletal than realistic design that would not seem too ponderous.

Problems developed from the start. For act one, Lee placed the Sphinx facing downstage, as one might expect, but Harrison objected because he would have to face upstage for his opening speech ("Hail, Sphinx: salutation from Julius Caesar!"). He insisted that the Sphinx face sideways, and Willman acquiesced. In that moment, Lee contends, the director lost control of the production. Thereafter, Harrison pretty much dictated all decisions. Willman was fired during the show's first performances at the Kennedy Center in Washington, D.C. (a fact he learned when asked about it by a reporter) and was replaced by Ellis Rabb, an actor and director with a solid background in the classics. But stepping into the production at this late date he, too, decided the focus should be on the star. Lee's set, as well as the production in general, were no match for the cavernous Kennedy Center theatre and fared little better at Broadway's Palace Theatre. As Brendan Gill remarked in his *New Yorker* review, "the theatre itself is so much grander than anything the set designer, Ming Cho Lee, could provide us with onstage; his Sphinx in the moonlit Egyptian desert, his lighthouse at Alexandria, and his royal quarters of the Queen were markedly less gorgeous than the auditorium they looked out upon" (March 14, 1977). Ultimately the show needed simplicity, but as a star vehicle, no one had really given the play itself much thought. It closed in a week and Lee, who normally keeps everything, has not so much as a pencil sketch.

At the same time, Ted Mann asked Lee to design *Romeo and Juliet* for Circle in the Square, where he had recently done *All God's Chillun Got Wings* and *The Glass Menagerie*. Mann wanted a straightforward Renaissance style, but Lee felt that "it kept us from really examining the play. Who are these kids? What is the Capulet family? What's really going on?" In fact, Mann cut the text fairly heavily to place most of the emphasis on the two lovers to the exclusion of everything else. Lee designed a background of arches and walls covered with frescoes inspired by Giotto. He was quite proud of the frescoes, which he created by drawing and painting the images, erasing them with sandpaper, then dry brushing over it with white gesso. He then arbitrarily cut the panels into smaller sections. The effect was remarkably realistic. But whereas Lee successfully incorporated the alley-like stage into the design for *All God's Chillun* and *Menagerie*, in this case the set was largely a background to action that was rather isolated on the long narrow strip of a stage. It was not a disastrous problem, but spatially the production lacked a sense of unity that might have strengthened it.

The Shadow Box, by Michael Cristofer, would go on to win the 1977 Pulitzer Prize as well as Tony and Drama Desk best-play awards. The action is located in an idyllic hospice in northern California where three families in three separate cottages cope with the impending death of a loved one. The dramaturgical structure posed specific design challenges—at times one family is the sole focus, while at other times the three stories intertwine—so that the set must create three discrete locales while retaining an overall unity. Gordon Davidson directed the original production at the Taper with a set by Robert Zentis, but wanted something different for the Long Wharf Theatre production in New Haven, Connecticut, and grabbed the opportunity to work with Lee again. Lee created a surround of redwood trees and a variety of platforms and posts with the feel of warm wood. The platforms were mostly placed on the Long Wharf's thrust stage, allowing the audience to look down at them, and while they were interconnected, the distinctions were fairly clear. When the production moved to the

CLIVE BARNES AND MING CHO LEE

British critic Clive Barnes was hired by the *New York Times* as dance critic in 1965, and in 1967 he also became the theatre critic. During his tenure he became Lee's most ardent supporter, heaping praise upon his sets and only rarely criticizing them. Reviewing the Arena Stage production of *The Iceman Cometh* he wrote, "For about the eighth time this season, I wondered why it was that whenever I admired a setting most and looked for the designer's name, that designer was Ming Cho Lee" (April 1, 1968). He was not, however, fond of Lee's mentor Jo Mielziner and in a review of the Mielziner-designed *Look to the Lilies* in 1970 Barnes suggested, "The style of the production and its staging would moreover have gained quite a lot from the delicately suggestive kind of verismo a designer such as Ming Cho Lee might have provided" (March 30, 1970). Lee was stunned upon reading the review, while Betsy received a call at home from Mielziner asking, "How did Ming like his review?"[2] A month later a letter from "Mr. and Mrs. Ming Cho Lee" appeared in the Drama Mailbag section of the *Times* stating that the review "has caused us deep concern." It went on to say,

> **The world of New York theatre designers is a remarkably cooperative one for all its reputation as being cut-throat and competitive. We see each other's work, criticize it, exchange thoughts and concepts, and learn and grow from being an artistic community. It is vitally necessary to all of us that there be as many different styles of design, as many different points of view, as there are working members of the profession. Only from this can we have a living, growing theatre. In this context we feel that one passage of the review...appears to pit designer against designer, and therefore is deeply embarrassing and not constructive, either for the designers, or for the theatre community** (April 26, 1970).

Morosco Theatre on Broadway, however, it had to be adapted for a proscenium. The cottages were arrayed horizontally across the stage, which worked against the cohesiveness of the locales. At the same time, the distinction between the cottages may not have been as clear: "We had a kind of gap between each cottage that only Gordon and I knew was there," says Lee. The grandeur of the redwood forest may have been too imposing, overwhelming the quotidian details of life and death. Lee recalls that when he removed the platform pieces from the model to send to the shop, leaving just the furniture, it suddenly looked better. "All I needed was the forest and the furniture." This was one of the rare instances in which the show was better received than Lee's set. Even Barnes, his usual champion, was disappointed: "Ming Cho Lee—a Houdini of a designer who can usually work with both arms and one leg tied behind his back—has come up with a dull multipurpose setting" (*New York Times*, April 1, 1977).

Lee returned to musical theatre in May 1978 with *Angel*, an adaptation of Thomas Wolfe's novel *Look Homeward, Angel*. Ketti Frings, who had earned a Pulitzer Prize in 1958 for his dramatic adaptation, now co-wrote the book for the musical version. It did not fare as well. *New York Times* critic Richard Eder was savage in his attack on the composer-lyricist team of Gary Geld and Peter Udell, concluding, "It is putting things too strongly to call *Angel* a disaster. It is a desert" (May 11, 1978). The set was a skeletal framework of a three-story house, another example of Lee's great love for American Victorianism. The sketch, in particular, lovingly captures the details of Wolfe's Asheville, North Carolina, house (Lee traveled to Wolfe's home for research), although the intersecting stair structure, the upper floor and even the thrust of wooden planks seem to contain the basic building blocks of the Delacorte and City Opera designs. It is a "Shakespearean" theatre with Victorian decor. The ghostly, evocative sketch [see page 155] also suggests a Mielziner-like haze of memory. This was not accidental. Lee was working in Mielziner's studio in 1957 when Mielziner was designing the play. Together with Mielziner's assistant John Harvey, Lee had built a ½" scale model of the house. "We made a white model with a lot of acetate and then used an eraser to create a scrim effect. When we finished, we turned the lights on and here is this floating Mielziner set. We thought it was heaven." But as much as Lee loved the model, he was a bit disappointed in Mielziner's actual design. "The scale seemed just a little bit small for the people. It became like a little dollhouse. So I always wanted to do a *Look Homeward, Angel* that actually was better than Jo's. And here was the musical that allowed me to do that."

Plans to produce *Angel* at the uptown Circle in the Square and then a different Broadway theatre fell through for financial reasons and the show wound up premiering at the Northstage Theatre Restaurant in Glen Cove. Not surprisingly, a musical based on Thomas Wolfe at a Long Island dinner theatre was a fiasco. Eventually there was a

Broadway production at the Minskoff Theatre in May 1978—where it closed after five performances.

Probably the only reason that Lee was offered one more musical was because it was directed by Freedman. *The Grand Tour,* now remembered only by musical theatre aficionados, was not a failure on the scale of the previous musicals. It had an estimable creative team with music and lyrics by Jerry Herman, book by Michael Stewart and Mark Bramble, and Joel Grey in the lead, and it ran for sixty-one performances. It was adapted from S.N. Behrman's 1944 play *Jacobowsky and the Colonel,* which in turn was adapted from Franz Werfel's play of the same name. It concerned a Polish-Jewish intellectual and a Polish aristocratic colonel who meet in Paris and team up to escape the approaching Nazis. Prior to being hired for *The Grand Tour,* Lee had been scheduled to design *Manon Lescaut* for the Met. He and Betsy had used that as an excuse to go to France for research, but discovered that much of the period architecture they hoped to see had been destroyed in the war. That research, however, turned out to be perfect for a story about evading the Nazis in France. (As *The Grand Tour* increasingly took up Lee's time and energy, he put *Manon Lescaut* on the back burner, and director Piero Faggione fired him. The Met, in turn, fired Faggione.)

The Grand Tour has fourteen scenes, and Lee employed a treadmill, appropriate given the "on the road" nature of the story. In one scene a barge on a river moved across the stage in one direction while trees moved behind in in the opposite direction. But the device was marred by inconsistencies. The *New York Times* review complained that "a scene on a railroad train…is quite ruined by carelessness. Lighting moves across the backdrop of the middle railroad carriage to convey this sense of motion; at the same time, the two carriages on either side are set against a plain unlit backdrop…obviously stationary" (January 12, 1979). The show premiered in San Francisco, but at the final run-through Stewart changed the brothel where Jacobowsky and the Colonel were hiding into a convent, so all the nude figures painted on the walls had to be transformed into angels.

The succession of Broadway musical failures during this thirteen-year period is staggering. Every successful designer, director or writer has the occasional bomb, but few could match this record. For whatever reason, Lee was hired for shows that seemed doomed to failure from the start. Yet Lee poured everything he had into each show, even when it was at a dinner theatre. A very real, if prosaic, effect of these failures, aside from the blow to the ego, was financial. Designers usually receive royalties from long-running shows. Musicals are expensive to design—the costs of assistants, maintaining a studio and materials can be prodigious, and the time commitment is great. Union-determined fees are barely sufficient to cover costs, and designers often lose money on shows that do not have an extended run. It is partly for this reason that designers such as Lee take on so many projects simultaneously, and it often contributes to the decision to teach.

But it may also be true that Lee simply was not the best person to design certain kinds of musical theatre. When pressed, Lee acknowledges this. "I think I'm afraid of it," he says, "because I worked on so many multi-scene musicals as an assistant to Jo and *Do Re Mi* for Boris. I pride myself as a technician who has enough knowledge to handle a musical in terms of scene changes, in terms of decking, in terms of turntables, wagons, working out scene change storage. I'm proud of that, but I'm not very good at it." Referring to Boris Aronson's contention that one could be an artist or a technician but not both, Lee says, "I guess I was trying to prove Boris wrong, that you're either Bob Randolph or you're Boris Aronson and there is no in between. I felt that I could do all aspects of a musical by myself."

Lee's problems could also be attributed to his approach. Anyone who has ever seen Lee in a critique knows that he will challenge students whose concepts ignore the necessities of the script, and yet to some extent that is what Lee was guilty of. "I always wanted to do a musical that has a look, like *Side Show*—a structural, real artsy look." In musicals, unlike much opera or Shakespeare, the transitions are often as important, even more so, than what happens during the scenes. Lee's Brechtianism sometimes missed crucial elements such as rhythm and movement. But there were moments in *Here's Where I Belong* and *Billy* that demonstrated Lee's ability to create show-stopping spectacle. A musical with a good book and score might have altered the course of his career.

It should be noted that condensing all these shows into one chapter takes them out of the context of Lee's overall career. While suffering through these debacles, he was simultaneously transforming the world of opera, producing outstanding dance design, continuing to do Shakespeare, putting his stamp on the American regional theatre movement, and commencing his career as the most influential teacher of stage design in history.

Master Teacher

1 Lee in his office at the Yale School of Drama, sometime in the 1980s.

THE MOST PROFOUND INFLUENCE that Lee has had on American theatre—and perhaps world theatre—may have come through his teaching. Since he began teaching at New York University's School of the Arts (now Tisch School of the Arts) in 1967, and at the Yale School of Drama in 1969, Lee has taught more than four hundred set design students—not to mention student costume and lighting designers, stage managers, playwrights and directors, as well as those who have taken his master classes and workshops around the world or participated in the renowned Clambake. No teacher of stage design has ever had the reach and impact of Ming Cho Lee. He is a committed, passionate and natural teacher.

Costume designer Susan Hilferty—a former Lee student and chair of the department of design for stage and film at Tisch since 1998—explains that as a teacher, "Ming brings an unstoppable passion for the work. He feeds off it. It's like nourishment for him."

"He was Dumbledore!" exclaims set designer Adrianne Lobel. "Of course, Dumbledore didn't exist yet, but when I look back at it, I feel like Harry Potter did. First of all, Yale is this fantastic Gothic set and Ming was like the great headmaster. He was the magician you wanted to please more than anything else."

1

The impetus to teach emerged in Lee's early years assisting Jo Mielziner. "I was so impressed that Jo Mielziner would see someone like me," he says. "Anyone could give Jo a ring and he would take the time to see their work. I thought I owed it to Jo to do the same." By the time he was offered the position at NYU, Lee's studio was probably the busiest in New York and had become a training ground for young designers, many of whom Lee helped prepare for the Union exam. His assistants learned everything from how to draw and build models to how to conceptualize space (and perhaps how to drink scotch and argue about politics). There were few other studios in New York that offered such possibilities. Lee had become a teacher—but largely at his own expense. "In the back of my mind I was thinking, I wish someone would pay me to do this," Lee recalls. "I'm going bankrupt." (During the summers the New York Shakespeare Festival paid for the assistants.)

Lee's first teaching job came in 1965, in the most unlikely setting—the Spence School, a rather posh all-girls school on the Upper East Side of Manhattan. One of his neighbors taught there and said they were looking for someone to teach stagecraft. Lee taught the class for a year ("the girls liked me because I treated them like adults") and oversaw a student design of a production of *The Cradle Song*. He was so worried that the young designer would not be up to the task that he created his own design as a backup, but it proved unnecessary. In 1967, while working on the Broadway production of *Little Murders*, lighting designer Jules Fisher asked if he would be interested in teaching in the graduate design program at the recently founded NYU School of the Arts, and Lee eagerly accepted. He was called in for an interview by the associate dean, J. Michael Miller, who remembers being rather surprised that Betsy accompanied him. Fred Voelpel and Wolfgang Roth were the primary set design teachers there and Robert Rabinowitz chaired the design program and taught painting. The first project Lee assigned was Richard Strauss's *Elektra*, a project he still often assigns to his first-year Yale students. At first the teaching was exciting and the students were stimulating, but after the first year, the promised eight or nine students per class grew to more than twenty, including undergraduates (the school wanted to generate more tuition revenue). Classes became unwieldy and difficult to teach, and Lee found that many of the younger students knew very little of the dramatic canon, making it hard to assign projects. The structure of the classes was not presentation and critique, but monitoring the work as it was being done, which Lee found to be a waste of time. He became increasingly frustrated and, as this also coincided with some of the busiest years of his career, he began to miss classes as he was called away to meet with directors or to rehearsals. In addition, he began to teach one class a week at Yale in the fall of 1969, stretching him even thinner. To top it off, he got caught in the midst of internal power struggles within the School of the Arts as well as squabbles within design department, and at the end of the 1970–71 academic year he was fired.

2 Donald Oenslager on his first return visit to Yale, c. 1972. Lee standing at left.

IN THE SPRING OF 1969 Lee had been invited up to New Haven to talk to the design students at the Yale School of Drama. By this time dean Robert Brustein knew that Donald Oenslager, who had taught at Yale for some forty years, was going to take a leave of absence the following year and he polled the students about whom they would like as a replacement. Tanya Moiseiwitsch was the first choice but she was not interested; Lee was second and he was offered a class for the fall. Oenslager's leave began with the spring semester and Lee took over the entire first- and second-year classes (each year usually had eight or nine set design students). Following his leave, Oenslager retired (Lee continued to invite him in to give lectures two or three times a year until he died in in 1975). At this point, the core design faculty consisted of Ariel Ballif, Lee and William Warfel, who taught lighting, and it was agreed that Lee would teach the first and second year set designers, while the third year would be a combined master class with the costume and lighting designers taught by all three of them. Ballif resigned from the faculty after the spring 1971 semester, so Warfel and Lee (who had just been fired from NYU) jointly, though unofficially, assumed leadership of the program. Warfel dealt with all the practical and administrative aspects, while Lee evolved into a kind of artistic director.

Until 1974 Lee's rank was instructor—a part-time teacher with no benefits, even though he was clearly doing full-time work. He was being exploited, as were most of the theatre faculty, but he had little to compare it to, and from his point of view it was the first time he had had a steady income, the first time, Betsy notes, that she knew there would be a set amount of money in the bank at the start of each month. But sometime around 1975, associate dean Howard Stein promoted him to associate professor, granting him benefits, though he was still technically part time. In 1979, when Lloyd Richards became dean, he made Warfel and Lee's co-chairmanship official. He also promoted Lee to full professor with a significant salary hike, partly in response to the attempt by the University of California, San Diego, to woo him away. The promotion did not increase the workload—he was already overworked. In addition to classes, Lee supervised design for fourteen productions a year: six at the Yale Repertory Theatre, which employed professional directors and actors but used student designers; four Winterfest productions, a festival of new plays that had been initiated by Richards, again designed by students; and four directors' thesis projects. Nonetheless, Lee was concerned, as only he could be, that he was not doing enough to merit the promotion. "I'm teaching only three days a week—is that full time?" he asked. None of this brought official job security as there is, to this day, no tenure system within the School of Drama and even full professors are on term contracts.

Lee's teaching style was as radically different from Oenslager's as was his approach to design. Michael Yeargan, who succeeded Lee as co-chair of the design department in 2012, was a student in the transitional year between Oenslager and Lee. "Oenslager was an old-world gentleman," remembers Yeargan. "Sketches had to be in ½" scale, mounted on black matte board; you had to do an ⅛" plan on graph paper; you had to be in class on time, sketches on your desk. After he closed the door you couldn't enter. Donald's classes were exactly two hours long." Lee's classes, on the other hand, were seemingly unstructured and could go on for hours. At least in the early years, there was a polemic aspect to his teaching. Lee, strongly influenced by Brecht, insisted that designs must make a statement; social and political commitment were inseparable from art. Of course, this was the height of the Vietnam War and political fervor enveloped much of the country, yet it was unlikely that any other design teacher in the country so thoroughly integrated politics and aesthetics in the classroom. Even a decade later, notes former student Chris Barreca, the questions and comments "were global, social and philosophical, inherently challenging one's role in society, and as an artist."

Probably the most significant pedagogical change Lee instituted was to shift the emphasis from sketches to models. To allow the students adequate time to construct their models, he altered Oenslager's practice of a new project every week to one every two weeks, something that was also necessitated by the amount of time Lee took on each individual critique.

Another change was to move the teaching of drafting from the technical department to the design department. As Lee explains, "There is technical drafting and design drafting and they are very different. Good drafting is simply good drawing. It is about how you hold a pencil and start a line. You need to press the pencil onto the paper very firmly, and until you are ready to move you shouldn't move, and once you move you go very fast and finish very strong. Start strong and finish strong, which is the foundation of calligraphy. Anyone who can sign their name can draw." For Lee, drawing is at the heart of the design experience and it is through drawing that he discovers the idea of the play. His criticism of much American design training is that drawing never gets beyond technique or illustration. "In theatre you really need to know how to draw things the way they are. You can't just start with abstraction. Composition, understanding the usage of what's onstage, how things are revealed to the audience is the basis of studying scenography." In the early 2000s he stopped teaching drafting, partly because of the change in culture and the reliance on computers, which he acknowledges can do many things more easily and more quickly. But he also notes their limitations, claiming that computers can't draw an old house with a sagging floor. "Jo's *Death of a Salesman* cannot be designed today."

Lee brought costume designer Jane Greenwood onto the faculty in 1976 and lighting designer Jennifer Tipton in 1981. Tipton remembers that after teaching lighting for a few years she wanted to have more interaction with the directors and set designers. "Finally I said, 'I'm going to go talk to Ming, even if I lose my job.' What Ming did, of course, was to say, 'Okay, let's include you in the master class and we'll add a master class on Monday as well as Wednesday.' So he did just the opposite of what I thought he was going to do. He opened himself and the school to me and made me part of everything." But it is Lee's Saturday class that is most famous—or perhaps notorious. This was an all-day marathon for first-year design students, that also included, at various times, directors, playwrights, stage managers and the occasional outside student (sculptor Maya Lin was a student one year). The class would begin at 10 A.M. and continue until 5 or 6 P.M. with only a short break. Lee could go the whole day without eating. Students presented their models and Lee would critique them. There was no preordained amount of time allocated for each student; Lee would discuss the project as long as he felt there was something to explore.

As a result of his experience at NYU, Lee vowed never to miss classes again, unless it was absolutely unavoidable. His dedication is legendary. He was willing to miss the occasional Monday or Wednesday class if he was abroad or if tech or dress rehearsals interfered, but he would fly back not only from around the country but from around the world for the Saturday class. When Lee was designing *Les Contes d'Hoffmann* in Hong Kong in 1991 he had already missed one Saturday class and did not want to miss a second. So he watched Friday rehearsals in Hong Kong, took an evening flight to New York and, taking advantage of the international dateline, was in the classroom at Yale at 10 A.M. Saturday morning. Saturday night he was on a plane back to Hong Kong and was there for the Monday morning rehearsal. No one would have faulted him for missing the second Saturday, but he could not imagine missing a potentially crucial step in a student's development. Lee seems to remember each of his former students and can often recall specific projects years, even decades, later. If one starts to add up the time commitment to teaching, advising and administration at Yale alone, and then calculate the time devoted to professional design work, which was increasingly taking him around the country and around the world, it does not seem humanly possible.

Lee's fundamental approach to teaching is to question, not to criticize—a Socratic approach as Barreca explains. He wants to understand how the student arrived at the design—what was the intention, the process? The probing is also intended to bring the student back to that starting point so that problems can be rethought. Lighting designer Stephen Strawbridge, co-chair of the design department since 1994, states, "Ming's genius as a teacher is bringing out what's best and most useful in a student's own response to a play or opera and developing that into an exciting, producible design. He sees, sometimes where others don't, the kernel of true value in the rough drafts and early versions that a student might present, and finds a way to incorporate that into a workable, finished design." Yeargan marvels, "He'll look at a student's work and I'll think it's hopeless, and he'll see something that will lead them into another direction." As Tipton explains, "He gets on the other side of students' problems and sees the path through." For Lee, the starting point is always the text and the practical needs of the play or opera. At critique sessions, when confronted by a seemingly spectacular or clever design, he will ask where a requisite bed or table will be placed, or wonder why there is no door when it may be necessary for a crucial dramatic entrance. Lobel describes a *Marriage of Figaro* project she designed with the walls a couple of feet off the floor. Lee asked, simply, "Well, how is Cherubino going to hide? They can see his feet." A student once proposed setting a production in a void. "Okay, what color is the void?" was Lee's response. Lee's knowledge of classical drama, opera

3 Lee at the Kennedy Center American College Theater Festival's Summer Intensive in 2008, part of a two-week workshop on the collaborative process taught by Lee and costume designer Constance Hoffman for scenic and costume designers and directors. The workshop was modeled on the Shakespeare project Lee assigned first-year designers and directors at Yale. Lee taught similar summer workshops, beginning in the 1970s at the Banff Centre in Canada, at several campuses of California State University in the 1980s, and at KCACTF.

3

and even a sizable portion of the modern canon is remarkable. Like a conductor who knows a score by heart, Lee knows each of these texts intimately—whether he has designed them or not—and knows the requirements of each act and scene. "A thorough and comprehensive knowledge of every character, their relationships to each other, exits, entrances and so on, is what makes Ming such a formidable teacher," declares Strawbridge. "Not to mention his ability to call to mind, and sometimes to voice, every passage of every opera in the canon."

While Lee's criticism is always meant to be constructive, and he is never intentionally cruel, he can be disconcertingly honest and blunt. No one who has ever been through a Ming Cho Lee critique would consider it a benign experience. At a minimum, Lee's questioning is so thorough that it can be exhausting for the recipient of his attention. At times it could be amusing. Yeargan remembers, as a student, having one model likened to the bottom of an aquarium and another to a bank in Dallas. At times it could be devastating. Hilferty recalls his frustration with another student in her class, asking, "Why did we admit you?" That may have been Lee's way of trying to remember the student's strengths so that he could bring her back to those qualities, but it is hard for a student to hear in the moment. Lobel remembers him asking, "Why is this drawing so bad?" Again, it was an attempt to figure out why something wasn't working, but it comes across as a harsh judgment. Occasionally it is simply, "I don't understand." Every one of Lee's students has such moments, good and bad, indelibly imprinted in their memories.

Lest it sound as if Lee is solely a stern taskmaster, he can also be warm, caring and nurturing. He and Betsy always took an interest in the personal lives of the students. Heidi Ettinger, the first woman admitted to the Yale set design program—one of Lee's goals when he began at Yale was to bring women into set design—recalls how he helped her get through a death in the family. Lobel, whose father had passed away a few years earlier, asked Ming to walk her down the aisle when she got married, which he did. ("I was walking very fast and he kept telling me to slow down.")

Sergio Villegas, a Mexico City–based designer, describes the "grading system" in the first-year class. "At the end of each critique, Ming can either move along to the next student, or he can shake your hand, or ask you to 'wrap' your model. A handshake is a valuable gesture of approval. Wrapping your model is the ultimate compliment, which meant that the project was successful enough for preservation, so he would recommend that you encase it in Saran Wrap." Villegas still keeps his first wrapped model above his desk.

First and second-year projects have varied over the years and have included Richard Strauss's *Salome* or *Elektra*, *Hedda Gabler*, *Iphigenia at Aulis*, *La Bohème*, Brecht and Weill's *The Seven Deadly Sins*, *Long Day's Journey into Night*, *The Marriage of Figaro*, several plays by Chekhov and Molière, a Shakespeare project with the directing students and something from the American musical theatre canon. For years *Guys and Dolls* was a standard project but it seemed increasingly difficult for students to relate to the work. Lee added one non-textual assignment that involves creating a scenario and design for a piece of music—the sublime second movement of Schubert's Quintet in C. The scenario can contain no adjectives or adverbs, only action. It must tell a story and have a payoff. In this situation it forces designers to think like writers.

Over the years there have been those who suggested that Lee was turning out clones of himself. Given the number of students, it is inevitable that were some who developed a "Ming Cho Lee style." But former students and colleagues alike emphasize that Lee does not teach a particular method or system. In fact, a recurring motif is his excitement and delight at being surprised by seeing something new in a design, something that he had never thought of. He teaches the students to make the play their own. As Hilferty explains, "If you are intimidated you want to copy. But if you trust him you can spring

4

4 Lee critiquing a model.

forward and find your own voice. He never tells anybody how to do it, which can be deeply frustrating for some people because they want to be told how."

That said, in his early years at NYU and Yale, Lee *was* rather dogmatic, insisting that the students take an emblematic, sculptural, nonrealistic approach to design—but this was at a time when scenography was dominated by naturalism or poetic realism and Lee was trying to get students to see other possibilities. Ettinger says that "he opened everybody's eyes to a kind of cerebral approach—very non-decorative, very conceptual. That was a fresh idea for a lot of the students." Ralph Funicello, a student at NYU, recalls seeing Lee's models for the first time and being overwhelmed. "His work always seemed to create a three-dimensional space for the play to live in," says Funicello. "A production never happened in front of his set, always within it, and the strength of his ideas always created a quiet dialogue between the actors and their environment. This may all be taken for granted now, but it was not as common in the American theatre of the sixties and early seventies."

The nature of academia inevitably changed over the decades of Lee's career. Part of what made the Yale design program so successful, he believes, was the ability to make decisions unencumbered by administrative regulations. Everything from admissions to hiring became more complex over the years. Lee also worries about the changes wrought by new technologies—not so much in terms of technique as attitude. He is concerned that students who grew up with new technologies have lost the ability and patience to enter into the measured and deliberate process that artistic creation requires. The underlying principles he teaches, however, are not bound by period, style or technologies. They are founded in trust of the text, meticulous research, discovery through drawing (the kinesthetic response of pencil on paper), and understanding space through the tactile experience of three-dimensional models. And he teaches patience. Hilferty compares it to planting a seed: "That is not the end of the event. It has to be husbanded, watered and watched, and with luck and care it will grow."

"The true enabler of Dad's lifestyle was and is his teaching," says Christopher Lee. "What began as a way for him to make some extra money became the driving force in his life and the true source of his legacy. As a designer, his work was gone when the shows closed. There are only photographs and the memories. And yet, Dad retains his position in the theatre world through the countless students who passed through his classes. They carry on his legacy not by copying or repeating his designs but by expressing their own voices in their work."

THE CLAMBAKE

Perhaps the single most important catalyst in the development of design training in the U.S. from 1990 through 2009 was an annual event affectionately known as Ming's Clambake.

Its origin dates back to the design portfolio review held under the auspices of the League of Professional Theatre Training Programs. Founded in 1972 as a consortium of thirteen schools with well-established acting-training curricula, the League's primary goal was to set standards for teaching and to help acting students make the transition into the regional theatres. In 1975 New York University's J. Michael Miller, one of the League's founders, suggested including design programs as well, and over a lunch meeting with Lee the idea for the design portfolio review was born. Lee, however, was not interested in setting standards for teaching. He felt the important goal was to let designers meet students and see their work, rather than depending on a barrage of inevitably repetitive letters of recommendation from teachers. Equally important was the opportunity for everyone to learn what was happening across the country since, Lee believed, students and teachers were isolated with little idea, in the pre-internet era, of what anyone else was doing.

But not all the League member schools had professional design-training programs. So the review, which commenced in 1976, included some schools that were not members of the League, and Lee played a major role in the selection process. Each selected student would set up models, sketches, photo documentation, etc., and teams of directors and designers would visit each exhibit. Unfortunately, the dynamics within these teams sometimes led to callous and even gratuitously cruel pronouncements. Lee's approach, however, while frank and uncompromising, was never intentionally harsh and always followed his method of questioning and probing to find the kernel of

5

the idea underlying the design. His critiques became legendary, and Lee quickly emerged as the de facto head of the event.

By 1987, however, the funding that had been provided by the National Endowment for the Arts was eliminated. Beyond the financial issues, Lee felt that the event had become an institution bogged down by too many rules. But its underlying purpose as a national town meeting of the design community was still important, and Miller encouraged Lee to organize an event himself. Meanwhile, in 1989, Robert Marx, the former head of theatre for the NEA, was appointed executive director of the New York Public Library for the Performing Arts at Lincoln Center. As part of his reorganization of the library, Marx insisted that "everything was to be artist-focused and artist-driven." He made a list of artists with whom he wanted to work, and Lee was at the top of the list. Lee broached the idea of holding the portfolio review there. When Ming and Betsy saw the vast second floor exhibition hall, says Marx, "it was like throwing a stake in the ground: 'This is where we will rebuild the design portfolio review.'"

5 Overview of a corner of the 2009 Clambake.

6 The logo from the final Clambake. The original was designed for the first Clambake by a student, Susan Branch. It depicts Ming on the half shell.

7 "Team Betsy" in 2009 with, from left, Martha Smith, Sharon Jensen and Betsy Lee.

As luck would have it, in 1989 the NEA awarded Lee a $25,000 Distinguished Artist Fellowship, and he decided to use the money to fund the new portfolio review. (It was a quintessential Lee gesture. Although he often bemoaned his personal financial state, whenever there was extra money he used it to pay assistants or to fund ventures such as this.) According to Miller, when Lee consulted him as to how he should organize the new event, Miller replied, "It's your clambake." Lee did not understand the reference, and Miller explained that the singer Bing Crosby used to host a charity golf tournament for professional golfers and his show-business friends. It was called Bing's Clambake, and the idea was that you could set your

6

own rules. So in 1990 *Ming's* Clambake was born, indirectly funded by the very organization whose withdrawal of funding contributed to the demise of the previous event. (In 1993 Lee was awarded the $5,000 Long Wharf Theatre Mary L. Murphy Award in Design, and he put that toward the Clambake as well.) Yale and eventually NYU contributed funding, as did some of the other participating schools. The Lees and the occasional anonymous donor always made up any shortfall. They held firmly to the belief that the participating students should not have to pay an entry fee. The library provided facilities, equipment and staff. The event was unique within the library's program, and Marx wanted to be sure the librarians and curators saw it as part of their venue. "I can guarantee you," Marx told them, "that of the living designers you collect here in dance, music and theatre, a great many of them will be here at the Clambake; and a great number of the designers you are *going* to collect in the future will also be here."

The organization of the event was a massive undertaking overseen by Betsy together with Sharon Jensen, who had been the executive director of the League. In the last years of the Clambake Martha Smith became an invaluable member of what by then was known as "Team Betsy." Betsy's centrality to the event was acknowledged by *American Theatre* magazine in its article on the final Clambake, titled "Last Call at Ming's (and Betsy's) Clambake."

The Clambake, which took place over a weekend in late May, began as a relatively small affair with fifty graduating students from eight MFA programs: Brandeis University, Carnegie Mellon University, NYU, the Universities of California (San Diego), Missouri, Texas and Wisconsin, and Yale. Virtually the whole design world and a broad group of directors from around the country were invited, and about sixty participated. Gone were the roving teams. Now all the professionals were encouraged to move about on their own and talk to any of the students they chose. It was a critique, but also a conversation. Sometimes a designer might sit with a student for an hour, sometimes five minutes. The sight of Lee sitting at a table with a student, studying a model and engaged in deep conversation, became iconic. It was a chance for schools to learn about each other which inevitably led to sharing of ideas for classes, workshops, projects, techniques and so forth. Students had a chance to meet their colleagues from other schools as well as professional designers and directors they would otherwise have never had the opportunity to encounter. By holding it at Lincoln Center rather than the campus of one of the participating schools, no one "owned" it—except, in a sense, Lee.

But this was much more than portfolio review. It was, in Marx's words, "a gathering of the tribe." It was a festive gathering—there was no other event like this in the theatre world. For many in the profession it was the one time a year to see old friends and colleagues, and not a few impromptu production meetings were held in corners and commandeered meeting rooms. There was an excitement and air of anticipation about new talents to be discovered. And as befits any festival, food was an essential ingredient. There was a lunch on both days—Saturday at the nearby Shun Lee West and Sunday at various other restaurants over the years—so that conversation among students and professionals could continue. This was the single largest budget item of the Clambake, and was paid for by Ming and Betsy.

Inevitably, the event grew. More and more schools wanted to participate, and participating schools wanted to send more students. Lee insisted on looking at portfolios from new schools before approving their participation, and this led to resentment in some quarters. The event began to be seen by some as a "cattle call"—a place for students to be seen by potential employers—not as an educational gathering. Betsy grew disenchanted with it, and Ming was getting tired. In its latter years some sixty-five set, costume and lighting design students exhibited (the maximum the space could accommodate), student directors from Yale and Columbia were invited to observe, and the guest list numbered 750. Betsy and her staff simply could no longer take on the responsibility of organization. The final Clambake was held in May 2009.

7

CHAPTER 10

City Opera to the Met 1970–74

1

1 ***Ariodante***, Kennedy Center, 1971, show curtain elevation. While the drops look very painterly, a lot of it was actually "fairly tight pencil drawings. The etching idea was kind of left over from *Giulio Cesare*. I discovered that if you have very good drawing as a foundation you can make color washes on top of it and then opaque white highlights. You can do highlights with just a little shadow without having to render everything."

2

3

Roberto Devereux

New York City Opera, 1970

2 Production photograph, Sara's chamber.

3 ¼" preliminary sketch, the great hall at Westminster. Lee's unit set transformed locale through the change of wall modules and tapestries.

LEE'S WORK AT NEW YORK CITY OPERA, beginning with *Don Rodrigo* in 1966 and continuing through *Idomeneo* in 1975 (plus two more operas in the early eighties), coincided with the institution's emergence as the most exciting and adventurous opera company in the United States. Between 1970 and 1973 Tito Capobianco, with Lee as designer, staged Gaetano Donizetti's "Three Queens" cycle as vehicles for Beverly Sills, beginning with *Roberto Devereux*, followed by *Maria Stuarda* in 1972 and *Anna Bolena* in 1973. (The Metropolitan Opera, by contrast, did not stage any of these until 2011.)

For all its newfound fame, City Opera worked on tight budgets, and when he began *Devereux*, Lee was told that one design might have to be adapted for all three operas of the cycle. Lee's solution, not surprisingly, was a unit set. The story of the opera is essentially a love triangle: Robert Devereux, Earl of Essex, is loved by Queen Elizabeth, but he is in love with Sara, the Duchess of Nottingham. In the end, he is beheaded. Three of the six scenes are set in the great hall at Westminster, so Lee created a framework of wooden columns and beams that suggested an enormously high Tudor hall with a remarkable feeling of depth, as well as a skeletal quality, as if looking into a giant rib cage. By plugging in additional scenic units and appropriate furniture the other locales could be created easily. For the Tower of London the Tudor structure was hidden by what appeared to be stone walls that were actually scrim, which could dissolve to reveal the soldiers coming for Roberto—a small though effective coup de théâtre.

Maria Stuarda, based on Friedrich Schiller's play about the rivalry between Queen Elizabeth and Mary, Queen of Scotland, leading to Mary's beheading, was produced a year and a half later, using an identical ground plan and essentially the same overall design. "The basic setup of the corridor with the posts is strictly from

4

5

4 ***Anna Bolena***, New York City Opera, 1973, preliminary ¼" sketch.

5 ***Maria Stuarda***, New York City Opera, 1972, production photograph of Fotheringay Park.

Devereux," explains Lee. "I added panels of painted scrim and little units to create various scenes, so it's all kind of pieced together. But somehow, when it was put together, the pieces looked better than they did in *Roberto Devereux*. It could have become a really boring job, but it was quite exciting because it turned out to be a wonderful opera." Harold Schonberg, the *New York Times* critic, made note of this (while attributing the sets to the costume designer): "If anybody thought Jose Varona's [sic] sets looked familiar, they were. The court scenes came largely from *Devereux*, as well they might, as the locale is the same" (March 9, 1972). He did acknowledge that the adaptation was "ingenious" and made particular note of the transformation into Fotheringay Park in act two.

Anna Bolena, about Henry VIII's second wife, was the first of the three operas that Donizetti composed, and the first in terms of historical chronology. "It does not have the kind of intimacy of *Devereux* or *Maria Stuarda*," notes Lee. The set employed roughly the same ground plan of flared walls and a raked central platform, but now the posts and beams were replaced by sculptural walls covered with a collage of heraldic emblems. Lee admits to borrowing the idea from his design for *Henry IV* the previous year at the Mark Taper Forum—stealing from himself, as he puts it. The walls were done in a foreshortened perspective so that the great depth of the first two operas here gave way to a more claustrophobic sense of enclosure.

Unfortunately, Hans Sondheimer, the powerful technical director and resident lighting designer of City Opera, with whom Lee often clashed, would not allow Lee to build the walls as high as he would have liked. The problem was the difficulties of changeovers between operas. City Opera had a limited staff, but even more restrictive were the stage elevators used for moving scenery. Although the New York State Theater was a new structure, built with opera production in mind, the technical infrastructure left something wanting. The elevators were just over nine feet tall and all scenery had to be able to break down to that size. Meanwhile, because Lee was simultaneously involved with plans for Arena Stage's trip to the Soviet Union, he was not present as much as he should have been. Capobianco and Sondheimer simply chose drops from *Devereux* and *Maria Stuarda*. "I think I lost interest," Lee remembers. "I didn't even attend opening night."

Nonetheless, the production was a huge success, especially for Sills, and even if Lee did not completely control every aspect of the design, the scenography and Capobianco's staging were as brilliantly integrated as anything they had worked on together. As described by *Village Voice* reviewer Leighton Kerner (a rare example of a critic who understands design): "Tito Capobianco has staged the opera as a bravura piece of romantic theatre.... Jane Seymour's confession of adultery with the King sends Anna groping along every cold-stone wall of the Ming Cho Lee's correctly claustrophobia inducing scenery as pity and fury fight for domination" (October 18, 1973).

In 1971, after *Devereux* but before the latter two Donizetti productions, Lee designed Handel's *Ariodante* as part of the opening festivities of the opera house at the Kennedy Center in Washington, D.C. Again directed by Capobianco and starring Sills, it was essentially a City Opera production, although it never moved to New York. It marked a radical shift for Lee as he created the first truly painterly, pictorial setting of his career. Even though he believed that this style was what baroque opera required, he had not taken that approach to *Giulio Cesare* a few years earlier. He attributes some of the shift to seeing a setting for *Manon* designed by former assistant Marsha Eck for Capobianco. She designed it in the style of Fragonard, and this was a revelation to Lee. "When I saw it on the opening night, I was overwhelmed by how fantastic the damn thing looked. And I said, 'Well, I've got to do something like that.'"[1]

The result was a series of ethereally painted drops and curtains with soft romantic imagery and clear influences of Mielziner and Eugene Berman. If the *Ariodante* designs were placed next to the more or less concurrent creations for *Two Gents* and *Timon of Athens* in the park and the pre-Broadway *Lolita, My Love*, it might be hard to imagine that they were all created by the same designer—the designer, no less, who had seemingly banished pictorialism from the American scenographic lexicon. "I have to say, I did a very beautifully painted show," Lee declares, "but it's the wrong period. For a baroque opera, the look is one hundred years too late. But architecturally it's okay." Nobody seemed troubled by the period disparity, perhaps because the set was framed by an eighteenth-century-style proscenium and side boxes. This is definitely what captured the attention of Paul Hume, the effusive critic of the *Washington Post*:

> **Ming Cho Lee, in devising the sets, used a gorgeous red and gold curtain that read "Ariodante." It serves both as screen and as a scrim through which, at times, the exquisite movement of dancers and singers could be seen. Lee's stage gave the look and**

feel of Handel's day, with side boxes from which the singers could view the stage silently or join in the music. His entire design enhanced the dramatic and musical implications of the score (September 16, 1971).

The same season also brought a production of *Susannah* at City Opera, directed by Robert Lewis, co-founder of the Actors Studio and a successful Broadway director. Written in 1955 by Carlisle Floyd, *Susannah* has remained one of the most popular American operas. Loosely based on the story of "Susannah and the Elders" from the Apocrypha, it is set in an Appalachian town in Tennessee. Lee saw it when it was first done at City Center in 1956 and fell in love with it. His design attempted to capture a feeling of southern humidity and dense woods, "where you can't get out of the foliage and mosquitoes are swarming all around." He used a burlap backdrop to create a rough texture and multiple layers of scrim painted with branches and leaves in the Chinese style. The basic set was very simple: a platform with ramps and scenic units of fragmented rotting buildings. But Lee felt, with some justification, that the units were too small for the enormous stage of the State Theater (Sondheimer couldn't handle bigger units), a problem noted by Donal Henahan in the *New York Times*, who was dismissive of the "small, raked platforms and conventionally fragmentary structures" and compared the sets unfavorably with those of the Met's National Company production of the opera designed by David Hays (November 2, 1971).

Lee also believes that the set should have been much more expressionistic. "What makes the *Susannah* design a little weak and a little pretty—which was not my intention—is the fact that it was all very reasonable instead of an unreasonable distortion. There isn't enough distortion." He still believes that he had not yet figured out how to do modern opera. "When the work had a kind of epic quality, like *Don Rodrigo* and so forth," explains Lee, "which is all set in pre-Shakespeare times, that seemed easy—right in the groove. But when I started doing opera that demanded something else in the contemporary period, I was still much too influenced by Jo and by Peter Brook's productions at the Met." Nonetheless, the sets were evocative and the layering was a sophisticated blend of soft-edged fabric with the natural reality of the wooden platforms. While the design certainly recalled the romantic realism of Mielziner, Lee successfully fused it with a Brechtian utilitarianism. In a certain way it was a harbinger of what came to dominate the American theatre in subsequent decades in the work of designers such as John Lee Beatty and Ralph Funicello. But at the time it may not have been "operatic" enough for some observers. A few years later Lee designed another Floyd opera, *Bilby's Doll*, at the Houston Grand Opera. Scenically it had many of the same elements, suggesting a rustic, poetic realism and including the signature floating branches and watercolor sky wash.

While the reception for *Susannah* may have been mixed, Offenbach's *Les Contes d'Hoffmann*, in the fall of 1972, was "a triumph for Ming Cho Lee," according to Irving Kolodin in the *Saturday Review* (October 21, 1972). Lee had distinct memories of seeing the opera as a child in Shanghai. "It scared the hell out of me. Even when I was very young I felt that that opera was psychologically very complex in the sense that Hoffmann had two sides—one is being a writer and being self-destructive and drinking too much; and then there is this evil side that manages to destroy whatever he builds up." Capobianco envisioned *Hoffmann* as a kind of Grand Guignol that could be both horrifying and humorous, and as with *Lolita, My Love* the previous year, he specifically wanted projections, although this time their use was more justifiable. For Lee this was an opera about theatre, and he wanted the design to reflect the theatricality of the opera itself. The basic set had a balcony ringing the upstage wall and a turntable platform in the middle. A cracked mirror hung overhead. The backdrop was made of Mylar which reflected light and distorted the projections, thereby creating, as the *New York Times* review stated, "a mysterious, psychedelic atmosphere, with a shimmering background, projections, strange physical distortions and a cumulative feeling of horror" (October 5, 1972). Images of dolls' heads, disembodied eyes and faces hovered eerily behind the scenes. Critics evoked "fun-house mirrors," Dali, phantasmagoria and "shimmering delirium" in an attempt to capture and convey the mood engendered by Lee's decor. This was still three years before Robin Wagner famously employed Mylar in the finale of *A Chorus Line*, and, as with *Animus* for the Joffrey Ballet a few years earlier, critics didn't know what to make of it, describing it as "some dark, shiny, vinyl-like material" (*Newsweek*, October 16,1972), "metallic-faced drapes" (*Saturday Review*, October 21, 1972), and, most amusingly, "some luminous new material called, I believe, 'Milo'" (*New York Post*, October 5, 1972).

The opera is structured as three stories told by Hoffmann to the students in the canteen of a theatre. The prologue creates the framework and the epilogue allows it to return to "reality." But Capobianco decided to eliminate the epilogue, which angered many

6

7

8

6, 7 ***Susannah***, New York City Opera, 1971, sketch of the church and dress rehearsal photograph.

8 ***Ariodante***, Kennedy Center, 1971, ¼" sketch. "We had two boxes on the stage to frame the baroque theatre and hanging chandeliers. Now, these boxes are okay, but they are taken from Josef Svoboda's *Don Giovanni*, which was based on the Tyl Theater in Prague. I just copied it and made it look more eighteenth century." Lee acknowledges Mielziner's influence in the painting of the trees.

9 Lee with Hans Sondheimer, technical director and production coordinator of New York City Opera.

9

10

12

14

11

13

15

Les Contes d'Hoffmann

New York City Opera, 1972

10, 11 Sketch and production photograph, act 1, "Olympia." "I thought that Spalanzani, who made the doll, would have a little baroque stage with all the mechanism for a curtain and so forth. I imagined that when Coppélius destroys the doll, all the rigging on that stage would all fall down." There are unfinished dolls hanging in cages, eyes projected on the Mylar and a mirror overhead.

12, 13 Production photographs, act 2, "Giulietta." A gondola is seen in the middle of the platform. "The bridge is kind of hung, and broken glass mirror and chandeliers fly in." Lee refers to the face embedded in the front of the balcony as "a little bit of *Bomarzo*."

14, 15 Sketch and production photograph, act 3, "Antonia." There is supposed to be a portrait of Antonia's mother in the scene and as Dr. Miracle tries to get Antonia to sing, the voice of the mother comes out of the portrait. Capobianco wanted Stella to come out of the portrait. "I said, 'How do you do that? The portrait is supposed to be upstairs.' He said, 'No, the portrait is actually going to be a mirror frame downstairs with a scrim stretched in front of it that has the painting of the mother on it. And then at the appropriate time, Beverly Sills will sneak in from behind, walk through the scrim and become Stella.' We all said, 'Okay,' and just did it."

critics, not to mention the conductor, Julius Rudel. Lee argued, "The whole thing about *The Tales of Hoffmann* is the irony. French opera is very melodious but there is always a sense of the human, a sense of ridicule and a sense of irony. Without the epilogue the whole irony is gone, and you might as well do an Italian opera." Ultimately, the financial backer sided with Capobianco. Kolodin facetiously attributed the excision to the design: "[The design] does, indeed, work so well that it is apparently impossible to make a shift back to the opening in Luther's Tavern, and the epilogue is omitted" (*Saturday Review*, October 21, 1972).

With the production of *Anna Bolena* the following season, the long partnership between Lee and Capobianco came to an end. There were undoubtedly many contributing factors, but Lee attributes some of it to a "slowly sliding death of City Opera," by which he means a shift from ensemble to a star system and focusing on effects over substance. No one was discussing the ideas inherent in the operas and how that might inform the repertoire. (There was, as it turned out, one more abortive collaboration—a production of Verdi's *Attila* in 1980, co-produced by City Opera, Lyric Opera of Chicago and San Diego Opera. Capobianco worked with Lee on the design but resigned before going into rehearsal, and it was directed in Chicago by Ernst Poettgen and in New York by Lotfi Mansouri with Lee's designs.) Lee and Capobianco had collaborated on seventeen operas and one Broadway musical over eight years, including *Bomarzo* and *Lucia di Lammermoor* at Teatro Colón in Buenos Aires and *Giulio Cesare* in Hamburg.

BACK TO SAN FRANCISCO OPERA AND THE MET

Early in 1973 Lee returned to San Francisco Opera, where he had been the resident designer in 1961. This was not quite a grand homecoming—more of a slipping in through the back door. The company produced an annual low-budget spring season at the Curran Theatre and opened its 1973 season with a staging of Bach's 1727 oratorio *The Passion According to Saint Matthew. The Passion*, of course, is not an opera, so when Kurt Herbert Adler asked Gerald Freedman to direct it, Freedman had to devise a theatrical structure:

> **I conceived of a layered production of both reality and time—three levels of reality: the present, the past and the time in which it was written. I thought of the soloists as penitents, and in their solos they are searching for a way back to Christ, to their spirituality. Eventually the penitents would break through the front scrim into His reality. They mingled there in contemporary dress with the Christ figures in biblical dress, surrounded by a chorus in neutral, kind of vestal costumes of Bach's time. For the front scrim I asked Ming to show other versions of the crucifixion—Rubens, Dali and so on—so that you saw other artists' impressions of the event. Ming created a sense of fantastic halo rays that were made of staffs that caught the light. It was one of the most exciting and thrilling collaborations we had.**

Lee's design was remarkably simple but effective. Using mostly stock platforming, he placed the chorus on a semicircular bank of steep risers surrounding a raked central platform that itself was surrounded by curved ramps. Radiating out from above the risers was what Lee describes as an abstract pipe sculpture which caught the light to give the impression of a heavenly emanation. An image of the crucifixion was projected at the back of the stage, along with the images on the front scrim. It was a well-received production, and even though Lee admits that Bach isn't his favorite composer ("a little bit of Bach goes a long way"), he nonetheless found it "strangely moving."

At almost the same time Lee returned to the Metropolitan Opera—or at least next door. In 1973, under the leadership of Schuyler Chapin, the Met acted upon an idea that had been kicking around for some time—a small space for chamber operas or other works that were inappropriate for the massive opera house. The location chosen for this venture was the Forum Theater (now the Mitzi E. Newhouse Theater) beneath the Vivian Beaumont at Lincoln Center. Officially known as Opera at the Forum, it was quickly dubbed the Mini-Met. The first—and what turned out to be only—season consisted of two bills in repertory: first, a double bill of Maurice Ohana's 1967 *Syllabaire pour Phèdre* and Henry Purcell's baroque *Dido and Aeneas*; and second, the Virgil Thomson–Gertrude Stein *Four Saints in Three Acts* from 1934, the latter directed by Alvin Ailey.

The stage of the Forum was essentially a circular thrust surrounded on roughly two-thirds of its circumference by seating—not an ideal space for opera. Lee says it was like doing a show in the lobby. Unlike the Mark Taper Forum in Los Angeles, which has a similar layout, it felt as if the audience and performers were in two separate spaces. Given the space and the repertory, the sets needed to be minimal and functional, something at which Lee normally excelled. But this time the space seemed to defeat him. His unit structure may have been functional, but it lacked the theatricality

THE EVOLUTION OF A DESIGN: JUILLIARD AMERICAN OPERA CENTER, 1972

Director Michael Cacoyannis wanted a very traditional setting and sketched out the garret and arcade for Lee. Says Lee: **"I have always told students that if a director wants to do a sketch you are lucky; you are not guessing what the hell he or she wants. I assure you, you will still have a lot to do because usually the director's sketch doesn't quite get there."** Lee went to Paris where Cacoyannis was living to research. **"We walked around Paris to look at various arcades. We had omelets at a small café, the best omelet I have had. Then I went back to the hotel and I started doing little sketches."**

16

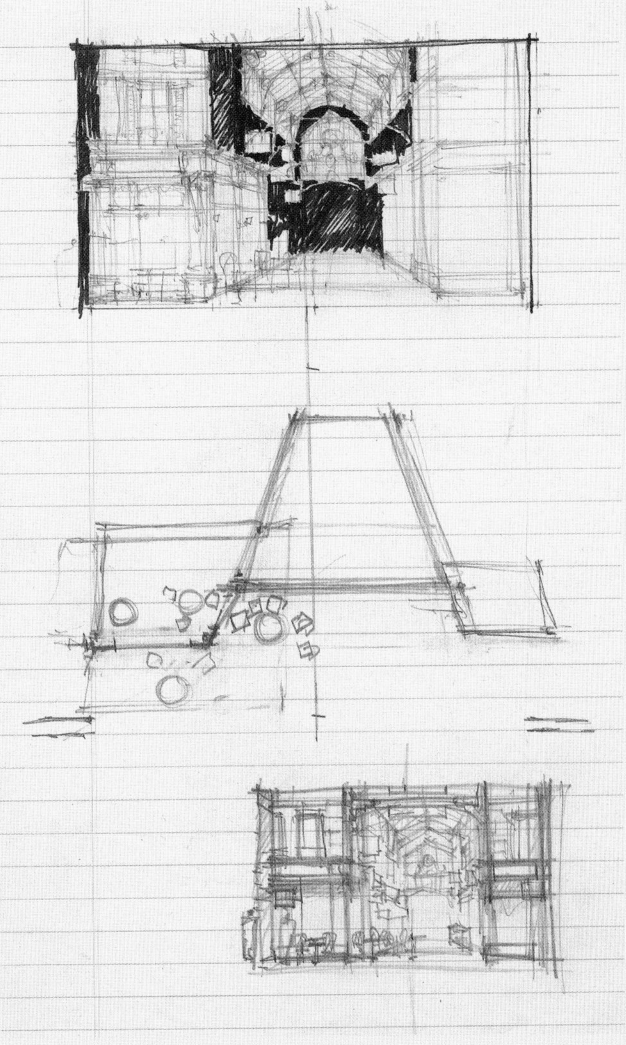

17

La Bohème

16 Director Michael Cacoyannis's sketch for the garret and Momus.

17 Based on Cacoyannis's sketch Lee made a ⅛" sketch and ground plan after visiting the actual Parisian arcade. But because he didn't know the details well enough, he did the 1/16" sketch at the bottom.

18

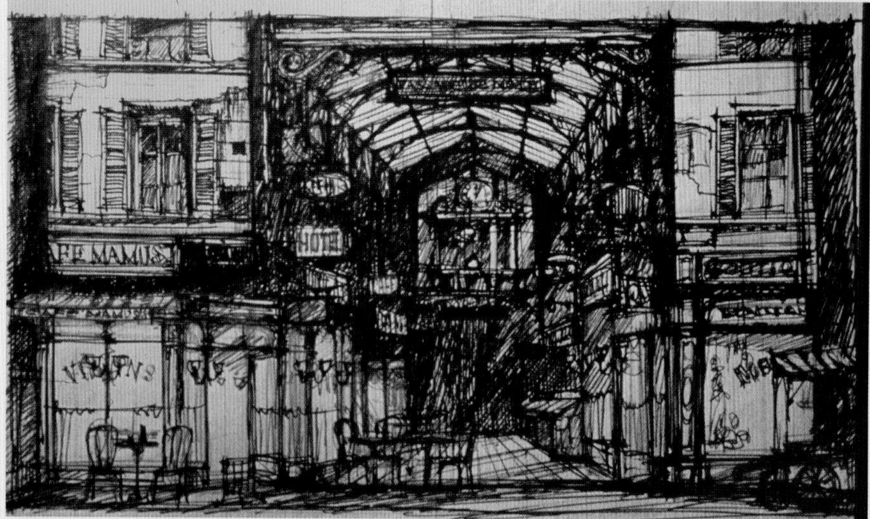
19

La Bohème

18 ¼" sketch of the garret, act 1.

19 ¼" sketch, Momus, act 2.

20 ¼" sketch for act 3. "We decided to have the third act happen at the end of the Metro line. I said, 'Well, all these European railroad stations always had a little inn, so perhaps we will have a little inn here.' It was based on a Utrillo painting. And there was a snow bank. This is where the customs people would go in and out."

21 ½" model, act 1. "Leigh Rand [head assistant at the time] made the model. It looks amazing. The set looked just like the model except that we made a mistake. Instead of using netting for the window, we thought we would use Plexiglas and make it really dirty. We didn't realize that the angle of the window exactly reflected the orchestra pit so that we saw the conductor in the window waving away and the orchestra playing. We had to put cardboard behind it, so the window ended up not having the feeling it does in the model."

22, 23 ½" model and production photograph, act 2.

20

21

PASSAGE
JEUX
JOUETS
MPR
PARISIENNE
MODES
EURS
PEDICURE
AU
PORT
SALUT
HOTEL
MOMUS
LA PETI
CAFE RESTAUTANT
MOMUS
CAFE MOMUS
BOUTIQUE
CURIOSIT

22

PASSAGE
PARISIENNE
MODES
HOTEL
JEUX
JOUETS
PEDICURE
MOMUS
LA PETITE
BOUTIQU

23

24

25

of previous analogous designs. Performers seemed isolated in space with only a scaffolding and the orchestra to frame them (there was no orchestra pit, so musicians were placed on the upper level of the upstage balcony). The presentational nature of opera almost demands the confines of a proscenium stage. Certainly these operas could work in alternative spaces, but these productions seemed lost, even in the intimacy of the Forum.

To further complicate matters, even getting the sets constructed was a hurdle. They were built by the Met shop, but as an afterthought to the mainstage productions, never getting the necessary attention. Furthermore, because of union agreements with the Teamsters, the sets, which could simply have been carried a short distance between the two theatres, were instead taken from the Met shop, loaded onto trucks, driven around the block, and then unloaded at the Forum, which was literally next door.

Paul-Emile Deiber, who directed the first double bill at the Mini-Met, was also the director of Donizetti's *La Favorita* which marked Lee's return to the main stage of San Francisco Opera that fall. The opera is set in fourteenth-century Spain and while Lee's settings were certainly attractive and appropriate, they were already derivative, with strong echoes of *Don Rodrigo* and even *Il Giuramento*. Deiber provided limited directorial guidance, leaving Lee to come up with a concept. "I just don't know how to go at it all by myself without a director with a strong point of view," he admits. The result was "just aesthetics and style and design and sculptural material. I did sketches and nobody rejected anything." When this production was moved to the Met in 1978, hanging the ceiling pieces was too complicated and a simple backdrop was used instead. This eliminated much of the theatricality of the design and Lee was so discouraged he did not even participate in the opening night curtain call.

Throughout this period there is a recurring use of drops or ceilings for opera and dance that are too complicated to be hung properly and are ultimately cut or simplified at the expense of the design. The problem, most often, had to do with time and space. Operas are done

24 ***The Passion According to Saint Matthew***, San Francisco Opera, 1973, production photograph with projected image.

25 ***Dido and Aeneas***, Mini-Met, 1973, production photograph.

26 ***Syllabaire pour Phèdre***, Mini-Met, 1973, production photograph.

26

27

28

27, 28 ***La Favorita***, San Francisco Opera, 1973, production photographs of the cloisters of the Monastery of St. James of Compostella (top) with Luciano Pavarotti, left, and Bonaldo Giaiotti, and the Palace of the Alcazar. The cloister was suggested by a colonnade of Moorish arches and a fragment of a bell tower, further theatricalized by being isolated within a surround of faux copper metal plates creating a sculptural, textured and almost surreal sky. The scene in the court added a staircase, some emblematic heraldry and Spanish grillwork, along with a floating ceiling and even the floating statues that first appeared in *Don Rodrigo* at City Opera in 1966 and again in *Henry IV* at the Delacorte in 1968.

29

30

29 ***Le Coq d'Or***, Dallas Civic Opera, 1973, sketch for act 1. Gouache, modeling paste, metallic paint and watercolor.

30 ***Idomeneo***, New York City Opera, 1974, sketch.

in rep and the fly space is often filled with drops and lights for more than one show. Anything that could not hang on one batten, such as diagonal drops or floating ceilings, took up too much overhead real estate, as it were. Furthermore, in the days before computer-controlled hydraulics, setting the trim was an inexact science, especially if there were multiple pieces at differing levels. This was further complicated in dance in which several different dances might be done in one evening, or in multi-scene operas which required rapid scene changes. Opera houses, even newly built mechanical marvels, such as the Met, were really functioning with nineteenth-century practices.

IDOMENEO

Before his true debut at the Met, Lee did two more operas: a serviceable production of *Le Coq d'Or* at the Dallas Civic Opera, directed by Jose Quintero (the design of which overlapped the trip to Russia with Arena and *Anna Bolena* at City Opera), and Mozart's *Idomeneo*, directed by Freedman and produced by City Opera at the Kennedy Center. The latter moved to the New York State Theater the following year—with some significant changes to the set. The *New York Times* reviewed it at both venues (two different critics), and the production was lambasted both times, earning Lee two of the worst reviews of his career.

At the time, *Idomeneo* was one of Mozart's less-produced operas, and it had never had a major production in New York. Set in Crete in the aftermath of the Trojan War, its mythological plot and the appearance of a sea monster seem more typical of baroque opera than the works for which Mozart became best known. Freedman, according to Lee, was more focused on the abstraction of the music than the demands of the story. Visually he wanted it to resemble a Martha Graham dance, and he returned to the idea of a Richard Lippold sculpture (as with the 1972 *Hamlet* at the Delacorte). Lee created a wire sculpture (that was never hung with the proper tension and thus tended to droop) and a basic set of platforms and steps. There were a Mylar cyc, metallic clouds, projections and a shadow-puppet-like sea monster. There is absolutely no reason why the opera could not work in an abstract setting, but there was no apparent connection between the design and the opera. Lee seemingly gave Freedman what he wanted without question without developing his own ideas about the opera's needs.

Whether or not the design was well executed is a matter of opinion. Schonberg in the *Times*, writing about the Kennedy Center production, had nothing good to say about the staging, which struck him as vulgar and amateurish, and as for the design he complained of a "cluttered and busy" stage, saying, "Instead of the classicism that the sets should have suggested, there were ugly ramps, staircases and crude symbolism" (May 25, 1974). Shortly after this devastating review Lee wrote an essay on designing for opera for *Contemporary Stage Design U.S.A.*, a book-length catalogue of a design exhibition of at Lincoln Center, and took the opportunity to respond:

> **Very recently, Harold Schonberg took me to task for my designs for the Mozart opera, *Idomeneo*. For him, the piece, being neoclassic in style, had to conform to his concept of neoclassic design—ruined temples and the like. Mozart's opera, however, has little to do with ruined temples. The music is clean, pure in line, lean—and my design reflected this. I used a simple, formal arrangement of cantilevered platforms and two-dimensional wire sculptures to give a sense of place: an open terrace, a harbor, a sacred place. In addition to this, the production had projections of primordial natural elements—the sea, storm clouds, a hot burning sunset—to support the very real human passions with which the opera deals. As long as the visual weight does not violate that of the music, you can go against the style—even abstraction for neoclassicism—in favor of other values in the work.**[2]

However harsh Schonberg's review may have been, and however conservative his scenographic aesthetic, it is not clear that he was dictating any specific scenic style. He was suggesting, perhaps with some justification, that the classicism of the opera—what Lee correctly understood as clean, pure in line and lean—was nowhere to be found in this production. Regardless, Lee did make changes for New York, giving it a more neoclassical look, eliminating the wire sculpture, but keeping the projections, which thus became a major scenic element. But all was for naught: Donal Henahan's *Times* review was, if anything, more scathing than Schonberg's regarding both Freedman's staging and Lee's sets, which he described as "minimal mock classic, against ugly, ineffective mock modern projections."

In a way, this design was on the cusp of the transition of much opera design from modern to postmodern, and perhaps the problem was that it did not go far enough. It made a gesture toward classicism, but not in a pure or recognizable form, but neither was it quoting classicism or making a bold contemporary statement. It was caught somewhere between. Freedman was not the director to make that transition, and Lee could not make the conceptual leap on his own.

CHAPTER 11

The Metropolitan Opera 1974–83

Boris Godunov

Metropolitan Opera, 1974

1 ½" model, coronation scene. Lee wanted the wooden bell towers on the sides to be over thirty feet tall, but the doors to the stage were only twenty-nine feet. He believes the smaller towers made the set feel unfinished on the sides. Also, "I made the front of the ramp just a little bit too high, so this long thirty-six foot ramp from the orchestra looks almost foreshortened. You have to see it from the boxes to get the full effect. It's a scene that should get an unbelievable amount of applause but it never quite did."

2 ¼" sketch, icon drop.

1

2

FOR ALL THE SUCCESS AND ACCLAIM that New York City Opera brought, the Metropolitan Opera was still pinnacle of the art in the U.S., the Mecca to which singers, directors and designers all aspired. When Lee finally made his mainstage debut at the end of 1974 it was monumental. The frenetic pace of the previous dozen years came to a halt as Lee devoted the next eighteen months to *Boris Godunov.*

BORIS GODUNOV

Lee had first encountered Modest Mussorgsky's opera in his season with San Francisco Opera, and then again when he designed a relatively small production with the Baltimore Civic Opera Company in 1967. *Boris* is the most well-known opera from the Russian repertoire and a major undertaking for any company. The Met had presented the American premiere in 1913, sung in Italian and conducted by Arturo Toscanini, using the Nikolai Rimsky-Korsakov orchestrations. That production, based on Serge Diaghilev's Paris production of 1908, would remain in the Met's repertoire for more than half a century. In the 1950s the Met introduced a new orchestration by Karol Rathaus and switched to an English libretto, but the physical production remained largely that of 1913. So the new production in 1974, in Russian, with Mussorgsky's orchestrations (a complicated matter since Mussorgsky made two distinct versions), was a momentous event in the opera world. It was staged by German director August Everding, who had made his Met debut in 1971 with *Tristan und Isolde.*

General manager Schuyler Chapin, who was trying to give the Met a more American identity, insisted on an American designer. Everding had not worked with any Americans previously, although he and Lee had met in 1969 when Lee and Capobianco staged *Giulio Cesare* at the Hamburg State Opera, and he asked to interview several designers, including Lee, Donald Oenslager and Robert O'Hearn. Lee met with Everding shortly before going to the Soviet Union with Arena Stage, and he proposed Russian icons as a dominant visual motif. "I thought, if you're the tsar and you are born into an environment with all these saints and whatever looking at you constantly, aren't you going to have a bad conscience, whether you have done anything or not?"

While in the Soviet Union Lee was surprised to discover the degree to which brick factored as a primary component of so many of the Kremlin's buildings. But the trip came and went, and there was still no word from the Met. Finally Everding, who could not make up his mind, asked for a scene from each candidate for his consideration—a request that all three refused. "This is not an audition," Lee explains. "It is not like you go and sing a tune from *South Pacific*. Designing has to be collaborative and evolve through discussions and give-and-take over time. And especially with something like *Boris*, how can you just design one scene?" Everding apparently accepted this argument and eventually settled on Lee because, as he described in a later interview, the opera "must be realistic, but without realistic sets.... I chose Ming Cho Lee as the designer because he is very good at making skeletons that hint at places and situations. He knows how to abbreviate and I know how to fill up a stage" (*New Yorker,* January 6, 1975). Chapin's concern was solely smooth, uninterrupted movement from scene to scene—no long scene changes. "This shows you the creativity of the American intendant," Lee remarks sardonically.

Nonetheless, he successfully met Chapin's challenge, taking advantage of the Met's famous wagons that allow entire sets to slide onstage as the previous one glides off. Reviewers seemed to view this as a noteworthy achievement: "[Lee] has worked up a semi-realistic set capable of fast scene changes. There was almost no wait last night as scene succeeded scene" (*New York Times,* December 17, 1974). Lee's true accomplishment, however, was to combine selective realism and heightened theatricality to create a powerfully imagistic set that established a believable atmosphere without total illusionism.

The first thing Lee designed was the icon drop, which remained throughout all the scenes—a constant presence that, in accordance with Lee's view, stood in judgment of the tsar and everyone on the stage and perhaps in the audience as well. A scrim in front of the drop filtered light onto the icons, bringing the faces to life with "softly iridescent color fusions" (*New York Post,* December 12, 1975). There was also a front scrim made of opera net—a fabric as transparent as bobbinet but stronger, available only from Germany at that time. The front scrim, which was painted in the same pattern as the icon drop, but without the faces or icons, remained through the first scene and was brought in for a few other scenes including Boris's study, the inn and St. Basil's Cathedral. It provided a softer or more mystical quality for those scenes, and of course when lit from the front to become opaque, helped mask the scene changes.

Boris Godunov

3–6 Production photographs of, from top, the exterior of the Novodievichy Monastery, where the crowd begs Boris to become tsar; the inn; Boris's study; and the exterior of St. Basil's Cathedral.

3

4

5

6

7

8

9

10

Boris Godunov

7 Production photograph, Marina's boudoir in Sandomir Castle.

8 Production photograph, garden of Sandomir Castle. Lee created a long staircase with three landings, each with a fountain. Everding insisted that the fountains have running water but the water made noise, so they were sometimes shut off in the quieter moments. The foliage was constructed from what Lee calls mosaic plates. "I was stealing from Boris Aronson. The plates stagger so they create a circle that creates a sense of foliage." *New Yorker* critic Andrew Porter described it as "an airy Cubist evocation of trees" (December 30, 1974).

9 ½" model, exterior of St. Basil's Cathedral. A mirror image of sorts of the Novodievichy Monastery scene.

10 Production photograph, throne room. "It's been traditional operatic staging for *every* Boris, from Chaliapin on, to fall down the staircase. That's because he dies while sitting on a throne, which should be elevated. I told Everding that every Boris falls, so should we pad the staircase? He said no, that the Met's Boris, Martti Talvela, wouldn't want to fall, that he was so good he could do it without falling. We left out the padding and then, at rehearsals, Talvela said, 'What do you mean I'm not going to fall?' So we rebuilt the staircase *with* padding" (*New York Times*, March 23, 1975).

11

11 ***I Puritani***, Metropolitan Opera, 1976, ½" sketch of act 1, scene 3 that was sold as a print by the Opera Guild.

In almost all the previous operas he had designed, Lee had employed a unit set; this was the first time he could create such a diversity of visual environments with substantially different ground plans for each of the opera's ten scenes. He exploited the possibilities for contrasting textures and color to create dramatic tension, a quality noted by *Time* magazine critic William Bender. "Lee's contrasts are myriad. The rough outer walls of Moscow do not prepare one for the tapestried, iconic splendor of the Kremlin rooms. After the gold be-crossed minarets of old Russia, the Renaissance fashion (all blues and whites) of an already Westernized Poland is breathtaking in its surprise" (December 30, 1974).

In a sense, Lee was able to accomplish with *Boris* what had eluded him in the Broadway musicals—a large-scale multi-scene show that flowed almost cinematically. Of course, he had the advantages vastly greater resources—not to mention Mussorgsky's music and a libretto based on Pushkin. This was not a work doomed to close in one night. Perhaps the most striking change was his use of color—still subtle by some standards but perhaps Lee's boldest use yet. The color, particularly red, played a dramatic role and worked as a visual complement to the music. Similarly, the varying textures of each scene emerged logically and powerfully as integral to the opera. The emblematic background was not merely ornamental or atmospheric as it was in, say, the Delacorte *Richard III* or the Mark Taper Forum *Henry IV.* It served a crucial thematic purpose. The production also demonstrated what Lee could accomplish with a strong director. The production remained in the repertoire for thirty years, and when a new production was mounted in 2010 there were those who lamented the loss of Lee's sets.

I PURITANI

Following this exhaustive endeavor Lee took a yearlong break from opera, other than remounting *Idomeneo* at City Opera. But he then did three productions at the Met in fairly rapid succession: Vincenzo Bellini's *I Puritani* and Richard Wagner's *Lohengrin,* both in 1976, and Donizetti's *La Favorita* in 1978. *I Puritani,* in its first Met revival since 1918, was overseen by the Italian theatre and film director Sandro Sequi. Initially, Pier Luigi Pizzi was slated to design, but he quit and Lee was brought in with only eight or nine months to create the design—more than sufficient in the world of theatre, but a short time in opera where plans are often made years in advance—and he was already working on *Lohengrin* with Everding. Given the nature of his

THE GHOST OF JO MIELZINER

On March 15, 1976, Jo Mielziner died in a taxi on the way back to his studio at the Dakota following a visit to his doctor. Betsy immediately went to the studio to help Jo's secretary, Phyllis Malinow, make arrangements. At the funeral service, Ming and Betsy functioned as unofficial hosts, and they were later part of a small group who cast his ashes into the New York harbor from the Staten Island Ferry.[1]

Mielziner had been working on a new musical, *The Baker's Wife*, based on the 1938 Marcel Pagnol film *La Femme du Boulanger*, produced by David Merrick, one of the last of the legendary Broadway impresarios. When Merrick asked Lee to take over the show, Lee insisted on being listed only as associate designer with the final third of the contractual payment going to Mielziner's estate. **"I insisted that Merrick pay to continue using the three assistants at Jo's studio. And I said that I must keep Jo's secretary, because none of us can answer all the phones, and there is still Jo's library to be put together. Then I had a fight with Eddie Kook [the executor of Mielziner's estate] who said that I was ruining the estate by keeping the studio open. But Eddie finally gave in."** Lee continued work on *Lohengrin* at his studio at home in the morning, and went to the Dakota in the afternoon to work on *The Baker's Wife*. He had the assistants make ½" white models, according to Mielziner's practice, and instead of his own watercolors and acrylics, he used Mielziner's cheap poster paints. **"They had a certain quality that made it Jo's,"** he notes.

The day before everything was due at Nolan's scene shop, I went to the Dakota after dinner to finish the elevations. I was by myself painting in Jo's studio. I even used the lighting room to test color. Suddenly I heard someone in the kitchen making tea, or plates clanking. So I went to the kitchen, and I didn't see anyone. I opened the front door to see if there was anyone in the hallway, and there was no one. I went back to the studio and started working, and shortly after that I again heard the plates clinking. I went to the kitchen, I saw no one, went to the hallway, I saw no one, and then I got very scared. I called Betsy and said, "I think I'm being visited by Jo's ghost." And I don't like ghosts, Jo Mielziner or not! It really got in the way of my finishing the painting. I wanted Betsy to come over, but she said no. So I called Larry Miller [Jo's assistant]. I said, "Larry, I don't care what you're doing, you have to come to the studio and sit with me while I finish the damn paint elevation, because I think there is a ghost." Larry came over. All was normal. I finished the thing, and then the next day we got it to the shop.

In Los Angeles the show was plagued by a series of problems. During the technical rehearsal two units crashed into each other. As Lee ran down the aisle to the stage, Merrick said, "I think Jo took the easy way out." The show never made it to New York.

---

work Lee was not an obvious choice to design a romatic opera, but it was the sort of opera he grew up with and he leapt at the chance.

With Joan Sutherland and Luciano Pavarotti in the leads, *I Puritani* was an enormous success. Rather than attempt anything innovative, Lee aimed for what he terms an "old-fashioned but still new look." Somewhat as with *Ariodante* at the Kennedy Center he went for a painterly style. The romanticism of Lee's painting may have been anachronistic for the baroque *Ariodante*, but it was absolutely appropriate for a nineteenth-century bel canto opera. He used J.M.W. Turner, the artist he emulated as a student in Shanghai, as inspiration for the sky drops. The sketches themselves were gorgeous, and despite Lee's disdain for "renderings," the Metropolitan Opera Guild made prints that they sold as a fundraiser: $5 unsigned, $25 signed by Lee.

Lee created a proscenium-like structure at the front which framed all the scenes. For the preshow there was a scrim depicting a landscape, and beneath was painted "*I Puritani* by Vincenzo Bellini." The first scene was played behind the scrim, which then flew out. Scrims were also used at the beginning of act two and in the storm scene of act three. The exterior scenes were done as perspective landscapes—the first time in his career Lee had attempted painted perspective scenery (as opposed to painted backdrops). His inexperience using wings and borders in this way led to the perspective of the castle wall on stage right being a bit too forced, so while it looked fine from the center seats, it was distorted from the sides. It also reduced the number of side entrances because anyone entering from far upstage would destroy the perspective illusion. Moreover, it created problems masking the upstage right corner. These complications seemed to go unnoticed by critics, but the response was divided into what might be thought of as traditionalists versus modernists. While German and British opera design by 1976 was increasingly conceptual or abstract, unconventional approaches were still rare in the U.S., at least at the Met. So a decidedly painterly decor that evoked the nineteenth century, done without a trace of irony or as a deliberate quotation, was seen in some quarters as "old and dusty," as Andrew Porter wrote in the *New Yorker* (April 5, 1976), while others, such as *Opera News*, found it to be exquisite and exemplary. In fact, when the opera was broadcast for the Met's weekly radio show, Peter Allen, the announcer, called Lee at home in the midst of the performance to tell him how beautiful he thought the set was. Lee would find himself caught in this cultural divide several times over the next decade.

12

13

14

15

16

17

Lohengrin

Metropolitan Opera, 1976

12 ½" model, act 1 (also used for act 3, scene 2).

13 Production photograph, act 2, scene 1, castle courtyard. "If I had done it ten years later, I probably would have just done a totally flat wall. Instead I put a certain amount of realism into it."

14, 15 ½" model and production photograph, act 2, scene 2, outside the cathedral. "I wanted to do a set that used the Met stage to create a sense of endless distance, which I did not achieve in *Boris*."

16 Production photograph, act 3, scene 1, bridal chamber. Everding suggested the tent, telling Lee this was common practice, but Lee never researched whether or not this was true. The three tapestry hangings behind the tent were added to emphasize that the tent was in an interior space rather than somewhere outdoors, though Lee worried that it made it seem like some of the Delacorte productions.

17 Production photograph, transition to act 3, scene 2. The set is the same for act 1. It struck many observers that the arrangement of the chorus resembled a military tank.

LOHENGRIN

Wieland Wagner had staged a very austere *Lohengrin* for the Met in 1966, but it never found favor with audiences or most critics and was retired after two years. So in 1976 the Met invited Everding to stage a new production. (This new *Lohengrin* was also significant as the first Wagner that James Levine, subsequently considered one of the world's great Wagnerians, conducted at the Met.)

Following on the successes of *Boris Godunov* and *I Puritani*, Lee went into *Lohengrin*, in his words, "a bit cocky." But while he knew the Italian, French and even Russian repertoire intimately, he had almost no knowledge of German opera. "It's not my favorite language," he admits. "I really found a good deal of Wagner kind of tedious." Also, *Lohengrin* dealt with aspects of European history and mythology that were completely unfamiliar to Lee. He notes that when medieval history was covered in his classes at Occidental, his English was still too inadequate to really understand the material. He would ultimately learn English and French history through Shakespeare, but German history remained unknown. "At the end of *Lohengrin*, he finally proclaims, 'I am the son of Parsifal. Lohengrin is my name.' It sounds wonderful in the aria, but I didn't know what Parsifal meant in German culture or where that myth came from." Musically, however, he found *Lohengrin* the most accessible of Wagner's operas. "The music fits the action, there is no need to explain it. It is beautiful and makes me want to express it in visual terms." But for Lee, that expression was Brechtian, intending to resist the beauty of the music while emphasizing the brutality and the demonization of otherness—what he saw as the roots of National Socialism. "I wanted to have a certain amount of ugliness attached to it." Everding was worried that Lee was just being politically correct, but Lee questioned, "What kind of marriage is that that you cannot ask your husband 'What is your name?' I thought that should somehow be reflected in the look of the opera."

Set in tenth-century Antwerp, there are three locales. The greatest challenge is the notorious arrival of Lohengrin on a swan which also reappears in the final scene. To begin with, Lee felt the place where the swan arrived should not be a decorative riverbank, but "a kind of wharf," with a wooden wall, a stone landing and a ramp, as if it were a port, a place of commerce. "The opera feels very, very linear, a kind of endless melody," explains Lee, and this inspired a design in the form of a loop or circle that could suggest a journey. There was a curved cyc made of scrim painted with clouds with a second scrim painted a deeper blue about six feet behind that. The end result, Lee thinks, looked too much like a watercolor painting which did not have the desired clarity.

The brutality that Lee sought was achieved most overtly in the second act, set outside the fortress. Lee designed a massive flat stone wall with only two openings: a balcony for Elsa and a door for soldiers and wedding guests. It spanned the stage and was almost overwhelming in its starkness; the two small openings suggested the insignificance of the individuals against the monumentality of this imposing edifice.

As the musical fanfare marking the transition to the next scene began, the wall parted and the two halves were pulled off to stage left and right, revealing the upstage stair unit, low wall and pillars of the cathedral exterior, as two side stairs were pushed into place and the chorus descended from all three stair units. This was done behind a scrim, and although the transition was achieved manually, critics commented on the beauty of the seemingly choreographed and stately convergence of scenery.

The second scene, outside the cathedral, accentuated depth and verticality, again seemingly dwarfing the performers through architecture. The long stairs and platform receding into the upstage darkness was an appropriately atmospheric echo and visual amplification of the processions within the scene. Lee acknowledged that he was once more "stealing" from *Don Rodrigo* with the columns and the floating figure—though only a solitary one this time. The emphatic diagonals of the set, with the fragmentary wall and the ramp, was not new in itself—it was there in *Boris*, for example—but the cascade of steps ascending mysteriously into a void and the wall that was part of no visible building created an eerie disembodied quality. The realism of the scenic textures combined with surrealism of the ground plan disturbed the more literalist critics. Irving Kolodin of the *Saturday Review*, who was otherwise enthusiastic about both the direction and scenography, complained that "the settings and direction came to a crisis of confusion in the last scene of act two, where Elsa and a crowd of attendants are directing their steps toward the Münster (cathedral), where she will marry Lohengrin. The procession persisted in doubling back to center stage, rather than proceeding to its objective. That might have been because there was no Münster visible to me, hence no objective" (January 8, 1977).

In a certain sense, the whole tone of the opera is determined by

18

18 ***Attila***, Lyric Opera of Chicago, 1980, sketch, act 1, scene 1.

19, 20 ***Il Trovatore***, Houston Grand Opera, 1980, ¼" models for gypsy camp (top) and convent.

21, 22 ***La Donna del Lago***, Houston Grand Opera, 1981, ⅛" sketches for Loch Katrine and ruins. The romanticism of the earlier *I Puritani* is even more apparent here, revealing an aesthetic not often associated with Lee's designs.

19

20

the way in which the swan is handled. It was agreed that a literal swan would be embarrassing, but if they went abstract, what was an abstract swan? Lee had been impressed by a German production designed by Rudolf Heinrich in which the swan was a projection within a halo of light, but he and Everding wanted something more concrete. Lee devised an abstract sculpture of metallic rods bathed in light, a bit like a small version of the Richard Lippold sculpture hanging in Avery Fisher Hall at Lincoln Center. The staging was complicated by a request from conductor James Levine. In most productions Lohengrin rides in on the swan from upstage, but Levine wanted it to come from the side. By placing a bank of reeds downstage, about three feet high, Lee was able to suggest the river flowing across the front of the stage. The swan sculpture followed a path through the reeds and Lohengrin rose up through a trap in the stage floor (several critics unkindly compared it to the surfacing of a submarine). Initially the lighting was being handled by the staff electrician, a not uncommon practice even in the mid-seventies, but it was soon evident that he did not know how to achieve the lighting effect Lee was after for Lohengrin's entrance, and he was replaced by Gil Hemsley, one of the great opera lighting designers. "It was such a relief," says Lee, "that suddenly you're at the Met and talking to a real lighting designer." Lee and Everding had timed the music for Lohengrin's entrance, about two and a half minutes. Hemsley, according to Lee, said, "Well, that is like a two-minute orgasm," and went on to create a lighting effect that built in intensity through that period of time. Whatever success this achieved, however, it did not really solve the issue of depicting the swan, which left Lee with a sense of disappointment that he had not felt with the previous two operas. (For the 1984 revival, Plácido Domingo, who took over the title role, insisted on reverting to the traditional upstage entrance.)

21

22

TURANDOT

Following *La Favorita*, which was brought to the Met from San Francisco Opera in 1978, Lee did a spate of operas around the country: *Boris Godunov* at Lyric Opera of Chicago, an adaptation of the Met production; *Attila*, a co-production of Lyric Opera of Chicago, San Diego Opera and City Opera; *Il Trovatore* and *La Donna del Lago* at Houston Grand Opera; *Madama Butterfly* in Santiago, Chile; his final two productions at Juilliard, Roger Sessions's *Montezuma* and Bellini's *I Capuleti e i Montecchi* [see chapter 12]; his final City Opera production, Gluck's *Alceste*; and *Turandot*, his reunion with Sarah Caldwell at the Opera Company of Boston.

Lee had always wanted to do Puccini's *Turandot*, so despite his previous experience with Sarah Caldwell on *Madama Butterfly* he accepted her offer. Caldwell had been traveling to China to study opera and music traditions there and intended to use Chinese costumes made by members of the Central Opera Theater in Beijing. Lee accompanied her on one of these trips to meet with the Chinese designers—and was able, for the first time, to bring Betsy with him. Lee had returned to China in 1978 while working on Astor Court for the Metropolitan Museum of Art, and then in 1981 as part of a cultural exchange with, among others, writer Susan Sontag, sculptor George Segal and filmmaker Robert M. Young. But this would be Betsy's first trip to China and her first meeting with the Lee family in Shanghai.

While in China they were taken to *La Bohème* performed by the graduates of the Academy of Opera. "I must confess," says Lee,

> **I never experienced such a performance of *La Bohème*. It was a shabby little auditorium, kids running around the room, cracking watermelon seeds, everyone was so noisy. On the stage were four standing microphones in front of the singers and the sloppiest scenery. The whole set was made of canvas. There was no coordination between the orchestra and the singers. The production was just...all you can say is really terrible. Then came act three and it caught the audience's attention and it became kind of quiet. You could suddenly hear the tenor, who was singing well, and the soprano, the baritone and the orchestra. And I realized that this must have been the kind of performance I saw as a kid in Shanghai. And I could not stop crying. *Bohème* just took over.**

Even before the trip Lee had decided to set *Turandot* in Beijing. He designed a "dark version" of Tiananmen Square and a fairly detailed and realistic Forbidden City. "I probably should have painted the whole thing blood red, but that was before my really jumping over the fence," he notes. But the shop that Caldwell was using could not build the set as Lee designed it, and he scaled it back. At the tech rehearsal the second act was only half finished, the third act was totally unpainted and the lighting designer quit. When Lee asked Caldwell what to do, she told him not to worry about it. "I was trying to light the second act, but the stagehands weren't there. I managed to cut some of the really embarrassing things so it looked somewhat decent. I don't even remember what the third act looked like. I think I just put a blue drop in front and went out and had a drink. I was so upset because I always thought that I should be the person who does a *Turandot*, but it turned out to be something that I'm so ashamed of."

A reviewer from the *New York Times* came to the dress rehearsal and Lee told him that third act was unfinished, and that was mentioned in the otherwise mostly positive review. The staff was furious with Lee for saying anything to the critic, but in her memoir Caldwell mentions none of this. She discusses the comedy of errors involved in getting the Chinese designers to the U.S., but otherwise notes that "*Turandot* was a smash hit. The reviews were ecstatic."[2]

23

24

25

23–25 ***Alceste***, New York City Opera, 1982, ⅛" sketches and production photograph. Lee was aiming for a formal classicism (he describes Gluck as a "clean" composer), and came up with a box-within-a-box motif. He designed a flat wall for the opening and closing scenes, but unlike the powerful wall in *Lohengrin*, the tight budgets of City Opera meant he had to settle for a drop. He had hoped that slashes of light—Gil Hemsley was the lighting designer—would add the necessary dramatic power, but that only emphasized the wrinkles in the drop, which was never stretched taut enough. The formalism was undercut by Lee's tendency toward romanticism. "I think my Mielziner influence got in the way," is how he puts it. Because Lee approaches his work through sketching, there are rarely straight edges or strong geometric lines in his designs. "If I had actually sketched with a straight edge, absolutely straight, then it may have had real power."

26

27

26, 27 ***Turandot***, Opera Company of Boston, 1983, sketches for act 1 (top) and act 2, scene 2, set in Tiananmen Square and the Forbidden City.

CHAPTER 12

The Monumental and the Minuscule—from K2 to the Kremlin 1982–85

1 ***Khovanshchina***, Metropolitan Opera, 1985, production photograph of the final scene. When "the Old Believers immolate themselves in their rickety two-story wooden church, [it] is a bloodcurdling image that few will soon forget," Peter G. Davis wrote in *New York Magazine*, one of the few positive critical comments the set received (October 25, 1985).

1

BEGINNING IN THE 1980s there was a discernable change in Lee's designs. The pipes and scaffolding, the wood planks and erosion cloth, collage—all seemed increasingly dated and clichéd. It was a modernist vocabulary in a postmodern world. What was once daringly new had become commonplace. Lee began to investigate new approaches, and this took him in seemingly opposite directions, though really more like two sides of the same coin. On the one hand he explored a heightened or superrealism in which he created work so detailed and so illusionistic that the audience could forget it was looking at a set. This could be interpreted as a scenographic equivalent of photorealism, which had emerged in the art of the 1970s, although that was not Lee's inspiration. The other direction, ultimately more interesting for him, rejected the coherence, logic, scale, texture and color of realism. This tendency was more self-consciously inspired by postmodern design, but it was also instigated by his work on a pair of small Off-Broadway plays written in the style of magic realism.

SUPERREALISM AND *K2*

Lee had toyed with extreme naturalism before, of course. It could be seen in the houses of *Wedding Band* at the Public Theater as early as 1972; the mountaintop for *The Ascent of Mt. Fuji* at Arena Stage in 1975, with its rocky surface and foliage; and the sunken gazebo for *Don Juan* in 1979, which could have been transplanted into a real garden. But for sheer superrealism, nothing could match the spectacular mountainside of *K2*.

Written by Patrick Meyers and directed by Jacques Levy, *K2* originated at Arena Stage in 1982, presented in the proscenium Kreeger Theatre. The plot was simple: two mountain climbers are trapped on a ledge 1,250 feet below the summit of K2, the second tallest mountain in the world. An avalanche has left one of them with a broken leg and caused the loss of most of their provisions. The only way for both of them to get down to the next ledge and possible rescue is to retrieve a section of rope on a ledge a couple hundred feet above them. Much of the dialogue is taken up with metaphysical discussions of life and death, but the appeal of the play is old-fashioned melodrama replete with spectacle, as the able-bodied climber attempts to scale the mountain to retrieve the rope. During the course of ninety minutes there is another avalanche; a climber falls, plummeting past the ledge; items are thrown or fall from the ledge into a seemingly bottomless chasm. In order for the play to succeed, the spectators must believe that they are viewing the sheer face of a mountain on which the climbers are trapped. Never for an instant can the audience remember that the climbers' perch is merely a few feet above a stage.

Lee's first impulse was to go for abstraction, but Levy insisted—quite rightly, Lee agrees—that it had to be utterly realistic. As always, he began by making some sketches, but it quickly became apparent that in this instance there was not much to sketch. He abandoned the sketches and went directly for a ¼" model. The mountain was carved out of Styrofoam blocks that were then assembled onto a wooden framework. To create the look of ice, the set was covered with tissue paper, then coated with acrylic paints to give it a glaze. Lee took inspiration from a visit to the Columbia Icefield while at the Banff Centre in Canada. "I discovered that when you stand on the ice field the ice is translucent, and sometimes you can see the crevices through the ice. It's not just a solid piece of ice, there is a certain depth." To achieve this effect the tissue paper was stretched over gaps to suggest looking through ice into crevices. Lee also turned to his training in Chinese painting to create the striations of the rock and the ice—even going up in a cherry picker to do some of the painting himself ("Scared the hell out of me!"). The sections on which the actors climbed—using real climbing gear such as pitons driven into the set—were reinforced with dense foam rubber, and those sections had to be touched up every night and replaced every week.

Lee and Levy decided not to use a front curtain, thus allowing the audience to contemplate the set during the preshow. The avalanche was created by enormous quantities of Styrofoam snow cascading from the grid along with a carefully composed soundscape by Jay Rosenberg and fog rising from the pit. The front of the ledge was hinged and a pin was pulled so that it would collapse, as if a section of ice had broken off. Even the temperature in the theatre was kept lower than usual so that the audience would feel cold. "It was really frightening," says Lee, and critics agreed. Lee gives a great deal of credit to the technical director David Glenn and master carpenter Jim Glendinning, who worked out the mountain's elaborate mechanics.

The most eloquent description of the set came from *New York Times* critic Frank Rich in his review of the Broadway production, which was scenically identical to that in Washington.

> **This scenic wonder is astounding.... What faces us is an enormous wall of simulated ice ascending from beneath stage level clear up**

2

3

4

K2
Arena Stage, 1982

2 Production photograph. Note the climber at the upper left. A crucial aspect was getting the right distance between the mountain and the auditorium. "It should be far enough from the edge that you don't feel like the actors can just jump and land in the theatre," explains Lee. "And if the ledge is too high up, you can't see a lot of the things that are happening." Lee's sense of proportion and scale served him well. The mountain was forty-three feet high, just two feet shy of the grid, so that the top rose beyond sightlines and the ascending climber could disappear above the stage. The stage floor in front of the set was removed so that objects dropped would plummet out of sight. Netting insured that they would not make a sound when they landed, thereby creating an illusion of unfathomable depth.

3 Photograph of the view from below, giving some sense of the height of the set.

4 Photograph looking down at the ledge (an angle the audience could not have), showing how narrow it was—about four-and-a-half feet.

5

6

7

Traveler in the Dark

Mark Taper Forum, 1985

5, 6 Preliminary sketches showing the house centered and stage left.

7 ⅛" model.

8 At first glance it almost seems like a photograph of an actual house and yard, until you look up and see the stage lights and grid.

beyond the proscenium arch. In its dark, icy shadows, its crevasse-scarred face looms like a prehistoric monster's. And it's not merely a feat of engineering. As designed by Ming Cho Lee and lighted with otherworldly mysteriousness by Allen Lee Hughes, this peak is a stage illusion that shoots past the clouds to arrive at the realm of pure sculpture.... When [the character of] Taylor uses a rope and ice axes to venture precariously up the mountain, finally rising above our view, the tension is so strong we forget we're in a theatre. When catastrophes occur—not the least of them another avalanche—we cringe with vicarious fright (March 31, 1983).

The show moved to Broadway, but not without some personnel issues. The playwright did not get along with Levy and insisted on a new director, Terry Schreiber. Lee actually found himself in a good bargaining position. He had a strong contract and the show could not transfer without his set. He tried to bargain for Levy to remain with the show, and when that was not possible he at least succeeded in getting Levy a percentage of the director's fee. He also negotiated a better fee for Arena Stage as the original producer. The set was cut apart and shipped to New York. The only alteration was the addition, at Schreiber's request, of a few more paths for the actor who climbed up. After the mountain was installed Lee realized that it was fifteen inches too far stage right, a distance that would probably not be noticed by almost anyone else, but one that kept Lee awake at night. As a result, the mountain became too centered in Lee's estimation and the audience saw a little too much of it and not enough of the sky. "It's better if it's either to one side or the other," he states. "If it's dead center it divides the stage in two and you don't see the middle." One major practical issue was the avalanche. The snow that hit the apron bounced into the first rows of the orchestra. A Plexiglas barrier was set up and seating was eliminated in the first three rows.

The most controversial change, however, was the introduction of a front curtain. At the start of the Broadway production the curtain rose very slowly, revealing the seemingly never-ending mountain inch by inch—"like a striptease," according to Rich, who observed that "the audience seems to stop breathing." This guaranteed applause for Lee, and no doubt contributed to his Tony, but he vehemently objected because he believed it would overwhelm the audience. "I said, 'Nobody will hear the first ten minutes of dialogue. It will *kill* the show.'" And this was essentially Rich's analysis: "Mr. Lee's mountain is so overpowering that the play itself may be a third through its ninety-five intermissionless minutes before you even

8

begin to start listening to the two characters trapped on a narrow ledge halfway up the ice" (March 31, 1983).

When Lee received the Tony Award that season, the applause from the theatre community seemed to acknowledge not only the spectacular production, but also what he had accomplished in the previous twenty-some years. But rather than leading to a revival of his Broadway career, it turned out to be a kind of swan song. Lee designed a poorly received revival of *The Glass Menagerie* on Broadway later that year, and three years later Emily Mann's *Execution of Justice* came to Broadway following productions at Arena and the Guthrie Theater. He never worked on Broadway after that.

An equally realistic, though certainly less monumental, example of superrealism came two years after *K2*, with Marsha Norman's *Traveler in the Dark* at Los Angeles's Mark Taper Forum, directed by Gordon Davidson. The play concerns the return of a doctor and his wife and child to an old farmhouse where the doctor's aging father still lives. Lee created the exterior of a farmhouse sitting on top of a gentle rise, surrounded by trees, the ground covered with autumn leaves. Once again, it was the set that captivated the critics.

The first thing you see on entering the Mark Taper Forum for *Traveler in the Dark* is Ming Cho Lee's set, and it is so true that it takes your breath away. An old frame house with porch steps slightly askew, a stand of bare trees, a floor of dead leaves, a ring of stones that used to be a fence.... Where are we? New Hampshire? Kentucky? Somewhere out in the country, anyway, in late fall or early spring. (The leaves would be wet underneath if we could touch them.) If this is a farm, the forest is ready to take it back. You wouldn't be surprised if a squirrel ran by (Dan Sullivan, *Los Angeles Times*, January 25, 1985).

The playwright wasn't mentioned until the fourth paragraph.

Though Norman had not specified the precise locale or season, Lee felt it was definitely not New England, but perhaps the Midwest. When Davidson and Lee asked Norman about the time of year, she said she envisioned the air filled with the sound of people walking on fallen leaves. That was all Lee needed to begin sketching. Because of the peculiar treadmill at the rear of the Taper stage, it is difficult to place scenery too far upstage, so the tendency is to put large scenic units toward the center. But Davidson felt that the house needed to be to one side, and it is precisely that asymmetry that instills the set with an even greater sense of realism.

At the center of the thrust stage was a ring of stones—Lee used real stones—where the doctor used to play as a child, and where his son now finds the old toys. It is quite literally at the center of the play both physically and thematically. The hill, as in *The Ascent of Mt. Fuji*, was created from Styrofoam and spray foam. Lee used real leaves, but this being Los Angeles, only green leaves were available, so they were dyed autumn colors. However, as the actors walked through the leaves the paint would come off, exposing the bright green underneath, necessitating touch ups after each performance. As for the trees, "I decided to take a chance—they are actually no deeper than six inches, so it's all almost flat cut outs with a little build out." But they were sufficiently far upstage that this would not be perceived by the audience. The house was designed to look as if it were sagging a bit, and the kitchen could be seen through the window, complete with cabinets. "There is not a place that doesn't feel like you're actually living in the environment," says Lee. Everyone working on the show began to treat the set as a real place. When costumes were washed they would be hung on a line onstage to dry; the boy playing the child would play with the toys in the stone ring when not rehearsing; and even Lee enjoyed sitting at the picnic table during breaks.

Comparing *K2* and *Traveler* Lee says that he felt that he had "kind of cheated" with *K2* because "it is really the novelty of seeing people actually climbing that high on the stage that gave it a breathtaking effect. I really didn't do a thing! *Traveler* went through a process. *K2* felt scenic, whereas *Traveler* felt real. It felt like Andrew Wyeth." This strikes at the heart of Lee's understanding of design. *Traveler in the Dark* is not a significantly better play than *K2* as a work of dramatic literature, but in order to arrive at the design Lee had to have an understanding of the characters, their lives and relationships. He needed to know the place, the season, the sounds. *K2* "merely" required him to recreate the side of a mountain. The fact that it was, in actuality, a monumental sculpture, that every crevice was carefully crafted to give the translucency of ice, that the set induced terror in the audience, was irrelevant. To him it was gimmickry, not design.

TOWARD THE POSTMODERN AND MAGIC REALISM

In the early 1980s Lee was becoming aware of postmodern trends in design evident particularly in the work of British colleagues and in much West German and French production, but increasingly in the U.S. as well. While postmodern design is not easily characterized because it is, almost by definition, typified by an inconsistency of style, it nonetheless has certain recurring characteristics: discordance, ugliness, the juxtaposition of styles and periods, incongruous elements and external references though quotation or appropriation. All this created a very intentional lack of unity among the visual elements, all done, of course, with a sense of irony. Hints of this could be seen in Lee's final production for the Juilliard American Opera Center in 1983, Bellini's *I Capuleti e i Montecchi*, adapted from an earlier opera by Nicola Vaccai called *Giuletta e Romeo*, itself taken from Italian sources rather than Shakespeare.

If one of the characteristic traits of postmodernism is the use of quotation or appropriation, what happens if it is the quotation itself that is then appropriated? This is what Lee did in *I Capuleti e i Montecchi*. Director Ian Strasfogel wanted to set it in the Italian Renaissance, but Lee was not interested in designing what would inevitably be another functional, historically accurate period design. So he did something cleverly postmodern. He created a courtyard that was essentially a copy of the lobby of Philip Johnson's AT&T Building (now the Sony Building), then under construction. The Johnson lobby was a postmodern quotation of neoclassical architecture so Lee's design was, in reality, a quotation of a quotation.

Lee's design for John Osborne's *The Entertainer* at the Guthrie Theater in Minneapolis later that year, with its spaciousness and oversized statues, could have been read as surrealistic, postmodern or—if viewed out of the context of performance—a hint of magic realism. The play, about a music hall performer whose career is on the wane, alternates locales between the entertainer's home and the music hall. Lee designed a virtually bare stage that served as both living room and music hall. There were footlights along the front, mid-century English parlor furniture and then two oversized statues—"icons that kind of say England or British Empire," Lee explains—that give the whole set an air of unreality. All was set against the bare brick wall of the theatre—an illusion since the Guthrie's back wall was actually cinder block.

The first production for which Lee made a very conscious effort to move away from naturalism and modernism came a year after *K2* at a very small Off-Broadway theatre, Intar, for a double bill of *Dog Lady* and *The Cuban Swimmer* by Milcha Sanchez-Scott. Intar Theatre was founded in 1966, dedicated to developing and

9

10

9 ***I Capuleti e i Montecchi***, Juilliard American Opera Center, 1983, production photograph, act 1, scene 1. By copying the AT&T lobby, Lee could provide an Italianate arcade as well as soaring verticality—pierced by the circular window above the arches taken directly from Johnson—while creating an ironic distance.

10 ***The Entertainer***, Guthrie Theater, 1983, photograph.

11 ***Dog Lady***, Intar, 1984, ½" model. "Instead of my usual little cloudy Mielziner watercolor, I painted it in almost flat colors, except for the house with the scrim that has a little bit of aging. I have vivid images of that neighborhood from when I was at Oxy. I remember those one-story houses. Without being absolutely, totally realistic, I was able to capture a sense of Los Angeles that

11

showcasing Latino artists, and at this time occupied a theatre with a tiny stage a mere twenty-two feet wide on Theatre Row on Forty-Second Street. Lee had agreed to do the design as a favor to Intar's artistic director, Max Ferra, with whom he had served on the theatre panel for the New York State Council on the Arts. *Dog Lady,* set in the Los Angeles barrio, was a piece of magic realism in which a runner is given a potion to make her run faster, but it causes her to run on all fours like an animal. Lee designed the neighborhood street in sharp perspective. "I decided you don't need logic to design a set and I thought it would be wonderful if the people entering upstage were twice as big as the house. And then when they arrive in front they are in the right proportion." The effect was heightened by having the actors walk slower as they moved upstage, and vice versa.

The second play takes place entirely in the ocean—a girl is swimming an endurance race from Long Beach to Santa Catalina Island, followed by her family in a boat. Lee created a series of ground row cutouts of waves. The boat was also a flat cutout on a platform, and the swimmer was lying on a platform hidden behind the waves. Throughout the entire show she did a swimming motion with her arms. There was a small helicopter seen through a translucent part of the backdrop. Once again the reviews focused on the scenography. Herbert Mitgang in the *New York Times* declared, "The sets designed by Ming Cho Lee are the hit of the evening.... Through the artistic techniques of perspective, suggestion and just plain legerdemain... Mr. Lee creates nothing less than a stretch of the Pacific Ocean, a tramp boat and a helicopter. The audience can almost feel the resisting tides and the California oil slick that are represented by a watery-blue floor and curtain." (May 10, 1984).

Despite his pride in the production, it was undeniably a step down from Broadway. While Lee never shortchanged a production because of venue or budget, the circumstances were appallingly unprofessional. There were problems with the shop, so Lee paid his assistants extra to build the set themselves and then carry it ten blocks from the shop to the theatre, and this consumed all of his minimal fee. He had to resort to threats in order for the costume designer to be paid. These were not the conditions one would expect for someone who had designed at the Metropolitan Opera and won a Tony on Broadway, but Lee rarely turned down a job.

KHOVANSHCHINA

Having consciously experimented with physical disparities of size, nonrealistic color and perspective, Lee expanded upon this on a grand scale with the Met production of *Khovanshchina* in 1985, his final work there. Like *Boris Godunov, Khovanshchina* (also by Mussorgsky and again directed by August Everding) dealt with a moment in Russian history, in this case the Streltsy Uprising of 1682 led by Prince Ivan Khovansky. The story is dense and complex and Lee and others argued for supertitles to help the audience follow the convoluted plot, but in 1985 this was still forbidden at the Met.

This was Lee's most deliberate effort to alter his approach to design. The result was not as radical as his 1964 *Electra,* if for no other reason than by this point designers such as John Conklin (who did the costumes for this production), Eugene Lee and a young George Tsypin were already pushing scenography into postmodern realms. But Lee still feels that *Khovanshchina* was a breakthrough for him. He was seeking a move toward a theatricality not confined by either sculptural aesthetics or the uniform logic of realism.

I didn't want to move back into the Shakespeare Delacorte abstract sculpture thing. That didn't fit the opera anyway. I was trying to move away from *Boris*, which had very realistic elements within an otherwise abstract, iconic design. Given the music and the story, I wanted to have a sense of brutality. I wanted the first act to be very big, and the small scenes to be very, very small—to be completely closed in. So right away, I was deliberately breaking a uniform scale of design. Then, I didn't want to lose the architecture of the Kremlin, but I also didn't want to get stuck illustrating it with real color. I wanted the white to be absolutely white, the black to be black. I wanted to go for the extreme. Instead of a lot of details and a lot of buildings, it should be concentrated onto one thing. I think I was struggling to have a postmodern look without fully understanding what postmodernism really was. But I was trying to capture the sense that postmodernism doesn't need to be logical. I ended up having a white box—I had actually never used a white box before—and the white box is really a sky, but with wooden doors so people are coming through the sky. That is as postmodern as I can ever get.

New productions were often funded by private or corporate donors but because *Khovanshchina* was such an unknown opera at the time, the Met was having difficulty finding adequate financial support. Despite an initial estimated cost of $1.5 to $2 million, it was ultimately budgeted at a mere $750,000—modest for the Met even then—and there was pressure to cut one or more scenes, but this seemed impossible within the complex narrative. Music director James Levine advised Lee to think about where the opera needed to wind up, what the final impression should be, and work backward from there. The immolation scene at the end of the opera was the coup de grâce and therefore had to be the most spectacular, but the audience would be more forgiving of simpler scenographic solutions at the beginning. Lee was working on *Traveler in the Dark* concurrently, and one day he was sitting by the stage door of the Taper working on *Khovanshchina*. "I sat at the doorman's desk with a little phone message pad, and I was drawing the scene where they arrest Golitsyn in St. Basil's Square [act four, scene two]. As I was drawing St. Basil's Cathedral with a red colored pencil I realized that it was basically the same scene as act one, which is set in Red Square just around the corner from St. Basil's. Why not use St. Basil's for both? In one stroke I cut out two big architectural elements."

The design for *Khovanshchina* was a landmark for Lee. It allowed him to approach space, scale, color and even the juxtaposition of realism and theatricality in ways he had never done before. But in a sense he was caught in the midst of an aesthetic and even generational shift. The design was neither the extreme postmodernism that was becoming increasingly common on opera stages around the world, nor was it a traditional historically accurate setting. Most critics were generally hostile to the set—the *New York Times* stated that "Ming Cho Lee's sets varied from starkly economical to plain ugly" (October 16, 1985), and even Peter G. Davis who gave a generally good review to the opera in *New York Magazine*, astonishingly called the sets "minimal" and "only functional." But by the 2012 revival the sets went largely unremarked by most critics.

Lee remains a bit baffled by the negative response. Some of it, of course, came from the traditionalists who balked at anything other than historical accuracy. Some of it Lee attributes to an inherent disjuncture in the opera itself. The overture is lyrical and beautiful, suggesting the sunrise over Red Square and the flowing Moscow River. But in terms of narrative, the night before the first scene the Streltsy Guard has revolted and slaughtered most of Peter's family and retainers. Everding made a deliberate decision to go against the beauty of the overture—which turns dark as the opera begins—and began the production showing the guard loading bodies onto a cart.

Lee also wonders if the response to the set had to do with scale. In *Boris*, he notes, everything was designed for the scale of the stage; much of the scenery was larger than life, which gave it a fairy-tale aura. But in *Khovanshchina* much of the scale is closer to reality—the architecture approached actual size in relation to the performers, which created a kind of realism but, ironically, seemed distorted on the stage. Whereas *Dog Lady* created a consistent world so that the audience understood the rules, with the opera Lee went for an intentional inconsistency of scale and color and decor, though rather subtly. In doing so, perhaps he did not go far enough, and it was not always obvious that the incongruities were intentional. It was a postmodern pastiche, but a somewhat timid one that perplexed the audience.

As it turned out, this was not only Lee's final opera for the Met, it was, for all intents and purposes, his final major opera. He had designed *La Donna del Lago* at the Royal Opera in London earlier the same year (recreating the Houston production of 1981) and would create a design for *Le Villi* in 1987 (which was never produced), as well as *Faust* at Opera Colorado in 1990 and *Les Contes d'Hoffmann* in Hong Kong in 1991. But, as with the leap from *K2* to *Dog Lady*, the work was decidedly a diminution. It is ironic, to say the least, that someone whose career was so closely entwined with opera, someone who played a major role in transforming American opera design, should spend the last fourteen years of his professional design career without a single new opera credit. Several of his designs lived on, of course, in revivals, or when his sets were rented or borrowed by other companies, including one instance in which he was able to change an earlier design. When Lotfi Mansouri produced *Attila* at San Francisco Opera in 1991 he used the City Opera sets but asked Lee to make some changes. Lee applied his recent experiments with color, introducing a bright red ground cloth and transforming act one, scene one from a neutral gray to a much more assertive red, "to reflect the energy of early Verdi." But there had been a seismic shift in opera throughout the world that went well beyond bolder use of color. Opera had become the locus for high-concept productions and postmodern design. Within the U.S. that revolution had been made possible in large part by Lee's innovations—but it had moved on, driven by a younger cadre of directors and designers with significantly different sensibilities.

12

13

14

15

16

17

18

Khovanshchina

Metropolitan Opera, 1985

12 ½" model for act 1, St. Basil's Square (Red Square). There was a white ground cloth and white sky cyc and St. Basil's was painted oxblood red and black.

13, 14 Preliminary ½" sketches of the Kremlin on onionskin paper. Not used.

15 Production photograph of act 3, scene 2, St. Basil's Square. One of the elements sacrificed for budgetary reasons was a wooden platform that was to cover much of the stage. Without it, in order to provide two levels—essential for sightlines—there was a trough in front. But since the trough was never explained, it may have confused audiences. "I think the mistake I made was adding the poles which added realism to what was essentially a nonrealistic set."

16 In this early sketch for St. Basil's Square Lee used forced perspective to make the cathedral appear small in the distance. He rejected it because he was afraid it would disappear behind the chorus. But he wonders if this more conventional sense of scale would have resulted in a better response to the set. "I would have been breaking my own rules by using this set, but the moral may be that when the rule is working you should go and break it."

17 Production photograph, act 2, Vasily Golitsyn's study.

18 ½" model, act 4, Ivan Khovansky's chamber—the Red Room.

19 Sketch of the hermitage in the woods.

19

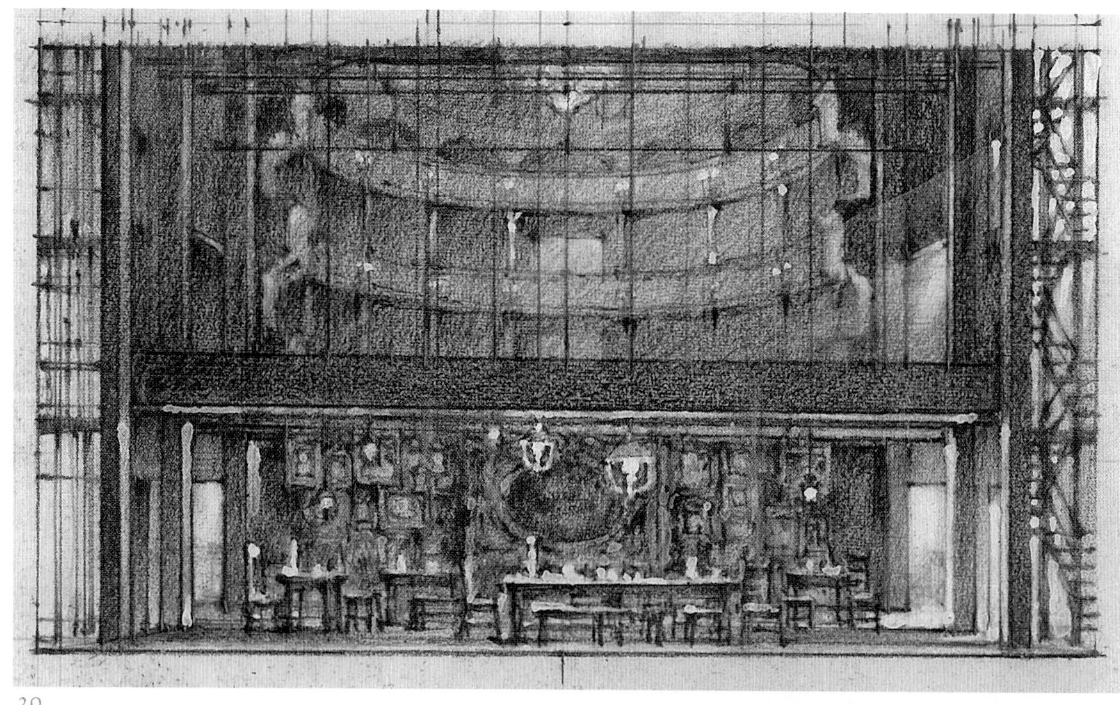

20

21

22

20, 21 ***Les Contes d'Hoffmann***, Hong Kong Cultural Festival, 1991, sketches for the tavern (top) and Antonia scene. Lee created a baroque theatre frame and a backdrop of a baroque opera house auditorium, which could be seen above and behind most of the scenes. The decor for each act filled only the lower half of the stage.

22 ***Faust***, Opera Colorado, 1990, photograph. This was done in the round. "I was looking at medieval paintings by Bruegel and Bosch. On the street you're forever being surrounded by horrible-looking creatures coming out of the ground. Then, when you're at home, you have all these angels with big wings in the rafters. The whole world is nothing but angels and demons. So I designed a round space with a lot of traps and demons, and overhead I had angels flying around. In Dürer's etchings you also see bats, so in addition to the angels I had bats flying overhead.

JOURNEY TO THE CENTER OF THE EARTH

In 1984 David Chambers was appointed artistic director of the Repertory Theatre of St. Louis. For the first full season under his leadership, 1985–86, he commissioned an original work based on Jules Verne's *Journey to the Center of the Earth*. It was intended as a visually spectacular production to be written by Richard Nelson working in close collaboration with Ming Cho Lee, with music by Richard Peaslee. Lee created a series of sketches depicting eighteen scenes, including the descent into the Earth, the underground ocean, and a pair of sea monsters. Given the magnitude of the production it could not be mounted for the 1985–86 season and was postponed to the following year, but was never done. Chambers was replaced as artistic director before the start of the 1986–87 season.

23

23 ***Journey to the Center of the Earth***, Repertory Theatre of St. Louis, 1985–86 (unproduced), sketch. This was a climactic scene depicting the raft and the sea monsters.

CHAPTER 13

New Paths in Dance 1973–2003

1 ***Whispers of Darkness***, National Ballet of Canada, 1974, ½" model. The design was intended to suggest an eclipse.

ALTHOUGH LEE'S REPUTATION lies primarily in classical drama and opera, he designed a considerable number of dances over the course of his career. What makes this body of work unusual is its eclecticism. The sculptural and minimalist scenography for Martha Graham and the Joffrey Ballet in the sixties and early seventies was a natural complement to his theatre and opera design of that period, but in 1973 he began to expand into classical ballet and narrative modern dance. The spatial demands of dance are somewhat different from those of theatre. The designer must create a sculptural space that envelops the dancer while simultaneously foregrounding the body which is the primary medium of expression. Lee struggled a bit with narrative dance and classical ballet, particularly if he was working with more traditionalist choreographers. He created some outstanding designs, such as *Romeo and Juliet* for the Pacific Northwest Ballet, but also some of his more disappointing, including the final dance design of his career, *Swan Lake*. On the other hand, *Nine Songs*, with Cloud Gate Dance Theatre of Taiwan, is among the most stunningly beautiful and effective designs Lee ever created.

COLLABORATIONS WITH TUDOR, GRAHAM AND FELD

Almost simultaneously with *Myth of a Voyage* for Graham in the spring of 1973, Lee was invited to do a production of *Don Juan* choreographed by Lew Christensen for San Francisco Ballet to composer Joaquín Rodrigo's *Concierto de Aranjuez* and *Fantasía para un Gentilhombre*. The design itself is not particularly noteworthy, but it forced Lee to think about dance in a new way. The ballet's literal narrative required detailed scenery, such as the façade of a Spanish house with balconies and a staircase, all for just a ten-minute scene in which Don Juan was chased from one apartment to another. Lee designed more scenery for this one-hour ballet than he had for many operas. This actually embarrassed him and he tried to pare it down, but Christensen insisted on keeping it.

Lee then did two dances with Canadian choreographer Norbert Vesak: a boring—in Lee's words—*Whispers of Darkness* with the National Ballet of Canada, and *In Quest of the Sun*, based loosely on the Peter Shaffer play *The Royal Hunt of the Sun*, at the Royal Winnipeg Ballet. The choreography of the latter was so weak that the scenery overwhelmed the dance and Lee spent the dress rehearsal eliminating much of the decor. (When asked why he worked with Vesak Lee responded, "A job is a job is a job.")

As if to compensate for these frustrating experiences, Lee soon got the opportunity to work with one of the great modern ballet choreographers, Antony Tudor. In fact, Lee would design Tudor's final two ballets, *The Leaves Are Fading* (1975) and *The Tiller in the Fields* (1978), both for American Ballet Theatre. Although *The Leaves Are Fading* had no plot—it was Tudor's first non-narrative ballet—it was nonetheless a very romantic piece, set to music by Dvorak, and embodying a nostalgic look back at youth from an autumnal point in life. Lee's first sketches were, in his words, "a typical kind of abstract, very lean, kind of grayish thing." But Tudor wanted something soft and romantic—something green to suggest the springtime of life. Lee came up with a backdrop of leaves and branches—"leafy wallpaper" as Clive Barnes described it in the *New York Times* (July 19, 1975). Lee had used Chinese-painting-inspired leaves since some of his earliest work, but this time, he felt, "I finally figured out how to do it." Lee found the dance deeply moving: "It was so beautiful that you just cried all the way through."

The Tiller in the Fields also used music by Dvorak and, like the previous dance, was lyrical and romantic in tone, but it resorted to a more narrative structure with a rather strange turn of events. A gypsy woman, danced by the great Gelsey Kirkland, seduces a young peasant boy and in the second half of the dance becomes very visibly pregnant, a rather startling image for a ballet. This time Lee began with a romantic design, but Tudor instead pointed him toward a kind of folk art that Lee found ugly. Nonetheless, he created a pastoral setting in bright colors that the *Washington Post* described as "flat, Chinese-lantern-style shapes and soft, fruity color" (December 14, 1978), while the *New York Times* remarked on the "lollipop trees" (May 7, 1979). Lee now wishes he had "just gone wild with it," but it was hard for him to break through his natural restraint, especially in terms of color.

Lee also had an ongoing—if peculiar—collaboration with Eliot Feld throughout the 1970s and '80s. Feld would ask him to design a dance, but Lee would argue that it didn't need a design. Sometimes Feld would prevail, sometimes Lee would. Their most elaborate production together was a revival of Stravinsky's *Les Noces*, the famous Bronislava Nijinska work from 1923, restaged by the choreographer's daughter, Irina Nijinska. Feld intended simply to reproduce the original Russian designs by Natalia Goncharova, with Lee as supervisory designer; Theoni

2

2 ***Don Juan***, San Francisco Ballet, 1973, 1/4" sketch.

3 ***The Leaves Are Fading***, American Ballet Theatre, 1975, paint elevation for backdrop.

4 ***The Owl and the Pussycat***, Martha Graham, 1978, 1/2" model.

5 ***Tangled Night***, Martha Graham, 1986, 1/2" model.

3

4

5

Aldredge essentially did that with the costumes. But Lee, rather astonishingly, felt that the great Russian artist's designs were ugly. "I think I let my ego get in the way," Lee admits. "I managed to convince Irina Nijinska and Eliot that to really reproduce the original you almost have to reproduce it from the original materials and reconstruct it from canvas flats and all that." Lee's concurrent work on *Khovanshchina*—it would open just a few days after the ballet—influenced his thinking about *Les Noces*, and he decided it would work better with a more folkloric Russian look. It apparently worked. Jack Anderson in the *New York Times* described the decor as "a set of low walls that appear to be made of planks. Convincingly rustic, they are in keeping with the essential spirit of the work" (October 10, 1985). But by the time he finished, Lee realized that perhaps Goncharova was right: "In my attempt to make it very Russian, it wasn't Russian enough. I think it should have been a cubistic painting."

Lee was having much the same experience with Martha Graham. In the mid-seventies she brought him in on a project for which she envisioned a piece of fabric unfolding. "She was doing something with Samuel Barber's music," remembers Lee, "with a song that had something to do with Cleopatra, and I designed a kind of macramé tent thing. She said, 'Good.' And then she called and said, 'I decided not to use the set.' I don't know why." This happened more than once. But in 1978 he designed a work for Graham to be danced to the children's poem "The Owl and the Pussycat," narrated by Liza Minelli. Graham asked for a sailboat-type structure and Lee created an elegant yet simple metal sculpture suggesting the skeletal outline of a sailboat, as well as a divan for the cat and a stepladder for the owl. Lee worried that the roughly eight foot by eight foot structure would be lost, sitting alone in the midst of the vast stage of the Metropolitan Opera, but Graham was not troubled by this, nor were the critics, who responded very positively.

A few more projects went nowhere, but Lee designed one last dance for Graham, *Tangled Night*, in 1986. It, too, depicted a sailboat, but was more complex and evocative. The music was by Norwegian composer Klaus Egge, and Graham initially asked Lee for something Nordic. He created a wooden sculpture that she felt was "too pure" for the dance. Her assistant brought out a watercolor of a Winslow Homer sailboat and Lee worked from that image. The result was something like *The Owl and the Pussycat*'s sculpture, but it now included a twisted sail and crossed wires, like a boat wracked by a storm. There was also a driftwood tree, serving as a vertical counterbalance to the ship.

PACIFIC NORTHWEST BALLET

In 1987 Lee designed *The Tragedy of Romeo and Juliet* for Kent Stowell, artistic director of Seattle's Pacific Northwest Ballet, the first of five dances he would do with Stowell over the next ten years. Stowell was not a particularly adventurous choreographer—the PNB repertoire included several faithfully recreated works by George Balanchine—but he did have artistic vision and integrity, and Lee's collaborations with him were far more rewarding than his earlier story ballet projects with Christensen or Vesak. PNB's *Romeo and Juliet* was not the well-known Prokofiev ballet; rather, Stowell created an entirely new piece out of twenty-five selections from some fifteen works by Tchaikovsky. Scenographically Stowell was not interested in gimmicks or updating. Lee devised a seemingly traditional design, but one that was minimalistic, combining a formal structure with a romantic sensibility. It consisted of a double row of arcades upstage, perfectly symmetrical and parallel to the front of the stage, with an upper balustrade along the front, and two towers. Scenic units or handkerchief drops could fly in to indicate various locales and the towers could also track in, thereby altering the configuration and volume of the stage. Thus, with a fairly simple vocabulary and a relatively limited number of set pieces, Lee was able to create a highly flexible space that could suggest several discrete locales while leaving the stage open for the dancers.

Stravinsky's *Firebird* followed two years later. Originally performed by the Ballets Russes in 1910 with choreography by Michel Fokine, *Firebird* was later adapted by Balanchine, but Stowell felt that both versions minimized the central story of the Tsarevich's love for the princess, and he decided to utilize the entire score in order to address that issue. The settings employed what for Lee were rather bold colors and elements of fantasy, though they were hardly as exotic or fanciful as the original Ballets Russes designs. Compared with his experimentation with scale and consistency in *Khovanshchina*, Lee's work here seems decidedly less adventurous (though the second act bears a certain resemblance to the Red Room of *Khovanshchina*), but he feels that "it was a very beautiful set and it's a little more whimsical than my usual design."

6

7

8

9

10

11

The Tragedy of Romeo and Juliet

Pacific Northwest Ballet, 1987.

6–9 1/8" sketches for, from left, the banquet, balcony, bedroom and tomb.

10 1/4" model.

11 Production photograph, Friar Laurence's cell.

12

13

14

Firebird
Pacific Northwest Ballet, 1989

12 ⅛" model for act 1, garden. "For the garden I did abstract trees with a white wall and a golden gate, and behind it I had a miniature Russian church and very, very blue sky. Kent felt that the garden should have some foliage, so I had a tree with big leaves and my typical floating foliage, except that this time it was all circular with flowers sprouting out—trying to look Russian, but it didn't look Russian at all."

13 ⅛" model, act 2, palace. Note the monster face peering out above the stage.

14 ⅛" model, finale, wedding.

15

16

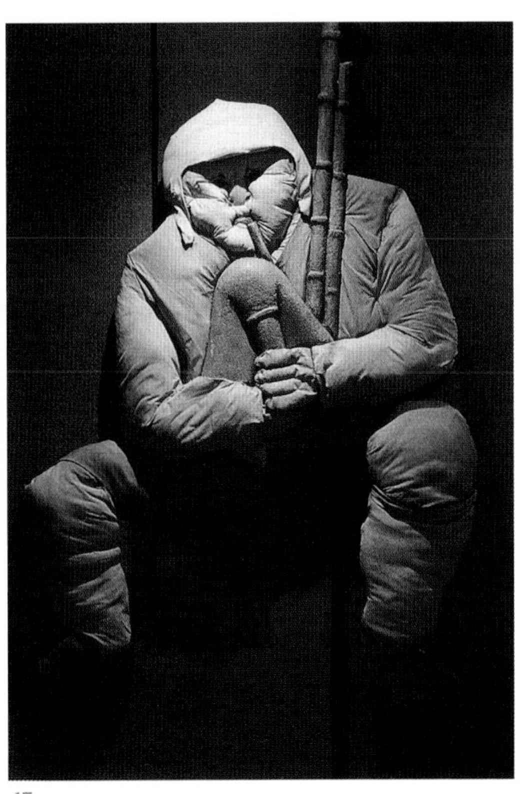

17

Carmina Burana

Pacific Northwest Ballet, 1993

15, 16 ¼" model and production photograph. For the tavern scenes Lee proposed a modern Bruegel-like setting "with the dancers as cowboys, and they're all Texans, and the dancers are wearing wooden clogs. That didn't go over very well with Kent."

17 Soft sculpture figure—one of three figures that descended onto the wheel for the tavern scene. This was a rare venture for Lee into design with fabric.

18

19

20

18, 19 ***Silver Lining***, Pacific Northwest Ballet, 1998, production photographs. Set to music by Jerome Kern, the ballet evoked the elegance of 1930s musicals. An art deco portal created a unifying frame for the flat cut-out backdrops for each segment.

20 ***Swan Lake***, Pacific Northwest Ballet, 2003, production photograph, act 1, scene 2. "I thought Kent did an amazing *Swan Lake*. While I did a very good design for *Swan Lake*, I failed him there a little bit." It was a simple, functional design of columns, wintry trees, shiny black floor and a moon, but no lake. One critic lamented, "One wanted to like Lee's decor, but really it is rather dull and devoid of imagination" (Seattlepi.com, February 2, 2007).

21 ***The Dream of the Red Chamber***, Cloud Gate Dance Theatre, 1983. The sketch was done in 2013 to show the horizontal aspect of the design.

21

What must be clear by now is that, for Lee, a good set has as much to do with process as with the final result. But when he decides to do something spectacular—not spectacle, per se, but something astonishing or breathtaking—there are few who can top him, whether it is an art nouveau gazebo or a mountain. For his next PNB production, a piece based on Carl Orff's *Carmina Burana*, he created a massive golden wheel of fortune that hovered over the stage and tilted at various angles while upstage were floating platforms that held the seventy-two-member chorus. One critic wrote, "It's all so impressive that you almost don't need to add dancers to the mix, and indeed the company sometimes seems dwarfed by all the other elements" (*Seattle Times*, April 16, 2012).

While Lee was somewhat disappointed with his final project with PNB, *Swan Lake* in 2003, his sixteen-year association with the company allowed him to do a very traditional style of design that he had had little opportunity to do previously—while simultaneously exploring increasingly non-romantic, postmodern design elsewhere. Lee's ability to juggle not only several genres of performance, but several styles of design was one of the remarkable characteristics of his work.

LIN HWAI-MIN AND CLOUD GATE DANCE THEATRE

In the midst of all this, Lee was contacted by a then-unknown choreographer, Lin Hwai-min, director of the equally unknown Cloud Gate Dance Theatre of Taiwan. Lin asked Lee to design *The Dream of the Red Chamber* and this led to one of the more important collaborative relationships of Lee's career.

Lin first came to the U.S. in the 1969 to study journalism at the University of Missouri, but was soon awarded a fellowship to the University of Iowa's International Writing Program. At Iowa he discovered dance, and when he moved to New York he took classes at the studios of Martha Graham and Merce Cunningham. Upon returning to Taiwan in 1973 he founded Cloud Gate, an unprecedented enterprise in Taiwan. At the time there was virtually no one in Taiwan with either design or technical training, so Cloud Gate's projects had been scenographically very simple. But for their tenth anniversary, with plans to open a new theatre, Lin wanted to make a bolder statement. Lee was legendary in the Chinese-speaking world, so Lin wrote to him. As recounted by Lin, "He wrote back saying that if I had the time we could sit down in New York and talk it over. I flew right away to New York to see him.... I was very surprised when I received his letter because he had no idea who I was but was willing to meet with me all the same. When we met, he plied me with nonstop big and small questions. He picked my brain and made me tell him everything I had on my mind.... Ming Cho Lee...is a true master."[1]

The Dream of the Red Chamber was written in the eighteenth century and is one of the most famous novels in Chinese literature, though Lee had never read it. It is an episodic narrative of the decline of a wealthy and powerful family, but Lin's dance focused more on the allegorical and Buddhist underpinnings of the story. In the midst of talking to Lee about colors Lin rather brashly suggested that they go over to the Metropolitan Museum of Art to look at the colors on Chinese porcelain. ("Who would dare to suggest that to Ming Cho Lee?" laughs Lin, recalling the story. "But I was so ignorant. And he was gracious and came with me.") Ultimately Lee suggested panels of stretched scrim or China silk painted in shades of green, plum and white to suggest the seasons. As simple as this was, the notion of broad swaths of color in horizontal patterns was a significant departure for Lee. The sculptural settings that had typified his work till this time were giving way to more layered planes and surfaces and, inevitably, a diminishment of verticality. Even the floor was done in alternating bands of gray and white marley. "You look at Chinese painting and it's all mist and horizontal bands. It just felt right," says Lee.

There were no scene shops in Taiwan capable of doing even something as simple as this, so Lee arranged for the panels to be made in New York and shipped over. Even so, there were problems. The theatre was still under construction, and because it was under the auspices of the Ministry of Education the stagehands were considered civil servants who therefore left work at 5 P.M. (Lin finally got the mayor to intervene so there could be a crew.) Nothing was allowed to be screwed into the floor and the stanchions and cables to hold the panels—which would move on and offstage—were supported offstage by blocks of concrete. The scenery ultimately worked, even if it sagged a bit.

"I felt that I was in the midst of a really big creative force," Lee recalls. "There is something remarkable about the dance in that it is

22

both very, very Chinese and very, very Western. They could do steps that come from Beijing Opera but at the same time that's integrated into Martha Graham's very earthbound movement." He was also impressed with the enthusiasm of the students he met and their thirst for knowledge. "In the U.S., especially after Reagan, you felt that art—artists—were tired. Very seldom did you feel the kind of thirst that I experienced talking to the students in Taiwan. It was a remarkable experience."

For Cloud Gate's twentieth anniversary, in 1993, Lin created a new work, *Nine Songs*. The company had achieved international fame in the intervening decade, and the fifteen performances sold out immediately, with twenty thousand people gathered in the plaza outside the National Theatre to watch the opening night simulcast. *Nine Songs* is based on a cycle of poems by Qu Yuan from the third century BCE, generally considered the pinnacle of Southern Chinese culture from the period. Lin added a section at the end, "Homage to the Fallen," a recitation of the names of those who died at the hands of oppressors, ranging from ancient China to the atrocities of Japanese occupation, to the 1947 massacres in Taiwan, to Tiananmen Square.

Lin envisioned lotus blossoms floating on water, a little like Monet's water lilies. The lotus, explained Lin, is the "flower of eternal life, of reincarnation, because the lotus buds in the spring, blossoms in summer, withers in autumn, dies and becomes part of the mud in winter, and then the following year the whole cycle repeats" (*Washington Post*, October 8, 1995). Something in Lin's description clicked instantly with Lee. "I did a very rough drawing on the spot," Lee recalls, "depicting the whole set as a series of panels flying up and down, moving side by side. Together they formed a painting of the lotus leaf. Then, some would fly away so that the lotus leaf gets deconstructed." Lee began researching Chinese paintings of lotus leaves, planning to paint it in the style of Chinese watercolor, but when he went to Taipei to see a rehearsal he realized that the dance was not lyrical, but rather very brutal with harsh music. He said to Lin, "I think the design you have just approved is wrong. Your dance is so brutal, and I have done a watercolor. It will never live up to the dance." The underlying idea was right, but Lee felt it needed something more formal and precise. They argued, but Lin gave in and sent more images to Lee back in New York, including one titled *Lotus*

Nine Songs
Cloud Gate Dance Theatre, 1993

22 Photograph of lotus panels in fully closed position.

23 ¼" model, with central section of panels open.

24 Model piece of the upstage wall from Lee's first design that he himself subsequently rejected.

25 Photograph of the final image with river of 800 votive candles receding upstage from the pool of wilted lotus blossoms.

23

24

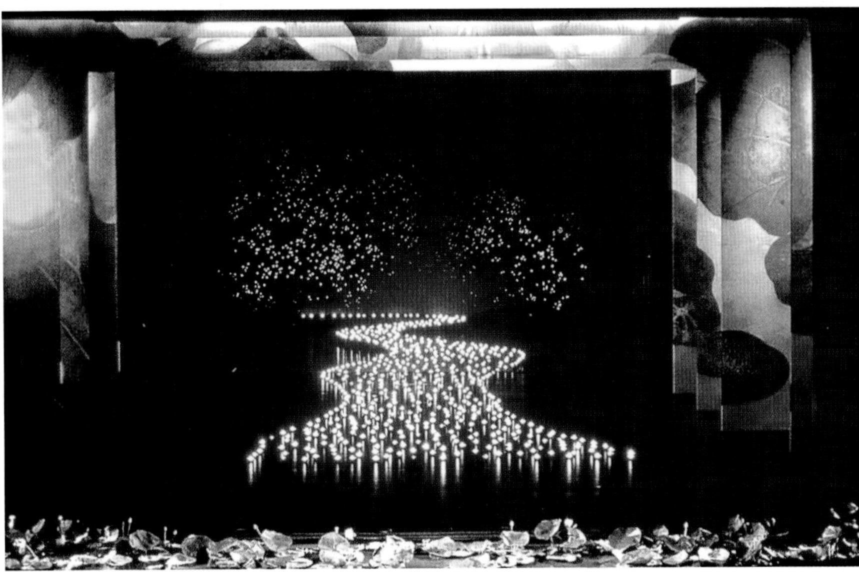

25

Pond by the noted Taiwanese painter Lin Yu-san. Lee actually used this painting, crediting the artist in the program. As finally designed, the panels moved to create openings of varying sizes, from a small door to a near full-stage opening to reveal a large moon.

By the 1990s there was a cadre of sophisticated Taiwanese technicians and designers who had studied in the U.S. and Great Britain, including Yale-educated Cloud Gate lighting designer Lin Keh-hua. The orchestra pit was transformed into a lotus pond, completely covered with real lotuses. Lotuses, once plucked from their roots, will wilt within two hours, even in water, so the dance was essentially timed to the wilting of the leaves. The imagery of the final part of the dance was taken from the executions during the Cultural Revolution when prisoners, wrists bound, were marched out with wicker baskets over their heads, lined up and shot. Lin had dancers come onstage in similar fashion—bound hands, baskets over their heads. To the insistent beats of wood blocks the dancers fell, one by one, until the stage was filled with bodies. Finally, one dancer was left standing downstage, back to audience, arms raised. A square opened in the upstage screen and four lights shone through, directly at the audience, suggesting the famous image of the student facing a tank in Tiananmen Square. There was the sound of the wood blocks again as the dancer fell. After a short time the dancers slowly began to rise and move off, returning over and over with the lighted candles until the stage was filled with four hundred candles in an undulating pattern. The back scrim then rose up revealing a curved ramp covered with another four hundred lit candles that seemed to merge into an infinite sky of stars. "The dance doesn't really end," says Lee. "After the applause it just continues. There were people who sat in the audience for ten minutes or more just watching the candles." Here was a design as stunningly beautiful and overwhelming as anything Lee had ever created, but it was not mere spectacle. It emerged organically from the demands of the affecting and disquieting dance. It was not a gimmick, not mimetic realism; it was a powerful visual counterpart to a dance that paid homage to two millennia of martyrs.

In 1996, Lin was asked to direct the premiere of *Rashomon*, an opera by Japanese composer Mayako Kubo, in Graz, Austria. Given Lee's vast experience with opera, as well as the success of *Nine Songs*, Lin asked him to design. The plot is based on the Kurosawa

26

27

28

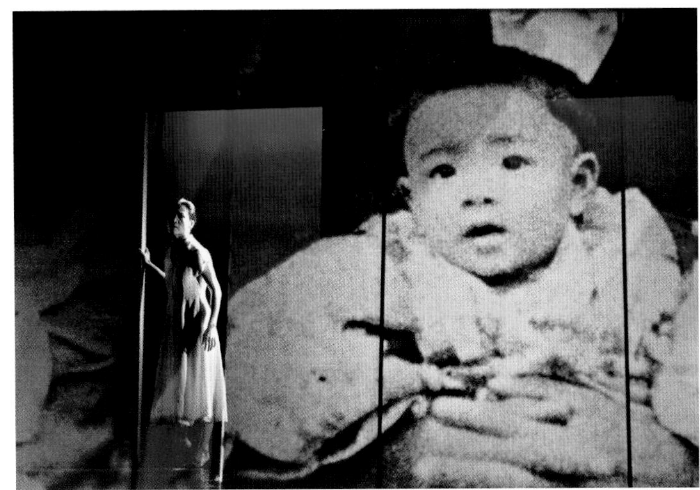
29

26, 27 ***Rashomon***, Oper Graz, Austria, 1996, production photograph and ¼" model. The set was a mirror image of the baroque theatre auditorium.

28, 29 ***Portrait of the Families***, Cloud Gate Dance Theatre, 1997, ¼" model and production photograph. A black rear projection screen was stretched above the portals.

30 ***Burning the Juniper Branches***, Cloud Gate Dance Theatre, 1999, production photograph.

30

film concerning four versions of an incident involving possible rape and murder. Lin came up with the idea of using a hanamichi—the traditional ramp through the auditorium of the Japanese Kabuki theatre—so that the performers could enter through the audience. But he had no clear idea of what the stage itself should be. "For some reason it hit me," recalls Lee. "I said we could have a mirror on the stage, and a turntable. Wouldn't it be wonderful if the singers came in from the auditorium, and we would have a pair of dancers, exactly like the husband and wife, coming from upstage? They would meet at both sides of the orchestra pit." While the final design had no mirror or turntable, Lee designed a set that mirrored the auditorium of the theatre as well as a walkway around the orchestra pit, and Lin did use the idea of doubles for the characters.

Portrait of the Families a year later was Lin's reflection upon the lifting of martial law in Taiwan ten years earlier. One result of the easing of restrictions was that photographs that had been hidden away out of fear, unseen for decades, were unearthed and these now formed the iconography of the dance. Lee created a rear projection screen out of scrim panels—the seams joining the panels were left visible, deliberately working against the fetishizing of the images—and more than thirty projectors created an ever-changing collage of hundreds of photos. This was accompanied by taped voices of individuals, in the different dialects of Taiwan, telling their stories of the massacre of 1947 and other horrors under martial law.

Lin and Lee's final work together was *Burning the Juniper Branches*, which Lin created with the turn of the millennium in mind. Lin explained that Tibetans burn juniper branches to pray for blessings and to predict the future. For Lee it was an odd mix of Martha Graham–like movement and the use of silk fabric on the one hand, and harsh, hard objects—rocks, chain-link fencing—on the other. The sides of the basically bare stage were covered with rocks that Lin had selected himself from a beach. Lee created a backdrop with an image of Buddha. During the course of the performance the dancers would hop from one rock to another, finally picking up the stones and throwing them at one performer, creating the illusion of stoning him to death and leaving the entire stage covered with stones.

Lee did only these four dances with Cloud Gate, but in essence he introduced design into their work. Over the years Lin turned increasingly to projection or design that emerged organically out of the rehearsal process. "I found that he has gone past me," says Lee somewhat wistfully. "I didn't know how to deal with his materials. And so much has to be done with the dance as it evolves, but I am a designer in my studio. He is moving elsewhere."

CHAPTER 14

Playing with the Canon 1979–99

1 ***The Glass Menagerie***, Guthrie Theater, 1979. (The sketch was originally done on blueprint paper so has yellowed over time.)

1

THE AMERICAN THEATRE HAS ALWAYS had a peculiar relationship with the classics of the Western canon. A limited number of Shakespeare's plays were very popular throughout the nineteenth century, fitting easily among the melodramas that dominated the stage, but until Joe Papp, that repertoire remained small. Outside of Shakespeare, even in the latter half of the twentieth century, the selection of pre-Ibsen and Strindberg classics was miniscule—a few Molières, the occasional Ben Jonson or Christopher Marlowe, and a handful of Greek tragedies. While the repertoire has slowly expanded, Lee's career was inevitably trapped within the confines of American taste. As a result, there are certain plays that Lee has designed multiple times, and this makes a fascinating way to look at the evolution of his work, as well as his relationship with a few directors with whom he has worked repeatedly. He designed *Romeo and Juliet* four times, plus once as a ballet and once as an opera; *The Tempest* four times; and *Othello* and *Antony and Cleopatra* three times each. From the modern American repertoire, he has done two productions of *Death of a Salesman* and four of *The Glass Menagerie*. With the exception of *Salesman*, Lee's initial productions of all these plays have been dealt with in earlier chapters; this chapter looks at some of the work from the late 1970s onward.

THE GLASS MENAGERIE AND EMILY MANN

The original Broadway production of *The Glass Menagerie* in 1945 established Tennessee Williams as a major playwright and was a landmark production for Lee's mentor Jo Mielziner, whose use of scrim became inextricably bound up with the theme and structure of the play. Lee first tackled the play at the Circle in the Square in 1975 [see chapter 8]. In 1979, he was teamed up with a young director, Emily Mann, for a production at the Guthrie Theater in Minneapolis. Alvin Epstein had recently become artistic director and was trying to broaden the roster of designers. Mann would be the first woman to direct on the Guthrie main stage. Given her inexperience Epstein wanted her to work with an established designer but left the choice to her and she chose Lee. As he often did with directors whose work he did not know, Lee asked her to explain why she wanted to do the play. "Ming put me at ease, allowed me to relax and express my ideas," recalls Mann. While Lee agreed with her basic interpretation—that "the play is about memory—what it is and how it shifts and changes. It has real points, but then it drifts through space"—he thought there might be less obvious ways of expressing a dream state, especially at the Guthrie, a theatre with a three-quarter round stage and an auditorium that had a fairly large capacity but a surprising sense of intimacy. He notes that, "In my experience, dreams are not abstract; dreams are very real, especially at the center of the dream. It's at the edges that it gets fuzzy. It goes from one place to another without logic, but the center of it is very, very real." He proposed treating the stage as an open expanse with "centers of reality, and between each reality there should be space. That's what memory is. It takes time to go from one reality to another. But it should be very, very, very real."

Lee did a sketch and model which showed the highly detailed set pieces in isolated areas on the stage. The ground cloth beneath each locus of reality was painted like flower-patterned linoleum, but the floor between these sites remained bare. The walls upstage and at the sides were made of multiple layers of scrim painted with wallpaper patterns so that they seemed to recede into the distance, and even the ceiling had wallpaper patterns and pictures so that the idea of memory was literally hanging over the characters. Several of the props were painted to be especially shiny, so that they seemed to sparkle in the light and heightened the sense of reality. Mann's concern upon seeing the sketch was whether the beautiful lighting as painted by Lee, so essential to the success of the design, could be recreated, but designer Duane Schuler captured it perfectly. As Lee has noted, light is part of the composition of the sketch, "but it would never occur to me that the lighting designer should recreate the composition. I'd be embarrassed. Just because it looks good in the sketch doesn't mean it will look good on the stage. Light is fluid; it's tied in the with the action of the play and the movement of the actor."

"Emily is steeped in the tradition of real theatre, I don't mean realistic but *real*, alive," Lee says. "There were things that happened during Emily's rehearsals that never happened elsewhere. It was really a beautiful, beautiful *Glass Menagerie*." Some twelve years later Mann chose *The Glass Menagerie* as her directorial debut at McCarter Theatre Center in Princeton, New Jersey, where she had been appointed artistic director in July 1990. "I wanted to lead with my best work, to show them what I could do," she says. McCarter is a frontal stage, but, in Lee's words, "like a barn," and given the intimacy of the play he felt he needed to transform the space. He designed a thrust to come out over the first two rows, which helped but never achieved the intimacy of the Guthrie. For the *New York Times* critic,

2

3

The Glass Menagerie

2 Guthrie Theater, 1979, ¼" model.

3 Guthrie Theater touring set, ¼" sketch. At the time the Guthrie often took productions on tour around the Midwest, which meant going into proscenium theatres, so Lee redesigned it. The fire escape was placed above, which in some ways worked better because Tom could look down at his memories and the audience could encompass past and present simultaneously.

4 McCarter Theatre, 1991, photograph.

5 Broadway, 1983, production photograph.

4

5

6

however, this was an advantage: "Unlike the transparent, closed-in representation of an apartment and the tenement exterior that one customarily associates with Tennessee Williams's first masterwork, the vision of Ms. Mann's production is of vastness. The lamplike fixtures hanging on high appear intermixed with the stage lights and the long narrow corridors that flank Ming Cho Lee's set design extend into the beyond.... At first sight, things seem all wrong. Before long, it all feels right" (January 27, 1991). Lee also added projections, such as the blue roses that Williams calls for in his stage directions.

In 1983, between the Guthrie and McCarter productions, Lee did yet another *Menagerie* on Broadway, directed by John Dexter. It was intended as a kind of homage to Williams, who had died earlier that year. When Dexter asked him to design Lee said, "You'd better be careful because every time I hit Broadway it's a flop. Not even Jessica Tandy [who was playing Amanda] is going to save me." And he was right: Tandy received rave reviews. Lee's set did not.

As with the Guthrie production, Lee was aiming for a contrast of memory and reality, but in this case the emphasis was reversed. Lee thought that Tom's monologues existed in a kind of limbo, and when he enters the scene it becomes more real, so instead of fragmentary pockets of reality, Lee designed a shabby apartment as an essentially naturalistic unit—though one without walls—enveloped in a surround of sky and clouds. It almost looked as if two different sets had been accidentally combined. There were towering vertical posts framing the set, perhaps to suggest the exterior of the house but functionally supporting the window and door units, and a tilted ceiling piece, oddly out of place in that context. It suggested to critic John Simon not a house but "the bottom of a huge elevator shaft...and the elevator halfway down to crushing the characters into pancakes" (*New York Magazine*, December 12, 1983)—an unfortunately accurate, if abrasive, appraisal. Lee had originally wanted to design it as a single room and to float the set—to remove the stage floor so that the set would seem to hover in a kind of void. Dexter had approved this version in the model, but changed his mind before the load-in, and insisted on covering the floor with black velour instead. Had the set floated, it might have given the tawdry reality a more ethereal context.

Lee went on to work with Mann on *Oedipus* at Brooklyn Academy of Music in 1981 and *Execution of Justice* at Arena Stage, the Guthrie and Broadway in 1985–86. The latter was a docudrama written by Mann based on the trial of San Francisco supervisor Dan White for the murder of mayor George Moscone and supervisor Harvey Milk. Lee created concentric squares of color on the floor—a red square at the center, which became the location for the witness stand, a blue surround for the rest of the stage floor, and a white border at the edge of the stage. A white cube suspended above functioned as a projection screen showing excerpts from the film *The Times of Harvey Milk*. To adapt it for the thrust stage of the Guthrie he designed a wall of Corinthian columns upstage that suggested the San Francisco city hall and placed a row of seating in front of that. He attempted to recreate that sense of intimacy for Broadway, including onstage seating, but the raised proscenium created a certain remoteness. While critics were generally sympathetic to the intentions of the play, the production was not well received and Lee's final Broadway venture closed after twelve performances.

THE TEMPEST AND ACTORS THEATRE OF LOUISVILLE

Lee's history with *The Tempest* dates back to 1962. It was the second show at the New York Shakespeare Festival, as well as Lee's first collaboration with Gerald Freedman, with whom he did the play again in the summer of 1979 at the American Shakespeare Theatre in Connecticut. But a few months earlier Lee did another *Tempest* with John Hirsch at the Mark Taper Forum in Los Angeles. (Lee refers to this production as *Tempest* West to distinguish it from the Connecticut production, dubbed *Tempest* East.) Lee, now in his post–Liviu Ciulei period, was eager for strong directorial collaborators, and Hirsch, a Hungarian-born Canadian director, proved to be someone with whom he could have extensive discussions about the play. Lee was quite taken with Hirsch's ability to make the play relate to personal experience. And whereas Lee found the magic of the play in the first Freedman production antithetical to his Brechtian inclinations at that time, Hirsch led him to see the play as Shakespeare's version of *The Magic Flute*, with an emphasis on spectacle. And just as Ciulei got Lee to move away from straight lines to Art Nouveau curves in *Don Juan*, Hirsch suggested a basic ground plan founded on a curvilinear design, inspired by, of all things, Radio City Music Hall.

7

8

The Tempest

6 Mark Taper Forum, 1979, production photograph.

7, 8 Actors Theatre of Louisville, 1989, ½" sketches of the ship deck depicting the pre-show (top) and island.

The opening sequence truly was spectacular. The entire set, including the floor, was draped in black sailcloth with a white sail rising up in the middle. At the end of the opening storm scene, the fabric was suddenly pulled down through the stage floor, like black water down a drain, revealing the set beneath. But following this coup de théâtre, Lee felt the production went downhill, an assessment shared by the critics. Lee crafted a gooey-looking volcanic mound, created of spray foam on bent metal tubing, rising up from the circular thrust stage covered with carpeting to suggest a sandy island. The overall impression was of something out of science fiction or fantasy. It inspired the *Los Angeles Times* critic to flights of rhetorical fancy, describing Prospero's cave as "rather like a large, sun-bleached vertebra cradled in receding, iridescent capiz shells" (May 18, 1979). Had the show captured the fun of the design, it might have worked, but Hirsch's production, which starred Anthony Hopkins, had a cold formality to it. Lee occasionally deems past designs "old-fashioned," though it is rarely a fair assessment. In this instance, however, the set, which Lee himself calls ugly, was very much a product of its time.

Ten years later he would do yet another *Tempest* at Actors Theatre of Louisville, marking the start of a highly productive decade-long collaboration with artistic director Jon Jory. In discussing this production, though, it is important to understand the timing and context in relation to Lee's life.

Lee's mother died unexpectedly in 1986, and this had a profound effect on him. It was his mother who introduced him to art and theatre, who took him to his first theatre in New York, who had opened her home to his friends in New York, and who helped raise his children. She was also, Lee came to understand, his primary audience throughout his life. "I realized that more important than doing theatre was that Betsy saw the work, and especially that my mother saw the work. She attended all my openings in New York. She was always there." Lee's response was inconceivable to anyone who knew him: he decided to take a year's sabbatical from designing. From the day he stumbled upon the theatre program at Occidental College in 1951, there had hardly been a moment that he was not doing theatre. "I kind of lost interest in designing because my mother was not going to see it. For the first time in my life I actually took a week off from teaching, and Betsy and I went to the Cape." Nevertheless, he would continue to teach at Yale during this period, and he would finish his existing obligations before stepping away from his drafting table. In 1986 his only designs were the Broadway production of *Execution of Justice* and *Tangled Night* for Martha Graham. In 1987 he designed the set for Puccini's seldom-produced opera *Le Villi* for Il Piccolo Teatro dell'Opera—a small New York opera company—which was not used, and *Romeo and Juliet* for the Pacific Northwest Ballet. And that was the starting point for the sabbatical. Following the opening of the ballet in Seattle, Ming and Betsy drove down the Pacific coast through Oregon and California, stopping to visit some relatives in Portland and San Francisco, but mostly taking time to do watercolor paintings along the route.

Lee also took advantage of this professional sabbatical to pursue a research project on education. Over the years, largely because he constantly gave lectures and workshops at schools around the country, he had become very interested in the state of liberal arts education at colleges and universities—where it stood in relation to the overall curriculum and how well it was integrated into theatre studies. He received a grant from the Guggenheim Foundation in 1987 to conduct a formal study. Over the course of the year he and Betsy visited liberal arts colleges across the country, returning to teach at Yale each week. This was at the height of the culture wars, and from both the right and left there were challenges to the canon, major overhauls of curricula and a questioning of the role of liberal arts within society. As someone who was a firm believer in the liberal arts as a necessary underpinning for all branches of education, Lee found that "the state of liberal arts education was *wretched*." The foundations of the liberal arts, particularly in the humanities, were eroding; theatre departments placed too much emphasis on practice at the expense of a broad-based liberal arts context, thereby short-changing their students. Partly because their findings were so discouraging, and partly because they did not know what to do with the material they amassed, a report was never generated.

An unexpected consequence of this respite from design was that for the first time in Lee's career, he was financially solvent. Because the expense of assistants and the cost of operating the studio often outstripped the income from the shows, Lee lost money on productions more often than breaking even. (Making a profit was almost impossible.) Without the expense of designing, he discovered that he could live off his salary as a professor.

The Tempest at Actors Theatre of Louisville was Lee's first show following his sabbatical year and he came back truly refreshed. "I was actually finishing shows early. I suddenly found that I had a lot of ideas, and it's the ideas that make designing easy. I was not fighting to do Broadway shows. I was actually not too worried about the Met."

Jory, who had been a co-founder of the Long Wharf Theatre in New Haven before moving to Louisville, had been familiar with Lee's work for years. Nonetheless, he says it took a lot of nerve to call Lee, who he describes as the great American designer of the period. As always, Lee grilled the director about his ideas for the production. Jory's initial concept for *The Tempest* was inspired by silent film, and he even had some thought of making Ariel a Charlie Chaplin figure. But Jory also describes Lee as a "remarkable dramaturg," and the evolution of this production was, in the end, a truly collaborative process, perhaps more so than any experience either Lee or Jory had had until then. Their first conversation about the production lasted more than an hour during which time, according to Jory, they never discussed the design. It was about the play and the ideas inherent within it. "I was nervous," Jory admits, "but he generously draws out your ideas and melds them with his own. Soon you begin to feel that you're pretty intelligent." Costume designer Marcia Dixcy, Jory's wife, designed four of the six shows Lee and Jory did together. "Ming was a guiding force dramaturgically and visually on every production we worked on," she says. "His insights into text and to how an audience may best perceive text are deeply felt and vividly theatrical. Few set designers discuss character with his humanity and compassion!"

With three *Tempest*s under his belt, Lee told Jory that the play always began to lose him in act two, scene one, when all the Neapolitans come onstage and "we have no idea who they are." The problem, as he saw it, was that everyone is introduced during the storm, but because of the special effects nobody hears it. Lee's proposed a preshow scene in which

> **they are on a yacht coming back from Carthage after the wedding, and it's calm. We have a little cart with all the bottles, and Stefano will serve a drink and then sneak another drink for himself. Ferdinand wants a drink, and Alonso says, "No, you're too young." Trinculo sings a song and then everyone goes downstairs. So now we know who they are. Then Antonio and Stefano, sitting on lounge chairs, begin to plot, and that's when the storm begins.**

The yacht would be suggested by a mast that rose into the fly space, and somewhat as with *Tempest* West, the ground was covered with black cloth. As the storm began the mast split in two, with part flying up and part descending into a trap along with the black cloth, revealing the island which, Lee thought, should be like Florida or the Caribbean, with Prospero's cell as a broken-down Art Deco hotel. Jory accepted most of Lee's proposal, although ultimately Dixcy's costumes were Renaissance rather than mid-nineteenth century as Lee had suggested. Prospero's cell became a ruined Palladian structure. The basic set was a mound, what Jory describes as "post-apocalyptic sand dunes." In retrospect, Lee thinks, "Had I just done an absolutely simple mound, like the garbage dump outside of New Haven, it would have been the perfect *Tempest*!"

Lee felt that Jory found an emotional connection in the play that none of the previous productions had. He describes the moment when Prospero asks Ariel how Ferdinand and his followers are faring and Ariel replies, "If you now beheld them, your affections would become tender." Prospero decides to give up his magic, and vows to break his staff and throw his book into the sea. Lee found this emotionally transformative. "For the first time," he declares, "it meant something. It was a great moment in the play. Also, I absolutely fell in love with Miranda. Suddenly the play meant a lot to me." Jory describes how this sense of forgiveness was manifested visually: "We wanted a sense of a new world, but there was no way to change the set. So Ming came up with the idea of a single flower growing up out of the ground. In the midst of the technical rehearsal we had to take a two-hour break as Ming experimented with color and shape. He wouldn't move past that moment until he got it right. He understands what details mean, and he would spare nothing to get the details right. He was brutally concentrated, and I mean brutal."

Over the next ten years Lee did five more productions at Louisville (he, Jory and Dixcy also worked on a production of Wendy Kesselman's *My Sister in this House* in Hamburg, Germany, which never came to fruition). Four were plays Lee had designed at least once previously: *Antony and Cleopatra*, *Romeo and Juliet*, *The Comedy of Errors* and *Othello*. In each case, Lee's response to working with Jory was similar—the production opened new insights and were often his most satisfying experience with those texts. For *Antony and Cleopatra* Jory had the idea of depicting the nearly twenty locales of the play through color rather than architecture. Lee created a set of sliding panels painted in primary colors. The gate of the monument was all blue (as was Octavian's cape that Dixcy designed

9

10

9, 10 ***Romeo and Juliet***, Actors Theatre of Louisville, 1994, ½" model (top) and ¼" model. The shop did not have a scene painter so the canvas for the flats was sent to New Haven where Ru-Jun Wang, a master scenic artist trained at the Central Academy of Drama in Beijing, executed the design and sent it back to Louisville to be reassembled.

11

12

13

14

11 ***The Comedy of Errors***, New York Shakespeare Festival, 1967, ½" model.

12, 13 ***The Comedy of Errors***, Actors Theatre of Louisville, 1996, production photographs.

14 ***Antony and Cleopatra***, Guthrie Theater, 2002, production photograph. The looming face was similar to one used in Louisville.

16

17

15

18

for his final entrance). Once again for Lee, the pleasure of working on the production came as much from the discussion of ideas as from design—examining what makes life worthwhile as you get older. "For Antony and Cleopatra it cost them a kingdom. It made them seem stupid. But what a great love!"

When he did the play again in 2002 with Mark Lamos at the Guthrie, Lee found none of that sense of purpose. The discussions focused on period and whether or not there should be multiple levels on the stage (Lee was opposed). And because of Lamos's other obligations, Lee had only limited input from him. Lee saw it as a production of tricks rather than ideas.

Lee had designed *Romeo and Juliet* at the Delacorte in 1968 and Circle in the Square in 1977, as well the ballet in 1987, and he did not want to do another Renaissance set for the 1994 Louisville production. Jory saw parallels with the breakup of Yugoslavia—ethnic conflict as a prelude not only to civil war but as an invitation for dictatorship. He wanted to draw a connection between authoritarianism in the family and its effects on social ethics, all of which led to the notion of setting the play in pre-fascist Italy, just before the rise of Mussolini. Lee began by basing his design on fascist architecture, but the monumentality and minimal decoration of that style did not mesh well with the sense of artistic decadence that Jory was also looking for. One day at Yale Lee walked past the drawing table of one of his students, Myung Hee Cho, and on it was a book called *Inside Rome* lying open to an image of an eighteenth-century Roman courtyard painted with decorative frescoes, with three window balconies and Ionic columns. "I said, 'Wow, that is *Romeo and Juliet*.'" The playful rococo frescoes gave a decidedly different feel than the faded, Giotto-inspired frescoes of the Circle in the Square production. And the absolutely frontal, two-story façade, with pediments and painted columns, provided a certain monumentality that was offset by the elegant painting. But Lee added one other touch that transformed the set from the merely decorative to the truly theatrical: bright white utilitarian, industrial stairwells on either side with walls seemingly made of concrete. The juxtaposition of the two radically opposite sensibilities emphasized the artificiality of the world of the Montagues and Capulets, a world of illusion surrounded by a cold, hard brutality.

Othello

Stratford Festival, Ontario, 1994

15 Preliminary sketch for scene 1 emphasizing the strong black and white contrast.

16, 17 Sketches for act 1, scene 2, in front of the Sagittary Inn (left) and Senate chamber. The imposing double door at the center of the rear wall for the Senate scene would recur three years later in *Mourning Becomes Electra* at the Shakespeare Theatre Company in Washington, D.C.

18 ½" model for the white courtyard in Cypress.

Othello

Actors Theatre of Louisville, 1998

19, 20 Production photographs of the Venetian ministry and soldiers' quarters in Cyprus. Jory comments, "When I first saw the barracks set I thought, 'Man, that's ugly'—but in a beautiful way, as anything by Ming would be. It was hard to look at."

19

20

Lee declares *The Comedy of Errors* his favorite comedy. "It's a really funny play if you leave it alone, but no one leaves it alone." When he first did the play in 1967 it was a real departure from the previous shows at the Delacorte Theater. There was no "above" at the rear of the stage and no visible stairs, but there was a bold—for Lee—use of color. Directed by Freedman, it was intended to be a joyful evocation of commedia dell'arte. "Instead of trying to make sculptural pieces with a great deal of depth," Lee later wrote, "we deliberately made the walls very flat and the colors very, very bright and flat—almost like a poster…not at all multi-layered."[1] All three units could rotate. The wooden platform was intended to suggest a commedia stage and the frame in front of the central structure held a curtain which was used to create the interior spaces.

The Actors Theatre production was a cartoonish a pastiche of vaguely Latin American and neoclassical elements though not exactly postmodern. Jory admits, "I didn't have strong ideas. It needed a certain comic sensibility that I didn't have." As a result, he said it "looked as if two good architects had created a motel."

OTHELLO

Othello, in 1994 at Stratford, Ontario, was the first of four productions Lee did with Brian Bedford. While the two never quite established the sort of intellectual give and take that characterized his collaboration with Jory or, a bit later, with Michael Kahn at the Shakespeare Theatre, it nonetheless allowed Lee to, as he puts it, "take a step forward" in regard to classic plays. Bedford wanted to emphasize the racial themes and initially proposed setting it during the Civil War, but Lee the dramaturg pointed out that the situation of the Union and the Confederacy was not the equivalent of Venice and Cyprus. Moreover, slavery was not the issue—Othello's race foregrounded his otherness within the society and that was the crux of the tragedy. (Also, he was afraid that costuming for a Civil War production would make it look like *Gone with the Wind.*) Lee proposed a more contemporary time frame, and ultimately it was set around 1939, not long before the U.S. entry into World War II. Venice became Washington, D.C., and Cyprus was a colonial outpost, perhaps the Philippines. Lee devised a black and white setting, inspired in part by a production of Verdi's *Otello* designed by Timothy O'Brien, that not only reflected the theme of the play but created a stark contrast between the two worlds. For act one in Venice, the set was shiny black, suggesting both elegance and a place of intrigue. For the remainder of the play in Cyprus, it was suggestive of colonial architecture—stark white with minimal decor, except for downstage which retained the shiny black surface and threw the rest of the set into relief.

The Louisville *Othello* four years later was, Lee declares, "The best *Othello* I had ever experienced." The contrast between the two locales in this production was created through a juxtaposition of beauty and ugliness. For the first act there was a backdrop based on a fifteenth-century painting by Carlo Crivelli (Lee would use it again in 2005 in *Lorenzaccio* at the Shakespeare Theatre Company). The painting is grotesque but with a richness of tone that created a Venetian atmosphere. The photorealism that Lee had been experimenting with in the 1980s was now turned into something harsh for the Cyprus portion of the play. Lee was inspired by the architecture of many American consulates: "You think, 'Here is America,' but instead you walk into a Holiday Inn. I envisioned Othello and Desdemona living in a totally soulless Holiday Inn. So in one sense it is absolutely abstract. On the other hand it is absolutely real." Thinking back on his first design for *Othello* in the park with Gladys Vaughan in 1964, he realized that he was spending too much time trying to get her to decide whether Cyprus should be more European or African; wood, brick or plaster? He felt that the quality of the ground on which the characters walked contributed to the nature of their actions. Now, doing *Othello* with Jory, the discussion revolved around larger thematic aspects such as the effect of an occupying army in a foreign country, and this freed him somewhat from worrying about the specificity of the material.

Lee's final production in Louisville was George Bernard Shaw's *Heartbreak House* in 1999. Jory left the theatre at the end of the 1999–2000 season to assume a teaching position at the University of Washington. "I consider myself one of Ming's students," he reflects, echoing what many of Lee's collaborators have felt. "He disguised his classes as productions. I have no degree beyond high school, but I have a master's degree from the University of Ming."

DEATH OF A SALESMAN

Lee almost designed *Death of a Salesman* in 1975 for George C. Scott, following *All God's Chillun Got Wings* at Circle in the Square. Any production of *Salesman* is inevitably haunted by Mielziner's iconic skeletal house, but in actuality most of the second act occurs elsewhere. Lee proposed to Scott doing a production without the house. "The stage should be filled with all the things that Willy Loman touches, that Linda touches," he explained. "All the props. And it should almost be like an attic with things all over. The car really should be on the stage." But Scott wanted something closer to Mielziner's set, except, bizarrely, the tombstone for the Requiem scene, which he wanted to be upstairs. Lee resigned and Marjorie Bradley Kellogg designed it. But Lee was able to put some of his ideas into practice in 1983 at Stratford.

What he designed was essentially a box set, but the walls, made of scrim, depicted an exterior world—the more idyllic Brooklyn of Willy's memory and the cityscape that came to surround the house—so that the house was a kind of void and Willy's world was totally enclosed by the exterior walls. The director, Guy Sprung, accepted Lee's ideas with one exception. He did not want the furniture to remain onstage all the time. As Lee designed it the walls sat about five feet above the stage so that furniture and props could glide on and off. But instead of a tracking or winch system, which would have been complicated given Stratford's repertory schedule, they decided to use air casters. The technical staff had little experience with this technology and, as Lee notes, "Every time you say okay to something like that, it becomes a nightmare." During the technical rehearsal the pressure had built up in the casters that moved the bed and dresser for the hotel scene. Instead of gliding on, it shot on as if launched from a cannon. Lee, who happened to be standing nearby, leapt onstage and pulled the actor playing Willy Loman out of the path of the speeding furniture, "saving Willy Loman's life," he jokes. Aside from such technical issues, the movement of furniture on and offstage became too repetitive, and Lee wishes he had fought harder to have the furniture remain onstage throughout. Lee also learned something about scrim. The upstage scrim worked well and allowed images to bleed through, creating the appropriate dissolves between present and past. But on the sides, where the scrim was at a right angle to the curtain line, the weave "tended to stack up" and became opaque. Lee found the production very moving. He remembers one moment in particular: "I arrived from New York and walked into a rehearsal. They were running through the scene between Willy and Biff, and Biff was shaking Willy saying, 'I'm a dime a dozen, and so are you.' And Willy responds, 'I am not a dime a dozen! I am Willy Loman.'

21

21 ***Heartbreak House***, Actors Theatre of Louisville, 1999, ¼" model. Lee considered alternatives to the detailed reality of the house, but finally decided that it could not be an abstraction. There was a surreal aspect to the design, however, what Jory describes as "abstract-realistic." As Shaw calls for in his stage directions, it resembled the prow of a ship, but was tilted. "It made you seasick to look at it (in a good way)," says Jory. In the final moments of the play there are explosions and Shaw's stage directions call for the sound of shattered glass falling from the windows. The theatre happened to have bags of broken sugar glass from other productions in storage and decided to use that here, cascading down onto the stage. Lee remembers that "the effect was chilling, seeing the whole stage covered with broken glass."

I had an experience of catharsis. I couldn't breathe. I was short of breath and I was weeping. It was unbelievable. Powerful. Once you have that experience you know what catharsis means."

Lee had the opportunity to design the play once more, at the Oregon Shakespeare Festival in Ashland. The set was essentially the same, but because of the curved thrust stage it was not quite like a box set. The back wall tilted slightly forward and the side walls came only partway downstage, with door and window frames hanging where the wall would have been had it extended all the way. The overall result was a sense of enclosure, yet instead of the claustrophobic encroaching walls, it was more frightening because Willy existed in a partial void. Lee, in a rare moment of satisfaction, declared it "as good a *Salesman* as I could do."

What is interesting about the Oregon *Salesman*, as well as the *Othello*s, and perhaps even the two *Antony and Cleopatra*s, is the total lack of romanticism. Rough textures have been replaced by hard surfaces, muted colors by saturated ones. The sets confront the audience head on; walls are at right angles. Verticality is still there, as is a sophisticated spatiality, but there is no sign of the old emblematic stage; the Constructivist scaffolding and all the modernist vocabulary that Lee brought to the American theatre is gone. There is a severity, a harsh reality, even a kind of desolation. If the set needed a door it was there, isolated against a bare wall or empty stage; if it needed a table and chair or a bed, those objects were there in stark relief against the stage. Lee may no longer have been at the forefront of scenographic innovation, but his design was constantly evolving and he had developed a visual and spatial vocabulary that meshed will with contemporary aesthetics.

22

23

24

Death of a Salesman

22, 23 Stratford Festival, Ontario, 1983. Sketches showing the present (top) and the Brooklyn of Willy Loman's memory.

24 Oregon Shakespeare Festival, 1997, photograph. The car could pivot. Willy put his valise in the trunk and got in the car which then rotated, shining its headlights at the audience, and there was a sound of a car crash. For the second act, appropriately period signs for the hotel and restaurant flew in so that it did not feel as if all the Boston scenes were simply happening in front of the scenery.

CHAPTER 15

New Directions 1994–2004

1 ***Angels in America, Part I: Millennium Approaches***, ¼" model.

2 ***Angels in America, Part 2: Perestroika***, ¼" model.

1

2

AT THE TIME I FIRST INTERVIEWED LEE in 1983 for my book *American Set Design*, he was searching for some way to move beyond the "spare and stark" quality of his Brechtian and industrial design on the one hand, and the romanticism of watercolor on the other. "Either it is very structural or very fuzzy," he said. In the work of director-designers such as Robert Wilson and Patrice Chéreau he saw a new pictorialism that used strong, almost surreal images that often had a photographic clarity—but, he lamented, "I've discovered that I don't have a foundation for it." By the 1990s, however, Lee's work *had* changed, and he was indeed moving in that new direction. Open stages and skeletal frameworks frequently gave way to solid, oppressive walls and claustrophobic enclosures; natural textures were replaced by glossy surfaces. There was a sharpness to the designs and a much bolder use of color and contrast. It was design for a post-industrial world. Most prominent was the emergence of the "sky box"—a box set with sky or exterior scenes painted on the walls so that entrances and exits were made through doors in the sky, as it were, as in the white box for *Khovanshchina* in 1985. Even Lee's distinctive verticality, on occasion, gave way to horizontality. Postmodern tropes found their way into various designs, though taken as a whole Lee's work was not really postmodern. It often seemed closer in spirit to Eastern European designs in which seemingly impenetrable walls projected a sense of inescapable entrapment.

A more immediate influence, however, came from British design. Just as he was strongly influenced by German design in the 1960s, Lee acknowledges the work of his British colleagues as the source for several of his ideas in the 1980s and '90s. Lee occasionally says, somewhat facetiously, that he "steals" or "copies" ideas from his colleagues and even his students, but it is really a process of inspiration, of becoming aware of potentially new approaches, and of breaking old habits. But there was also an element of insecurity. "I always felt I was a step behind," he explains. Despite a long friendship with John Bury, the most influential British designer of the era, Lee's inspirations now came more from Stefanos Lazaridis, Richard Hudson, Timothy O'Brien and especially Ralph Koltai (an abstract circular structure Koltai used in a Royal Ballet production of *The Planets*, for example, directly influenced the wheel of fortune in Pacific Northwest Ballet's *Carmina Burana*). These designers frequently employed distorted or exaggerated architecture, iconic and allegorical scenic elements, and heightened or nonrealistic color schemes—all elements that found their way into Lee's work. Given the clear relation of these stylistic devices to the German expressionist scenography of the early twentieth century, Lee's new style might best be designated as neo-expressionist. (Lee was not overtly influenced by the art movement known as neo-expressionism from this same period, although one could find analogous elements, particularly in the emotional use of color and figuration, and even in the interest in graffiti.)

Elements of his new approach could be seen as far back as the 1966 *Measure for Measure*, directed by Michael Kahn, with its grim, post-industrial, urban façade and emphatic frontality, or in A.J. Antoon's *Cymbeline* in 1971 with its cool, reflective, Plexiglas surfaces. But the first true example of Lee's neo-expressionist postmodernism is Friedrich Schiller's *Mary Stuart* at the Stratford Festival, directed by John Hirsch in 1982. Though it shared much of the same narrative material as City Opera's "Three Queens" trilogy of the early 1970s, the Stratford production was spare and confining as opposed to richly textured and spacious. A right-angled box set of barren gray stone walls and a beamed ceiling was transformed into different locales through simple scenic units, such as the fireplace for Elizabeth's great hall. The dramatic use of light, particularly in Mary's chamber, was highly reminiscent of German expressionist design. (Beverly Emmons was the lighting designer.) The most startling scenic image appeared in the garden scene when the back wall flew out, revealing a sky drop and trees, while the side walls and ceiling remained. The scene was simultaneously interior and exterior, and the framing of the garden within the confines of the existing set worked against illusionism, creating instead a pictorial reference—a garden captured within a stage setting.

As discussed in the previous chapter, the Stratford *Death of a Salesman* the following year also placed the play within a box. But this technique of containment would not appear as a dominant motif until the mid-1990s.

THE HORIZONTAL SETTING

Meanwhile, a different stylistic transformation was emerging. The horizontal movement patterns of modern dance led to horizontality in design, notably in the horizontal panels for some of the Eliot Feld works and for Cloud Gate Dance Theatre's *The Dream of the Red*

3

4

3, 4 ***Mary Stuart***, Stratford Festival, Ontario, 1982, sketches for Elizabeth's great hall and the garden that was simultaneously interior and exterior.

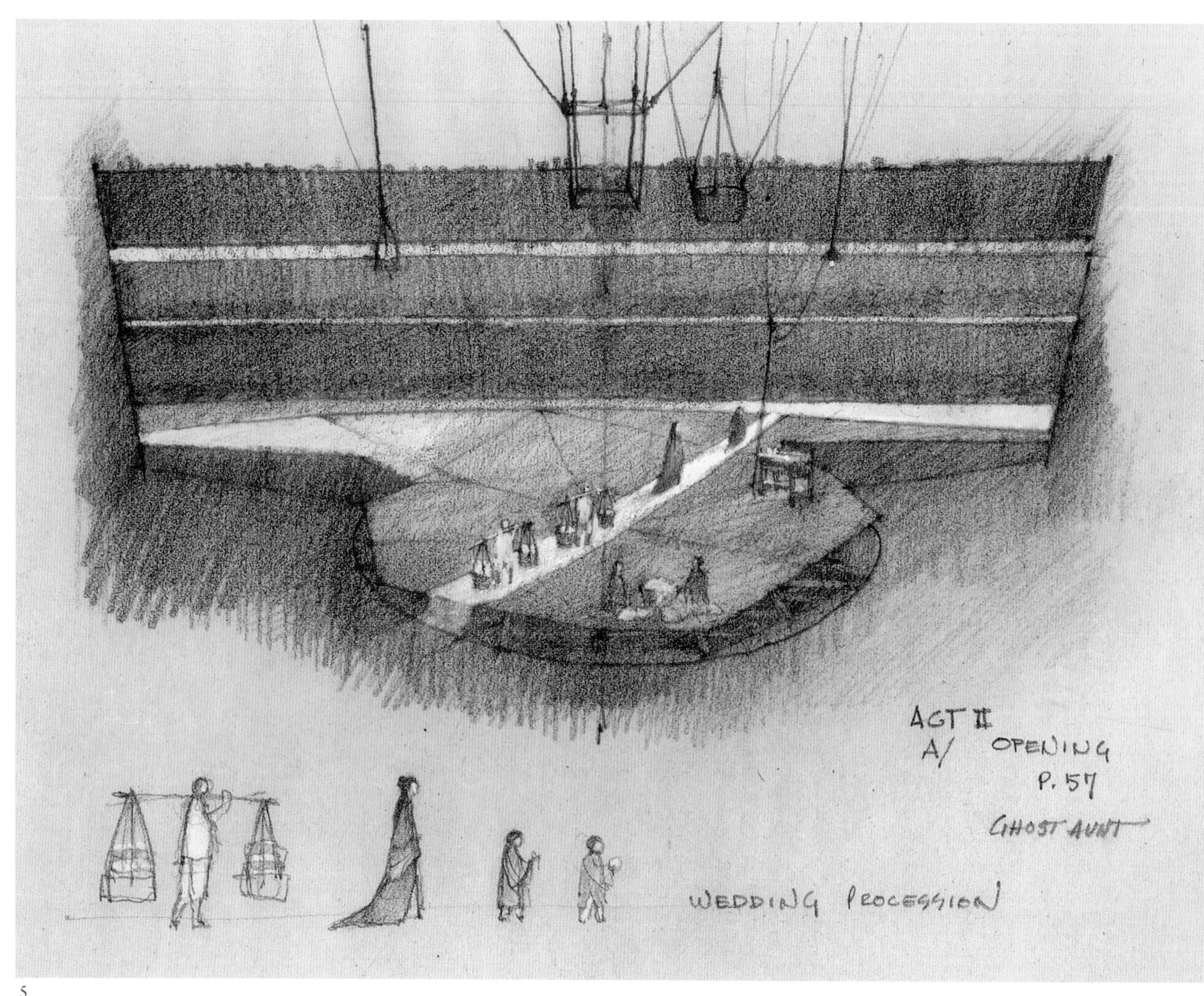

5

The Woman Warrior

Berkeley Repertory Theatre, 1994

5 Sketch of the wedding procession for the unrealized production at the Mark Taper Forum, 1984.

6 ¼" model for the wedding scene.

7 ¼" model of Maxine, isolated, floating above stage in her bed. Costume designer Susan Hilferty recalls, "Ming found the most gorgeous solution to a whole section of the piece, a fever-driven scene. He had the bed lifted up and facing the audience so that the girl was constantly present, while all sorts of activity swirled around below her. It was an incredible visual, but also a practical solution that allowed many things to be happening at the same time."

8 Backdrop from ¼" model showing Chinese graffiti projection. Lee suggested that "when the girl goes out of her mind, we should have projections of Chinese graffiti with all the words that say 'little sister,' 'pretty girl,' all these endearing names that Chinese have for young women. And I did a graffiti projection on top."

6

7

8

Chamber in 1983. Lee first applied it—or intended to apply it—to a theatrical production in 1984 when he began working with Gordon Davidson on an adaptation of Maxine Hong Kingston's novels *The Woman Warrior* and *China Men* at the Mark Taper Forum. Unfortunately, the production did not come to fruition at that time, but in his preliminary designs Lee treated the Taper in a new way, with bold horizontal bands across the entire rear of the stage, emphasizing width in a manner almost unprecedented in his work. He felt that this visual gesture was "very Chinese, like the horizontal cloud banks in Chinese paintings" and also showed the influence of Japanese painting that contained "all these horizontal fog banks and in between you'll see a pavilion showing through. I have always loved that."

The play was finally produced in 1994 at Berkeley Repertory Theatre, directed by Sharon Ott, as a collaboration between Berkeley, the Taper and Boston's Huntington Theatre Company. The horizontality now was even more pronounced. The set consisted of a white background and white floor, with bands of China silk in various shades of red and pink stretched across the stage. As costume designer Susan Hilferty describes, "The set felt like it was nothing, but at the same time it was a wildly sophisticated box that allowed almost effortless transitions from big crowds to intimate moments to dream sequences."

The Kingston books, which Lee had not previously read, opened him up to a world of Chinese immigrant experience and history about which he frankly knew very little.

Reading Maxine Hong Kingston's novels was like entering into a totally new culture. I was not aware of any of that history. There were waves of Chinese immigrants starting in the nineteenth century, when they simply came to make a living and send money home, and this is why they worked on the railroad. Then, when immigration began to open up a little, and women were allowed to immigrate, the Chinese community began to be established in the U.S. They were all uneducated, from the farms, or they were manual laborers. So when they came here, aside from building railroads and working in factories, they would open laundries and restaurants. The women worked in sweatshops sewing garments. You still find them when you go to Chinatown. That is a culture and life that I had never experienced. I belong to another wave of Chinese immigrants that started during the late thirties and forties. Those immigrants tended to be very wealthy Chinese who realized that the situation in China, because of the Japanese, would not be good for their children. We were the people who came to the U.S. to get into college. We entered into professions—teaching, physicists getting Nobel Prizes, businessmen. And odd people like me getting into theatre. The reason most of us naturalized and became citizens is that after we came here we had no place to go. We couldn't go back to China; we couldn't go back to Hong Kong because we weren't British subjects; we couldn't go back to Formosa because we were really emigrants from the mainland. So we were left here. We were called the Uptown Chinese. Most of us came from Shanghai and the coastal region, or from Beijing because of the great universities there. The only contact we had with the Chinatown Chinese was when the housewives, like my mother, went to get Chinese staples for cooking, or to get dim sum for breakfast. We had almost nothing to do with the earlier immigrants.

THE SKY BOX PERIOD

There is no single show, such as *Electra* in 1964, that marks the shift into Lee's fin de siècle style, but *Millennium Approaches*, the first part of Tony Kushner's *Angels in America*, at Dallas Theater Center in 1996 comes close. Emphasizing the circular thrust of the Frank Lloyd Wright–designed Kalita Humphreys Theater, Lee designed what was, for all intents and purposes, a cutaway cylinder. In the rough sketches it looks almost futuristic. The curved upstage wall depicted a sky with white clouds. But this was not simply a sky drop—a large overhead cornice enclosed the sky within an interior space. Furthermore, there was a tall, narrow opening in the center—an angel-shaped hole would appear—which also suggested a rupture within the cosmos, or perhaps the "fabric of the sky unravel[ing]," as the Angel herself says in *Perestroika*, the second part of *Angels*. The sky might be understood symbolically as the domain of the angels, but for Lee it was also a representation of Utah, the home of Mormonism, which plays a significant role in the play. "For me, Utah is almost pristine blue sky," Lee says, and by placing that sky deliberately within an interior space, he could suggest the continuous presence of the expansive American West and its concomitant conservatism within the urban New York world of the characters. The sky was treated as a wall; there were light switches, the television of the hospital room and so on. Because much of *Millennium Approaches* takes place in law offices and institutional locales, Lee made the floor glossy and reflective, creating a high-tech look and further emphasizing the artificiality of the sky, and placing the pedestrian objects such as a bed and other furniture in high relief. "*Angels in America* combined many elements into one environment that is even less logical than *Khovanshchina*, but at the same time, the elements are much more real," Lee notes. "I was going beyond *Khovanshchina* and not worrying about realism or reality. Without having done *Khovanshchina* I would not have been able to take that step."

Most productions use the same set for both parts of the play, but believing that the atmosphere and environment of *Perestroika* was completely different, Lee created a different set for the production of that play in Dallas later the same year. In *Millennium*, notes Lee, "people live very well, so it requires slick interiors. But in *Perestroika*, Louis runs away to the East Village, to a tenement. And Heaven is no better—it's also a tenement. Everything is earthbound." Lee played against the natural curve of the stage and created a square box set. The sky was gone, replaced by tenements "like the ones in *Death of a Salesman*."

The sky box motif continued in the Cincinnati Playhouse in the Park production of *The Notebook of Trigorin*, Tennessee Williams's adaptation of Chekhov's *The Seagull*, and *Jeanne La Pucelle*, at the Place des Arts in Montreal, Canada. The latter was a large-scale musical based on the story of Joan of Arc, directed by Martin Charnin, with an elaborate set of soaring walls, sliding panels and, as the Montreal *Gazette* described it, "eye-popping cathedral trappings" (February 14, 1997). Everything was placed at an angle and set pieces tracked on and off and flew in with "cinematic fluidity," including wheat fields, a gothic stained-glass window and—depending on the critic's point of view—a dazzling "Dali-like Christ" (*Gazette*) or "a giant, overbearing, crucifix that descends over Joan's head" (*Variety.com*, March 1, 1997). Unfortunately, while the show played to fairly enthusiastic audiences, it received largely negative reviews, mostly from the French-language press, and never made it to Broadway as hoped. The curse of Broadway extended even to Montreal.

Lee may have the distinction of being the only designer to work on two productions of Eugene O'Neill's *A Touch of the Poet* simultaneously, one at Arena Stage, to be directed by Doug Wager in his final year as artistic director, and one at the Oregon Shakespeare Festival, to be directed by Jose Quintero. They opened about ten months apart, in October 1997 and July 1998, but the design process overlapped. Work began on the Arena production first. The play is set outside Boston in 1828 in a tavern run by an impoverished Irish immigrant. Given the scenic limitations of designing in the round, Lee and Wager agreed upon a basic platform of gray wood with four windows hanging above the stage, "windows that seem designed more to keep out the light than admit it," as described in the *Washington Post* (October 10, 1997). The family living quarters are above the tavern and, while never seen in the play, the implied presence is important. Lee proposed a staircase above one of the voms, but Wager rejected the idea. Before rehearsals began, however, Wager was hired to work on the television series *Law and Order* and left the production, asking Michael Kahn to take over. Kahn agreed to work with the existing design.

Lee began work on the Oregon production and met with Quintero at his home in Florida. Quintero, who at this point used a voice box to speak, having lost his larynx to throat cancer, described it as a romantic play and said all he needed was a large round table. Lee came up with several designs for Quintero to consider, including one based on Robert Edmond Jones's design for an unrealized production of the play in 1946. Quintero selected that one. Meanwhile, the Arena production was scheduled to transfer to the Denver Center Theatre Company and Lee was working on adapting the set when, on January 1, Quintero called Lee to say he was resigning for health reasons—he would die a little over a year later. Oregon Shakespeare Festival artistic director Libby Appel scrambled to find a new director. Lee told her, "I have about eleven versions of this show. I don't care how you're going to get another director, but he must look through my eleven versions." In an ironic twist, Appel found Doug Wager—so Lee and Wager resumed the process they had begun months earlier, though this time for a thrust stage. Wager liked the idea of adapting the Jones design, but as Lee was about to finalize the design, "I looked at it and realized that it was absolutely predictable; it had no personality. I just didn't believe in it. I called Doug and said, 'I'm going to design a twelfth version.'" This was not simply a case of being unhappy with the design; it was Lee at his dramaturgical best. He told Wager, "I think the play is more than just realistic. I would like to see the staircase because Sara [the daughter] keeps going up, and that is her future, right there."

The result was a near-surrealist design. The tavern was set within a sky box; a miniature iconic mansion representing Con Melody's ancestral Irish home seemed to float amidst the clouds; and a long staircase ascended upstage to a door in the sky. Without the sky box

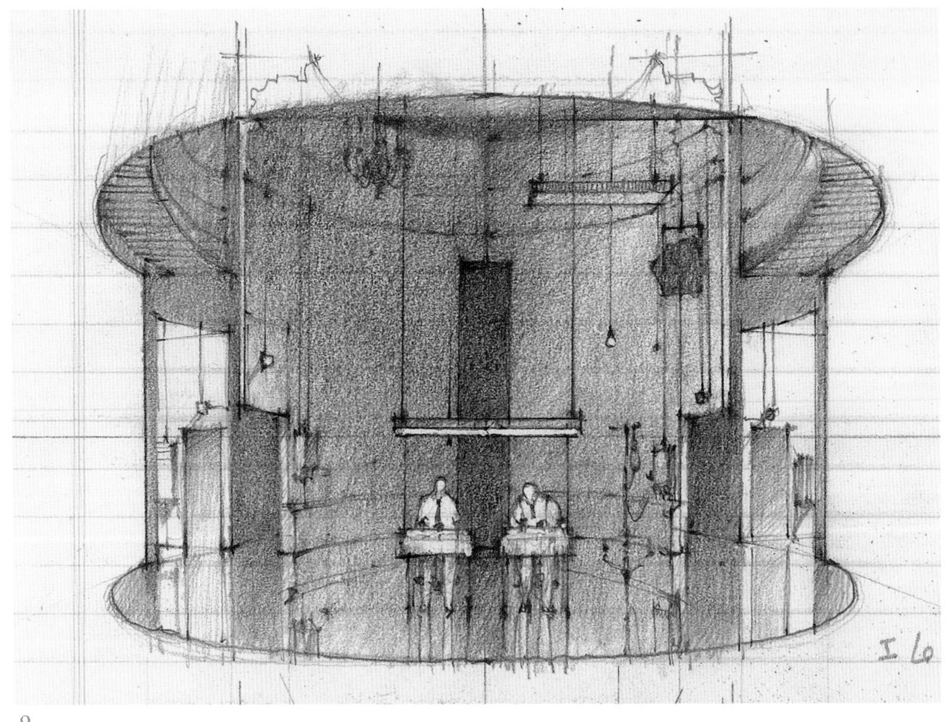

9

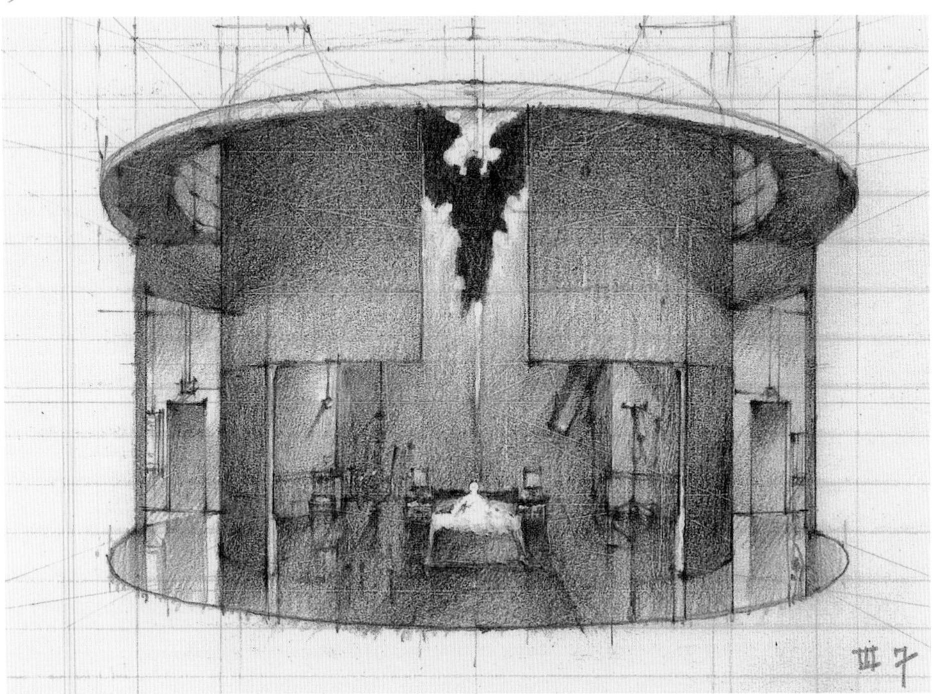

10

11

9–11 ***Angels in America, Part I: Millennium Approaches***, Dallas Theater Center, 1996, sketches.

12, 13 ***Jeanne La Pucelle***, Montreal, 1997, ½" models.

14 ***A Touch of the Poet***, Oregon Shakespeare Festival, 1998, photograph. "Halfway through the dress rehearsal I began to feel sorry for the actress who had to keep climbing that long staircase. She was exhausted."

12

13

14

15

16

it was an utterly simple set whose sparse islands of furniture recalled the Guthrie productions of *The Glass Menagerie* and *The Entertainer*. But with the sky box, the floating mansion and the stairway to the sky, it became one of Lee's most eerily beautiful sets and a superb example of his neo-expressionism.

In the summer of 1999 Lee designed yet another O'Neill play, this time the playwright's only comedy, *Ah, Wilderness!*, at the Guthrie Theater, also directed by Wager. And once again Lee used what he described as "a cheerful blue sky box." The floor was a bright, glossy green—an ironic representation of grass. The four-act play has multiple locations, including a scene at the beach. Because that scene is unique within the play it is often done as an in-one, but Lee decided to begin by designing the beach, and that led to the sky box. He then designed the tavern, but as he began the living and dining room scenes he said to himself, "The hell with it. I have so much research from *Long Day's Journey into Night* [at Arizona Theatre Company the previous year]. I'll design the whole house." He designed the façade as a semi-built-out scenic unit. He thought it might be possible to do the entire production simply in front of the house exterior—an inspired idea—but Wager felt that the demands of the play required detailed interiors. The house wound up being used only for the curtain call. "I regret that decision," says Lee. "I wish I had the guts to do it in front of the house. At the curtain call the whole show was there. I wonder if I hadn't had all this realistic scenery if it would have taken the play into more of a musical comedy vein." It is interesting to compare this house with the one he designed for *Angel*, based on Thomas Wolfe's Asheville home. In the latter, the house is an ethereal creation, still highly influenced by Mielziner. In contrast, the *Ah, Wilderness!* house has absolute clarity of line; it is a perfect replica of the facade of a Victorian house, yet its total isolation on the nearly candy-colored stage makes it a hauntingly unreal entity.

Howard Korder's *The Hollow Lands*, directed by David Chambers, premiered at South Coast Repertory, in Costa Mesa,

17

15 ***Enigma Variations***, Mark Taper Forum, 1999, ¼" model. Lee did not exactly create a sky box, but the sky cyc was the dominant element behind the bay window.

16 ***Long Day's Journey into Night***, Arizona Theatre Company, 1998, ¼" model.

17 ***Ah, Wilderness***, Guthrie Theater, 1999, production photograph.

California, in 2000. Like *A Touch of the Poet*, it concerns an Irish immigrant in the U.S. in the early nineteenth century, but it is a far more epic and brutal play, as Lee described it, "tough, unsentimental, violent and yet strangely moving."[1] South Coast is a moderate-sized theatre with a wide, shallow stage and a low opening, not really equipped for an epic with fifteen sets, but Lee and Chambers "decided to design the play as written, giving each scene its full value."[2] Though Chambers dealt with the play in a very realistic manner, Lee wanted to push it beyond reality, "to find a style that reflects the violence." The result, declared *Time* magazine, was "some of the most strikingly eccentric sets in recent memory, full of skewed angles and semiabstract swatches of color" (January 23, 2000). When the audience entered, the stage was shuttered with only a tiny opening visible. As the show began, it opened a bit more to reveal the hold of the ship coming to New York, and then opened to reveal the shop near the New York docks run by the family. There was a sky drop behind the exterior scenes also seen through the windows of the interiors. Forced perspective, skewed angles, distortions and a collapsed bed place the design firmly in the tradition of expressionism, but the use of color, including a bright red floor, sharp lines and clarity of scenic elements against sky drops, made it the most forceful and iconic example to that time of Lee's new style. Lee also acknowledges the influence of Robert Wilson, which seems most evident in several of the exterior scenes.

The design for *The Hollow Lands* was probably as good and as cutting edge as anything being done in the American theatre in the 1990s; *A Touch of the Poet* and at least the final scene of *Ah, Wilderness!* were equally outstanding examples of neo-expressionism. Yet the unfortunate reality of the American theatre is that if it happens outside of New York, it is invisible. The cognoscenti knew what Lee was doing—creating startling imagistic design—but for many in the theatre world who had not seen his work since the mid-1980s, Lee had slipped off the radar.

18

19

20

The Hollow Lands

South Coast Repertory, 2000,

18 ¼" model of the hotel room in St. Louis.

19 ¼" model of the Missouri River scene with the angled wall inspired by Ben Shahn.

20 ¼" model of the skeletal shack for the cult scene.

MICHAEL KAHN AND THE SHAKESPEARE THEATRE COMPANY

In 1997 Lee and director Michael Kahn reconnected, twenty-nine years after the Broadway debacle of *Here's Where I Belong.* Kahn would have been happy to collaborate more with Lee over the years, but in 1969 he became artistic director of the American Shakespeare Theatre in Connecticut, and Joe Papp would not have allowed Lee to work for a "rival" company. In 1986 Kahn became artistic director of the Shakespeare Theatre at the Folger in Washington, D.C. (now the Shakespeare Theatre Company), although it still took another decade before he and Lee could work together again. Under Kahn's direction the Shakespeare Theatre presented a repertoire of classics seldom produced in the American theatre, and among the plays Lee designed there were *Mourning Becomes Electra, Peer Gynt, King John, Don Carlos* and the almost unknown *Lorenzaccio.* The Shakespeare Theatre Company became Lee's primary home for the remainder of his career, with six productions in the eight years before he retired. He might have done even more, but he found Kahn's sometimes quixotic personality exhausting.

Lee's first production with the Shakespeare Theatre—*Macbeth* in 1995—was directed by Joe Dowling, not Kahn, and was a frustrating experience as Dowling provided virtually no guidance. Lee created a spare, off-white box whose stage right wall curved into the wooden plank floor. Visible through the portals of the blood-stained back wall was a field of wheat, while a barren, blood-red tree, resembling a diseased heart and arteries, dominated the set. Lee told the *Washington Post* that he was inspired by a paperback copy of the play that had a photo of a tree on the cover. "I thought it was perfect because I had never seen a *Macbeth* that had frightened me. So I just lifted it right off, because it looked really spooky" (September 23, 1995). To satisfy actor Stacy Keach's desire for an "above" Lee provided metal scaffolding upstage—a sort of last hurrah for his early scenic vocabulary. None of this evolved from any coherent conceptual idea, but despite the haphazard genesis, the set worked remarkably well, and the bloody tree was a perfect metaphor for the play.

Shortly afterward Kahn asked Lee to design his production of *Mourning Becomes Electra.* The play is O'Neill's adaptation of the House of Atreus story, transplanted to nineteenth-century New England. For the mansion of the Mannon family, Lee designed a symmetrical box set, aptly described by the *Washington Post* as a "high, cold, neoclassical tomb" (May 7, 1997). It was dominated by what Kahn describes, with a degree of awe, as an "absolutely amazing, extraordinary" pair of seventeen-foot-high doors virtually bisecting the upstage wall, and a pair of equally tall louvered doors on either side wall. For other scenes, there were another fourteen doors, all eight feet tall. The shop had to cut some thousand louver pieces by hand, and the technical director sliced off part of his thumb in the process. The set was on a turntable built on a subtle ½" rake to make everything appropriately off kilter. While the turntable facilitated scene changes, it also created technical nightmares—the tilt placed an enormous strain on the tall and very heavy set as it rotated and nearly broke apart in technical rehearsals and had to be reinforced. As Lee says, "Sometimes lack of knowledge is a good thing because you don't know what the hell you're getting into."

Mourning was done in May; *A Touch of the Poet* directed by Kahn at Arena opened in October, while the design process for *Peer Gynt* was already under way for a January opening at the Shakespeare Theatre. Lee jokes that he can handle two Michael Kahns a year, but three is one too many.

Thirty years separate Kahn's *Peer Gynt* from the one Lee did at the Delacorte with Gerald Freedman. Thirty years of life—of raising a family, of career ups and downs, of human experience—makes *Peer Gynt* a significantly different play, and Lee approached it from a totally different perspective. "I just found a lot of connections with childhood, with myth. I felt that I reached another point of understanding *Peer Gynt.*" He had also been assigning it as a class project for many years and found that the students often had startling insights into the play and clever solutions for the many design challenges. Whereas the Delacorte production had been an abstract constructivist roller coaster, this time, Lee felt, "I should respect every item—every piece of imagery—that is mentioned in the script: the pig, the ladle, the sphinx, the insane asylum, the palm trees and orange sky of Morocco, the moon for the Troll scene, the black ocean of the drowning scene, the miniature ocean liner that moves across the stage and sinks. I thought the set should reflect and embody the fjords—the Norwegian landscape and its folkloric culture."[3] For research Lee looked at the paintings of Edvard Munch, particularly his depictions of domestic scenes and summer nights with people dancing under moonlight. But Lee also discovered Norwegian painter Harald Sohlberg, who used very bold colors in an expressionistic manner. He designed curved wings that glided on and offstage, creating a landscape of stylized

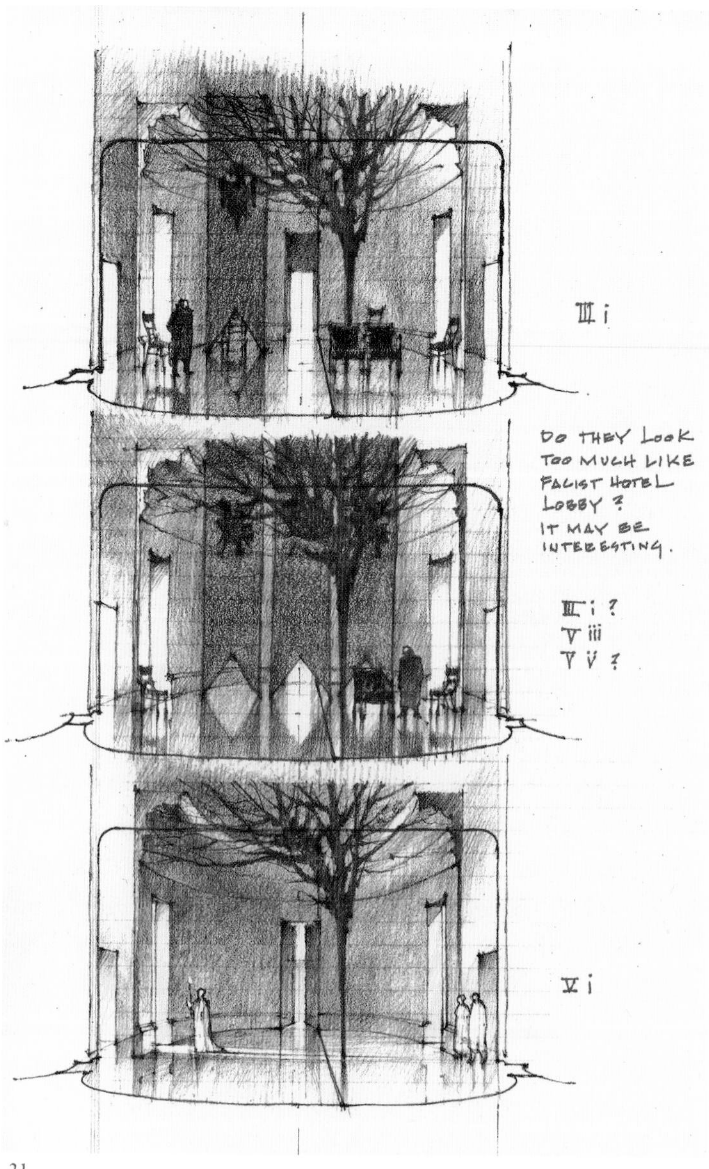

21

Macbeth
Shakespeare Theatre Company, 1995

21 Storyboard images, ⅛" scale.

22 ¼" model.

Mourning Becomes Electra
Shakespeare Theatre Company, 1997

23–25 Production photographs of the sitting room (top and bottom) and outside the mansion (middle). The portraits were on the floor leaning against the wall rather than hung. Thus, rather than looking down on the scene as such portraits appear to do, they occupied the same space as the characters. The doors were three-and-a-half feet wide to accommodate the hoop skirts, but it turned out that, because of the skirts, the women could not close the doors behind them after they entered.

22

23

24

25

Peer Gynt
Shakespeare Theatre Company, 1998

26 Production photograph. The Lady in Green rode to the Troll Kingdom on a green pig, an idea that came from a pink pig Adrianne Lobel had designed as a student at Yale. This pig was modeled on Lee's granddaughter's piggy bank.

27 ½" model, a composite of several scenes, including the troll kingdom.

28 ½" model, Morocco.

26

27

28

fjords. The backdrop, often punctuated by a sun or moon, shimmered in an array of vibrant colors, depending on the mood and locale of the scene. (In building the models in the studio he used a lot of bright Krylon spray paint until neighbors complained about the fumes.) A slanted bridge that could rise up and down cut across the width of the stage (inspired by a student design). As Kahn points out, Lee's great strength is his ability to shape space, and while his sets are rightly known for their verticality, there is usually something that cuts across the horizontal plane that restricts or transforms the space. The bridge certainly did that, and also figured prominently in the drowning scene in act five, which Lee was particularly proud of.

I had pictures of the Black Sea, and when it storms, it's really black. So instead of using blue china silk to represent the sea, as we did at the Delacorte, I suggested we use black. Michael had three rows of china silk going on and offstage. We had people on the sides waving the cloth. Peer and the Cook were on the bridge and they would try to walk up and kept sliding down. Then they dropped into the undulating china silk. I had a floating barrel with black china silk around it and they held onto it. It was spectacular. Then the china silk disappeared, like in *The Tempest*. Suddenly we were in the middle of Norway and the funeral scene. A lot of umbrellas. It never failed.

King John is one of Shakespeare's less-frequently produced plays, perhaps because it sits uneasily between history and farce, lacking the grandeur and intrigue of the other history plays. Initially Kahn and Lee saw it primarily as a political play and Lee designed a parapet with a red balcony and a gate below, which allowed a rostrum for speeches. There were towers on either side which moved in and out to delineate the different scenes. Once again, the basic ground plan was a formal box perforated by rectangular openings. During rehearsals, however, it became clear that the strength of the play lay in the moments of personal interaction among the characters. "Both Michael and I agreed that this was one show we miscalculated at the beginning, thinking it was a cold, impersonal political play," says Lee "It turned out to be an impersonal climate that contained a lot of intimate details about the life of people involved." Scenic elements were added to mitigate the original formality of the design.

The Merchant of Venice followed later that spring with what Lee refers to, with some justification, as a "safe set," essentially a Shakespeare in the Park Renaissance set adapted for a proscenium

THE MING CHO LEE TEMPLATE

I learned about gobos from Jo Mielziner. Jo had used gobos for *Death of a Salesman*. He created a template for *Death of a Salesman* as if the light was coming through and hitting the leaves, so the bright part of the template was the leaves. When I first worked for Jo I drew up the template for *The Most Happy Fella* and it was designed as if light was coming through the open area of the trees, so the dark part is the leaves and the light parts are the openings. When I saw *The Most Happy Fella* for the first time, I was absolutely overwhelmed by how well the leaf gobos worked. I realized that what Jo did was very carefully have areas with no gobos, so there are large patches that are dark, as if they were the body of the tree. At that time, a lot of people didn't know how to use the leaf gobo. They tended to just throw gobos all over the stage and it looked messy. At first glance it may look like sunlight through the leaves, but when you look carefully it's a lot of dappled light breaking up the space. The minute I started working for Joe Papp I created a template based on the design I did for Jo. But in a Broadway theatre the lights are at a higher angle [than at the Delacorte]. Jo adjusted the template so the holes are bigger on the lower part than the top to compensate for the angle. I decided not to do that, which gave us a little more freedom. That template became a stock unit, and it's called the Ming Cho Lee template. You can still get it. Then Tony Walton did a template. And Jules Fisher has a template. But I still feel most people really don't know how to use gobos properly.

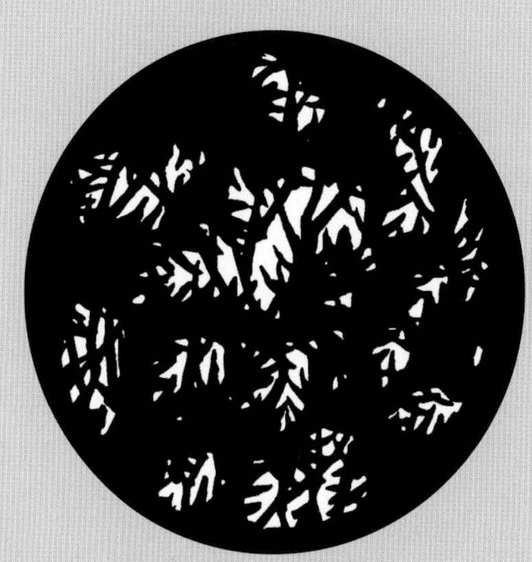

29

30

31

29 ***King John***, Shakespeare Theatre Company, 1999, production photograph. "*King John* eventually looked better than I had expected. I had gone through a period of hating Shakespeare's histories, with everyone carrying banners. I *hate* it. That's because I had done so much of it at Shakespeare in the Park. There, you always expect a sound cue—trumpets—and all the banners come on. But in *King John*, when the red banners come out on top on the red parapet, it had a real look."

30, 31 ***The Merchant of Venice***, Shakespeare Theatre Company, 1999, sketch and production photograph.

32 ***Don Carlos***, Shakespeare Theatre, 2001, ¼" model. Panels, often with doors embedded in them, slid in from the sides and could alter the depth of the stage.

32

stage. "If you do it in the period," Lee asserts, "you cannot do a bad set. And I did not do a bad set. But it was not a great set." For Schiller's *Don Carlos,* however, another play rarely done in the U.S., Lee reverted to the spare postmodernist grayish-white box. In this case the walls, penetrated on both sides by Italian Renaissance door frames with windows above, were not at right angles but flared out, creating a perspective effect. A huge crucifix hung above the scenes with Philip II. For the opening garden scene Lee designed a flat cutout tree with leaves that sat partway upstage, essentially reducing the stage depth by half. "It looked great and it felt absolutely right to have a somewhat more artificial scenic look for garden," says Lee. But as the actors began to rehearse on the set, Kahn realized he needed more depth. "It forced the actors to flatten out and address the audience rather than each other. It became more of a political declamatory approach." The tree was eliminated and the garden was created instead through gobo patterns [see sidebar, page 267].

Lee is clearly more enamored of Verdi's *Don Carlos,* although he never designed the opera, but he is passionate about the democratic ideals that are the underpinnings of Schiller and the other Romantics. The plays, operas and literature of this era resonate with the politics that informed Lee's aesthetics all his life. "Those people were at the forefront of human rights, liberty and freedom and anti-authoritarianism," Lee declares.

> **They were not afraid of making grand statements or preaching about liberty, about freedom. It is in their guts. They felt it and they fought for it. You cannot listen to Beethoven's Fifth Symphony without feeling that here are artists that are at the beginning of creating a society, and we are the products of those people who somehow brought that whole idea into reality. When you work on *Don Carlos,* and when Don Roderigo begins to talk about the need for Flanders to be independent, you want to stand up and cheer. You're not embarrassed by it. They are great plays and great operas. Deeply political. I swear I don't find that in today's plays.**

A CHRISTMAS CAROL

It may seem odd to end a chapter on new directions with the warhorse of the regional theatre, *A Christmas Carol,* but Lee finally joined the crowd, designing a production at McCarter Theatre Center in 2000 that has continued to be performed annually. When Emily Mann asked him to do it, he was skeptical, but also intrigued by the challenge. The resulting design was deeply informed by Lee's work of the previous decade—he compares the design to that of *The Hollow Lands*—and it is undoubtedly one of the more somber, expressionistic and deeply Victorian scenographic examples of the story being done today.

From the start Lee functioned as a counterbalance to the impulses of the writer, David Thompson, and director Michael Unger. Of course *A Christmas Carol* has to be a family entertainment, but Lee fought the sentimentality. The script called for a narrative framing device of a father telling the story to a little girl in bed. Lee, never one to be reticent, refused. "I rebelled, saying that is a terrible way of starting!" Lee instead proposed starting with the stage covered in a dirty-white ground cloth, representing snow, a vista of dark Victorian London buildings, and "a really sad Christmas tree" in the middle of the stage, with Tiny Tim sitting beside it—and that is how the show ultimately began. Many scenes employed expressionist distortion and angularity that, in combination with the dark hues, gave it an ominous, even frightening, aspect.

Lee's design career seemed to be winding down. He was getting fewer calls and, after nearly five decades of designing, he began to contemplate retirement. In 2001 there were only two shows, *Don Carlos* at the Shakespeare Theatre and a dance, *Firecracker,* an adaptation of *The Nutcracker* set in Shanghai at Chinese New Year, for the little-known Michael Mao Dance Company. Lee did the initial designs, but passed it on to an assistant, Adam Stockhausen, to complete. The following year he did *Antony and Cleopatra* at the Guthrie and a double bill of Molière comedies, *School for Husbands* and *The Imaginary Cuckold,* directed by Brian Bedford, at the Taper, which was reprised at Chicago Shakespeare Theater in 2004, his only production that year.

In 2003 he designed a dance for the Joffrey Ballet for the first time in thirty-four years, *I/DNA,* Gerald Arpino's response to the Illinois death penalty controversy in which DNA samples proved the innocence of some death-row inmates. In the dance a Christ figure is set to be executed in what one critic termed "Ming Cho Lee's mother of all electric chairs, a towering wooden set piece" (*Chicago Tribune,* April 25, 2003). And finally, Pacific Northwest Ballet's *Swan Lake* in 2003. But the fates intervened, and while Lee would, in fact, retire, he went out with a bang—a burst of four major designs in 2005.

33

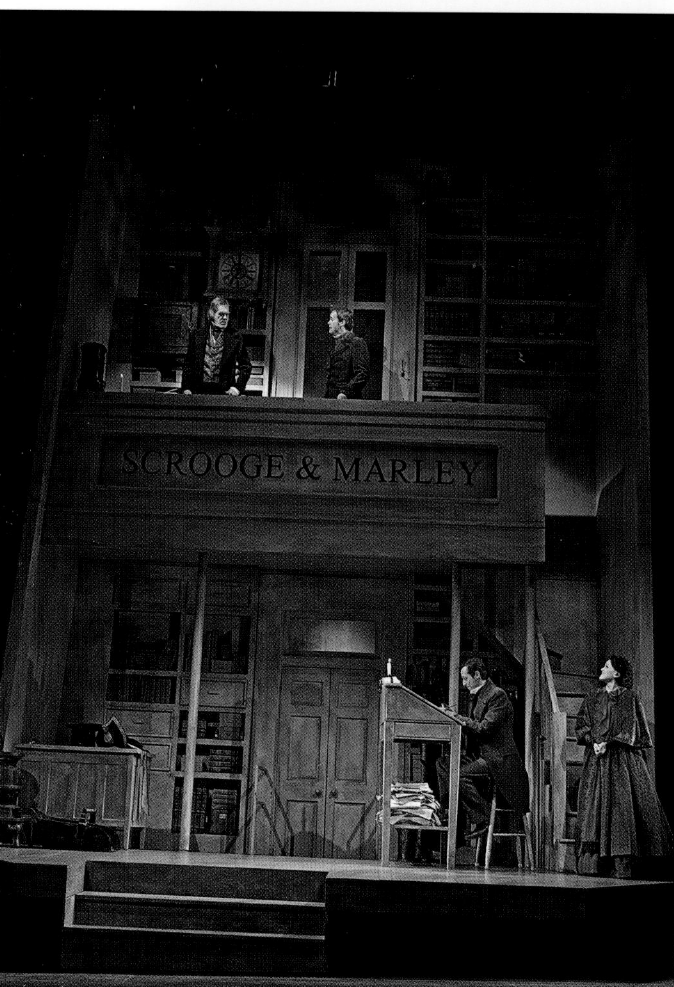

34

35

A Christmas Carol

McCarter Theatre Center, 2000

33 Production photograph of the opening scene with "a really sad Christmas tree," Tiny Tim and a photo-blowup of St. Paul's Cathedral.

34 Production photograph of Scrooge and Marley's office showing the expressionist angling of the set.

35 Photograph, exterior of Scrooge's house. The building was copied from Ian MacNeil's design for *An Inspector Calls* (1994). When the director expressed surprise that Lee would copy someone else's design, Lee responded, "By the time I'm finished it won't be the same," though the resemblance is clear. (It is worth noting that before MacNeil designed *An Inspector Calls,* he studied with Lee to get a better grasp of designing for the American theatre and was thus influenced by Lee's work. So there is a degree of mutual borrowing or inspiration.)

36

37

36 ***The School for Husbands***, Mark Taper Forum, 2002, photograph. Lee set the play in the French classical style of François Mansart. "I wanted it to look like the French stage designs of the 1950s."

37 ***The Imaginary Cuckold***, Mark Taper Forum, 2002, photograph. In contrast to *The School for Husbands* Lee designed a gothic cottage against a park-like backdrop to create a more informal atmosphere.

CHAPTER 16

2005 and Beyond

1

1 ***Annie***, national tour, 2005, ¼" model, Times Square. Lee felt this design marked a coming full circle since his first professional design was Times Square for *Guys and Dolls* at the Grist Mill Playhouse in 1955.

2 Lee, fourth from left, after receiving the National Medal of Arts with, from left, Karen Lerner-Lee, President Bush, Katherine Lerner-Lee, Betsy, Richard Lee, stepsister Fay Loo, Laura Bush and cousin Billy Ming Sing Lee.

THE YEAR 2004 MARKED FIFTY YEARS since Lee moved to New York. Now in his seventies, the long hours and the rigors of travel were taking their toll. Opera companies were looking for younger, hipper designers, his long-time collaborators were retiring and young directors were not calling. It seemed time to retire from designing—a decision that Lee did not regret. He would still be teaching, overseeing the Clambake and continuing to do master classes around the country. As if to emphasize the end of a career, he received the 2002 National Medal of Arts, the country's highest honor for artistic excellence. This posed a conundrum for Lee. President George W. Bush, who would present the award, epitomized the opposite of everything Lee stood for, and the thought of having to shake his hand was distasteful. But after long discussions with his family Lee agreed to accept, reasoning that the award was granted by the National Endowment for the Arts and nominations came from fellow artists and arts organizations. Furthermore, unless you are a high-profile individual, few people would even know that you turned it down. (Adrienne Rich, Stephen Sondheim, Wallace Stegner and Leonard Bernstein had previously rejected the award.) And it would be a once-in-a-lifetime chance for his granddaughter Katie to visit the White House.

With no new productions in 2004, he had reached a logical endpoint. But sometime that year he got a call from Gordon Davidson who told him that he, too, was retiring as artistic director of Center Theatre Group (the Mark Taper Forum, Ahmanson Theatre and Kirk Douglas Theatre) and wanted Lee to design his final production. It was a touching gesture and a most appropriate conclusion for both of them. The only problem was that Davidson was not sure what play he wanted to direct—possibly two Shakespeares in rep. Then Gordon Edelstein, artistic director of Long Wharf Theatre in New Haven, asked him to design Eugene O'Neill's *A Moon for the Misbegotten*. At almost the same time, Michael Kahn at the Shakespeare Theatre Company asked him to design Alfred de Musset's *Lorenzaccio*. Suddenly Lee had three shows, all scheduled to open in the first half of 2005. Then, with the design process underway for *Lorenzaccio* and *Moon*, Lee received a call from Martin Charnin, who asked him to design a touring revival of *Annie* which might possibly end up on Broadway to coincide with the show's thirtieth anniversary. It was hard to resist one last chance at a musical and possibly one last shot at Broadway. He gave Davidson a mid-December deadline for choosing a play if he hoped to have it designed in time for a May or June opening. That deadline came and went. But with three shows in the works simultaneously, the studio was back up and running.

Lorenzaccio is a French romantic closet drama, set in the sixteenth-century world of the Medicis. The convoluted plot of intrigue and decadence, adapted for this production by John Strand, is fundamentally an examination of the failure of republican ideals in the face of power and corruption. Lee's set was a sort of amalgamation of his sky boxes and the telescoping panels of *Nine Songs*. The basic design was a box with a kind of minimalist colonnade on the bottom half of the three walls. The ever-shifting panels of the back wall allowed rapid changes from bedroom to tavern to garden. Covering the walls was a detail of a fifteenth-century painting by Carlo Crivelli, *St. Jerome and St. Augustine* (the same painting used in the Louisville *Othello*). In the Crivelli painting the two men are depicted full length, St. Augustine in resplendent bishop's garb staring at the dour St. Jerome in cardinal red. But Lee cropped the painting, focusing it so tightly that not even the full faces of the two saints are visible, and thus all religious reference and iconography is eradicated. The image is enlarged to an overpowering size, making them brooding, terrifying figures, "people who control the world," Lee told the *Washington Post* (February 4, 2005). In certain ways, this

3

3 *Lorenzaccio,* Shakespeare Theatre, 2005, ¼" model of great hall with the faces of St. Jerome and St. Augustine from the Crivelli painting looming over the set.

4

5

6

Lorenzaccio

Shakespeare Theatre, 2005

4 Production photograph of the cathedral.

5 Production photograph of the bedroom. Sliding panels could create a strong sense of enclosure

6 Production photograph of the final scene in which the red panels were removed and a simple wooden scaffold took center stage for the coronation of Duke Cosimo.

7

8

A Moon for the Misbegotten

Long Wharf Theatre, 2005

7 Production photograph. The smaller rocks were real, but the big boulder O'Neill required had to be built. In order not to call attention to its difference from the other rocks, a few more boulders were constructed as well. Despite the two poles on either side of the stage, and the low light grid, there was a quality of absolute reality. To achieve the weathered look of the house, Lee used his "dirty-water wash"—dirty water mixed with sizing, "then you take a big brush and do Jackson Pollock."

8 Lee with lighting designer Jennifer Tipton, center, and costume designer Jennifer von Mayrhauser on the set of *A Moon for the Misbegotten.*

9

10

Stuff Happens

Mark Taper Forum, 2005

9 Photograph of the set with the projection that Lee wanted (eliminated after the first preview). Pictured, from left, are Colin Powell, Dick Cheney, President Bush, Condoleezza Rice, Paul Wolfowitz (whom Lee substituted for chief of staff Andrew Card), George Tenet and Donald Rumsfeld. The basic structure of the back wall was the same as for *Portrait of the Families* for Cloud Gate Dance Theatre.

10 Set with the White House image that was ultimately used throughout the show.

set, one of his last, calls to mind two of his most important earlier works. Like the icon wall of *Boris Godunov* the faces—the eyes—are inescapable. Because of the angle of St. Jerome's gaze, he seems to be sitting in judgment of the spectators even more than the characters. And while the structure is admittedly different, the set echoes the floating walls of *Electra*. The earthbound characters operate on the plane of the stage, while hovering around them is the realm of power with only slim fragments of the painting anchoring it to the world below.

Lee's design for *A Moon for the Misbegotten*, O'Neill's sequel to *Long Day's Journey into Night*, was a return to the superrealism of *Traveler in the Dark*, with which it shared a similar ground plan. Lee had seen the original production at the Bijou Theatre in 1957 as well as a production at Arena Stage in 2002. There was one aspect of the latter production that had bothered him. Although the setting suggested the rugged dirt terrain of the Hogan farm, when Josie ran onstage barefoot her feet were absolutely clean and, remarks Lee, "It took any sense of reality out of the show. And when you don't believe the people, *Moon for the Misbegotten* can be a big bore." He and Edelstein agreed that everything had to be as real as possible, especially the ground, and Lee visited old farms off Connecticut back roads for research. There was a layer of dirt and grass mats on the sloped stage floor, a working pump and rocks.

By this time, with several O'Neill productions to his credit, Lee felt that the way to approach the play was to ignore his detailed stage directions and work from a close reading of the text. The crucial element was the porch on which much of the play transpired, and the whole ground plan was determined by the siting of the porch. The slightly surreal sky cyc placed the setting in relief and further foregrounded its reality. Parts of the front of the house were cut away to reveal the interior, particularly Josie's bedroom. When Jennifer Tipton's lighting revealed Josie on the bed, "it was so real you felt you were seeing something out of an Ingmar Bergman film," Lee recalls. (Tipton uses only the bare essential number of lighting instruments, a rarity in the contemporary theatre, but the result, says Lee, is "exquisite.") The production was subsequently remounted at Hartford Stage and the Alley Theatre in Houston. "*Lorenzaccio* was a good show, and *Moon for the Misbegotten* was a very, very good show," says Lee. "It was a good way to finish up at places where I had worked."

STUFF HAPPENS

Meanwhile, in late January, Gordon Davidson finally called to say he had a play that Lee could not refuse—not a classic, as he had originally intended, but *Stuff Happens* by British playwright David Hare. Betsy told him there was no longer enough time to design it, but Davidson begged her to take a look and emailed the script. Betsy read it, called Ming at Yale and said, "It's unbelievable," and forwarded it to him. Lee read it on the train on they way home. When he walked in the door, recalls Betsy, "We looked at each other and said, 'We cannot *not* do this show.'" This was the sort of political play that Lee had been hungering for, a type that was largely absent from the contemporary American theatre. The title came from Donald Rumsfeld's response to the looting in Baghdad after the fall of Saddam Hussein, and the play took verbatim dialogue from public speeches and press conferences and combined it with imagined scenarios of private meetings, particularly between Bush and British Prime Minister Tony Blair.

What better way for Lee to end his career than with a play that appeared to condemn the policies of George W. Bush and the White House coterie that manipulated the country into the Iraq War? Perhaps it was a chance to express the things he couldn't say when he was presented with the National Medal of Arts.

Lee had worked with Hare once before, on a production of *Plenty* at Arena Stage in 1980, directed by David Chambers. Lee had designed a technically ambitious set that ran into serious complications, and Lee believes that Hare blamed him for all the problems and was not happy to have to work with him again in Los Angeles. From the start Hare was resistant to Lee's ideas. The basic ground plan for *Stuff Happens* was simple. There was a platform upstage about four feet high with steps on either side descending to the thrust, which was level with the auditorium floor. There were four office cubicles around the perimeter of the thrust, turning it into a kind of pit in which the many scenes unfolded. Lee wanted projected images on the arcade-like back wall, but the question was, what would these be?

Lee's original thought was to reproduce the cover of the British edition of the published play that showed Rumsfeld speaking with Bush at his side. But Davidson didn't think this was quite right. He suggested an image of the White House, but Lee thought that was boring. "How many chances do we have in the American theatre

Annie

National tour, 2005

11–14 ¼" models for, from top, the orphanage, St. Mark's Place, Hooverville and the East Room.

to make a statement like this?" asked Lee. "If we are going to do something, we should do something that if you were doing it in Communist China you would be arrested. We should at least do something that's arrestable." But Hare insisted that his play was not propaganda or a polemic. As Lee remembers, Hare said, "I didn't write a play for Americans to vent their anger. A good deal of it is about Tony Blair, and I want it to remain a theatre piece." Lee relented and provided an image of the White House. But then he came across an Annie Leibovitz photograph of the Bush inner circle in an issue of *Vanity Fair* and thought it would be perfect for the close of the show. The White House would fade out and this would fade in, confronting the audience with the perpetrators of the war. He convinced Davidson to try it for a preview performance, and Hare reluctantly agreed. But the projection was not really readable for spectators on the sides, and Davidson, probably worried about Hare's reaction, used that as an excuse to cut it after the first preview. Perhaps it would have been too blatant, but given the docudrama aspect of the play, it was not an unreasonable idea—and it was a haunting final image.

ANNIE

Lee's final project was *Annie*, and he had a history of sorts with the musical. The original show, with sets by Lee's former assistant David Mitchell, opened on Broadway in 1977 and ran for almost 2,400 performances. In 1992, lyricist and original director Martin Charnin created a sequel, *Annie Warbucks*, which premiered in Chicago with sets by Thomas M. Ryan. Charnin asked Lee to design a Broadway-bound version. There was a five-city pre-Broadway tour, but at the last minute the curse of Broadway struck again, and the financial backing for the New York production fell through. The play eventually made it to New York in 1993, but as a totally revised low-budget Off-Broadway production with a flat cutout cartoon-style design. This turned out to be the last show Lee designed in New York City.

Despite his history with musicals, Lee still enjoyed designing them, and he was determined to have fun with the revival of *Annie*. The set—conceived as a series of single drops with translucencies in order to accommodate touring and a rather limited budget—is an unabashedly exuberant musical comedy design. Although he thought that Mitchell's design for the original was a "masterpiece," Lee wanted to make it his own. He employed elements of the expressionist vocabulary he had used in *The Hollow Lands* and *A Christmas Carol*, and there is an underlying sense of menace in several of the scenes. The orphanage has a postmodern nightmarish quality; the melancholy Hooverville scene under the Fifty-Ninth Street Bridge was inspired by Jo Mielziner's famous design for *Winterset*; the slanted buildings surrounding the construction site for the St. Mark's scene throw everything off kilter. Lee was particularly proud of his Times Square drop. "It took me two *Guys and Dolls*, but I finally got it right in *Annie*." *Annie* opened shortly before Lee's seventy-fifth birthday, almost fifty years to the day after his first professional show, *Guys and Dolls* at the Grist Mill Playhouse. There were multiple touring companies and the first actually made it to New York, though not Broadway. It played at the Theater at Madison Square Garden in December 2006 as a holiday attraction. Lee refused to see it there—"It's a horrible place to see a show. Terrible." The tour continued until 2010.

Officially retired from designing, Lee continued to teach and co-chair the design department at Yale, commuting to New Haven on Wednesdays and Saturdays. He thought he would return to his first love—watercolors. His first paintings were done along the coast of Maine. It took him longer than he expected to rid himself of the theatre habit of beginning with rough sketches. He soon tired of the Maine landscape and tried other subjects, but it remained unsatisfying. "I felt these were not true watercolors. They were not *me*." He felt, oddly, that his technique was too good. But in studying some of J.M.W. Turner's late paintings he came across one with the ocean horizon created by a single big brush stroke, leaving the edges rough. And there were some that seemed as if they were "painted by an old person with a shaky hand—like me." Lee tried leaving the paintings purposely incomplete, with empty space, but "no matter how I tried, they became cleaner—just the opposite effect." Finally, "I dropped it. Washed all the brushes and put them back."

He developed some physical ailments, including a broken hip, which made getting around much more difficult, and pretty much put an end to any theatregoing, though he did travel to China in June 2011 for an exhibition of his work in Shanghai and Ningbo. The next summer he stepped down as co-chair of the design department, though continuing to teach—it is impossible for Lee, or anyone, to imagine what he would do if he stopped teaching.

11

12

13

14

THE LEGACY OF MING CHO LEE

Lee transformed American design in the mid-twentieth century and holds a place in theatre history alongside Robert Edmond Jones, Jo Mielziner and Boris Aronson. Lee moved American scenography away from the painterly and imagistic toward the emblematic and iconic. He made the stage a sculptural place. Particularly with the pipework scaffolding for which he became known, he replaced poetic realism with a modern industrial sensibility. But he never became trapped in a particular style, and his design continued to evolve throughout his career. Lee understood the stage as a cubic volume in which each dimension was equally important, particularly the vertical, which was virtually unknown in the American theatre when his career began. When asked to comment on Lee's work, his colleague, lighting designer Jennifer Tipton, made a vertical soaring motion with her hands. Perhaps language is inadequate—the verticality evokes a visceral or kinesthetic response.

Lee was the catalyst who transformed American design, and yet he never became a "household name" (not that the public is ever much aware of designers). This is really to say that he never established a Broadway career, and even in opera, which defined much of his life, he did not have a sustained career at any of the major opera houses. There is a sense in which Lee was slightly out of sync with developments in the American theatre. He was inspired in part by German designers—but those designers tended to work closely with equally iconoclastic directors or were, like Wieland Wagner, director-designers. Lee was fortunate to work with outstanding directors, including Gerald Freedman, Tito Capobianco, Gordon Davidson and Jon Jory, directors who were open to exploration and embraced the new visual aesthetic that Lee introduced, but who could not be described as iconoclastic. Lee's collaborations with somewhat more radical directors such as A.J. Antoon, Andre Gregory, Liviu Ciulei and Michael Kahn produced some of his most adventurous designs, but these collaborations were few and far between or, as with the majority of his work with Kahn, late in his career. It would take a new generation of directors, inspired by the avant-garde and experimental theatre of the 1960s and '70s as well as in developments in parts of Europe, to radicalize theatre and opera and move these forms into the realm of the postmodern, and these directors most often wanted to work with designers from their own generation who shared a cultural aesthetic. But Lee's presence could be felt even there, as many of the new generation of designers were his former students.

Lee often expresses his fear that changes in theatre, art and technology have somehow left him behind. In regard to certain aspects of technology that may be true, but as an artist he proved time and again, down to his final designs, that he has few equals. The specific styles and techniques of Lee's work, like those of his predecessors, will be superseded by others, as they should be. But he also has something that none of his mentors had—generations of students. This may be his true legacy—not any particular scenographic aesthetic he may have taught them, but rather an approach to design and a belief, as Susan Hilferty says, "in the power of art, in the voice of the individual. He believes that if he is truthful, that has the possibility of changing the world." Lee offered an example of living a life in art. His son Christopher may have the most insightful analysis:

> **He found a way to succeed in a nearly impossible task: to make a living as a working artist. How many people who try to eke out an existence as an artist are able to do so the way my father has? Very few. In many ways it is an unrealistic model to hold up for anyone, and yet there it is, a testament to the possible. In the end, the sheer breadth of his work and vision demands respect, and combined with his work at Yale, the legacy of the Clambake and his personal history as an immigrant to this country, they paint a portrait of a unique and important man, and a truly American artist.**

15

15 Lee family portrait, 2013. Back row, from left, David Vi Fa Lee, Eileen Malyszko Lee, Christopher Vi Gning Lee, Karen Lerner-Lee, Richard Vi Sung Lee; middle row, from left, Ming Cho Lee, Betsy Lee; front row, from left, Oona Ru Anh Lee, Eamon Anthony Ru Cho Lee, Katherine Shulamit Ru-Ying Lerner-Lee.

Watercolors

Los Angeles 1950, watercolor on paperboard, 18½" × 24"

As a teenager in Shanghai, Lee studied watercolor painting for two years with the master Chang Kwo Nyen. He resumed his study at Occidental College, where he took several art courses, partly to offset his poor grades in other classes as a result of his still shaky English. Painting provided a much more personal outlet for Lee's creativity, and it also seemed to provide a kind of refuge during times of stress or transition. Some of his most prolific periods as a painter coincided with his move to New York, the death of his mother, and his retirement from professional designing, as well as on rare vacations. For this portfolio Lee selected a small sampling of his work between 1950—his second year at Occidental—and 2007, when he stopped painting.

Los Angeles 1952, gouache and watercolor on paperboard, 22" × 28"

New York 1955, watercolor on paperboard, 15" × 21½"

New York, 72nd Street and Broadway 1955, watercolor on paperboard, 28¾" × 19⅝"

New York, West 100th Street 1956, watercolor on paperboard, 21½" × 15"

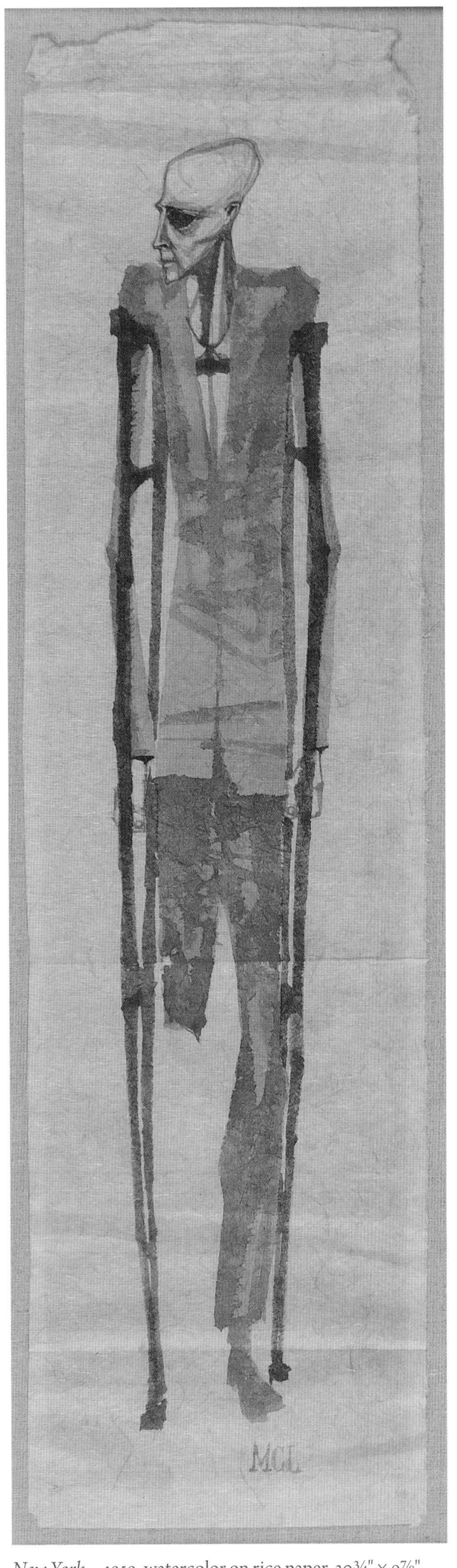

New York 1959, watercolor on rice paper, 30¾" × 9⅞"

Cape Cod 1986, watercolor on watercolor paper, 14¼" × 20"

Cape Cod 1986, watercolor on watercolor paper , 14½" × 20"

Cape Cod 1986, watercolor on watercolor paper, 14¼" × 20"

Oregon Coast (A & B) 1987, watercolor on watercolor paper, 18¼" × 24⅛"

Washington Coast 1987, watercolor on watercolor paper, 18¼" × 24⅛"

Eureka, CA 1987, watercolor on watercolor paper, 18" × 23¼"

San Francisco 1987, watercolor on watercolor paper, 16¼" × 12¼"

Near Bar Harbor, ME   late 1980s, watercolor on watercolor paper, 23¾" × 18"

Phippsburg, ME late 1980s, watercolor on watercolor paper, 7¼" × 10½"

Bar Harbor, ME   2007, watercolor on watercolor paper, 14¼" × 20"

Bar Harbor, ME (A, B & C)   2007, watercolor on watercolor paper, each 10¼" × 14¼"

Near Bar Harbor, ME 2007, watercolor on watercolor paper, 14¼" × 20"

Maine Coast 2007, watercolor on watercolor paper, 14¼" × 20"

Maine Coast 2007, watercolor on watercolor paper, 14¼" × 20"

Maine 2007, watercolor on watercolor paper, 14¼" × 20"

Chronology

1930 OCT 3 Ming Cho Lee is born in Shanghai

Lee painting scenery in Indianapolis for the Met's National Company tour of *The Marriage of Figaro*, 1966.

Unless otherwise noted, all sets designed by Ming Cho Lee.

1948

NOV Moves to Hong Kong with his family

1949

OCT Arrives in Los Angeles to begin studying at Occidental College

1952

THE SILVER WHISTLE

FEB 29–MAR 1 Occidental College, Los Angeles; by Robert E. McEnroe, directed by Omar M. Paxson

THE ADDING MACHINE

APR 25–26 Occidental College, Los Angeles; by Elmer Rice, directed by Omar M. Paxson

LADY IN THE DARK

SUMMER Camden Hills Playhouse, ME; book by Moss Hart, music by Kurt Weill, lyrics by Ira Gershwin

THE MADWOMAN OF CHAILLOT

DEC 5–6 Occidental College, Los Angeles; by Jean Giraudoux, directed by Omar M. Paxson

1953

LADY AUDLEY'S SECRET

MAR 5–7 Occidental College, Los Angeles; by C.H. Hazlewood, directed by Omar M. Paxson

MUCH ADO ABOUT NOTHING

APR 24–25 Occidental College, Los Angeles; by Shakespeare, directed by LanNor Lombard

SEP Begins master's program at University of California, Los Angeles

1954

THE PEARL

APR 20 Royce Hall, University of California, Los Angeles; adapted and directed by John Jones

SUMMER Moves to New York City

NOV Starts working for Jo Mielziner

1955

THE REHEARSAL CLUB REVUE

MAR 2–3 Carl Fischer Concert Hall, New York City; by Carol Burnett et al., directed by Don Saroyan, sets and lighting by Ming Cho Lee

JUN Passes United Scenic Artists union exam

GUYS AND DOLLS

JUL 2–10 Grist Mill Playhouse, Andover, NJ; book by Abe Burrows and Jo Swerling, music and lyrics by Frank Loesser, directed by Nick Mayo, choreography by Mark West, costumes by Alvin Colt

OH, MEN! OH, WOMEN!

JUL 12–17 Grist Mill Playhouse, Andover, NJ; by Edward Chodorov

1956

HAPPY HUNTING

DEC 6–NOV 30, 1957 Majestic Theatre, Broadway; book by Howard Lindsay and Russel Crouse, music by Harold Karr, lyrics by Matt Dubey, directed by Abe Burrows, choreography by Alex Romero and Bob Herget, sets and lighting by Jo Mielziner, costumes by Irene Sharaff; technical assistant, Ming Cho Lee

1957

THE SQUARE ROOT OF WONDERFUL

OCT 30–DEC 7 National Theatre, Broadway; by Carson McCullers, directed by George Keathley, sets and lighting by Jo Mielziner, costumes by Noel Taylor; assistant scenic designer, Ming Cho Lee

LOOK HOMEWARD, ANGEL

NOV 28–APR 4, 1959 Ethel Barrymore Theatre, Broadway; by Ketti Frings, directed by George Roy Hill, sets and lighting by Jo Mielziner, costumes by Motley; assistant scenic designer, Ming Cho Lee

1958

THE INFERNAL MACHINE

FEB 3–MAR 9 Phoenix Theatre, Off Broadway; by Jean Cocteau, adapted by Albert Bermel, directed by Herbert Berghof, costumes by Alvin Colt, lighting by Tharon Musser

MADAMA BUTTERFLY

PREMIERED FEB 19 Metropolitan Opera, New York City; music by Puccini, libretto by Luigi Illica and Giuseppe Giacosa, conducted by Dimitri Mitropoulos, directed by Yoshio Aoyama, sets and costumes by Motohiro Nagasaka, lighting by Rudolph Kuntner; supervisory costume designer, Ming Cho Lee

THE CRUCIBLE

MAR 11–JUN 14, 1959 Martinique Theatre, Off Broadway; by Arthur Miller, directed by Word Baker, sets and lighting by Ming Cho Lee, costumes by Patricia Zipprodt

MAR 21 Marries Elizabeth (Betsy) Rapport

MISSA BREVIS

PREMIERED APR 11–12 Juilliard Dance Theater, New York City; choreography by José Limón, music by Zoltán Kodály, projection and costumes by Ming Cho Lee, lighting by Thomas DeGaetani

THE WORLD OF SUZIE WONG

OCT 14–JAN 2, 1960 Broadhurst Theatre, Broadway; by Paul Osborn, directed by Joshua Logan, sets and lighting by Jo Mielziner, costumes by Dorothy Jeakins; assistant scenic designer, Ming Cho Lee

TRIAD (*The Dress*, *Tale for a Deaf Ear* and *Sweet Betsy from Pike*)

NOV 21–DEC 20 Theatre Marquee, Off Broadway; music and libretto by Mark Bucci, directed by Richard Altman, sets and lighting by Ming Cho Lee

WHOOP-UP

DEC 22–FEB 7, 1959 Shubert Theatre, Broadway; book by Cy Feuer, Ernest H. Martin and Dan Cushman, music by Moose Charlap, lyrics by Norman Gimbel, directed by Feuer, choreography by Onna White, sets and lighting by Jo Mielziner, costumes by Anna Hill Johnstone; assistant scenic designer, Ming Cho Lee

DEC Starts working for Boris Aronson

1959

GYPSY

MAY 21–MAR 25, 1961 Broadway Theatre, Broadway; book by Arthur Laurents, music by Jule Styne, lyrics by Stephen Sondheim, directed and choreographed by Jerome Robbins, sets and lighting by Jo Mielziner, costumes by Raoul Pène Du Bois; assistant scenic designer, Ming Cho Lee

JUN 15 Son Richard is born

TENEBRAE, 1914

AUG 13–14 American Dance Festival, Palmer Auditorium, New London, CT; choreography by José Limón, music by John Wilson, costumes by Pauline Lawrence, lighting by Thomas Skelton

THE APOSTATE

AUG 15 American Dance Festival, Palmer Auditorium, New London, CT; choreography by José Limón, music by Ernst Krenek, costumes by Pauline Lawrence, lighting by Thomas Skelton

IL TROVATORE

PREMIERED OCT 26 Metropolitan Opera, New York City; music by Verdi, libretto by Salvadore Cammarano, conducted by Fausto Cleva, directed by Herbert Graf, sets and costumes by Motley, lighting by Rudolph Kuntner; assistant designer, Ming Cho Lee

LE NOZZE DI FIGARO

PREMIERED OCT 30 Metropolitan Opera, New York City; music by Mozart, libretto by Lorenzo Da Ponte, conducted by Erich Leinsdorf, directed by Cyril Ritchard, choreography by John Butler, sets and costumes by Oliver Messel, lighting by Rudolph Kuntner; assistant to Messel, Ming Cho Lee

A LOSS OF ROSES

NOV 28–DEC 19 Eugene O'Neill Theatre, Broadway; by William Inge, directed by Daniel Mann, sets by Boris Aronson, costumes by Lucinda Ballard, lighting by Abe Feder; assistant to Aronson, Ming Cho Lee

THE TURK IN ITALY

DEC 15–17 Peabody Art Theatre, Baltimore; music by Rossini, libretto by Felice Romani, translated by George and Phyllis Mead, conducted by Laszlo Halasz, directed by Lee Williams, choreography by Carol Lynn

1960

THERE WAS A LITTLE GIRL

FEB 29–MAR 12 Cort Theatre, Broadway; by Daniel Taradash, directed by Joshua Logan, sets and lighting by Jo Mielziner, costumes by Patton Campbell; assistant scenic designer, Ming Cho Lee

THE FALL OF THE CITY

MAR 1 Peabody Art Theatre, Baltimore; music by James Cohn, libretto by Archibald MacLeish, conducted by Laszlo Halasz, directed by Lucas Hoving

THE OLD MAID AND THE THIEF

MAR 1 Peabody Art Theatre, Baltimore; music, libretto and direction by Gian Carlo Menotti, conducted by Laszlo Halasz

THE BEST MAN

MAR 31–JUL 8, 1961 Morosco Theatre, Broadway; by Gore Vidal, directed by Joseph Anthony, sets and lighting by Jo Mielziner, costumes by Theoni V. Aldredge; assistant scenic designer, Ming Cho Lee

LA BOHÈME

APR 26–30 Peabody Art Theatre, Baltimore; music by Puccini, libretto by Luigi Illica and Giuseppe Giacosa, translated by Joseph Machlis, conducted by Laszlo Halasz, directed by Désirè Defrère

THE RIDDLE OF SHEBA

MAY 21–22 Temple Emanu-El, Yonkers, NY; book and lyrics by Morton Wishengrad, music by Mildred Kayden, directed and choreographed by Lucas Hoving, costumes by Lavina Nielsen

PETER IBBETSON

JUL 22–29 Empire State Music Festival, Bear Mountain, NY; music by Deems Taylor, libretto by Constance Collier and Taylor, conducted by Wilfrid Pelletier, directed by Désirè Defrère

KÁTYA KABANOVÁ

JUL 30 Empire State Music Festival, Bear Mountain, NY; music by Leoš Janáček, libretto by Norman Tucker, conducted by Laszlo Halasz, directed by Christopher West, sets and lighting by Ming Cho Lee

NOV 3 Son Christopher is born

THE OLD MAID AND THE THIEF

DEC 8 Peabody Art Theatre, Baltimore; music, libretto and direction by Gian Carlo Menotti, conducted by Laszlo Halasz

AMAHL AND THE NIGHT VISITORS

DEC 8 Peabody Art Theatre, Baltimore; music, libretto and direction by Gian Carlo Menotti, conducted by Herbert Grossman, choreography by Carol Lynn

DO RE MI

DEC 26–JAN 19, 1962 St. James Theatre, Broadway; book and direction by Garson Kanin, music by Jule Styne, lyrics by Betty Comden and Adolph Green, choreography by Marc Breaux and Dee Dee Wood, sets by Boris Aronson, costumes by Irene Sharaff, lighting by Al Alloy; assistant to Aronson, Ming Cho Lee

1961

LES PÊCHEURS DE PERLES
(*The Pearl Fishers*)

MAR 23 Peabody Art Theatre, Baltimore; music by Georges Bizet, libretto by Michel Carré and Eugène Cormon, conducted by Laszlo Halasz, directed by Hugh Thompson, choreography by Carol Lynn, sets and costumes by Ming Cho Lee

THREE TIMES OFFENBACH
(*The Magic Fife*, *Mariage aux Lanternes* and *The Island of Tulipatan*)

MAY 4 Peabody Art Theatre, Baltimore; music by Jacques Offenbach, librettos by Charles Nuitter and Étienne Tréfeu (*Fife*), Michel Carré and Léon Battu (*Mariage*) and Henri Chivot and Alfred Duru (*Tulipatan*), translated by Robert Simon, conducted by Laszlo Halasz, directed by Salvatore Baccaloni, sets and costumes by Ming Cho Lee

MAY Moves to San Francisco

THE PEARL FISHERS

JUL 12–21 Empire State Music Festival, Bear Mountain, NY; music by Georges Bizet, libretto by Michel Carré and Eugène Cormon, conducted by Laszlo Halasz, directed by Hugh Thompson, sets and costumes by Ming Cho Lee

LUCIA DI LAMMERMOOR

SEP 15–OCT 25 San Francisco Opera, War Memorial Opera House; OCT 29–NOV 4 on tour, Los Angeles and San Diego; music by Donizetti, libretto by Salvadore Cammarano, conducted by Francesco Molinari-Pradelli, directed by Dino Yannopoulos, choreography by Lew Christensen, production design by Leni Bauer-Ecsy with Ming Cho Lee

UN BALLO IN MASCHERA

OCT 12–20 San Francisco Opera, War Memorial Opera House; OCT 22–NOV 4 on tour, Sacramento and Los Angeles; music by Verdi, libretto by Antonio Somma, conducted by Francesco Molinari-Pradelli, directed by Dino Yannopoulos, choreography by Lew Christensen, costumes by Goldstein & Co.

DEC Returns to New York City

1962

DON GIOVANNI

JAN 19–21 Peabody Art Theatre, Baltimore; music by Mozart, libretto by Lorenzo da Ponte, translated by Edward J. Dent, conducted by Laszlo Halasz, directed by Hugh Thompson, sets and costumes by David Dekker, lighting by Ming Cho Lee

TRISTAN UND ISOLDE

MAR 5 Baltimore Opera Club and Peabody Conservatory of Music, Lyric Theatre; music and libretto by Richard Wagner, conducted by Laszlo Halasz, directed by Herbert Graf

A LOOK AT LIGHTNING

MAR 5–18 Martha Graham Dance Company, Broadway Theatre, New York City; choreography and costumes by Martha Graham, music by Halim El-Dabh, lighting by Jean Rosenthal

WERTHER

APR 25–29 Peabody Art Theatre, Baltimore; music by Jules Massenet, libretto by Edouard Blau, Paul Milliet and Georges Hartmann, conducted by Laszlo Halasz, directed by Margaret Fairbank, sets and lighting by Ming Cho Lee

THE MERCHANT OF VENICE

JUN 21–JUL 14 New York Shakespeare Festival, Delacorte Theater; by Shakespeare, directed by Joseph Papp and Gladys Vaughan, sets and lighting by Ming Cho Lee, costumes by Theoni V. Aldredge

THE TEMPEST

JUL 16–AUG 4 New York Shakespeare Festival, Delacorte Theater; by Shakespeare, directed by Gerald Freedman, choreography by Donald McKayle, sets and lighting by Ming Cho Lee, costumes by Theoni V. Aldredge

KING LEAR

AUG 13–SEP 1 New York Shakespeare Festival, Delacorte Theater; by Shakespeare, directed by Joseph Papp and Gladys Vaughan, sets and lighting by Ming Cho Lee, costumes by Theoni V. Aldredge

MACBETH

NOV 5–30 New York Shakespeare Festival, Heckscher Theatre; DEC–APR 1963 school tour; by Shakespeare, directed by Gladys Vaughan, sets and lighting by Ming Cho Lee, costumes by Theoni V. Aldredge

HAMLET

NOV 9–11 Peabody Art Theatre, Baltimore; music by Sergius Kagen, libretto by Shakespeare, conducted by Laszlo Halasz, directed by Joseph Papp, sets and lighting by Ming Cho Lee, costumes by Andrew Trimingham

MADAMA BUTTERFLY

DEC 2–6 Opera Company of Boston, Wellesley High School Auditorium, Harvard Square Theater, Winchester High School Auditorium; music by Puccini, libretto by Luigi Illica and Giuseppe Giacosa, translated by Ruth and Thomas Martin, conducted and directed by Sarah Caldwell, sets and lighting by Ming Cho Lee, costumes by Patricia Zipprodt

THE MOON BESIEGED

DEC 5 Lyceum Theatre, Broadway; by Seyril Schocken, directed by Lloyd Richards, sets and lighting by Ming Cho Lee, costumes by Robert Fletcher

1963

MOTHER COURAGE AND HER CHILDREN

MAR 28–MAY 11 Martin Beck Theatre, Broadway; by Bertolt Brecht, adapted by Eric Bentley, music by Paul Dessau, directed by Jerome Robbins, costumes by Motley, lighting by Tharon Musser

APR 10 Son David is born

ANTONY AND CLEOPATRA

JUN 13–JUL 6 New York Shakespeare Festival, Delacorte Theater; by Shakespeare, directed by Joseph Papp, sets and lighting by Ming Cho Lee, costumes by Theoni V. Aldredge

AS YOU LIKE IT

JUL 11–AUG 3 New York Shakespeare Festival, Delacorte Theater; by Shakespeare, directed by Gerald Freedman, sets and lighting by Ming Cho Lee, costumes by Theoni V. Aldredge

THE WINTER'S TALE

AUG 8–31 New York Shakespeare Festival, Delacorte Theater; by Shakespeare, directed by Gladys Vaughan, costumes by Theoni V. Aldredge, lighting by Martin Aronstein

TWELFTH NIGHT

OCT 7–27 New York Shakespeare Festival, Heckscher Theatre; OCT 28–DEC 19 school tour; by Shakespeare, directed by Joseph Papp, costumes by Theoni V. Aldredge, lighting by Martin Aronstein

WALK IN DARKNESS

OCT 28–NOV Greenwich Mews Theatre, Off Broadway; by William Hairston, directed by Sidney Walters, sets and lighting by Ming Cho Lee, costumes by Irish Ayres

CONVERSATIONS IN THE DARK
DEC 23–JAN 4 Walnut Street Theatre, Philadelphia; JAN 13–25 National Theatre, Washington, DC; by William Hanley, directed by Daniel Petrie, costumes by Michael Travis

1964

THE CLOAK (_Il Tabarro_)
JAN 24–25 Juilliard Opera Theater, New York City; music by Puccini, libretto by Giuseppe Adami, translated by Joseph Machlis, conducted by Emanuel Balaban, directed by Christopher West, costumes by Patton Campbell, lighting by Sidney Bennett

GIANNI SCHICCHI
JAN 24–25 Juilliard Opera Theater, New York City; music by Puccini, libretto by Giovacchino Forzano, translated by Percy Pitt, conducted by Frederic Waldman, directed by Christopher West, costumes by Patton Campbell, lighting by Sidney Bennett

ANYONE CAN WHISTLE
(formerly _Side Show_)
APR 4–11 Majestic Theatre, Broadway; book and direction by Arthur Laurents, music and lyrics by Stephen Sondheim, choreography by Herbert Ross, sets by William and Jean Eckart, costumes by Theoni V. Aldredge, lighting by Jules Fisher; Ming Cho Lee's designs not used

KÁTYA KABANOVÁ
MAY 1–3 Juilliard Opera Theater, New York City; music and libretto by Leoš Janáček, translated by Norman Tucker, conducted by Frederic Waldman, directed by Christopher West, costumes by Patton Campbell, lighting by Sidney Bennett

HAMLET
JUN 10–JUL 4 New York Shakespeare Festival, Delacorte Theater; by Shakespeare, directed by Joseph Papp, sets and lighting by Ming Cho Lee, costumes by Theoni V. Aldredge

A MIDSUMMER NIGHT'S DREAM

JUN 27–AUG 29 New York Shakespeare Festival, Mobile Unit; by Shakespeare, directed by Jack Sydow, sets by William Ritman, costumes by Willa Kim, lighting by Martin Aronstein; Mobile Unit design by Ming Cho Lee

OTHELLO
JUL 8–AUG 1 New York Shakespeare Festival, Delacorte Theater; by Shakespeare, directed by Gladys Vaughan, costumes by Theoni V. Aldredge, lighting by Martin Aronstein

ELECTRA
AUG 5–29 New York Shakespeare Festival, Delacorte Theater; by Sophocles, translated by H.D.F. Kitto, directed by Gerald Freedman, costumes by Theoni V. Aldredge, lighting by Martin Aronstein

OTHELLO
OCT 8–JUL 4, 1965 Martinique Theatre, Off Broadway; by Shakespeare, directed by Gladys Vaughan, costumes by Theoni V. Aldredge, lighting by Roger Morgan

1965

FIDELIO
JAN 28–30 Juilliard Opera Theater, New York City; music by Beethoven, libretto by Joseph Sonnleithner and Georg Friedrich Treitschke, conducted by Jean Morel, directed by Christopher West, costumes by Hal George, lighting by Sidney Bennett

ARIADNE
PREMIERED MAR 12 Harkness Ballet, Opéra Comique, Paris; choreography by Alvin Ailey, music by André Jolivet, libretto by Pierre-Alain Jolivet and Ailey, costumes by Theoni V. Aldredge, lighting by Nicola Cernovich

LOVE'S LABOR'S LOST
JUN 9–JUL 3 New York Shakespeare Festival, Delacorte Theater; by Shakespeare, directed by Gerald Freeman, costumes by Theoni V. Aldredge, lighting by Martin Aronstein

HENRY V

JUN 28–AUG 25 New York Shakespeare Festival, Mobile Unit; by Shakespeare, directed by Joseph Papp, costumes by Sonia Lowenstein

THE TAMING OF THE SHREW

JUN 29–AUG 25 New York Shakespeare Festival, Mobile Unit; by Shakespeare, directed by Joseph Papp, costumes by Sonia Lowenstein

CORIOLANUS
JUL 7–31 New York Shakespeare Festival, Delacorte Theater; by Shakespeare, directed by Gladys Vaughan, costumes by Theoni V. Aldredge and Ray Diffen, lighting by Martin Aronstein

TROILUS AND CRESSIDA
AUG 4–28 New York Shakespeare Festival, Delacorte Theater; by Shakespeare, directed by Joseph Papp, costumes by Theoni V. Aldredge, lighting by Martin Aronstein

MADAMA BUTTERFLY
SEP 22–JUNE 12, 1966 Metropolitan Opera National Company, on tour; music by Puccini, libretto by Luigi Illica and Giuseppe Giacosa, translated by Ruth and Thomas Martin, directed by Yoshio Aoyama, sets and costumes by Ming Cho Lee and Motohiro Nagasaka

CARMEN

SEP 25–JUNE 12, 1966 Metropolitan Opera National Company, on tour; music by Georges Bizet, libretto by Henri Meilhac and Ludovic Halévy, translated by John Gutman, directed by Louis Ducreux, sets and costumes by Bernard Daydé; associate designer, Ming Cho Lee

THE WITCH OF ENDOR

NOV 2–20 Martha Graham Dance Company, 54th Street Theatre, New York City; choreography by Martha Graham, music by William Schuman, lighting by Jean Rosenthal

THE MAGIC FLUTE

DEC 9–11 Juilliard Opera Theater, New York City; music by Mozart, libretto by Emanuel Schikaneder and Karl Ludwig Giesecke, translated by Edward J. Dent, conducted by Alfred Wallenstein, directed by Christopher West, costumes by Hal George, lighting by Sidney Bennett

1966

SLAPSTICK TRAGEDY
(*The Mutilated* and *The Gnadiges Fraulein*)

FEB 22–26 Longacre Theatre, Broadway; by Tennessee Williams, directed by Alan Schneider, costumes by Noel Taylor, lighting by Martin Aronstein

DON RODRIGO

FEB 22–MAR 28 New York City Opera, New York State Theater; music by Alberto Ginastera, libretto by Alejandro Casona, conducted by Julius Rudel, directed by Tito Capobianco, costumes by Theoni V. Aldredge

SEA SHADOW

MAR 30–APR 3, Joffrey Ballet, New York City Center; choreography by Gerald Arpino, music by Maurice Ravel and Michael Colgrass, costumes by A. Christina Giannini, lighting by Thomas Skelton

OLYMPICS

MAR 31–APR 3 Joffrey Ballet, New York City Center; choreography by Gerald Arpino, music by Toshiro Mayazumi, lighting by Jennifer Tipton

THE TRIAL OF LUCULLUS

MAY 19–21 Juilliard Opera Theater, New York City; music by Roger Sessions, libretto by Bertolt Brecht, conducted by Jorge Mester, directed by Ian Strasfogel, sets and projections by Ming Cho Lee, costumes by Hal George, lighting by Sidney Bennett

A TIME FOR SINGING

MAY 21–JUN 25 Broadway Theatre, Broadway; book and lyrics by Gerald Freedman and John Morris, music by Morris, directed by Freedman, choreography by Donald McKayle, costumes by Theoni V. Aldredge, lighting by Jean Rosenthal

ALL'S WELL THAT ENDS WELL

JUN 8–JUL 2 New York Shakespeare Festival, Delacorte Theater; by Shakespeare, directed by Joseph Papp, costumes by Theoni V. Aldredge, lighting by Martin Aronstein

MEASURE FOR MEASURE

JUL 6–30 New York Shakespeare Festival, Delacorte Theater; by Shakespeare, directed by Michael Kahn, costumes by Theoni V. Aldredge, lighting by Martin Aronstein

RICHARD III

AUG 3–27 New York Shakespeare Festival, Delacorte Theater; by Shakespeare, directed by Gerald Freedman, costumes by Theoni V. Aldredge, lighting by Martin Aronstein

NIGHTWINGS

SEP 7–25 Joffrey Ballet, New York City Center; choreography by Gerald Arpino, music by John La Montaine, costumes by Willa Kim, lighting by Thomas Skelton

THE MARRIAGE OF FIGARO

SEP 15–JUNE Metropolitan Opera National Company, on tour; music by Mozart, libretto by Lorenzo Da Ponte, translated by Ruth and Thomas Martin, conducted by Robert La Marina, directed by Kirk Browning, choreography by Rhoda Levine, sets and lighting by Ming Cho Lee, costumes by Jane Greenwood

GIULIO CESARE

SEP 27–NOV 14 New York City Opera, New York State Theater; music by Handel, libretto by Nicola Francesco Haym, conducted by Julius Rudel, directed by Tito Capobianco, costumes by Jose Varona, lighting by Hans Sondheimer

1967

THE CRUCIBLE

JAN 17–FEB 19 Arena Stage, Washington, DC; by Arthur Miller, directed by Milton Katselas, costumes by Nancy Potts, lighting by William Eggleston

LITTLE MURDERS

APR 25–29 Broadhurst Theatre, Broadway; by Jules Feiffer, directed by George L. Sherman, costumes by Theoni V. Aldredge, lighting by Jules Fisher

THE RAPE OF LUCRETIA

MAY 17–20 Juilliard Opera Theater, New York City; music by Benjamin Britten, libretto by Ronald Duncan, conducted by Frederic Waldman, directed by Christopher West, costumes by Constance Mellen, lighting by Sidney Bennett

BOMARZO
MAY 19–22 Opera Society of Washington, Lisner Auditorium; music by Alberto Ginastera, libretto by Manuel Mujica Láinez, conducted by Julius Rudel, directed by Tito Capobianco, choreography by Jack Cole, costumes by Jose Varona

THE COMEDY OF ERRORS
JUN 7–JUL 1 New York Shakespeare Festival, Delacorte Theater; by Shakespeare, directed by Gerald Freedman, costumes by Theoni V. Aldredge, lighting by Martin Aronstein

TITUS ANDRONICUS
AUG 2–26 New York Shakespeare Festival, Delacorte Theater; by Shakespeare, directed by Gerald Freedman, costumes by Theoni V. Aldredge, lighting by Martin Aronstein

ELEGY
PREMIERED AUG 17 Joffrey Ballet, Opera House, Seattle; choreography by Gerald Arpino, music by Andrzej Panufnik, costumes by Edith Lutyens Bel Geddes

FALL Begins teaching at New York University

LE COQ D'OR
SEP 21–OCT 7 New York City Opera, New York State Theater; music by Nikolai Rimsky-Korsakov, libretto by Vladimir Bielsky, translated by Antal Dorati and James Gibson, conducted by Julius Rudel, directed by Tito Capobianco, costumes by Jose Varona, lighting by Hans Sondheimer

HAIR
OCT 17–DEC 10 Public Theater, Anspacher Theater; DEC 22–JAN 28, 1968 Cheetah, New York City; book and lyrics by Gerome Ragni and James Rado, music by Galt MacDermot, directed by Gerald Freedman, costumes by Theoni V. Aldredge, lighting by Martin Aronstein

BORIS GODUNOV
NOV 2–6 Baltimore Civic Opera, Lyric Theatre; music by Modest Mussorgsky and revised by Nikolai Rimsky-Korsakov, libretto by Mussorgsky, translated by John Gutman, conducted by Leo Mueller, directed by Tito Capobianco, costumes by Jose Varona

1968

THE TENTH MAN
FEB 13–JUN 2 Arena Stage, Washington, DC; by Paddy Chayefsky, directed by Donald Moreland, costumes by Marjorie Slaiman, lighting by William Eggleston

ROOM SERVICE
FEB 14–JUN 2 Arena Stage, Washington, DC; by John Murray and Allan Boretz, directed by Donald Moreland, costumes by Marjorie Slaiman, lighting by William Eggleston

SECRET PLACES

FEB 20–MAR 12 Joffrey Ballet, New York City Center; choreography and costumes by Gerald Arpino, music by Mozart, lighting by Thomas Skelton

ERGO
FEB 20–APR 14 Public Theater, Anspacher Theater, New York City; by Jakov Lind, directed by Gerald Freedman, costumes by Theoni V. Aldredge, lighting by Martin Aronstein

HERE'S WHERE I BELONG
MAR 3 Billy Rose Theatre, Broadway; book by Alex Gordon, music by Robert Waldman, lyrics by Alfred Uhry, directed by Michael Kahn, choreography by Tony Mordente, costumes by Ruth Morley, lighting by Jules Fisher

BOMARZO
MAR 14–APR 6 New York City Opera, New York State Theater; music by Alberto Ginastera, libretto by Manuel Mujica Láinez, conducted by Julius Rudel, directed by Tito Capobianco, choreography by Jack Cole, costumes by Jose Varona

THE ICEMAN COMETH
MAR 26–JUN 2 Arena Stage, Washington, DC; by Eugene O'Neill, directed by Edwin Sherin, costumes by Marjorie Slaiman, lighting by William Eggleston

ORMINDO
APR 25–27 Juilliard Opera Theater, New York City; music by Francesco Cavalli and adapted by Raymond Leppard, libretto by Giovanni Faustino, translated by Geoffrey Dunn, conducted by Jorge Mester, directed by Roy Lazarus, costumes by Hal George, lighting by Sidney Bennett

THE LADY OF THE HOUSE OF SLEEP
MAY 30–JUN 9 Martha Graham Dance Company, George Abbott Theatre, New York City; choreography and costumes by Martha Graham, music by Robert Starer, lighting by Jean Rosenthal

HENRY IV, PART 1
JUN 11–AUG 3 New York Shakespeare Festival, Delacorte Theater; by Shakespeare, directed by Gerald Freedman, costumes by Theoni V. Aldredge, lighting by Martin Aronstein

HENRY IV, PART 2
JUN 18–AUG 3 New York Shakespeare Festival, Delacorte Theater; by Shakespeare, directed by Gerald Freedman, costumes by Theoni V. Aldredge, lighting by Martin Aronstein

ROMEO AND JULIET

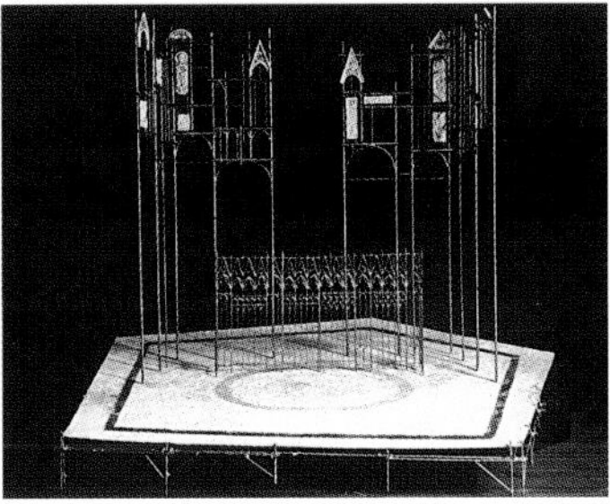

AUG 7–30 New York Shakespeare Festival, Delacorte Theater; by Shakespeare, directed by Joseph Papp, costumes by Theoni V. Aldredge, lighting by Martin Aronstein

A LIGHT FANTASTIC
SEP 25–OCT 19 Joffrey Ballet, New York City Center; choreography by Gerald Arpino, music by Benjamin Britten and adapted by Rayburn Wright, costumes by Bruce Harrow, lighting by Thomas Skelton

FAUST
OCT 17–NOV 14 New York City Opera, New York State Theater; music by Charles Gounod, libretto by Jules Barbier and Michel Carré, conducted by Julius Rudel, directed by Frank Corsaro, choreography by Robert Joffrey, costumes by Jose Varona

KING LEAR

NOV 7–FEB 12, 1969 Repertory Theater of Lincoln Center, Vivian Beaumont Theater, New York City; by Shakespeare, directed by Gerald Freedman, costumes by Theoni V. Aldredge, lighting by John Gleason

THE BARBER OF SEVILLE

DEC 11–14 Juilliard Opera Theater, New York City; music by Rossini, libretto by Cesare Sterbini, translated by George Mead, conducted by Alfred Wallenstein, directed by Tito Capobianco, costumes by Hal George, lighting by Sidney Bennett

1969

CITIES IN BEZIQUE

JAN 4–MAR 2 Public Theater, Anspacher Theater, New York City; by Adrienne Kennedy, directed by Gerald Freedman, costumes by Theoni V. Aldredge, lighting by Martin Aronstein

ANIMUS

MAR 5–6 Joffrey Ballet, New York City Center; choreography by Gerald Arpino, music by Jacob Druckman, lighting by Thomas Skelton

INVITATION TO A BEHEADING

MAR 8–MAY 4 Public Theater, Anspacher Theater, New York City; by Vladimir Nabokov, adapted by Russell McGrath, directed by Gerald Freedman, costumes by Theoni V. Aldredge, lighting by Martin Aronstein

BILLY

MAR 22 Billy Rose Theatre, Broadway; book by Stephen Glassman, music and lyrics by Ron Dante and Gene Allan, directed by Arthur Allan Seidelman, choreography by Grover Dale, costumes by Theoni V. Aldredge, lighting by Martin Aronstein

PEER GYNT

JUL 8–AUG 2 New York Shakespeare Festival, Delacorte Theater; by Henrik Ibsen, translated by Michael Meyer, directed by Gerald Freedman, costumes by Theoni V. Aldredge, lighting by Martin Aronstein

ELECTRA

JUL 29–AUG 30 New York Shakespeare Festival, Mobile Unit; by Sophocles, translated by H.D.F. Kitto, directed by Gerald Freedman, costumes by Theoni V. Aldredge, lighting by Lawrence Metzler

FALL Begins teaching at Yale School of Drama

THE POPPET

OCT 9–NOV 2 Joffrey Ballet, New York City Center; choreography by Gerald Arpino, music by Hans Werner Henze, costumes by Patricia Zipprodt, lighting by Jennifer Tipton

MADAMA BUTTERFLY

OCT 13–31 Lyric Opera of Chicago; music by Puccini, libretto by Luigi Illica and Giuseppe Giacosa, conducted by Argeo Quadri, directed by Yoshio Aoyama, sets and costumes by Ming Cho Lee, lighting by John Harvey

GIULIO CESARE

NOV 9–DEC Hamburg State Opera, Germany; music by Handel, libretto by Nicola Francesco Haym, conducted by Richard Bonynge, directed by Tito Capobianco

SAMBO

DEC 12–JAN 11, 1970 Public Theater, Anspacher Theater, New York City; music by Ron Steward and Neal Tate, lyrics by Steward, directed by Gerald Freedman, sets by Ming Cho Lee and Marjorie Bradley Kellogg, costumes by Milo Morrow, lighting by Martin Aronstein

LA STRADA

DEC 14 Lunt-Fontanne Theatre, Broadway; book by Charles K. Peck Jr., music and lyrics by Lionel Bart, directed by Alan Schneider, choreography by Alvin Ailey, costumes by Nancy Potts, lighting by Martin Aronstein

HELP, HELP, THE GLOBOLINKS!

DEC 22–JAN 4, 1970 New York City Center; music, libretto and direction by Gian Carlo Menotti, conducted by Charles Wilson, choreography by Alwin Nikolais, costumes by Nikolais and Willa Kim

1970

THE RAKE'S PROGRESS

APR 23–26 Juilliard American Opera Center, New York City; music by Stravinsky, libretto by W.H. Auden and Chester Kallman, conducted by Erich Leinsdorf, directed by Tito Capobianco, costumes by Jose Varona

IL GIURAMENTO

MAY 15–17 Juilliard American Opera Center, New York City; music by Saverio Mercadante, libretto by Gaetano Rossi, conducted by Bruno Maderna, directed by Tito Capobianco, choreography by José Limón, costumes by Jose Varona

THE WARS OF THE ROSES (Henry VI, Parts 1, 2 and 3; Richard III)
JUN 23–AUG 22 New York Shakespeare Festival, Delacorte Theater; by Shakespeare, directed by Stuart Vaughan, costumes by Theoni V. Aldredge, lighting by Martin Aronstein

SAMBO
JUL 21–AUG 8 New York Shakespeare Festival, Mobile Unit; music by Ron Steward and Neal Tate, lyrics by Steward, directed by Michael Schultz, choreography by Tommy Jonsen, costumes by Milo Morrow, lighting by Lawrence Metzler

ROBERTO DEVEREUX
OCT 15–NOV 8 New York City Opera, New York State Theater; music by Donizetti, libretto by Salvadore Cammarano, conducted by Julius Rudel, directed by Tito Capobianco, costumes by Jose Varona, lighting by Hans Sondheimer

GANDHI
OCT 20 Playhouse Theatre, New York City; by Gurney Campbell, directed by Jose Quintero, costumes by Jane Greenwood, lighting by Roger Morgan

THE NIGHT THOREAU SPENT IN JAIL
OCT 23–NOV 29 Arena Stage, Washington, DC; by Jerome Lawrence and Robert E. Lee, directed by Norman Gevanthor, costumes by Marjorie Slaiman, lighting by Lee Watson

JACK MACGOWRAN IN THE WORKS OF SAMUEL BECKETT
NOV 19–JAN 25, 1971 Public Theater, Newman Theater, New York City adapted by Jack MacGowran from Samuel Beckett, costumes by Theoni V. Aldredge, lighting by Martin Aronstein

REMOTE ASYLUM

DEC 1–JAN 9, 1971 Center Theatre Group, Ahmanson Theatre, Los Angeles; by Mart Crowley, directed by Edward Parone, costumes by Donald Brooks, lighting by Thomas Skelton

1971

LOLITA, MY LOVE
FEB 16–27 Shubert Theatre, Philadelphia; MAR 23–27 Shubert Theatre, Boston; book and lyrics by Alan Jay Lerner, music by John Barry, directed by Tito Capobianco (replaced by Noel Willman in Boston), costumes by Jose Varona, lighting by Jules Fisher

TIMON OF ATHENS
JUN 29–JUL 18 New York Shakespeare Festival, Delacorte Theater; by Shakespeare, directed by Gerald Freedman, costumes by Theoni V. Aldredge, lighting by Martin Aronstein

TWO GENTLEMEN OF VERONA
JUL 22–AUG 8 New York Shakespeare Festival, Delacorte Theater; AUG 11–29 Mobile Unit; by Shakespeare, adapted by John Guare and Mel Shapiro, music by Galt MacDermot, lyrics by Guare, directed by Shapiro, choreography by Jean Erdman, costumes by Theoni V. Aldredge, lighting by Lawrence Metzler

THE TALE OF CYMBELINE
AUG 12–29 New York Shakespeare Festival, Delacorte Theater; by Shakespeare, directed by A.J. Antoon, costumes by Theoni V. Aldredge, lighting by Martin Aronstein

ARIODANTE
SEP 14–15 Kennedy Center, Washington, DC; music by Handel, conducted by Julius Rudel, directed by Tito Capobianco, choreography by Lew Christensen, costumes by Jose Varona

SUSANNAH
OCT 31–NOV 14 New York City Opera, New York State Theater; music and libretto by Carlisle Floyd, conducted by Julius Rudel, directed by Robert Lewis, choreography by Thomas Andrew, costumes by Patton Campbell

TWO GENTLEMEN OF VERONA
DEC 1–MAY 20, 1973 St. James Theatre, Broadway; by Shakespeare, adapted by John Guare and Mel Shapiro, music by Galt MacDermot, lyrics by Guare, directed by Shapiro, choreography by Jean Erdman, costumes by Theoni V. Aldredge, lighting by Lawrence Metzler

1972

LA BOHÈME
FEB 10–13 Juilliard American Opera Center, New York City; music by Puccini, libretto by Luigi Illica and Giuseppe Giacosa, conducted by James Conlon, directed by Michael Cacoyannis, costumes by Hal George, lighting by Joe Pacitti

VOLPONE
FEB 26–APR 23 Center Theatre Group, Mark Taper Forum, Los Angeles; by Ben Jonson, directed by Edward Parone, costumes by Noel Taylor, lighting by Martin Aronstein

MARIA STUARDA
MAR 7–21 New York City Opera, New York State Theater; music by Donizetti, libretto by Giuseppe Bardari, conducted by Charles Wilson, costumes by Jose Varona, lighting by Hans Sondheimer

BOMARZO
APR 29–MAY 9 Teatro Colón, Buenos Aires; music by Alberto Ginastera, libretto by Manuel Mujica Láinez, conducted by Antonio Tauriello, directed by Tito Capobianco, costumes by Jose Varona

OLDER PEOPLE
MAY 14–JUL 1 Public Theater, Aspacher Theater, New York City; by John Ford Noonan, directed by Mel Shapiro, costumes by Theoni V. Aldredge, lighting by Roger Morgan

HAMLET
JUN 20–JUL 16 New York Shakespeare Festival, Delacorte Theater; by Shakespeare, directed by Gerald Freedman, costumes by Theoni V. Aldredge, lighting by Martin Aronstein

LUCIA DI LAMMERMOOR

JUN 23–JUL 4 Teatro Colón, Buenos Aires; music by Donizetti, libretto by Salvadore Cammarano, conducted by Juan Emilio Martini, directed by Tito Capobianco, costumes by Jose Varona

MUCH ADO ABOUT NOTHING
AUG 10-SEP 3 New York Shakespeare Festival, Delacorte Theater; by Shakespeare, directed by A.J. Antoon, costumes by Theoni V. Aldredge, lighting by Martin Aronstein

LES CONTES D'HOFFMANN
OCT 4-25 New York City Opera, New York State Theater; music by Jacques Offenbach, libretto by Jules Barbier, conducted by Julius Rudel, directed by Tito Capobianco, costumes by Jose Varona, lighting by Hans Sondheimer

HENRY IV, PART 1
OCT 14-DEC 10 Center Theatre Group, Mark Taper Forum, Los Angeles; by Shakespeare, directed by Gordon Davidson, costumes by Lewis Brown, lighting by Martin Aronstein

WEDDING BAND
OCT 25-FEB 25, 1973 Public Theater, Newman Theater, New York City; by Alice Childress, directed by Childress and Joseph Papp, costumes by Theoni V. Aldredge, lighting by Martin Aronstein

MUCH ADO ABOUT NOTHING
NOV 11-FEB 11, 1973 Winter Garden Theatre, Broadway; by Shakespeare, directed by A.J. Antoon, costumes by Theoni V. Aldredge, lighting by Martin Aronstein

OUR TOWN
DEC 15-JAN 21, 1973 Arena Stage, Washington, DC; by Thornton Wilder, directed by Alan Schneider, costumes by Marjorie Slaiman, lighting by Hugh Lester

1973

THE PASSION ACCORDING TO SAINT MATTHEW
FEB 13-22 San Francisco Opera, Curran Theatre; music by Bach, libretto by Picander, conducted by Abraham Kaplan, directed by Gerald Freedman, costumes by Ming Cho Lee and Pat Woodbridge

SYLLABAIRE POUR PHÈDRE
FEB 17-MAR 9 Metropolitan Opera, Forum Theater, New York City; music by Maurice Ohana, libretto by Raphael Cluzel, conducted by Richard Dufallo, directed by Paul-Emile Deiber, choreography by Richard Tanner, costumes by Jane Greenwood, lighting by Shirley Prendergast

DIDO AND AENEAS
FEB 17-MAR 9 Metropolitan Opera, Forum Theater, New York City; music and libretto by Henry Purcell, conducted by Richard Dufallo, directed by Paul-Emile Deiber, choreography by Richard Tanner, costumes by Jane Greenwood, lighting by Shirley Prendergast

FOUR SAINTS IN THREE ACTS

FEB 20-MAR 10 Metropolitan Opera, Forum Theater, New York City; music by Virgil Thomson, libretto by Gertrude Stein, conducted by Roland Gagnon, directed and choreographed by Alvin Ailey, costumes by Jane Greenwood, lighting by Shirley Prendergast

LEAR

APR 13-MAY 19 Yale Repertory Theatre, New Haven, CT; by Edward Bond, directed by David Giles, costumes by Jeanne Button, lighting by William B. Warfel

MYTH OF A VOYAGE
MAY 3-13 Martha Graham Dance Company, Alvin Theatre, New York City; music by Alan Hovhaness, choreography and costumes by Martha Graham, lighting by William H. Batchelder

DON JUAN
PREMIERED JUN 10 San Francisco Ballet, War Memorial Opera House; music by Joaquín Rodrigo, choreography by Lew Christensen, costumes by Jose Varona

LA FAVORITA
SEP 7-29 San Francisco Opera, War Memorial Opera House; music by Donizetti, libretto by Alphonse Royer and Gustave Vaëz, translated by Francesco Jannetti, conducted by Carlo Felice Cillario, directed by Paul-Emile Deiber, choreography by Norbert Vesak, costumes by Jane Greenwood, lighting by Robert Brand

INHERIT THE WIND
SEP 21-23 Arena Stage, Hartke Theatre, Catholic University of America, Washington, DC; SEP 29-OCT 17 Moscow Art Theatre and Pushkin Theatre, Leningrad, U.S.S.R.; OCT 24-27 Arena Stage; by Jerome Lawrence and Robert E. Lee, directed by Zelda Fichandler, costumes by Marjorie Slaiman, lighting by Hugh Lester

OUR TOWN
SEP 26-27 Arena Stage, Hartke Theatre, Catholic University of America, Washington, DC; SEP 29-OCT 17 Moscow Art Theatre and Pushkin Theatre, Leningrad, U.S.S.R.; OCT 24-27 Arena Stage, Kreeger Theater; by Thornton Wilder, directed by Alan Schneider, costumes by Marjorie Slaiman, lighting by Hugh Lester

ANNA BOLENA
OCT 3-18 New York City Opera, New York State Theater; music by Donizetti, libretto by Felice Romani, conducted by Julius Rudel, directed by Tito Capobianco, costumes by Jose Varona, lighting by Hans Sondheimer

LE COQ D'OR
NOV 2-6 Dallas Civic Opera Company, Music Hall at Fair Park; music by Nikolai Rimsky-Korsakov, libretto by Vladimir Bielsky, conducted by Nicola Rescigno, directed by Jose Quintero, choreography by Luciana Novaro, costumes by Peter J. Hall, lighting by Ken Billington

1974

IDOMENEO
MAY 23-26 Kennedy Center, Washington, DC; music by Mozart, libretto by Giambattista Varesco, conducted by Julius Rudel, directed by Gerald Freedman, choreography by Ben Stevenson, costumes by Theoni V. Aldredge, lighting by Hans Sondheimer

SEPHARDIC SONG

MAY 28–JUL 7 Eliot Feld Ballet, Public Theater, Newman Theater, New York City; choreography by Eliot Feld, sets and costumes by Santo Loquasto, lighting by Jennifer Tipton; Ming Cho Lee's design not used

WHISPERS OF DARKNESS

PREMIERED OCT 5 National Ballet of Canada, Toronto; choreography and lighting by Norbert Vesak, music by Gustav Mahler

BORIS GODUNOV

PREMIERED DEC 16 Metropolitan Opera, New York City; music and libretto by Modest Mussorgsky, conducted by Thomas Schippers, directed by August Everding, costumes by Peter J. Hall, lighting by Rudolph Kuntner

1975

THE SEAGULL

JAN 8–APR 5 Manhattan Project, Public Theater, Martinson Hall, New York City; by Anton Chekhov, directed by Andre Gregory, costumes by Nanzi Adzima, lighting by Victor En Yu Tan

JULIUS CAESAR

FEB 26–APR 6 Arena Stage, Washington, DC; by Shakespeare, directed by Carl Weber, costumes by Marjorie Slaiman, lighting by William Mintzer

IDOMENEO

MAR 16–27 New York City Opera, New York State Theater; music by Mozart, libretto by Giambattista Varesco, conducted by Julius Rudel, directed by Gerald Freedman, choreography by Thomas Andrew, costumes by Theoni V. Aldredge, lighting by Hans Sondheimer

ALL GOD'S CHILLUN GOT WINGS

MAR 20–MAY 4 Circle in the Square Theatre, Broadway; by Eugene O'Neill, directed by George C. Scott, costumes by Patricia Zipprodt, lighting by Thomas Skelton

IN QUEST OF THE SUN

APR 9–13 Royal Winnipeg Ballet, Centennial Concert Hall; choreography and lighting by Norbert Vesak, music by Gregory Martindale

THE ASCENT OF MT. FUJI

MAY 27–JUL 6 Arena Stage, Kreeger Theater, Washington, DC; by Chingiz Aitmatov and Kaltai Mukhamedzhanov, translated by Nicholas Bethell, directed by Zelda Fichandler, costumes by Marjorie Slaiman, lighting by Hugh Lester

THE LEAVES ARE FADING

JUL 17–AUG 7 American Ballet Theatre, New York State Theater; choreography by Antony Tudor, music by Antonin Dvorak, costumes by Patricia Zipprodt, lighting by Jennifer Tipton

THE GLASS MENAGERIE

DEC 18–FEB 22, 1976 Circle in the Square Theatre, Broadway; by Tennessee Williams, directed by Theodore Mann, costumes by Sydney Brooks, lighting by Thomas Skelton

1976

I PURITANI

PREMIERED FEB 25 Metropolitan Opera, New York City; music by Vincenzo Bellini, libretto by Carlo Pepoli, conducted by Richard Bonynge, directed by Sandro Sequi, costumes by Peter J. Hall, lighting by Rudolph Kuntner

BILBY'S DOLL

FEB 27–MAR 5 Houston Grand Opera; music and libretto by Carlisle Floyd, conducted by Christopher Keene, directed by David Pountney, costumes by Suzanne Mess, lighting by Duane Schuler

MAR 15 Jo Mielziner dies

WAITING FOR GODOT

MAR 19–APR 26 Arena Stage, Washington, DC; by Samuel Beckett, directed by Gene Lesser, costumes by Marjorie Slaiman, lighting by Hugh Lester

THE BAKER'S WIFE

MAY 11–JUN 26 Dorothy Chandler Pavilion, Los Angeles; book by Joseph Stein, music and lyrics by Stephen Schwartz, directed by Joseph Hardy, choreography by Dan Siretta, sets by Jo Mielziner, costumes by Theoni V. Aldredge, lighting by Jennifer Tipton; associate set design, Ming Cho Lee

FOR COLORED GIRLS WHO HAVE CONSIDERED SUICIDE/WHEN THE RAINBOW IS ENUF

SEP 15–JUL 16, 1978 Booth Theatre, Broadway; by Ntozake Shange, directed by Oz Scott, choreography by Paula Moss, costumes by Judy Dearing, lighting by Jennifer Tipton

IMPROMPTU

OCT 18–NOV 7, Eliot Feld Ballet, Public Theater, Newman Theater, New York City; choreography by Eliot Feld, music by Albert Roussel, costumes by Willa Kim, lighting by Thomas Skelton

LOHENGRIN

PREMIERED NOV 4 Metropolitan Opera, New York City; music and libretto by Richard Wagner, conducted by James Levine, directed by August Everding, costumes by Peter J. Hall, lighting by Gilbert V. Hemsley Jr. and Rudolph Kuntner

1977

THE SHADOW BOX

JAN 21–FEB 18 Long Wharf Theatre, New Haven, CT; MAR 31–DEC 31 Morosco Theatre, Broadway; by Michael Cristofer, directed by Gordon Davidson, costumes by Bill Walker, lighting by Ronald Wallace

CAESAR AND CLEOPATRA

FEB 24–MAR 5 Palace Theatre, Broadway; by George Bernard Shaw, directed by Ellis Rabb, costumes by Jane Greenwood, lighting by Thomas Skelton

ROMEO AND JULIET

MAR 17–MAY 22 Circle in the Square Theatre, Broadway; by Shakespeare, directed by Theodore Mann, costumes by John Conklin, lighting by Thomas Skelton

1978

LA FAVORITA

PREMIERED FEB 21 Metropolitan Opera, New York City; music by Donizetti, libretto by Alphonse Royer and Gustave Vaëz, conducted by Jesús López-Cobos, directed by Patrick Tavernia, choreography by Thomas Pazik, costumes by Jane Greenwood, lighting by Gil Wechsler

HAMLET

MAR 24–APR 30 Arena Stage, Washington, DC; by Shakespeare, directed by Liviu Ciulei, costumes by Marjorie Slaiman, lighting by Hugh Lester

MOTHER COURAGE AND HER CHILDREN

APR 5–23 Acting Company, American Place Theatre, Off Broadway; by Bertolt Brecht, translated by Ralph Manheim, directed by Alan Schneider, costumes by Jeanne Button, lighting by David F. Segal

KING LEAR

APR 9–23 Acting Company, American Place Theatre, Off Broadway; by Shakespeare, directed by John Houseman, costumes by Nancy Potts, lighting by David F. Segal

ANGEL

MAY 10–13 Minskoff Theatre, Broadway; book by Ketti Frings and Peter Udell, music by Gary Geld, lyrics by Udell, directed by Philip Rose, choreography by Robert Tucker, costumes by Pearl Somner, lighting by John Gleason

THE OWL AND THE PUSSYCAT

JUN 26–JUL 1 Martha Graham Dance Company, Metropolitan Opera, New York City; choreography by Martha Graham, music by Carlos Surinach, costumes by Graham and Halston, lighting by Gilbert V. Hemsley Jr.

TWELFTH NIGHT

JUL 14–AUG 6 American Shakespeare Theatre, Stratford, CT; by Shakespeare, directed by Gerald Freedman, costumes by Jeanne Button, lighting by David F. Segal

THE TILLER IN THE FIELDS

PREMIERED DEC 13 American Ballet Theatre, Kennedy Center, Washington, DC; choreography by Antony Tudor, music by Antonin Dvorak, costumes by Dunya Ramicova, lighting by Thomas Skelton

1979

THE GRAND TOUR

JAN 11–MAR 4 Palace Theatre, Broadway; book by Michael Stewart and Mark Bramble, music and lyrics by Jerry Herman, directed by Gerald Freedman, choreography by Donald Saddler, costumes by Theoni V. Aldredge, lighting by Martin Aronstein

DON JUAN

MAR 30–MAY 6 Arena Stage, Washington, DC; by Molière, translated by Richard Nelson, directed by Liviu Ciulei, costumes by Dunya Ramicova, lighting by Hugh Lester

THE TEMPEST

MAY 6–JUL 1 Center Theatre Group, Mark Taper Forum, Los Angeles; by Shakespeare, directed by John Hirsch, costumes by Carrie F. Robbins, lighting by David F. Segal

THE GLASS MENAGERIE

JUN 18–NOV 10 Guthrie Theater, Minneapolis; 1979–80 on tour; by Tennessee Williams, directed by Emily Mann, costumes by Jennifer von Mayrhauser, lighting by Duane Schuler

THE TEMPEST

JUL 18–SEP 2 American Shakespeare Theatre, Stratford, CT; by Shakespeare, directed by Gerald Freedman, costumes by Ray Diffen, lighting by Martin Aronstein

SAINT JOAN

OCT 24–NOV 18 Seattle Repertory Theatre; by George Bernard Shaw, directed by John Hirsch, costumes by Carrie F. Robbins, lighting by David F. Segal

1980

PLENTY

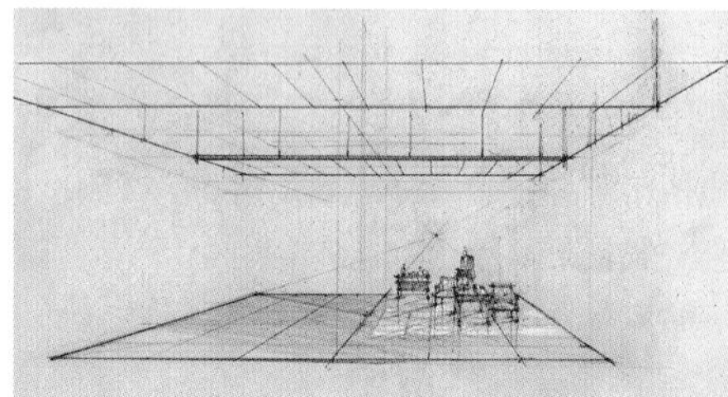

APR 4–MAY 11 Arena Stage, Washington, DC; by David Hare, directed by David Chambers, costumes by Marjorie Slaiman, lighting by William Mintzer

BORIS GODUNOV

SEP 20–OCT 14 Lyric Opera of Chicago; music and libretto by Modest Mussorgsky, conducted by Bruno Bartoletti, directed by August Everding, choreography by George Skibine, costumes by Peter J. Hall, lighting by Duane Schuler

IL TROVATORE
OCT 10-17 Houston Grand Opera; music by Verdi, libretto by Salvadore Cammarano, conducted by Miguel Gomez-Martinez, directed by Giancarlo Del Monaco, costumes by Annette Beck, lighting by Patricia Collins

ATTILA
OCT 25-NOV 14 Lyric Opera of Chicago; music by Verdi, libretto by Temistocle Solera, conducted by Bruno Bartoletti, directed by Ernst Poettgen, costumes by Hal George, lighting by Duane Schuler

1981

ATTILA
MAR 13-22 New York City Opera, New York State Theater; music by Verdi, libretto by Temistocle Solera, conducted by Sergiu Comissiona, directed by Lotfi Mansouri, choreography by Margo Sappington, costumes by Hal George, lighting by Gilbert V. Hemsley Jr.

OEDIPUS THE KING

APR 16-MAY 10 Brooklyn Academy of Music; by Sophocles, adapted by Stephen Berg and Diskin Clay, directed by Emily Mann, costumes by Jennifer von Mayrhauser, lighting by Arden Fingerhut

MADAMA BUTTERFLY

SEP 15-22 Teatro Municipal de Santiago, Chile; music by Puccini, libretto by Luigi Illica and Giuseppe Giacosa, conducted by Juan Pablo Izquierdo, directed by Sarah Ventura, costumes by Nan Cibula, lighting by Bernardo Trumper

LA DONNA DEL LAGO
OCT 15-23 Houston Grand Opera; music by Rossini, libretto by Andrea Leone Tottola, conducted by Claudio Scimone, directed by Frank Corsaro, costumes by Jane Greenwood, lighting by Christine Wopat

1982

MONTEZUMA

FEB 19-23 Juilliard American Opera Center, New York City; music by Roger Sessions, libretto by G.A. Borgese, conducted by Frederik Prausnitz, directed by Ian Strasfogel, costumes by Nan Cibula, lighting by Beverly Emmons

K2
APR 23-JUN 6 Arena Stage, Kreeger Theater, Washington, DC; by Patrick Meyers, directed by Jacques Levy, costumes by Noel Borden, lighting by Allen Lee Hughes

MARY STUART
AUG 4-OCT 20 Stratford Festival, Avon Theatre, Ontario; by Friedrich Schiller, directed by John Hirsch, costumes by Tanya Moiseiwitsch, lighting by Beverly Emmons

ALCESTE
OCT 1-16 New York City Opera, New York State Theater; music by Christoph Willibald Gluck, libretto by Ranieri Calzabigi, translated by Le Blanc du Roullet, conducted by Raymond Leppard, directed and choreographed by Brian Macdonald, costumes by Suzanne Mess, lighting by Gilbert V. Hemsley Jr.

CYMBELINE

DEC 3-JAN 9, 1983 Arena Stage, Washington, DC; by Shakespeare, directed by David Chambers, costumes by Marjorie Slaiman, lighting by Frances Aronson

1983

I CAPULETI E I MONTECCHI
FEB 23-27 Juilliard American Opera Center, New York City; music by Vincenzo Bellini, libretto by Felice Romani, conducted by Denis Vaughan, directed by Ian Strasfogel, costumes by Nan Cibula, lighting by Craig Miller

DESIRE UNDER THE ELMS

MAR 15-APR 10 Indiana Repertory Theatre, Indianapolis; by Eugene O'Neill, directed by Tom Haas, costumes by Susan Hilferty, lighting by Rachel Budin

K2
MAR 30-JUN 11 Brooks Atkinson Theatre, Broadway; by Patrick Meyers, directed by Terry Schreiber, costumes by Noel Borden, lighting by Allen Lee Hughes

DEATH OF A SALESMAN
AUG 30-OCT 22 Stratford Festival, Avon Theatre, Ontario; by Arthur Miller, directed by Guy Sprung, costumes by Debra Hanson, lighting by Harry Frehner

THE ENTERTAINER
SEP 23-OCT Guthrie Theater, Minneapolis; by John Osborne, directed by Edward Payson Call, costumes by Ann Wallace, lighting by Dawn Chiang

TURANDOT
NOV 13-27 Opera Company of Boston, Boston Opera House; music by Puccini, libretto by Giuseppe Adami and Renato Simoni, conducted and directed by Sarah Caldwell, costumes by Wang Linyou, lighting by Graham Walne

BORIS GODUNOV
NOV 23-DEC 11 San Francisco Opera, War Memorial Opera House; music and libretto by Modest Mussorgsky, conducted by Marek Janowski, directed by August Everding and David Kneuss, costumes by Peter J. Hall, lighting by Thomas J. Mann

THE GLASS MENAGERIE
DEC 1-FEB 19, 1984 Eugene O'Neill Theatre, Broadway; by Tennessee Williams, directed by John Dexter, costumes by Patricia Zipprodt, lighting by Andy Phillips

THE DREAM OF THE RED CHAMBER
PREMIERED DEC 3 Cloud Gate Dance Theatre of Taiwan, Social Education Hall, Taipei; choreography by Lin Hwai-min, music by Lai Deh-ho, costumes by Lin Jing-ru, lighting by Lin Keh-hua

1984

THE CUBAN SWIMMER* AND *DOG LADY
APR 27-MAY 27 Intar, New York City; by Milcha Sanchez-Scott, directed by Max Ferra, lighting by Anne E. Militello, costumes by Connie Singer

AN DI (Anna Christie)

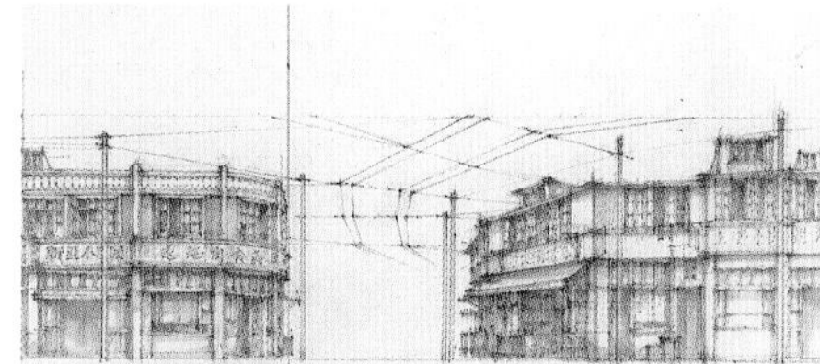

PREMIERED OCT 16 Central Academy of Drama, Beijing; by Eugene O'Neill, translated by Huang Zongjiang, directed by George C. White, costumes by Patricia Zipprodt, lighting by Ian Calderon

1985

TRAVELER IN THE DARK
JAN 12-MAR 10 Center Theatre Group, Mark Taper Forum, Los Angeles; by Marsha Norman, directed by Gordon Davidson, costumes by Susan Denison, lighting by Marilyn Rennagel

EXECUTION OF JUSTICE
MAY 10-JUN 16 Arena Stage, Washington, DC; by Emily Mann, directed by Douglas C. Wager, costumes by Marjorie Slaiman, lighting by Allen Lee Hughes

LA DONNA DEL LAGO
JUN 27 Royal Opera House, London; music by Rossini, libretto by Andrea Leone Tottola, conducted by Lawrence Foster, directed by Frank Corsaro, costumes by Jane Greenwood, lighting by Robert Bryan

LES NOCES
OCT 9-NOV 2 Eliot Feld Ballet, Joyce Theater, New York City; choreography by Bronislava Nijinska as staged by Irina Nijinska, music by Stravinsky, costumes by Theoni V. Aldredge, lighting by Allen Lee Hughes

EXECUTION OF JUSTICE
OCT 12-24 Guthrie Theater, Minneapolis; written and directed by Emily Mann, costumes by Jennifer von Mayrhauser, lighting by Pat Collins

KHOVANSHCHINA
PREMIERED OCT 14 Metropolitan Opera, New York City; music by Modest Mussorgsky, libretto by Mussorgsky and Vladimir Stasov, conducted by Neeme Järvi, directed by August Everding, choreography by David Toguri, costumes by John Conklin, lighting by Gil Wechsler

1986

JAN 19 Ing Tang Yung dies (born JAN 15, 1903)

JOURNEY TO THE CENTER OF THE EARTH
NEVER PRODUCED Repertory Theatre of St. Louis; book by Richard Nelson and Ming Cho Lee, music by Richard Peaslee

EXECUTION OF JUSTICE
MAR 13-22 Virginia Theatre, Broadway written and directed by Emily Mann, costumes by Jennifer von Mayrhauser, lighting by Pat Collins

TANGLED NIGHT
JUN 4-14 Martha Graham Dance Company, New York City Center; choreography by Martha Graham, music by Klaus Egge, costumes by Halston, lighting by Richard Nelson

CAMILLE

NOV 28-JAN 11, 1987 Long Wharf Theatre, New Haven, CT; by Pat Gems, directed by Ron Daniels, costumes by Jess Goldstein, lighting by Ronald Wallace

1987

LE VILLI

MAY 16 Il Piccolo Teatro dell'Opera, Brooklyn Academy of Music; music by Puccini, libretto by Ferdinando Fontana, conducted by Giampaolo Bracali; Ming Cho Lee's design not used

THE TRAGEDY OF ROMEO AND JULIET
PREMIERED JUN 3 Pacific Northwest Ballet, Seattle; choreography by Kent Stowell, music by Tchaikovsky, costumes by Theoni V. Aldredge, lighting by Randall G. Chiarelli

1989

THE TEMPEST
MAY 18-JUN 11 Actors Theatre of Louisville, KY; by Shakespeare, directed by Jon Jory, costumes by Marcia Dixcy, lighting by Allen Lee Hughes

THE FIREBIRD
PREMIERED SEP 29 Pacific Northwest Ballet, Kennedy Center, Washington, DC; choreography by Kent Stowell, music by Stravinsky, costumes by Theoni V. Aldredge, lighting by Randall G. Chiarelli

1990

FAUST

APR 28–MAY 13 Opera Colorado, Denver; music by Charles Gounod, libretto by Jules Barbier and Michel Carré, conducted by Anton Guadagno, directed by Nathaniel Merrill, choreography by David Taylor, costumes by Suzanne Mess, lighting by James Sale

1991

THE GLASS MENAGERIE

JAN 15–FEB 3 McCarter Theatre Center, Princeton, NJ; by Tennessee Williams, directed by Emily Mann, costumes by Jennifer von Mayrhauser, lighting by Robert Wierzel

THE SEAGULL

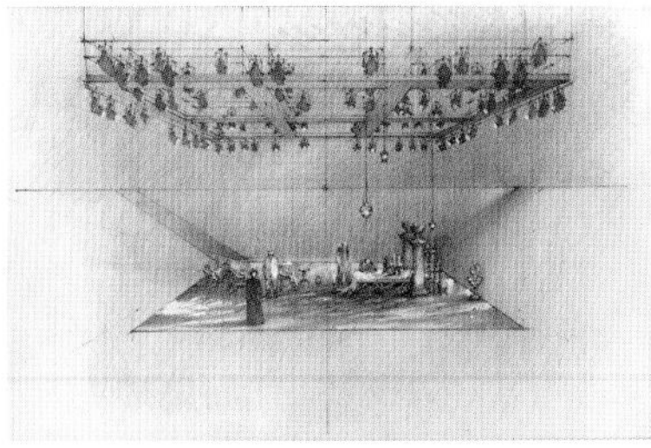

MAY 17–JUN 23 Arena Stage, Washington, DC; by Anton Chekhov, translated by Jean-Claude von Itallie, directed by Douglas C. Wager, costumes by Marjorie Slaiman, lighting by Arden Fingerhut

LES CONTES D'HOFFMANN

SEP 26–29 Hong Kong Cultural Centre, Grand Theatre; music by Jacques Offenbach, libretto by Jules Barbier and Michel Carré, conducted by Constantine Kitsopoulos, directed by Lo King-man, costumes by Candice Donnelly, lighting by Lin Keh-hua

I PURITANI

OCT 23–NOV 16 Lyric Opera of Chicago; music by Vincenzo Bellini, libretto by Carlo Pepoli, conducted by Donato Renzetti, directed by Sandro Sequi, costumes by Peter J. Hall, lighting by Duane Schuler

ATTILA

NOV 21–DEC 8 San Francisco Opera, War Memorial Opera House; music by Verdi, libretto by Temistocle Solera, conducted by Gabriele Ferro, directed by Laura Alley, choreography by Kirk Peterson, costumes by Hal George, lighting by Joan Arhelger

1992

ANTONY AND CLEOPATRA

MAY 7–31 Actors Theatre of Louisville, KY; by Shakespeare, directed by Jon Jory, costumes by Marcia Dixcy, lighting by Stephen Strawbridge

A SMALL DELEGATION

JUN 3–20 Philadelphia Festival Theatre for New Plays, Annenberg Center; by Janet Neipris, directed by Susan H. Schulman, costumes by Vickie Esposito, lighting by Curt Senie

ANNIE WARBUCKS

AUG 17–NOV 2 on tour; AUG 9, 1993–JAN 30, 1994 Variety Arts Theatre, Off Broadway; book by Thomas Meehan, music by Charles Strouse, lyrics and direction by Martin Charnin, choreography by Peter Gennaro, costumes by Theoni V. Aldredge, lighting by Ken Billington

1993

A PERFECT GANESH

JUN 4–SEP 19 Manhattan Theatre Club, New York City Center; by Terrence McNally, directed by John Tillinger, costumes by Santo Loquasto, lighting by Stephen Strawbridge

THE JOY LUCK CLUB

AUG 6–MAR 1994 Long Wharf Theatre and Shanghai People's Art Theatre, on tour, China and Hong Kong; adapted by Susan Kim, directed by Arvin Brown, costumes by Susan Tsu

NINE SONGS

PREMIERED AUG 10 Cloud Gate Dance Theatre of Taiwan, National Theatre, Taipei; choreography by Lin Hwai-min, costumes by Lin Hwai-min and Lo Ruey-chi, lighting by Lin Keh-hua

CARMINA BURANA

PREMIERED OCT 5 Pacific Northwest Ballet, Seattle; choreography by Kent Stowell, music by Carl Orff, costumes by Theoni V. Aldredge and Larae Theige Hascall, lighting by Randall G. Chiarelli

MY SISTER IN THIS HOUSE

NEVER PRODUCED Deutsches Schauspielhaus, Hamburg; by Wendy Kesselman, directed by Jon Jory, costumes by Marcia Dixcy

1994

ROMEO AND JULIET

MAY 12–JUN 4 Actors Theatre of Louisville, KY; by Shakespeare, directed by Jon Jory, costumes by Marcia Dixcy, lighting by Scott Zielinski

THE WOMAN WARRIOR

MAY 13–JUL 10 Berkeley Repertory Theatre; SEP 9–AUG 9 Huntington Theatre Company, Boston; FEB 16–APR 23, 1995 Center Theatre Group, Doolittle Theatre, Los Angeles; by Deborah Rogin, directed by Sharon Ott, costumes by Susan Hilferty, lighting by Peter Maradudin

OTHELLO

JUN 22–OCT 15 Stratford Festival, Avon Theatre, Ontario; by Shakespeare, directed by Brian Bedford, costumes by Ann Curtis, lighting by Michael J. Whitfield

JUL 4 Tsu-Fa Lee dies (born MAY 13, 1897)

1995

LONG DAY'S JOURNEY INTO NIGHT

JAN 6–FEB 12 Arena Stage, Washington, DC; by Eugene O'Neill, directed by Douglas C. Wager, costumes by Paul Tazewell, lighting by Scott Zielinski

THE CHERRY ORCHARD

MAY 27–JUL 3 South Coast Repertory, Costa Mesa, CA; by Anton Chekhov, directed by Martin Benson, costumes by Walker Hicklin, lighting by Peter Maradudin

MACBETH

SEP 12–NOV 5 Shakespeare Theatre Company, Washington, DC; by Shakespeare, directed by Joe Dowling, costumes by Marina Draghici, lighting by Howell Binkley

AS YOU LIKE IT

OCT 10–NOV 19 Long Wharf Theatre, New Haven, CT; by Shakespeare, directed by John Tillinger, costumes by Marcia Dixcy, lighting by Brian Nason

1996

ANGELS IN AMERICA, PART 1: MILLENNIUM APPROACHES

MAR 21–APR 28 Dallas Theater Center, Kalita Humphreys Theater; by Tony Kushner, directed by Richard Hamburger, costumes by Katherine B. Roth, lighting by Howell Binkley

THE COMEDY OF ERRORS

MAY 8–JUN 2 Actors Theatre of Louisville, KY; by Shakespeare, directed by Jon Jory, costumes by Ilona Somogyi, lighting by Brian Nason

WAITING FOR GODOT

JUL 7–SEP 3 Stratford Festival, Patterson Theatre, Ontario; by Samuel Beckett, directed by Brian Bedford, lighting by Michael J. Whitfield

THE NOTEBOOK OF TRIGORIN

SEP 3–OCT 4 Cincinnati Playhouse in Park, Robert S. Marx Theatre; by Tennessee Williams, directed by Stephen Hollis, costumes by Candice Donnelly, lighting by Brian Nason

RASHOMON

PREMIERED SEP 29 Oper Graz, Austria; music and libretto by Mayako Kubo, conducted by Stefan Lano, directed and choreographed by Lin Hwai-min, costumes by Yip Kam-tim, lighting by Reinhard Traub

ANGELS IN AMERICA, PART 2: PERESTROIKA

OCT 17–NOV 17 Dallas Theater Center, Kalita Humphreys Theater; by Tony Kushner, directed by Richard Hamburger, costumes by Katherine B. Roth, lighting by Howell Binkley

1997

JEANNE LA PUCELLE

PREMIERED FEB 12 Place des Arts, Théâtre Maisonneuve, Montreal; book and lyrics by Vincent de Tourdonnet, translated by Antonine Maillet, music by Peter Sipos, directed by Martin Charnin, choreography by Michele Assaf, costumes by Jean Blanchette, lighting by Ken Billington

DEATH OF A SALESMAN

FEB 23–NOV 1 Oregon Shakespeare Festival, Angus Bowmer Theatre, Ashland; by Arthur Miller, directed by Penny Metropulos, costumes by Emily Beck, lighting by Dennis Parichy

THE JOY LUCK CLUB

APR 15–MAY 25 Long Wharf Theatre, New Haven, CT; adapted by Susan Kim, directed by Seret Scott, costumes by Candice Donnelly, lighting by Mark Stanley

MOURNING BECOMES ELECTRA

APR 29–JUN 15 Shakespeare Theatre Company, Washington, DC; by Eugene O'Neill, directed by Michael Kahn, costumes by Jane Greenwood, lighting by Howell Binkley

PORTRAIT OF THE FAMILIES

PREMIERED SEP 20 Cloud Gate Dance Theatre of Taiwan, National Theatre, Taipei; choreography by Lin Hwai-min, music by Arvo Pärt and Nan Kouan, costumes by Chen Wan-lee, lighting by Lin Keh-hua, projections by Elaine McCarthy

A TOUCH OF THE POET

OCT 3–NOV 9 Arena Stage, Washington, DC; by Eugene O'Neill, directed by Michael Kahn, costumes by Patricia Zipprodt, lighting by Allen Lee Hughes

UNCLE VANYA

DEC 12–JAN 18, 1998 Arena Stage, Washington, DC; by Anton Chekhov, translated by Carol Rocamora, directed by Zelda Fichandler, costumes by Lindsay W. Davis, lighting by Nancy Schertler

1998

PEER GYNT

JAN 20–MAR 8 Shakespeare Theatre Company, Washington, DC; by Henrik Ibsen, translated by Kenneth MacLeish, directed by Michael Kahn, costumes by Paul Tazewell, lighting by Howell Binkley

ROMEO AND JULIET

JAN 29–FEB 8 Acting Company, New Victory Theatre, Off Broadway; by Shakespeare, directed by James Bundy, costumes by Ann Hould-Ward, lighting by Robert Wierzel

OTHELLO

MAY 6–31 Actors Theatre of Louisville, KY; by Shakespeare, directed by Jon Jory, costumes by Marcia Dixcy, lighting by Stephen Strawbridge

SILVER LINING

PREMIERED MAY 26 Pacific Northwest Ballet, Seattle; choreography by Kent Stowell, music by Jerome Kern, costumes by David Murin, lighting by Randall G. Chiarelli

THE WINTER'S TALE

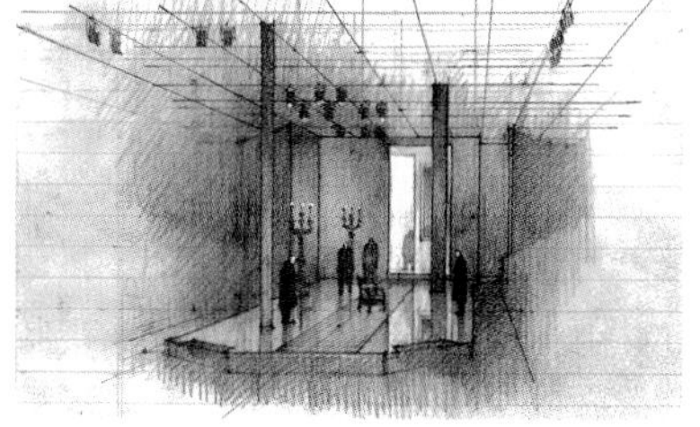

JUN 9–NOV 8 Stratford Festival, Patterson Theatre, Ontario; by Shakespeare, directed by Brian Bedford, costumes by Ann Curtis, lighting by Kevin Fraser

A TOUCH OF THE POET

JUL 29–NOV 1 Oregon Shakespeare Festival, Angus Bowmer Theatre, Ashland; by Eugene O'Neill, directed by Douglas C. Wager, costumes by Noel Taylor, lighting by Chris Parry

LONG DAY'S JOURNEY INTO NIGHT

OCT 17–NOV 28 Arizona Theatre Company, Temple of Music and Art, Tucson, and Herberger Theater Center, Phoenix; by Eugene O'Neill, directed by Marshall W. Mason, costumes by Laura Crow

THE FARAWAY NEARBY

DEC 11–JAN 24, 1999 Arena Stage, Washington, DC; by John Murrell, directed by Roberta Levitow, costumes by Lindsay W. Davis, lighting by Allen Lee Hughes

BURNING THE JUNIPER BRANCHES

PREMIERED DEC 31 Cloud Gate Dance Theatre of Taiwan, National Theatre, Taipei; choreography by Lin Hwai-min, music by Henry Wolff, Nancy Hennings and Alain Presencer, lighting by Lin Keh-hua, costumes by Yip Kam-tim and Yang Yu-teh

1999

KING JOHN

JAN 19–MAR 6 Shakespeare Theatre Company, Washington, DC; by Shakespeare, directed by Michael Kahn, costumes by Robert Perdziola, lighting by Howell Binkley

ENIGMA VARIATIONS

APR 24–JUN 13 Center Theatre Group, Mark Taper Forum, Los Angeles; by Eric-Emmanuel Schmitt, translated by Roeg Jacob, directed by Daniel Roussel, costumes by Candice Cain, lighting by Robert Wierzel

THE MERCHANT OF VENICE

MAY 25–JUL 18 Shakespeare Theatre Company, Washington, DC; by Shakespeare, directed by Michael Kahn, costumes by Martin Pakledinaz, lighting by Howell Binkley

AH, WILDERNESS!

JUL 30–AUG 29 Guthrie Theater, Minneapolis; FEB 22–MAY 11, 2002 on tour; by Eugene O'Neill, directed by Douglas C. Wager, costumes by Zack Brown, lighting by Allen Lee Hughes

HEARTBREAK HOUSE

OCT 28–NOV 20 Actors Theatre of Louisville, KY; by George Bernard Shaw, directed by Jon Jory, costumes by Deborah Trout, lighting by Mark McCullough

2000

THE HOLLOW LANDS

JAN 7–FEB 13 South Coast Repertory, Costa Mesa, CA; by Howard Korder, directed by David Chambers, costumes by Shigeru Yagi, lighting by Chris Parry

ENIGMA VARIATIONS
(as *Enigmatic Variations* in London)

FEB 24–APR 1 Royal Alexandra Theatre, Toronto; MAY 31–JUL 29 Savoy Theatre, London; by Eric-Emmanuel Schmitt, translated by Roeg Sutherland, directed by Anthony Page, costumes by Candice Cain, lighting by Robert Wierzel

GUYS AND DOLLS

MAR 29–APR 23 Dallas Theater Center, Arts District Theater; book by Abe Burrows and Jo Swerling, music and lyrics by Frank Loesser, directed by Richard Hamburger, choreography by Willie Rosario, costumes by Meg Neville, lighting by Howell Binkley

A CHRISTMAS CAROL

DEC 5–24 McCarter Theatre Center, Princeton, NJ; by Charles Dickens, adapted by David Thompson, directed by Michael Unger, costumes by Jess Goldstein, lighting by Stephen Strawbridge

2001

DON CARLOS

JAN 16–MAR 11 Shakespeare Theatre Company, Washington, DC; by Friedrich Schiller, translated by Robert David, directed by Michael Kahn, costumes by Robert Perdziola, lighting by Chris Parry

FIRECRACKER

DEC 8-9 Michael Mao Dance Company, PepsiCo Theatre, Performing Arts Center at Purchase College, NY; choreography by Michael Mao, sets by Ming Cho Lee and Adam Stockhausen, costumes by Linda Cho, lighting by Brian Haynsworth

2002

ANTONY AND CLEOPATRA

JAN 25-FEB 24 Guthrie Theater, Minneapolis; by Shakespeare, directed by Mark Lamos, costumes by Jane Greenwood, lighting by Stephen Strawbridge

THE MOLIÈRE COMEDIES (School for Husbands* and *The Imaginary Cuckold)

FEB 10-APR 7 Center Theatre Group, Mark Taper Forum, Los Angeles; JAN 30-FEB 24, 2004 Chicago Shakespeare Theater, Shubert Theatre; by Molière, translated by Richard Wilbur, directed by Brian Bedford, costumes by Jane Greenwood, lighting by Robert Wierzel

2003

MAR 4 Receives the National Medal of Arts from President George W. Bush

I/DNA

APR 23-27 Joffrey Ballet, Auditorium Theatre, Chicago; choreography by Gerald Arpino, music by Arnold Roth and Charles Ives, costumes by Nan Zabriskie, lighting by Howell Binkley

SWAN LAKE

PREMIERED SEP 25 Pacific Northwest Ballet, Seattle; choreography by Kent Stowell, music by Tchaikovsky, costumes by Paul Tazewell, lighting by Randall G. Chiarelli

2005

LORENZACCIO

JAN 18-MAR 6 Shakespeare Theatre Company, Washington, DC; by Alfred de Musset, translated and adapted by John Strand, directed by Michael Kahn, costumes by Murell Horton, lighting by Howell Binkley

A MOON FOR THE MISBEGOTTEN

FEB 23-MAR 27, Long Wharf Theatre, New Haven, CT; JAN 5-FEB 5, 2006 Hartford Stage; JAN 12-FEB 4, 2007 Alley Theatre, Houston; by Eugene O'Neill, directed by Gordon Edelstein, costumes by Jennifer von Mayrhauser, lighting by Jennifer Tipton

STUFF HAPPENS

MAY 25-JUL 17 Center Theatre Group, Mark Taper Forum, Los Angeles; by David Hare, directed by Gordon Davidson, costumes by Candice Cain, lighting by Christopher Akerlind

ANNIE

PREMIERED AUG 21 Paramount Theatre, Seattle; on tour through 2010; book by Thomas Meehan, music by Charles Strouse, lyrics and direction by Martin Charnin, choreography by Liza Gennaro, costumes by Theoni V. Aldredge and Jim Halliday, lighting by Ken Billington

2013

JUN 9 Receives the Special Tony Award for Lifetime Achievement in the Theatre

Arnold Aronson and Ming Cho Lee in front of the Shanghai Art Theatre in 1989. When Lee was growing up it was called the Lyceum Theatre and his mother took him to many productions there.

NOTES

INTRODUCTION

1 The term scenography can be problematic. In its broadest definition, it refers to any and all aspects of scenic art, and that is generally how I am using the word here. In Europe, however, and increasingly in the U.S., scenography is often used interchangeably with scene design (as distinct from costumes, lights, projections, etc.), and a set designer is referred to as a scenographer. But as I have argued elsewhere [see my book *Looking into the Abyss: Essays on Scenography*], scenography rightfully describes the totality of all the visual and spatial elements of a production.

2 An excellent, concise history of the New Stagecraft can be found in the introduction to Mary C. Henderson's *Mielziner: Master of Modern Stage Design* (New York: Back Stage Books, 2000).

3 No relation to this author.

4 Frank Rich, *The Theatre Art of Boris Aronson*, with Lisa Aronson (New York: Knopf, 1987).

5 Tony Davis, *Stage Design* (Crans-près-Céligny, Switzerland: RotoVision, 2001), 40.

6 Ming Cho Lee, interview by James Leverett, New York City, February 28, 1989, New York Public Library, Theatre on Film and Tape Archive, videocassette, 115 minutes.

7 Rich, *The Theatre Art of Boris Aronson*, 85.

8 He saw the photo in *Stage Design Throughout the World Since 1935* by René Hainaux (New York: Theatre Arts Books, 1956).

9 Bertolt Brecht, *Brecht on Theatre: The Development of an Aesthetic*, ed. and trans. John Willett (New York: Hill and Wang, 1964), 230.

10 Davis, *Stage Design*, 40.

11 Davis, *Stage Design*, 40.

CHAPTER 1

1 In traditional Chinese nomenclature, all siblings and cousins of the same generation share the same name and are distinguished by their "middle" names. Each family has a generation poem that determines the names; in the case of the Lee family it covers seventy-two generations. If Ming Cho Lee had had brothers they would all be "Ming," which is the thirty-first or thirty-second generation name of the poem.

2 In actuality, Canton did not completely fall to the Communists until October 14, 1949.

3 David Nils Flaten, "Ming Cho Lee: American Stage Designer" (PhD diss., University of California, Santa Barbara, 1979), 22.

CHAPTER 2

1 In 2013, Paul Libin, Bernard Gersten and Lee were all presented with special Tony Awards for lifetime achievement.

CHAPTER 3

1 Rich and Aronson, *The Theatre Art of Boris Aronson*, 129.

2 Rich and Aronson, *The Theatre Art of Boris Aronson*, 22.

3 Henderson, *Mielziner: Master of Modern Stage Design*, 226–27.

CHAPTER 4

1 Lynn Pecktal, *Designing and Painting for the Theatre* (New York: Holt, Rinehart and Winston, 1975), 243.

2 Helen Epstein, *Joe Papp: An American Life* (Boston: Little, Brown, 1994), 175.

3 Flaten, "Ming Cho Lee: American Stage Designer," 75.

4 Kenneth Turan and Joseph Papp, *Free for All: Joe Papp, the Public, and the Greatest Theater Story Ever Told* (New York: Doubleday, 2009), 161.

5 Arnold Aronson, *American Set Design* (New York: Theatre Communications Group, 1985), 92.

6 Sarah Caldwell and Rebecca Matlock, *Challenges: A Memoir of My Life in Opera* (Middletown, CT: Wesleyan University Press, 2008), 102.

7 Daniel Kessler, *Sarah Caldwell: The First Woman of Opera* (Lanham, MD: Scarecrow Press, 2008), 41.

CHAPTER 5

1 Epstein, *Joe Papp: An American Life*, 179.

2 Ming Cho Lee, "Ming Cho Lee on Six of His Sets," *Theatre Design & Technology*, no. 24 (February 1971): 6.

3 Flaten, "Ming Cho Lee: American Stage Designer," 87.

4 Lee, "Ming Cho Lee on Six of His Sets," 6.

5 Ming Cho Lee, "Ming Cho Lee: A Life of Design," discussion with Gerald Freedman, Winston-Salem, May 30, 2008, University of North Carolina School of the Arts, Semans Library, DVD.

6 Aronson, *American Set Design*, 92.

INTERLUDE: THE STUDIO

1 Zelda Fichandler, introductory remarks for Mary B. Murphy Award in Design, Long Wharf Theatre, New Haven, CT, May 6, 1993.

2 Not all the Lee sons saw it quite that way. Middle son Christopher, while agreeing that it was a kind of extended family, always thought of the assistants as his parents' friends and associates.

3 Lee, interview by James Leverett.

4 James Leverett, "The Art of Ming Cho Lee," unknown publication, 18.

5 Lee, interview by James Leverett.

CHAPTER 6

1 Sasha Anawalt, *The Joffrey Ballet: Robert Joffrey and the Making of an American Dance Company* (New York: Scribner, 1996), 226.

2 The rights to the Ravel score had never been obtained and at the final rehearsal at City Center lawyers for the music publisher confiscated the scores. A young composer, Michael Colgrass, who was part of the Joffrey orchestra, wrote a new score for the twelve-minute dance literally overnight. (Anawalt, *The Joffrey Ballet*, 219.)

3 Jennifer Dunning, *Alvin Ailey: A Life in Dance* (Reading, MA: Addison-Wesley, 1996), 192.

4 Ming Cho Lee, "Designing Opera," *Contemporary Stage Design U.S.A.*, ed. Elizabeth B. Burdick, Peggy C. Hansen and Brenda Zanger . (New York: International Theatre Institute/U.S., 1974), 43.

5 Lee, "Ming Cho Lee on Six of His Sets," 7–9.

6 Lee, "Designing Opera," 41.

7 Aronson, *American Set Design*, 94.

8 Lee, "Ming Cho Lee on Six of His Sets," 9.

CHAPTER 7

1 Robert Marx, "Ground Plans," *Opera News* 67, no. 2 (August 2002): 20.

2 Aronson, *American Set Design*, 92.

3 Lee, "Ming Cho Lee on Six of His Sets," 9.

4 Epstein, *Joe Papp*, 191.

5 Rich, *The Theatre Art of Boris Aronson*, 156.

6 Lee worked as a consultant and designer of theatre spaces on three more projects during his career: for the 380-seat Patricia Corbett Theater at the University of Cincinnati's College-Conservatory of Music (in 1971); for three of the four theatres at the SUNY Purchase Performing Arts Center (throughout the 1970s); and the Duke on 42nd Street, a flexible-space black-box theatre in New York, in 2000.

CHAPTER 8

1 Flaten, "Ming Cho Lee: American Stage Designer," 162–63.

2 Amy S. Green, *The Revisionist Stage: American Directors Reinvent the Classics* (New York: Cambridge University Press, 1994), 138.

CHAPTER 9

1 Pecktal, "A Conversation with Ming Cho Lee," 243.

2 Delbert Unruh, *The Designs of Ming Cho Lee* (Syracuse, NY: United States Institute for Theatre Technology, 2006), 26.

CHAPTER 10

1 Flaten, "Ming Cho Lee: American Stage Designer," 253.

2 Lee, "Designing Opera," 43.

CHAPTER 11

1 Henderson, *Mielziner: Master of Modern Stage Design*, 298–99.

2 Caldwell, *Challenges*, 160.

CHAPTER 12

1 Aronson, *American Set Design*, 100.

CHAPTER 13

1 Cheng Ching-wen, "An Encounter between stage designer Ming Cho Lee and director/choreographer Lin Hwai-Min," trans. Paul Frank, Culture.tw, Feb. 15, 2007, http://www.culture.tw/index.php?option=com_content&task=view&id=280&Itemid=157.

CHAPTER 14

1 Lee, "Ming Cho Lee on Six of His Sets," 7.

CHAPTER 15

1 Davis, *Stage Design*, 49.

2 Ibid.

3 Unruh, *The Designs of Ming Cho Lee*, 69.

IMAGE CREDITS

FRONT COVER

Boris Godunov, Metropolitan Opera, 1974, ½" model, coronation scene. Photograph © T. Charles Erickson.

BACK COVER

The Silver Whistle, Occidental College, 1952, sketch. Courtesy Ming Cho Lee (MCL).

ENDPAPERS

The Leaves Are Fading, American Ballet Theatre, 1975, paint elevation for backdrop. Courtesy MCL.

FRONTISPIECE

© Mark Ostow Photography

INTRODUCTION

1 courtesy MCL; 2 courtesy Jules Fisher; 3 courtesy Marc Aronson; 4 from René Hainaux, *Stage Design Throughout the World Since 1935* (New York: Theatre Arts Books, 1956), page 117; 5 © 2014 The Isamu Noguchi Foundation and Garden Museum, New York/Artists Rights Society (ARS), New York; 6 collection of the McNay Art Museum, gift of the Tobin Endowment

CHAPTER 1

1–11 courtesy MCL; 12–14 courtesy Omar and Helen Paxson; 15 courtesy Occidental College Special Collections and College Archives, photo by Howard & Ted Miller; 16–17 courtesy Omar and Helen Paxson; 18 courtesy Occidental College Special Collections and College Archives, photo by Howard & Ted Miller; 19 courtesy Occidental College Special Collections and College Archives; 20–23 courtesy MCL; 24 courtesy University of California, Los Angeles; 25 courtesy MCL

CHAPTER 2

1–3 courtesy MCL; 4 courtesy Arnold Aronson; 5–10 courtesy MCL

CHAPTER 3

1–5 courtesy MCL; 6 courtesy MCL, photo by Blakeslee-Lane, Inc.; 7–8 courtesy MCL; 9 courtesy MCL, photo by Blakeslee-Lane, Inc.; 10–17 courtesy MCL

CHAPTER 4

1–3 courtesy MCL; 4 Billy Rose Theatre Division, the New York Public Library for the Performing Arts, Astor, Lenox and Tilden Foundations; 5–15 courtesy MCL

CHAPTER 5

1–3 courtesy MCL; 4 from *The Best Plays of 1962–1963*, edited by Henry Hewes (New York: Dodd, Mead & Company, 1963); 5–10 courtesy MCL; 11 used by permission of the Juilliard School, photo by Milton Oleaga 12 courtesy MCL; 13 used by permission of the Juilliard School, photo by Milton Oleaga; 14–17 courtesy MCL; 18 Billy Rose Theatre Division, the New York Public Library for the Performing Arts, Astor, Lenox and Tilden Foundations; 19 Billy Rose Theatre Division, the New York Public Library for the Performing Arts, Astor, Lenox and Tilden Foundations, photo by George E. Joseph; 20–27 courtesy MCL; 28 from René Hainaux, *Stage Design Throughout the World Since 1950* (New York: Theatre Art Books, 1963), page 65.

INTERLUDE: THE STUDIO

1 Billy Rose Theatre Division, the New York Public Library for the Performing Arts, Astor, Lenox and Tilden Foundations; 2 courtesy MCL; 3–4 Nathaniel Tileston for *Theatre Crafts*, 1984; 5 courtesy MCL

CHAPTER 6

1–12 courtesy MCL; 13 used by permission of the Juilliard School, photo by Milton Oleaga; 14–15 courtesy MCL; 16 © Beth Bergman; 17 used by permission of the Juilliard School; 18 © Beth Bergman; 19 courtesy MCL; 20 © Beth Bergman; 21–23 courtesy MCL; 24–25 © Beth Bergman; 26 courtesy Gabriel Pinski, photo by Fred Fehl; 27–28 courtesy MCL; 29 courtesy Gabriel Pinski, photo by Fred Fehl; 30 courtesy MCL; 31 courtesy Gabriel Pinski, photo by Fred Fehl; 32 courtesy MCL; 33 courtesy Gabriel Pinski, photo by Fred Fehl; 34 © Beth Bergman; 36 courtesy MCL; 37 courtesy Gabriel Pinski, photo by Fred Fehl; 38–39 © Beth Bergman; 40–41 courtesy MCL; 42 © Beth Bergman; 43–48 courtesy MCL

CHAPTER 7

1–5 courtesy MCL; 6 Billy Rose Theatre Division, the New York Public Library for the Performing Arts, photo by George E. Joseph; 7 courtesy Marty New, TEOMing, photo by Rebeka Bieber; 8–12 courtesy MCL; 13 Billy Rose Theatre Division, the New York Public Library for the Performing Arts, photo by George E. Joseph; 14 Billy Rose Theatre Division, the New York Public Library for the Performing Arts, Astor, Lenox and Tilden Foundations, photo by George Cserna; 15–28 courtesy MCL

CHAPTER 8

1–6 courtesy MCL; 7–8 courtesy Center Theatre Group, photo by Steven Keull; 9 courtesy Arena Stage, photo by Fletcher Drake; 10–13 courtesy MCL; 14 © T. Charles Erickson; 15–16 courtesy MCL; 17–19 courtesy Arena Stage, photo Joe B. Mann; 20 courtesy MCL; 21 © The Metropolitan Museum of Art, sourced from Art Resource, NY

CHAPTER 9

1–12 courtesy MCL; 13 © T. Charles Erickson; 14–17 courtesy MCL

INTERLUDE: MASTER TEACHER

1–4 courtesy MCL, 5 courtesy Marty New, TEOMing, photo by Rebeka Bieber; 6 courtesy MCL; 7 courtesy Marty New, TEOMing, photo by Rebeka Bieber

CHAPTER 10

1 courtesy MCL; 2 © Beth Bergman; 3–4 courtesy MCL; 5 courtesy New York City Opera; 6 courtesy MCL; 7 © Beth Bergman; 8 courtesy MCL; 9 © Beth Bergman; 10 courtesy MCL; 11 © Beth Bergman; 12 courtesy MCL; 13 © Beth Bergman; 14 courtesy MCL; 15 © Beth Bergman; 16–22 courtesy MCL; 23 © Beth Bergman; 24 courtesy MCL; 25–26 © Beth Bergman; 27–28 courtesy Metropolitan Opera Archives, photo by James Heffernan; 29–30 courtesy MCL

CHAPTER 11

1–2 courtesy MCL; 3–8 © Beth Bergman; 9 courtesy MCL; 10 © Beth Bergman; 11–12 courtesy MCL; 13 © Beth Bergman; 14 courtesy MCL; 15 © Beth Bergman; 16 courtesy Metropolitan Opera Archives, photo by James Heffernan; 17–24 courtesy MCL; 25 © Beth Bergman; 26–27 courtesy MCL

CHAPTER 12

1 © Ken Howard/Metropolitan Opera; 2–3 courtesy Arena Stage, photo by George de Vincent; 4 courtesy MCL, photo by John Heckler; 5–6 courtesy MCL; 7 © T. Charles Erickson; 8 courtesy MCL; 9 © Beth Bergman; 10 © Joseph Giannetti; 11 © T. Charles Erickson; 12–14 courtesy MCL; 15 © Beth Bergman; 16–25 courtesy MCL

CHAPTER 13

1–15 courtesy MCL; 16 © Angela Sterling; 17 courtesy MCL; 18–19 © Kurt Smith; 20 © Angela Sterling; 21 courtesy MCL; 22 courtesy the Cloud Gate Dance Foundation, photo by Liu Chen-hsiang; 23–24 courtesy MCL; 25 courtesy the Cloud Gate Dance Foundation, photo by Liu Chen-hsiang; 26 courtesy MCL; 27 © T. Charles Erickson; 28 courtesy MCL; 29 courtesy the Cloud Gate Dance Foundation; 30 courtesy the Cloud Gate Dance Foundation, photo by Hsieh An

CHAPTER 14

1–3 courtesy MCL; 4 © T. Charles Erickson; 5–11 courtesy MCL; 12–13 courtesy Actors Theatre of Louisville, photo by Richard C. Trigg; 14 © T. Charles Erickson; 15–18 courtesy MCL; 19–20 courtesy Actors Theatre of Louisville, photo by Richard C. Trigg; 21–24 courtesy MCL

CHAPTER 15

1–2 © T. Charles Erickson; 3–6 courtesy MCL; 7 © T. Charles Erickson; 8–16 courtesy MCL; 17 © Michal Daniel; 18–22 courtesy MCL; 23–26 courtesy the Shakespeare Theatre Company, © Carol Rosegg; 27–28 courtesy MCL; 29 courtesy the Shakespeare Theatre Company, © Carol Rosegg; 30 courtesy MCL; 31 © courtesy the Shakespeare Theatre Company, © Carol Rosegg; 32–35 © T. Charles Erickson; 36–37 Jay Thompson/Craig Schwartz

CHAPTER 16

1 courtesy MCL; 2 courtesy George W. Bush Presidential Library and Museum, used by permission; 3 courtesy MCL; 4–6 courtesy the Shakespeare Theatre Company, © Carol Rosegg; 7–8 © T. Charles Erickson; 9–10 Craig Schwartz; 11–15 courtesy MCL

WATERCOLORS

1–24 courtesy MCL

CHRONOLOGY

page 298 Billy Rose Theatre Division, the New York Public Library for the Performing Arts, Astor, Lenox and Tilden Foundations; *Hamlet* (1962) courtesy the Peabody Institute Archives, Johns Hopkins University, photo by Blakeslee-Lane, Inc.; *Help, Help, the Globolinks!* (1969) © Beth Bergman; *Four Saints in Three Acts* (1973) courtesy Metropolitan Opera Archives, photo by Louis Melançon; *Saint Joan* (1979) courtesy Seattle Repertory Theatre; *Antony and Cleopatra* (1992) courtesy Actors Theatre of Louisville, photo by Richard C. Trigg; *The Joy Luck Club* (1993) © T. Charles Erickson; *As You Like It* (1995) © T. Charles Erickson; *Uncle Vanya* (1997) courtesy Arena Stage, photo by Stan Barouh; *The Faraway Nearby* (1998) courtesy Arena Stage, photo by Carol Pratt; *Guys and Dolls* (2000) courtesy Dallas Theater Center; all other images courtesy MCL

AUTHOR PHOTOGRAPH

© Lorie Novak

INDEX

Page references followed by *fig.* indicate illustrations or material contained in their captions.

ABOUT THE AUTHOR

Arnold Aronson is a professor of theatre at the Columbia University School of the Arts. He frequently writes about scenography and contemporary theatre, and his books include *The History and Theory of Environmental Scenography*, *American Set Design*, *American Avant-Garde Theatre: A History*, *Looking into the Abyss: Essays on Scenography* and *The Disappearing Stage: Reflections on the 2011 Prague Quadrennial*, as well as the introductory essay for volume three of *The Cambridge History of American Theatre*. He served as general commissioner of the Prague Quadrennial in 2007.